I0819357

The Art of Darkness

First published in 2022
by Frances Lincoln,
an imprint of The Quarto Group.
1 Triptych Place, 2nd Floor,
London, SE1 9SH,
United Kingdom
T (0)20 7700 9000
www.Quarto.com

EEA Representation, WTS Tax d.o.o.,
Žanova ulica 3, 4000 Kranj, Slovenia.
www.wts-tax.si

A catalogue record for this book is available from the British Library.

ISBN 978-0-7112-6920-0
Ebook ISBN 978-0-7112-6921-7

10 9 8 7

Design by Masumi Briozzo

Printed in Huizhou, Guangdong, China, TT092025

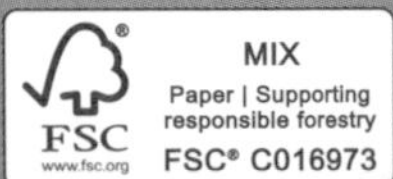

For the weirdos and freaks who doodled flying eyeballs and burning hearts in the margins of their school books instead of paying attention in class. We saw things differently, felt things deeply, daydreamed darkly. This world of strangeness and beauty has always existed for us.

Front cover: AntiquityV
Alex Eckman-Lawn
2019, cut paper/collage.
© Alex Eckman-Lawn

Back cover: How to Hold, Chris Mrozik, 2018, acrylic on paper.
© Chris Mrozik

S. Elizabeth

The Art of Darkness

A Treasury of the Morbid, Melancholic and Macabre

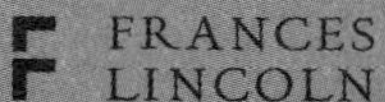
FRANCES LINCOLN

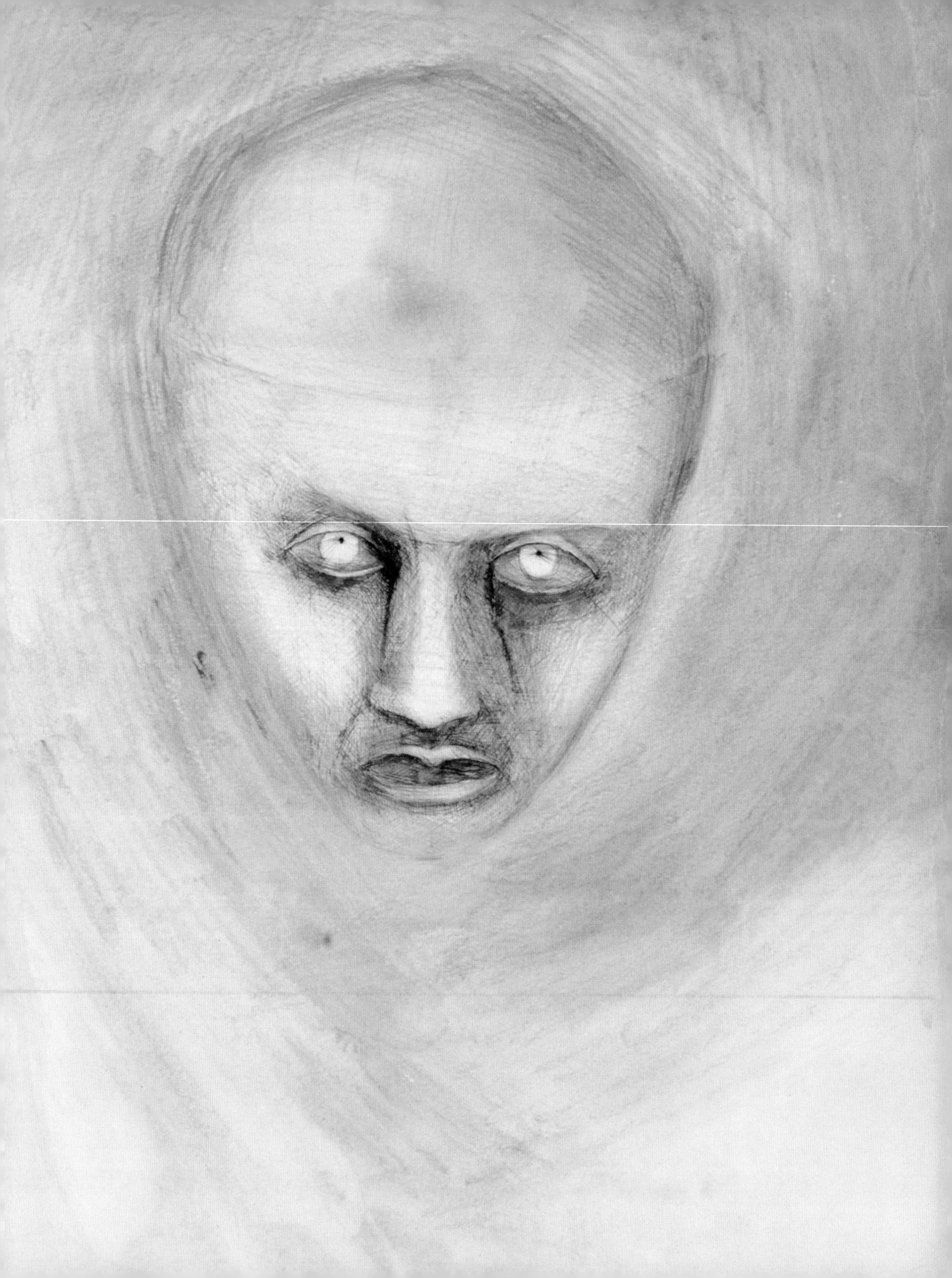

Introduction: In Praise of Shadow

In the beginning, there was darkness. And we're terrified of it. Although, I once heard that it's not that we're afraid of being alone in the dark. Not exactly. What we are actually afraid of is that we are NOT alone in the dark.

That's an interesting idea to sit with, isn't it? Momentarily ruling out the monsters, what is it that we fear? Sitting in the gloom, our thoughts tend to crowd in on us. Fears and anxieties, loneliness and despair, regret for our pasts, concern for our future, anger that we're alone in the dark with nothing better to do but think about any of this in the first place. No wonder we don't want to be alone with it. So we avoid it. We don't think about the unpleasantness potentially lurking in the shadows and we stay positive. It's fine, I'm fine, we're all fine here!

But here's something else to think about. If we're eternally living in the light where it's always bright and happy, where we ignore or evade our distressing, uncomfortable feelings, then we are starved of shadows, of nuance, and risk an existence robbed of the richness of contrast. When we only validate our positive feelings, we vastly restrict our tools for looking at the world. We are neither dealing with reality as it is nor adequately readying ourselves for the random pains and struggles that life has in store for us. We deny our inner darkness at our own peril. Because tragedies and calamities are inevitable and darkness will descend at some point in your life, no matter what sort of mindset you have. Despite what you may have heard, good things don't only happen to good people, and bad things don't only happen to bad people, and whatever it is, your positive or negative thoughts did not make it happen. Shit happens. Pain is pain, feelings are feelings. And as humans, for our emotional health, it is important that we experience and embody the full spectrum of emotions.

'Leave the door open for the unknown, the door into the dark. That's where the most important things come from . . .'

– REBECCA SOLNIT, 'A FIELD GUIDE TO GETTING LOST'

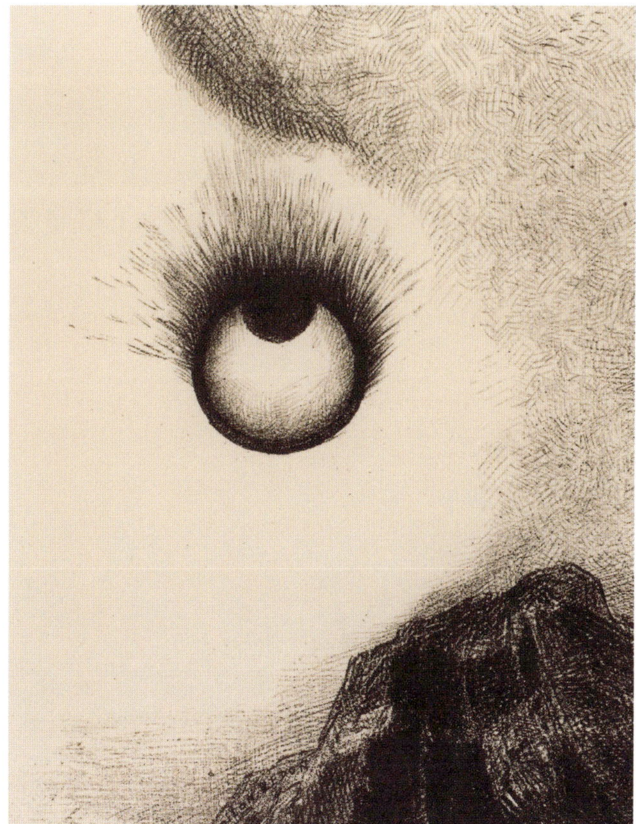

Right: Everywhere eyeballs are aflame, plate 9 from *The Temptation of Saint Anthony* (1st series), Odilon Redon, 1888, lithograph in black on ivory China paper, laid down on ivory wove paper.

Previous spread: Head, Leonora Carrington, c. 1940, pencil, ink and watercolour on paper.

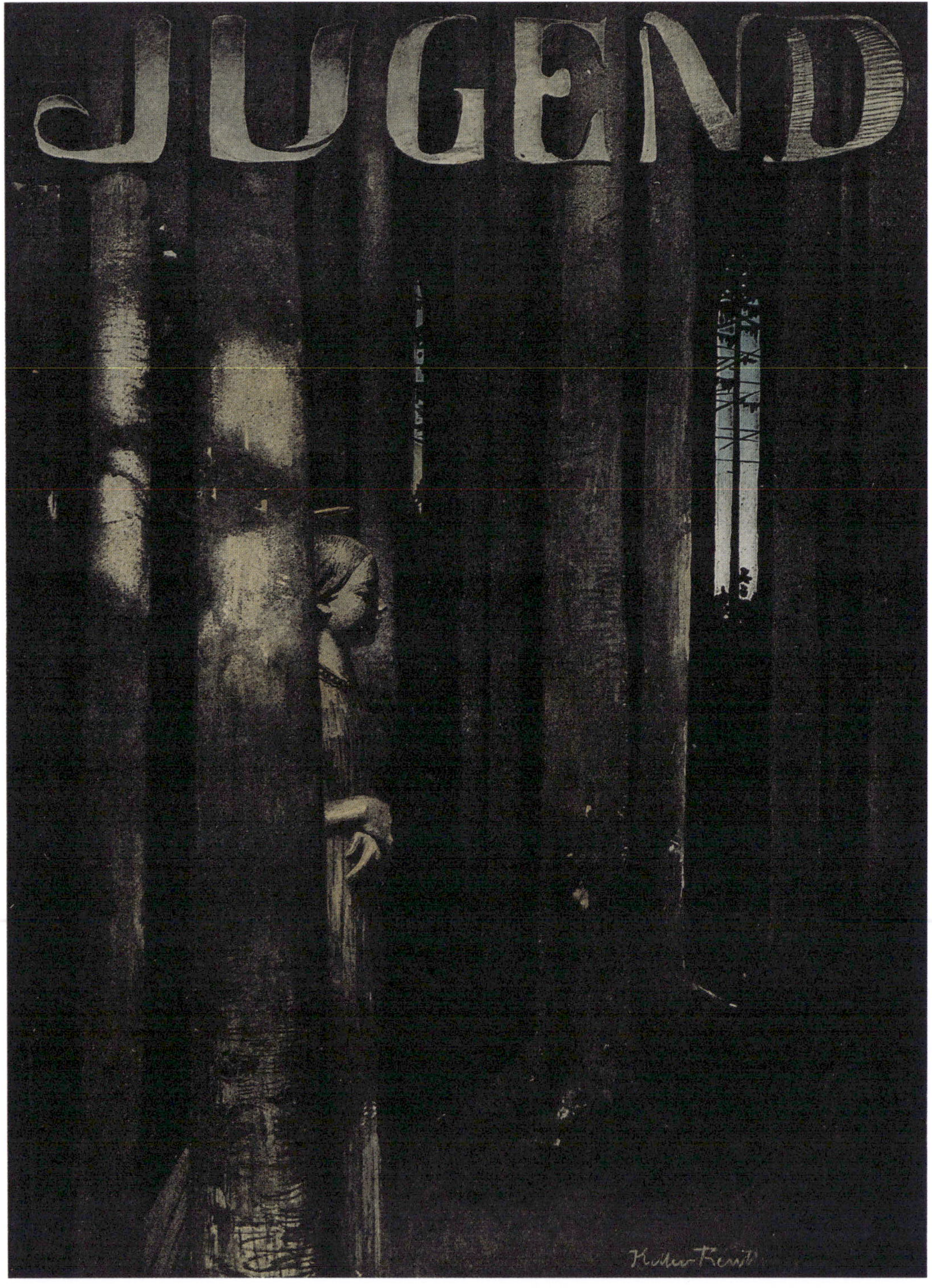
JUGEND

Opposite: Umschlag der Kunst und Literaturzeitschrift 'Jugend' (Cover of the art and literary magazine 'Youth'), *Ausgabe Nr. 15/1896*, Paul Wilhelm Keller-Reutlingen, 1896, oil on canvas.

We should think of this human darkness as a spectrum as well, with many elements along its continuum worth exploring. James Thurber wrote that there are two types of light: the glow that illuminates, and the glare that obscures, and I can't help but think of the obscuring glare here in terms of the phony light of that 'good vibes only' doctrine. Perhaps we can instead confront our darkness straight on and head into it with the illuminating glow of courageous curiosity to guide us through our explorations. And who better to lift the lantern along our pathway than the artists who have engaged with these impulses and have painted canvases awash in unpalatable feelings across the centuries? While the themes and imagery presented in many of these works can be difficult to confront, their beauty and truth lies in laying bare the universality of our struggles and allowing us a bit of distance to sit with something outside ourselves that we also recognize internally. Who hasn't gazed upon the infernal phantasmagoric chaos in the third panel of Hieronymus Bosch's *The Garden of Earthly Delights* triptych and seen their inner pandemonium mirrored right back at them? Surely, it's not just me!

Within the following chapters is a gallery of artworks reflecting these anxieties and aversions, tensions and terrors that transcend time and which have long plagued our psyches – a Stygian kaleidoscope through which tumble our inner demons and our deepest, darkest feelings. Among the push and pull of these seductive and repellent images, we'll traverse the realm of dreams and nightmares, observe the visual culture of struggle and violence, and examine our ingrained and inherent fear of death and decay. And in indulging our fears for a time, in reconciling with our dark halves, our human experience will become closer to whole.

It's important to note that while many of these works are visually stunning and quite beautiful, they also have themes that are considered disturbing or shocking. It is never my intent to share horror for horror's sake but consider this a content warning: these works run the gamut of subject matter and motifs that might provoke distress and discomfort. Please be forewarned and treat yourself gently when perusing these pages.

Once more for the people in the back! Denial of our darkness leads us to fear it. Let's create a connection with our shadows instead, and revel in all the inspiration and wonder we may find there.

PART ONE

—

It's All in Your Mind

'I used to think I was the strangest person in the world but then I thought there are so many people in the world, there must be someone just like me who feels bizarre and flawed in the same ways I do . . .'

– FRIDA KAHLO

'Art enables us to find ourselves and lose ourselves at the same time,' wrote modern monk and man of contradictions Thomas Merton, a prolific poet, essayist and artist. It's no joke that creative people spend a lot of time in their heads. And it's easy to get lost in there.

If you have spent any time with a highly creative person, you have probably experienced moments when it seems like they live in a totally different world from yours, a completely different plane of reality. These dreamers are life's observers and explorers, asking the big questions, discovering the patterns, connecting all the dots. They focus intensely, feel deeply, their minds and hearts on fire, seemingly on the edge of mania and melancholy, exhilaration and existential despair, all at once. A feverish, fraught, frenetic existence.

History is full of long-suffering creative geniuses who have a burning need to express themselves through the medium of their art. The list is so extensive that great art has almost become synonymous with pain. If popular culture is to be believed, in order to be truly creative, one must be touched by mental affliction.

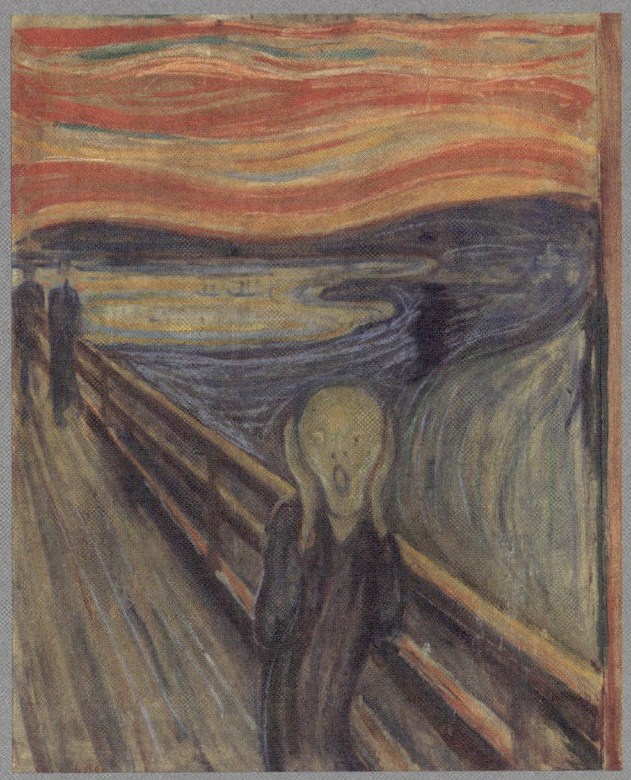

Right: The Scream, Edvard Munch, 1893, oil, tempera and pastel on cardboard.

Opposite: Mad Kate, Henry Fuseli, 1806–07, oil on canvas.

Van Gogh painted *The Starry Night* (1889) while battling anxiety and addiction. Frida Kahlo obsessively painted her physical and emotional pain. Edvard Munch wrote that 'sickness, madness and death were the black angels that guarded my crib', and he even came to be diagnosed with neurasthenia, a clinical condition associated with hysteria and hypochondria. Aristotle expressed this phenomenon when he claimed that 'no great genius has ever existed without a strain of madness'.

The theory that achieving greatness requires some degree of suffering on the part of the creator dates at least as far back as the Greek myth of Philoctetes. In this story a man is exiled on an island as a result of a wound. While there, he invents the bow and arrow from scraps of material he finds in a cave – an invention which becomes an important weapon for the Greeks in their battles. Much like many artists, Philoctetes exists in the margins, and his wound, a symbol of his emotional suffering, is the reason he is rejected from society, but it has also given him a kind of insight and is seen as the facilitator for his invention.

We still don't have the full picture of how the imaginative mind works. Research has suggested that creativity involves the coming together of a multitude of traits, behaviours and social influences in a single person, and neuroscience paints a complicated picture of creativity, which is thought to involve a number of cognitive processes, neural pathways and emotions. Psychologically speaking, creative personality types are difficult to understand, largely because they're complex, paradoxical and tend to avoid habit or routine. So perhaps the 'tortured artist' isn't just a stereotype – perhaps the brain of an artist is hardwired in a unique way.

But the concept of turning one's pain into art is a tired old chestnut and the 'tortured artist', with a scorpion-filled mind that succumbs to its nightmares, is a harmful myth. It suggests that these two states are mutually exclusive – an intensely disturbing notion for anyone who practises a creative craft. Let us then instead gaze upon these beautiful, bold and sometimes baffling works of art with appreciation. Let us celebrate these masters of their craft – tormented by maladies of the body, mind and spirit – and their capability to create great art despite their suffering, not because of it.

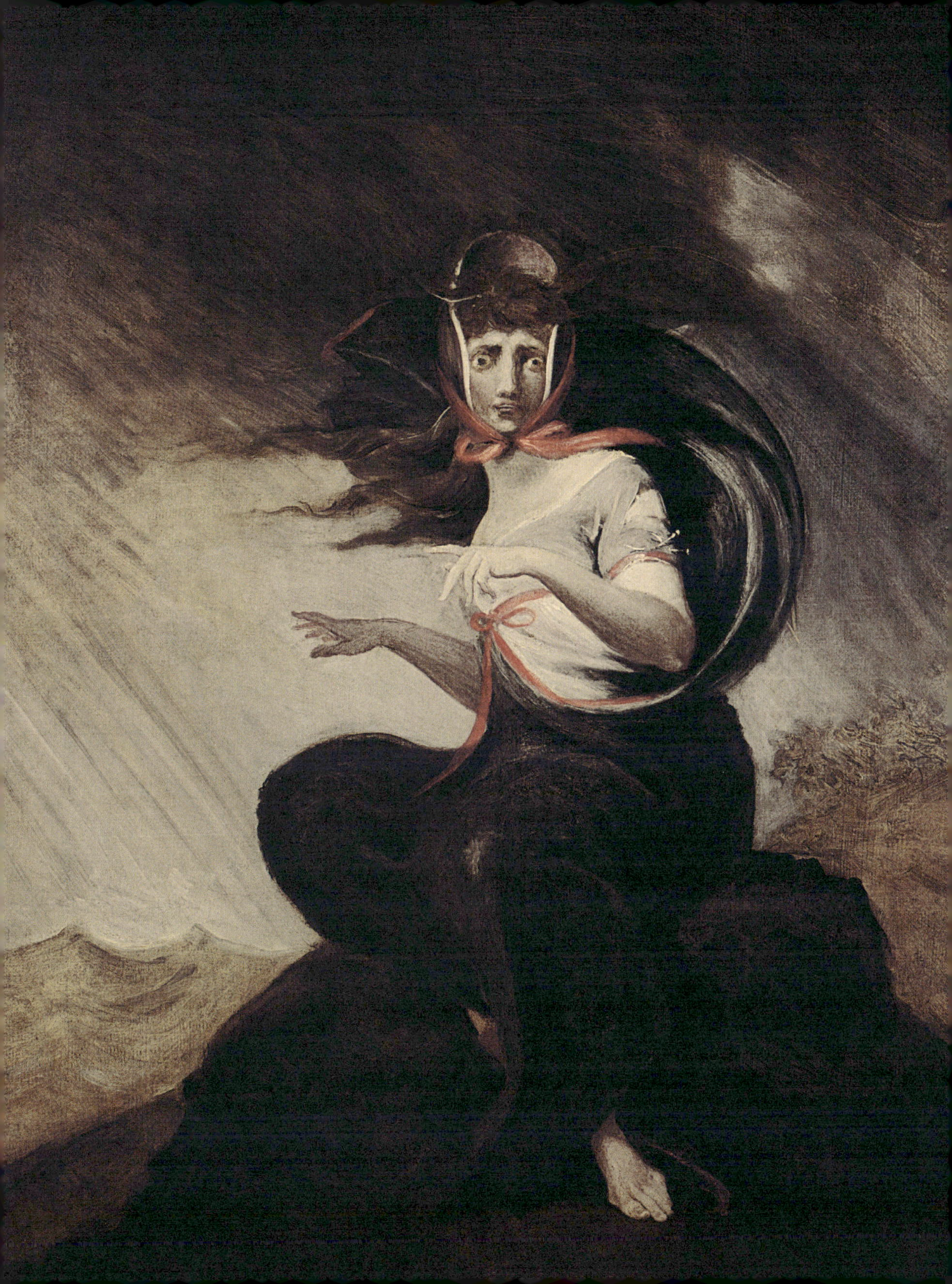

I

—

Dreams & Nightmares

'When we fall asleep, where do we go?'

– BILLIE EILISH

Think back on your last nightmare. Remember the harrowing nocturnal visions that wrench you awake in the 2 a.m. gloom with a shudder and a sob, the visions of vivid and mordant splendour that render you terror-stricken, make your heart pound and you pray desperately that the scenario you've just encountered while slumbering is, in fact, not real. Powerless and sleepless, you lie under the blankets, paralysed, the darkness teeming with awful possibility, your nerves jangled and at the edge of your skin, until the sky lightens with morning, the room's dim shadows scatter, and you finally see that you are alone. Or, at least, you are alone now.

. . . or are you? In the following pages we will explore the imagery of some of the dark, dangerous fantasies and mind-bending scenarios of these dreams and nightmares, as well as the artists who coax forth those phantom filaments from the darker recesses of our disturbed slumbers and conjure them to the canvas in the form of horror- and macabre-fantasy-inspired artwork.

Dreams and nightmares are an indispensable part of the artistic imagination and have long proved a lush, fruitful and inexhaustible wellspring for human creativity and expression. Whenever we drift into sleep, we slip into a world saturated in fabulous and frightening fancies of surreal creativity far beyond what our waking minds can conceive of. The shifting ciphers of these midnight riddles, possibly caused by random neural firings alongside emotion and memory, are perhaps the perfect vehicle for those artists looking to uncover the ineffable fears and desires that lie submerged, and to bring to light these elusive truths the waking mind has buried deep.

Although early human beings and ancient cultures had varying ideas concerning what dreams are, we can certainly say that they all invested dreams with great significance. The ancient Greeks and Romans believed that dreams were messages from the gods or from the deceased, while Renaissance scholars believed that dreams could be both instructional and amusing – that the same dream had different meanings depending on a person's dominant humour and the time of year. Dreams and nightmares were especially important to artists of the late eighteenth- and early nineteenth-century Romantic movement; one of the most notable examples is seen in the theatrical gothic drama of Henry Fuseli's painting *The Nightmare* (1781). On this canvas swoons a woman awash in glowing light. A disagreeable imp-like figure crouches on her chest while a horse with malevolently glowing eyes and flared nostrils lurks in the shadows. When *The Nightmare* was first displayed at the annual Royal Academy Exhibition in London in 1782, the original visitors found the subject matter awfully shocking, as these late eighteenth-century exhibits were typically the domain of portraits, landscapes or scenes illustrating literature and history. Viewers, however, were also intrigued. *The Nightmare* did not fit into any of these usual categories. What did it mean? Was the painting meant to be an allegory of some sort, or simply a bizarre fantasy? The art critics were mystified, and the work proved so popular that Fuseli created another three versions, making it the popular painting of the day. Interpretations vary. An icon of horror, it has inspired mystery and speculation for generations.

On the topic of analysis, one wonders what Sigmund Freud would have to say about all of this? He was, after all, rumoured to have kept a reproduction of *The Nightmare* on the wall of his apartment in Vienna. Freud emphasized the importance of dreams in understanding the mind, and his work inspired the work of the Surrealists and later artists. Surrealists were also deeply interested in interpreting dreams as conduits for unspoken feelings and desires, and many artists of the movement would use the motifs they found in their dreams to construct intense and provocative pieces.

While Freud thought that dreams expressed forbidden wishes in disguise, Swiss psychologist and psychiatrist Carl Jung saw dreams as expressing things openly, telling us things we already

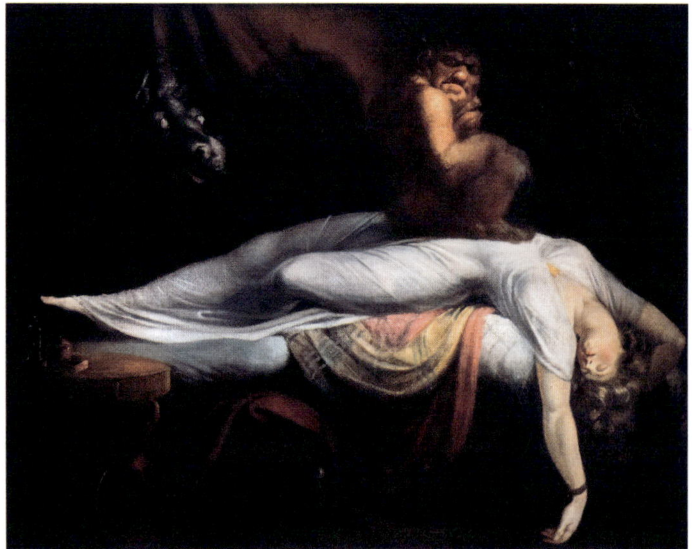

Left: The Nightmare, Henry Fuseli, 1781, oil on canvas.

This famous painting by Swiss-English painter Henry Fuseli (born Johann Heinrich Füssli, 1741–1825) showed dark, irrational forces at play in its dreamlike and haunting erotic evocation of infatuation and obsession. How could this combination of titillating themes not be a massively popular success? After its first showing, at London's 1782 Royal Academy Exhibition, critics and patrons reacted with horrified fascination and the work became widely popular, to the extent that it was parodied in political satire and an engraved version was widely distributed. In response, Fuseli produced at least three other versions.

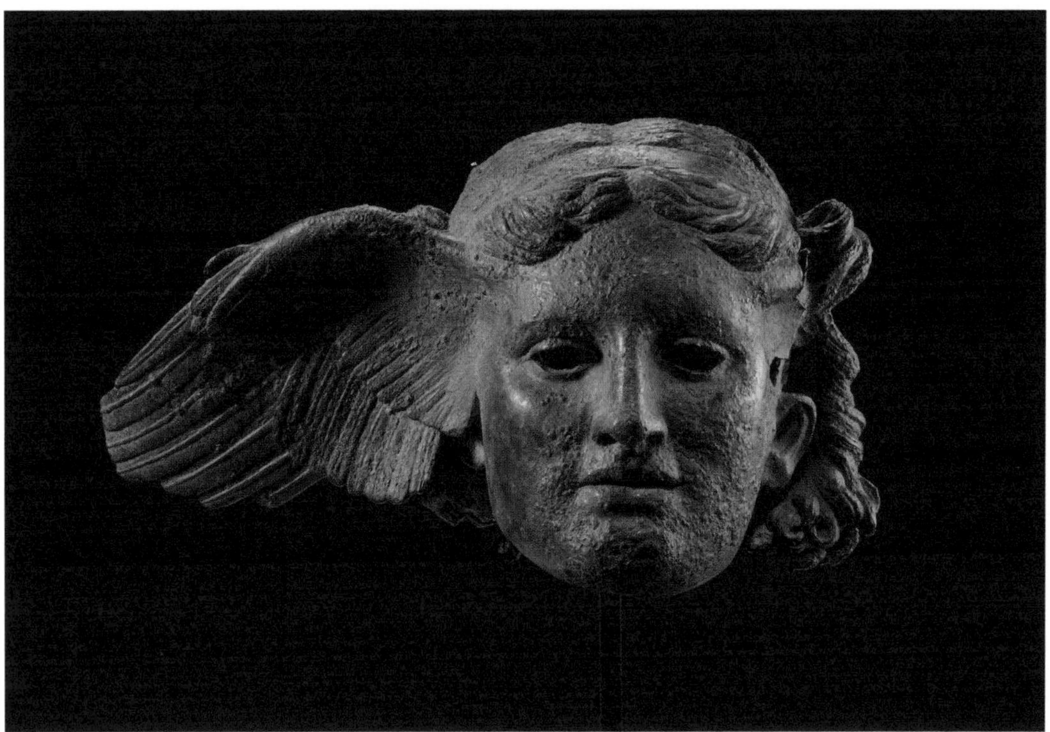

Above: Bronze head of Hypnos, copy of a Hellenistic original found at Civitella d'Arno (near Perugia, Italy), 1st–2nd century CE, bronze.

Hypnos first appears in mythology in the works of one of the earliest Greek poets, Hesiod. In them, Hypnos (Sleep) and Thanatos (Death) were the terrible sons of Nyx (Night). Hypnos's wings allowed him to move swiftly over land and sea, and to fan the foreheads of the weary until they fell asleep. His son Morpheus served as the dream messenger, and Morpheus's brother Phobetor was the bringer of nightmares. His name translates from Greek as 'to be feared' and be-fear he does, as he emerges from the land of eternal darkness every night as a winged demon to infest the dreams of the living. Phobetor's children are the shapes of nightmares themselves, allowing him to extend his reach to all the sleeping people of the world.

know, albeit through the use of symbols. Seekers have looked to these theories and archetypes – before and beyond – to find meaning and purpose in their dreams, translating these illogical musings into the visual language of brushstrokes on canvas. Perhaps this is why so many artists, from the Symbolists to the Surrealists to contemporary creators today, turn to their dreams and nightmares, exploring the warped shadows of that disruptive eeriness and unreality with the hopes of returning to wakefulness with greater truths and creative flashes of genius. It is not surprising then, that born from the throb and thrumming and contradictory electrical chaos of deep sleep brain waves, these nocturnal cerebral meditations have entered the works of artists and creators throughout the ages.

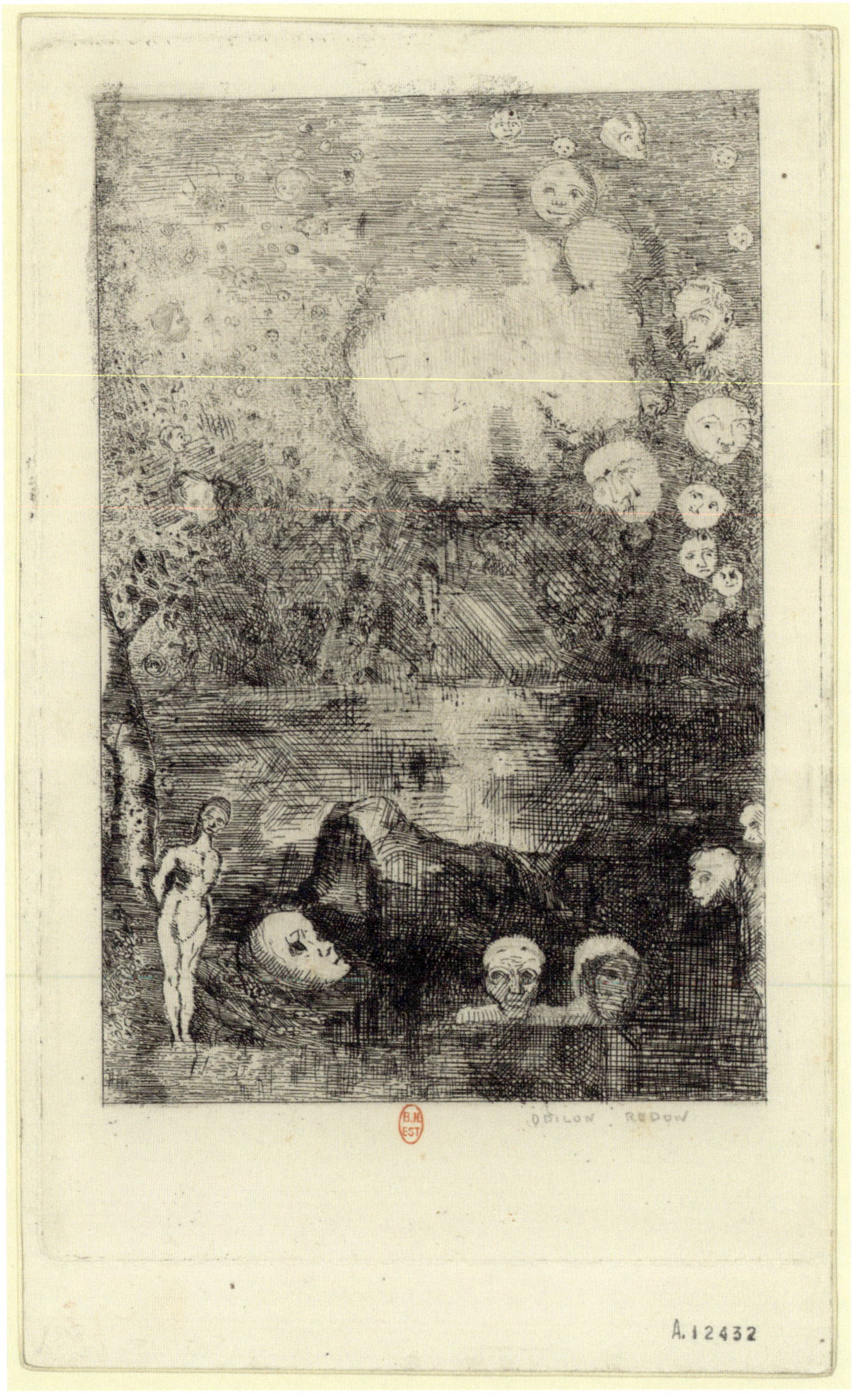
ODILON REDON
A.12432

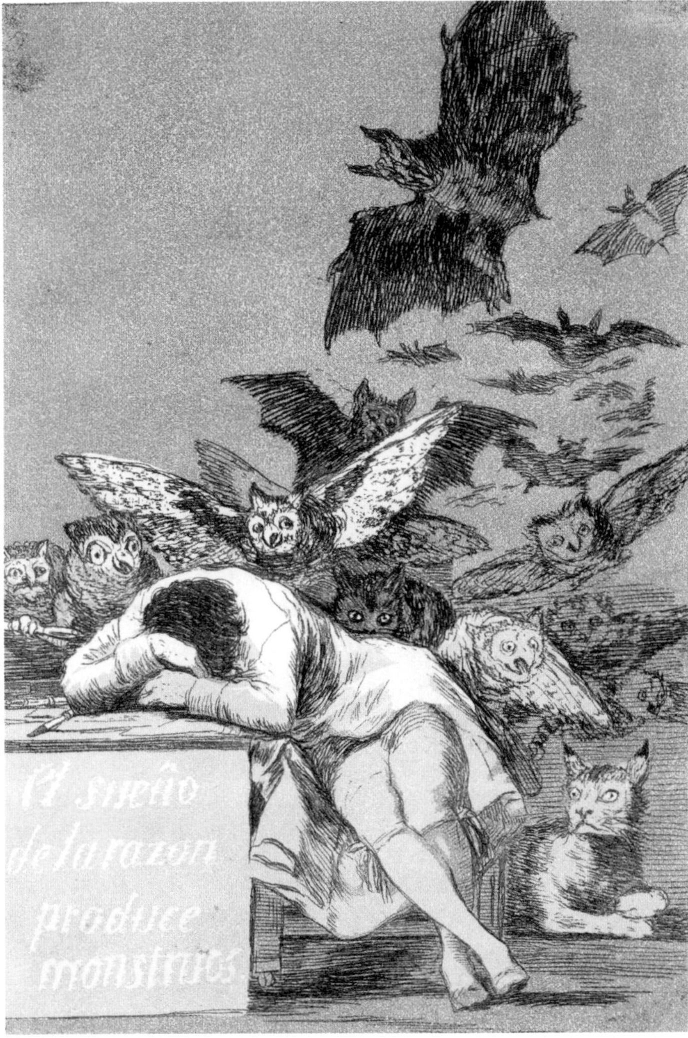

Left: The Sleep of Reason Produces Monsters, No. 43, from Los Caprichos (The Caprices), Francisco Goya, 1796–98, engraving.

In this lively scene, a chaotic throng of malefic creatures bedevils the sleeper in *The Sleep of Reason Produces Monsters*, numbered 43 in a series of 80 aquatint etchings published in 1799 by Francisco Goya (1746-1828). Known as Los Caprichos, this series is generally understood as the artist's criticism of the society in which he lived. Various creatures, including bats and owls, animals symbolizing evil and mystery in Spanish folklore, swarm around the slumbering artist, and a vigilant lynx standing sentinel at the lower right alerts us to the monstrous forces that we are unable to control when sleep takes us. The epigraph for the work contains a warning, a proclamation of Goya's adherence to the values of the Enlightenment: 'Imagination abandoned by reason produces impossible monsters; united with her, she is the mother of the arts and source of their wonders.'

Opposite: Vision de Rêve (Dream Vision), Odilon Redon, 1878–82, engraving.

Odilon Redon (1840-1916) was one of the most recognized and original of Symbolist artists, and a master of interior worlds. His visionary works occupy the spaces of dreams, fantasy and the imagination. His Noirs Series, monochromatic compositions that comprise the first half of his career, are some of his most famous works, and typify Symbolism in their mysterious subjects and bizarre, dreamlike inventions. Redon's expressive and suggestive images led French writer Joris Karl Huysmans to christen him as 'the prince of mysterious dreams'.

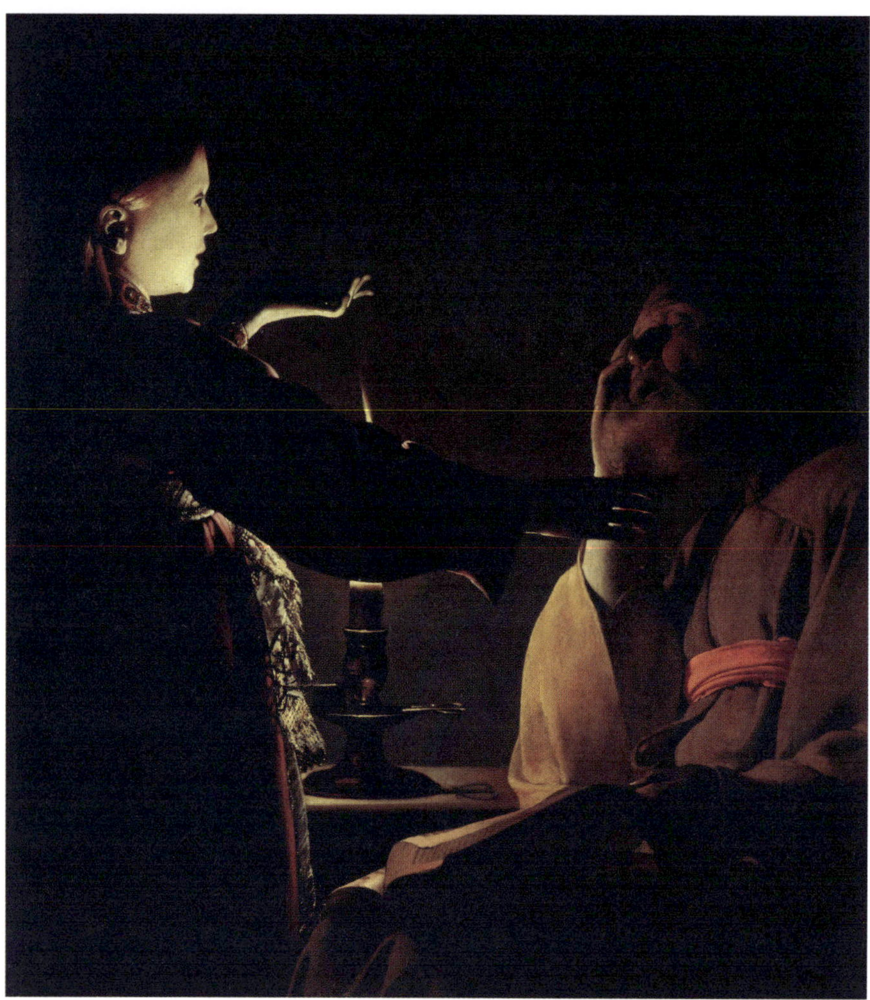

Above: The Dream of St Joseph, Georges de La Tour, c. 1640, oil on canvas.

Unlike those who have been contacted by burning bushes, earthquakes or the roar of thunder, St Joseph only heard God in the quietest of ways. He dreamed of angels and received God's missives through these celestial messengers while he slept. In this candlelit scene, French Baroque painter Georges de La Tour (1593–1652) painted St Joseph, the father of Jesus, being visited in a dream by an angel with a message. According to the New Testament he was visited four times with various messages and it is not clear which visit is portrayed in this scene, but whatever game of holy telephone this messenger was playing, Joseph is a man who appears to be missing out on a solid night's sleep.

Right: The Garden of Earthly Delights (right panel), Hieronymus Bosch, 1490–1500, oil on oak panels.

Do works of art get any more nightmarish than the paintings of Jheronimus van Aken, better known as Hieronymus Bosch (c. 1450–1516)? I'd wager not. The paintings of this fanatical late-medieval artist, about whom surprisingly little is known, are infamous for their chaotic dreamscapes brimming with strange and surreal details. Though his works may not be depicting literal nightmares, who can say that on occasion their dream terrors do not in some way resemble the grotesqueries that cavort and caper within the carnival atmosphere of this artist's lurid canvases? In this panel from Bosch's most complex and enigmatic creation, *The Garden of Earthly Delights,* we are treated to the wild ecstasy of a hellishly remarkable menagerie where, among other scenes of eyeball-scarring strangeness, man-eating bird-monsters placidly devour their wriggling meals and a pink froggy monster blob croaks out a song from a score inscribed on a human backside. A drop of dream-fuel, indeed!

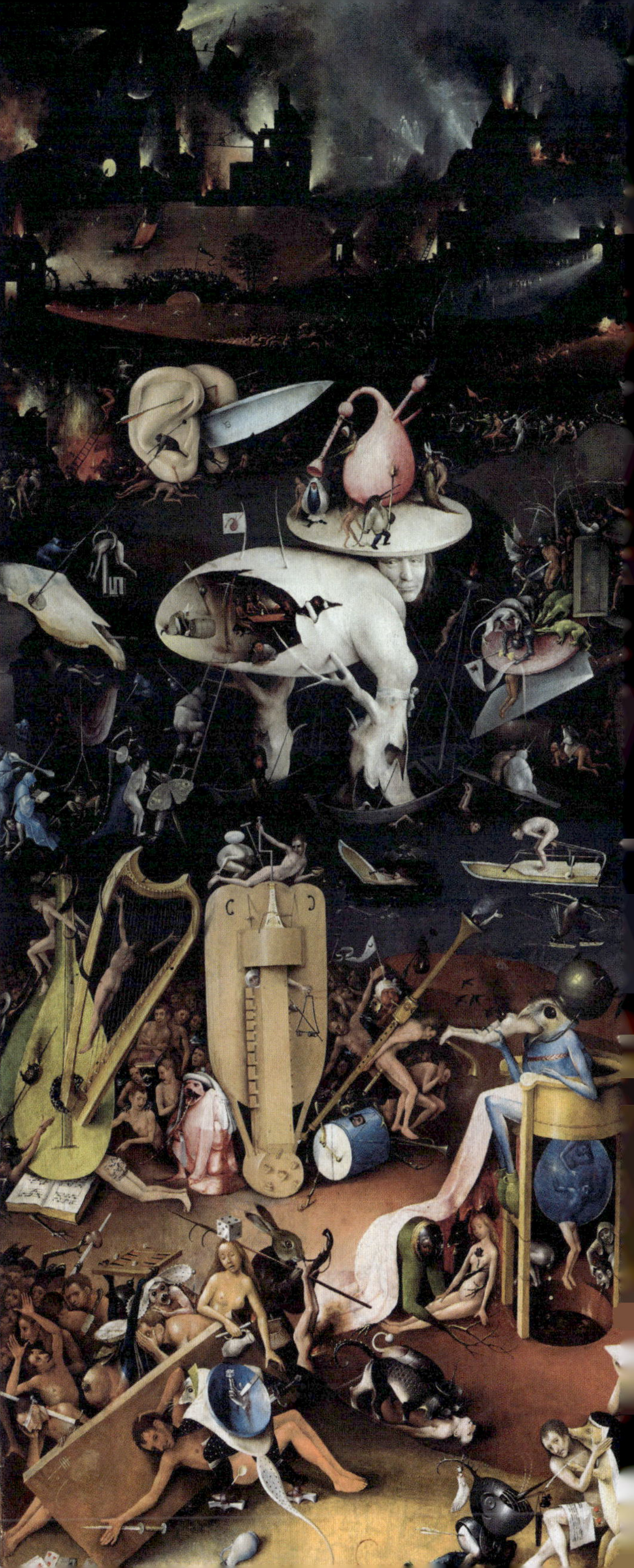

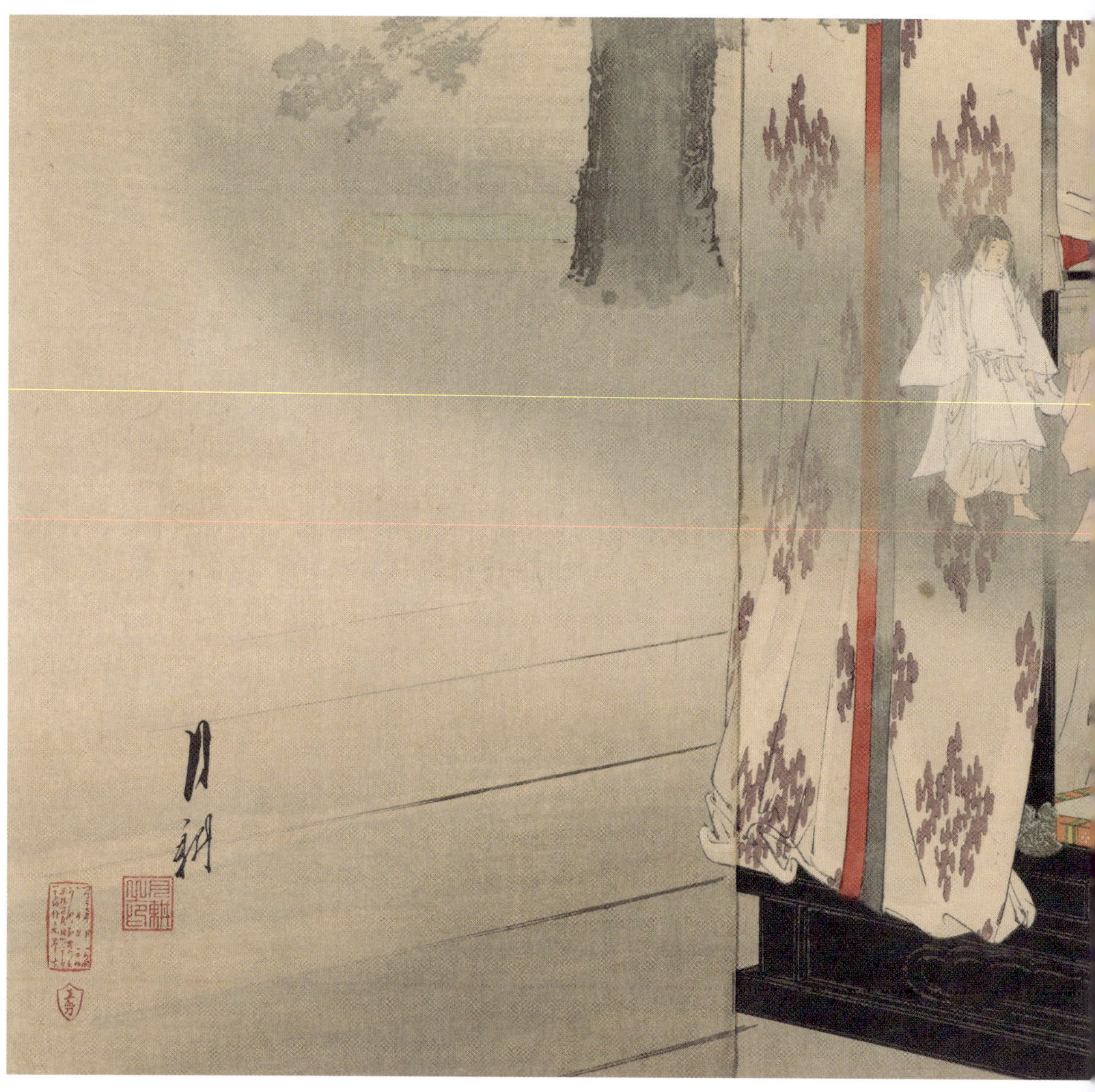

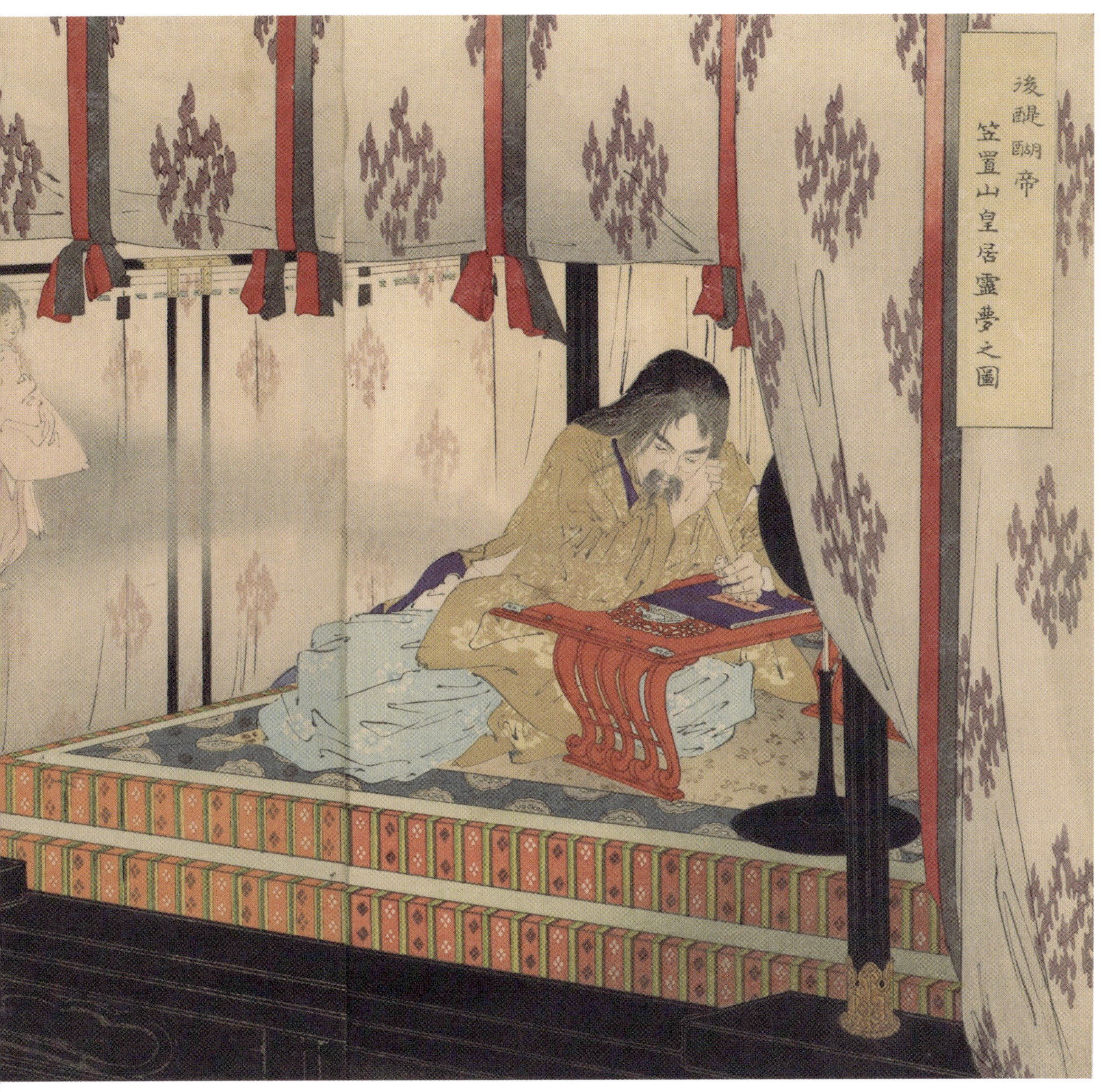

Above: Emperor Go-Daigo, Dreaming of Ghosts at his Palace in Kasagiyama, Ogata Gekkō, 1890, wood block triptych.

Ogata Gekkō (1859–1920) was a Japanese artist best known as a painter and a designer of ukiyo-e woodblock prints. He was considered to be one of the important ukiyo-e artists of the Meiji era and was among the earliest Japanese artists to win an international audience. He had developed his own artistic style, influenced by traditional Japanese painting, and his works are typically genre scenes from the everyday lives of people, and reveal interesting insights into daily life in Japan at the turn of the century. In this intimate scene, we get a peek at Emperor Go-Daigo whose efforts to overthrow the shogunate and restore the monarchy led to civil war and divided the imperial family into two rival factions. In this phantasmal image, the ghosts of two small children appear in a dream to advise the emperor. One assumes, from the calm and resolute atmosphere, that this is with regard to military strategy, but one hopes it's to suggest a peaceful resolution with less innocent bloodshed.

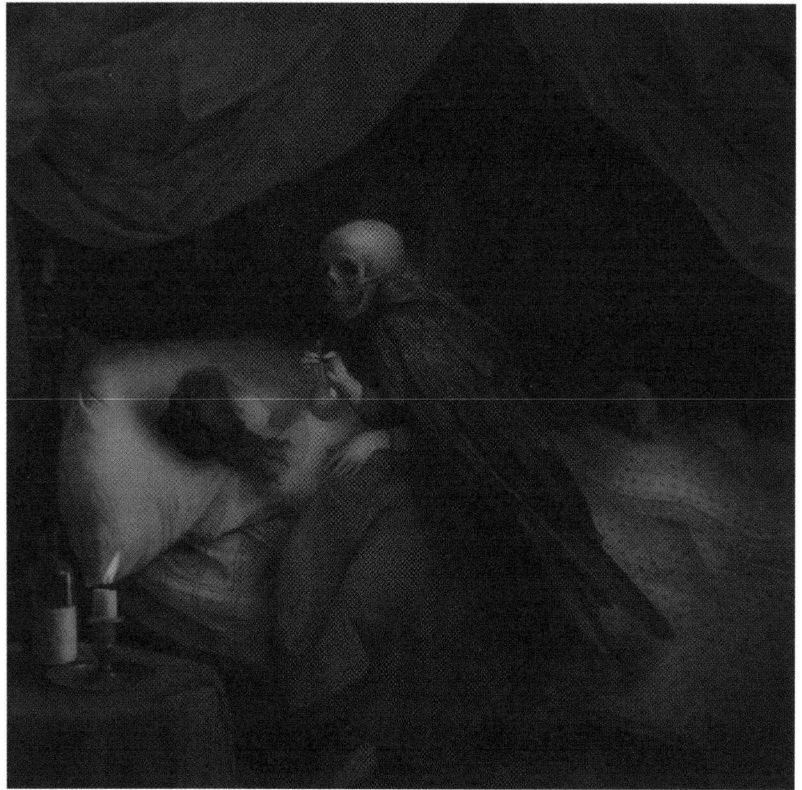

Above: The Sandman, Stephen Mackey, 2020, oil on panel.

British artist Stephen Mackey comments wryly about his cryptic creative persona, 'No information = mystique . . . You can have any facts you want, but you're sworn to secrecy.' Keep your secrets, then, Mr Mackey! Self-taught and inspired by the great French, Dutch and Italian masters of the Renaissance, Mackey's works portray fantasy settings and the magic of imaginary worlds. They are full of Symbolism, both exciting and ambiguous, and feature gossamer beings in scenarios that feel as ethereal and elusive as a dream.
In this scene of velvety textures, one senses that the sleeper may awaken at any moment, and this mysterious figure may never have been there at all.

Opposite: Night Terrors, David Whitlam, 2017, pencil and digital.

Contemporary British artist David Whitlam (b. 1977) showed an interest in and talent for drawing at a young age. While studying graphic art at Leeds Metropolitan University, he developed a curiosity for Surrealism and the workings of the unconscious. Working in a variety of media, often combining traditional drawings and paintings with digital art, his goal is to 'tap into the desires and anxieties within the subconscious', allowing his images to evolve into their own identities rather than attempting to capture reality.

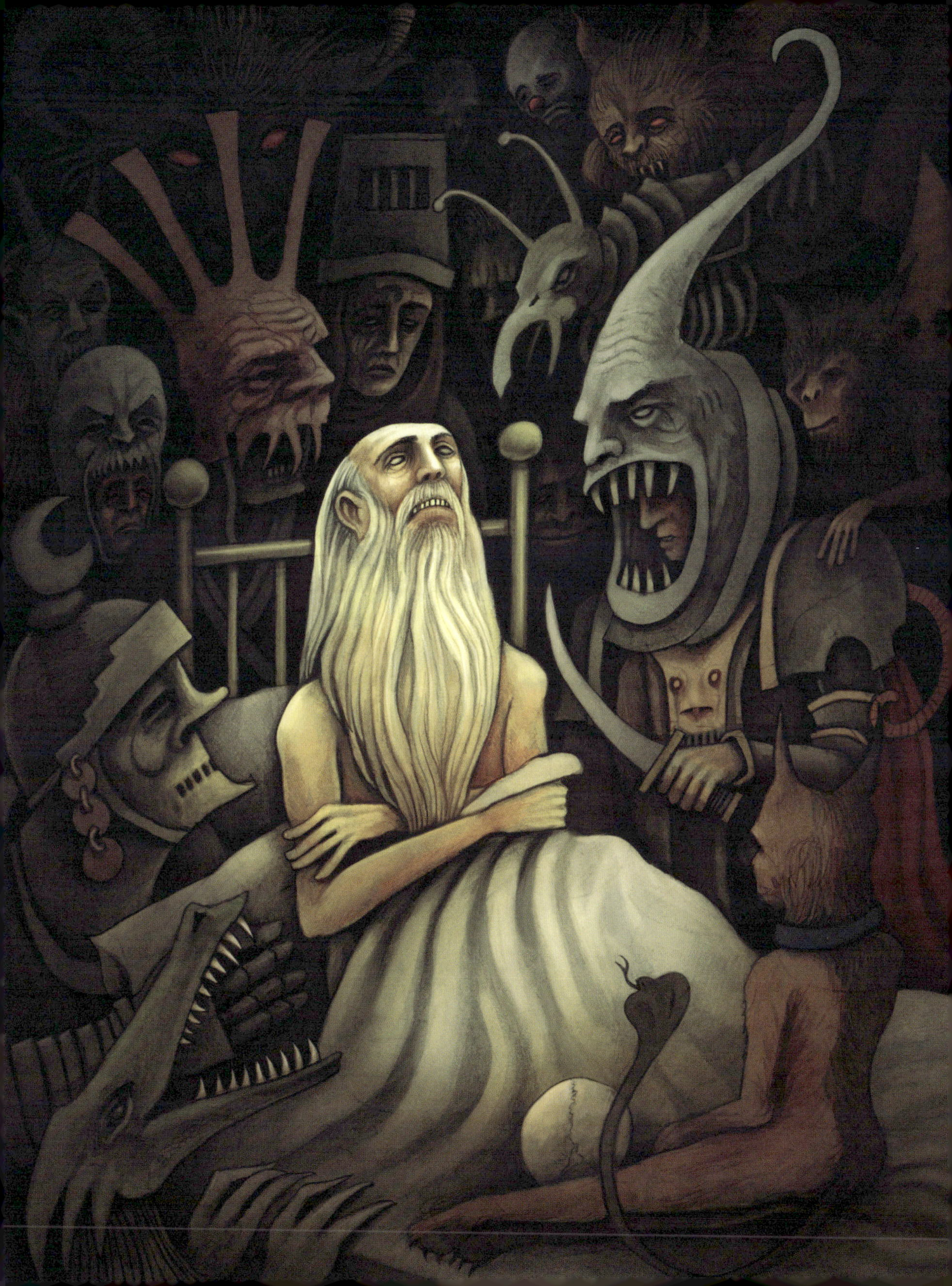

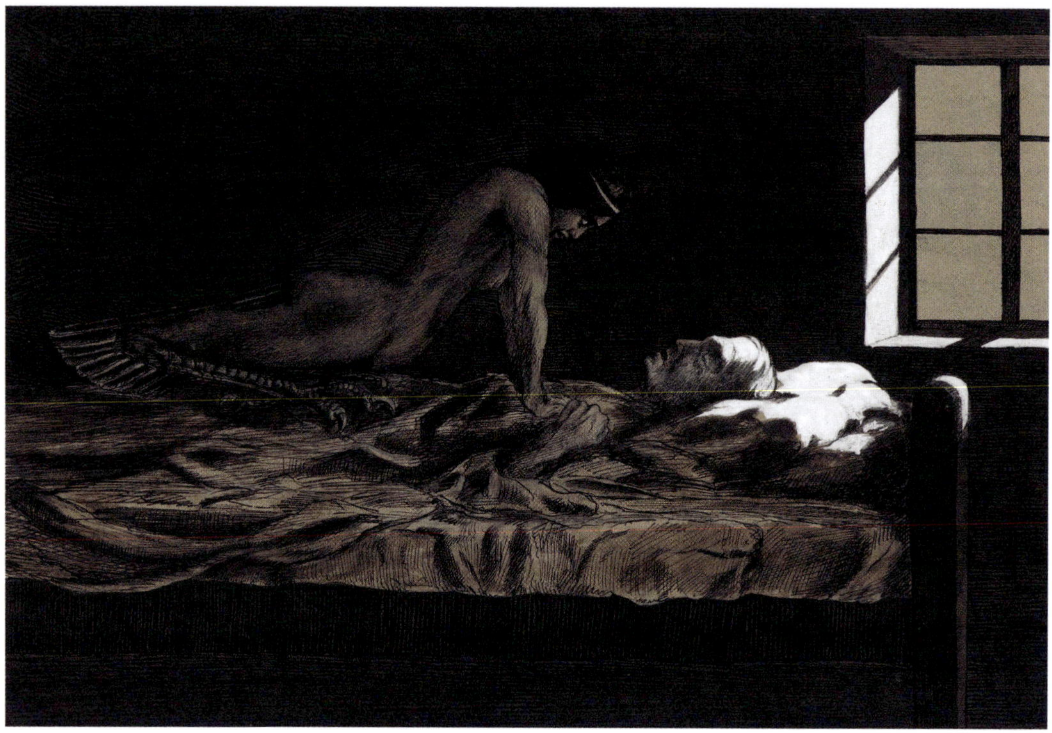

Above: My Dream, My Bad Dream, Fritz Schwimbeck, 1915, pen and ink, wash and gouache on paper.

This imagery of a terrifying nocturnal visitation is no doubt a feeling that all cat-owners are familiar with, although fuzzy paws are certainly preferable to the iron grip of the succubus. Fritz Schwimbeck (1889–1972) was a German artist best known for his atmospheric psychological pen-and-ink illustrations, engrossing narrative prints and graphic drawings. Schwimbeck's many notable accomplishments include illustrations for art books and editions of works by Arnold Strindberg, William Shakespeare, Edgar Allen Poe and E.T.A. Hoffmann.

Opposite: The Somnambulist, John Everett Millais, 1871, oil on canvas.

In John Everett Millais' (1829–96) nerve-wracking painting, *The Somnambulist*, we observe a barefoot young woman sleepwalking perilously close to the shadowy edge of a cliff. Her candle has been snuffed out by the wind, which renders this nail-biting scene even more tense as she walks ahead in the moonlit darkness, unaware of the danger close at hand. Where is she going? What is she dreaming? Sleepwalking, also known as somnambulism or noctambulism, is a phenomenon of combined sleep and wakefulness and is classified as a sleep disorder belonging to the parasomnia family. Millais, an English painter and illustrator who was one of the founders of the Pre-Raphaelite Brotherhood, was 41 years old and at the height of his powers at the time he painted this strange, sleepy drama.

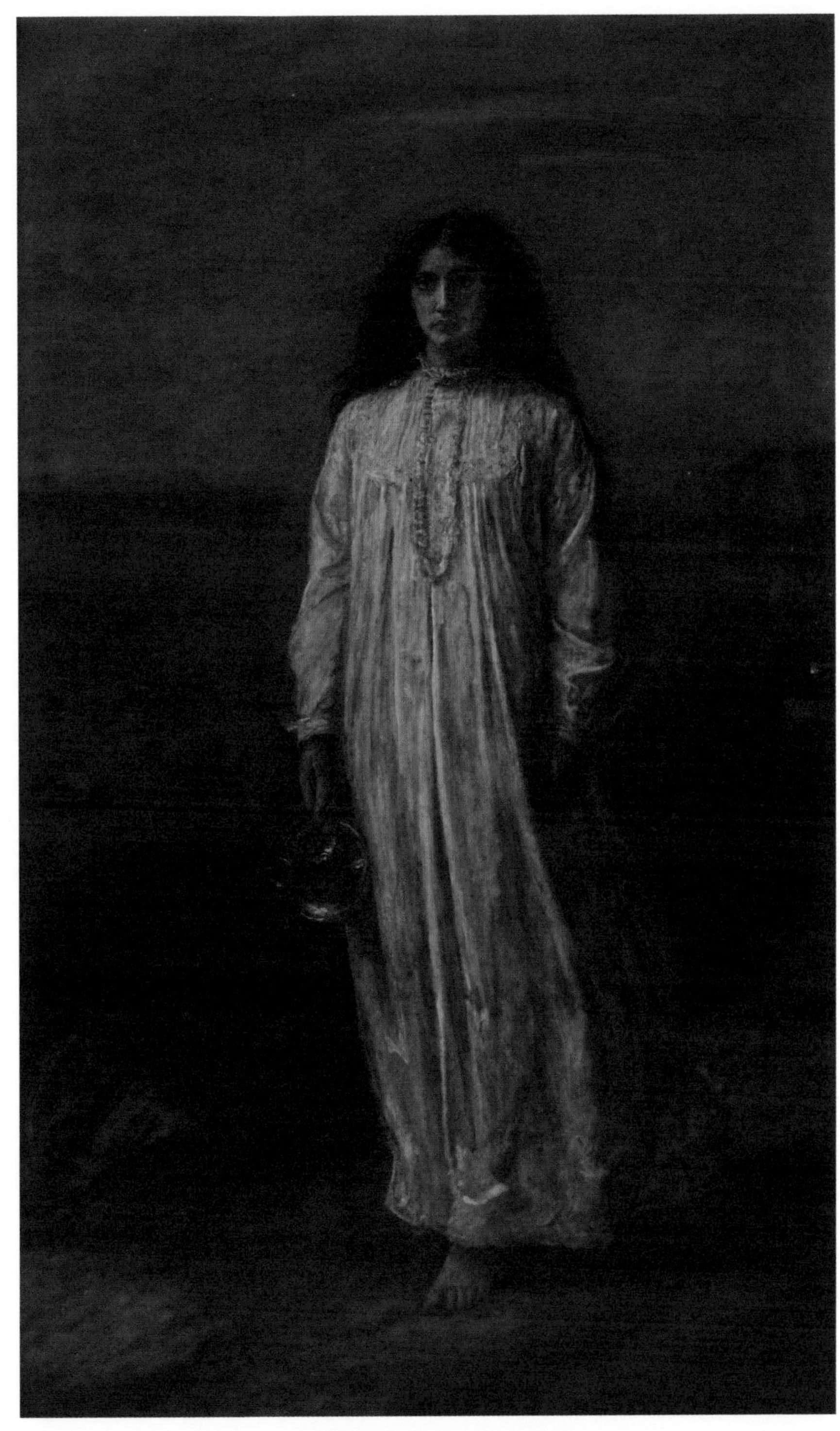

II

Psychological Distress

'I put my heart and my soul into my work and lost my mind in the process.'

– VINCENT VAN GOGH

When it comes to articulating our inner emotional landscapes, it's possible that painter Georgia O'Keeffe, who endured a nervous breakdown in 1933, put it best: 'I found I could say things with color and shapes that I couldn't say any other way–things I had no words for.'

For much of human history, creative expression has been a powerful means of communicating our dreams, visions, stories and ideas, and torments of the mind – depression, anxiety, angst, grief and loneliness – are no different. Mental illness has for centuries been linked in the popular imagination with extraordinary creativity and great works of art, and while much in the history and treatment of 'madness' has changed over time, one of the most consistent features has been the presence of the visual arts, and our speculation and cultural fascination with madness as a creative force.

This celebration of emotion through art is not always of the champagne and roses, 'good vibes only' variety. In this chapter, we will visit works depicting psychological distress, desperate inner turmoil, and deeply scarring trauma. But is there a danger in glorifying art created under the pressures of a suffering artist, or should we celebrate these works as salvation? Art challenges our awareness and understanding of mental illness and it casts a light on a part of what it means to be human. According to the NIMH (National Institute of Mental Health) nearly one in five adults lives with a mental illness. Historically, this can be seen in some of our most revered artworks depicting internal trauma, and many renowned artists have struggled with mental health issues, even if they were not diagnosed with such at the time. Early Renaissance artists, such as Vittore Carpaccio, translate mental illness through the lens of religious and spiritual imagery. Later Renaissance artists, such as Albrecht Dürer wirh his intellect, introspection and ruthless perfectionism, may have elicited a state of melancholia – what is now known as depression. Romantic artist Francisco Goya's work captured the turbulence of his times, but also documented his personal struggles with a tormented mind. Fantastical visual artist Leonora Carrington was deemed 'incurably insane', sent to an asylum in Spain and subjected to a pharmaceutical that produced effects akin to those of electroshock treatment. Describing the harsh realities of her time in the Spanish asylum and her horrifying treatment there in terms of a forced incarceration,

Carrington once remarked that 'I suddenly became aware that I was both mortal and touchable and that I could be destroyed.' In 1970, whilst entrapped by dissociative states and debilitating depression, and after over a decade of intermittent hospitalization for mental illness, outsider artist Unica Zürn, known for her anagrammatic poetry as well as her intricate and entrancing visual art, died by suicide by jumping out of the window of the apartment of her long-time companion, Surrealist artist Hans Bellmer. Zürn's artistic practice was entangled with her bouts of mental illness and she produced much of her art during the time she spent in mental institutions.

What is the relationship between psychological state, the artistic impulse and the creative process? What can artworks produced by people struggling with mental illness illuminate for us about 'artistic genius'? Can art therapy help in the treatment of the mentally ill? Data confirms that the creation of art can aid in calming and relieving stress. Through the studies from which this data comes we have learned that many patients had lower levels of the stress hormone cortisol and increased levels of dopamine, regardless of artistic ability. Even if it doesn't help that person with their particular mental health issues, art creation is shown to be a great tool to access our innermost thoughts and provides time for introspection. Consumed by their illness, many people living with mental health issues aren't able to create at all, despite desperately wanting to. And yet, there are some incredible individuals who persevere and create magnificent works of art despite their challenges.

Although it is a common occurrence in people's lives, and despite the many current attempts to destigmatize mental health, discussion of psychological distress and suffering remains a difficult undertaking. Yet for centuries, these disturbed and disturbing aspects of our psyches have served as inspiration to artists who have portrayed these profoundly human experiences with sensitivity, nuance and empathy. The pain experienced by these artists rendered as paint on canvas, carved in clay or seen through a photographic lens can make for fraught and difficult viewing, and we may want to close our eyes, or look away – but these challenging works of art can help us better understand the darkness experienced by our fellow humans and hold a mirror up to our own darkness as well.

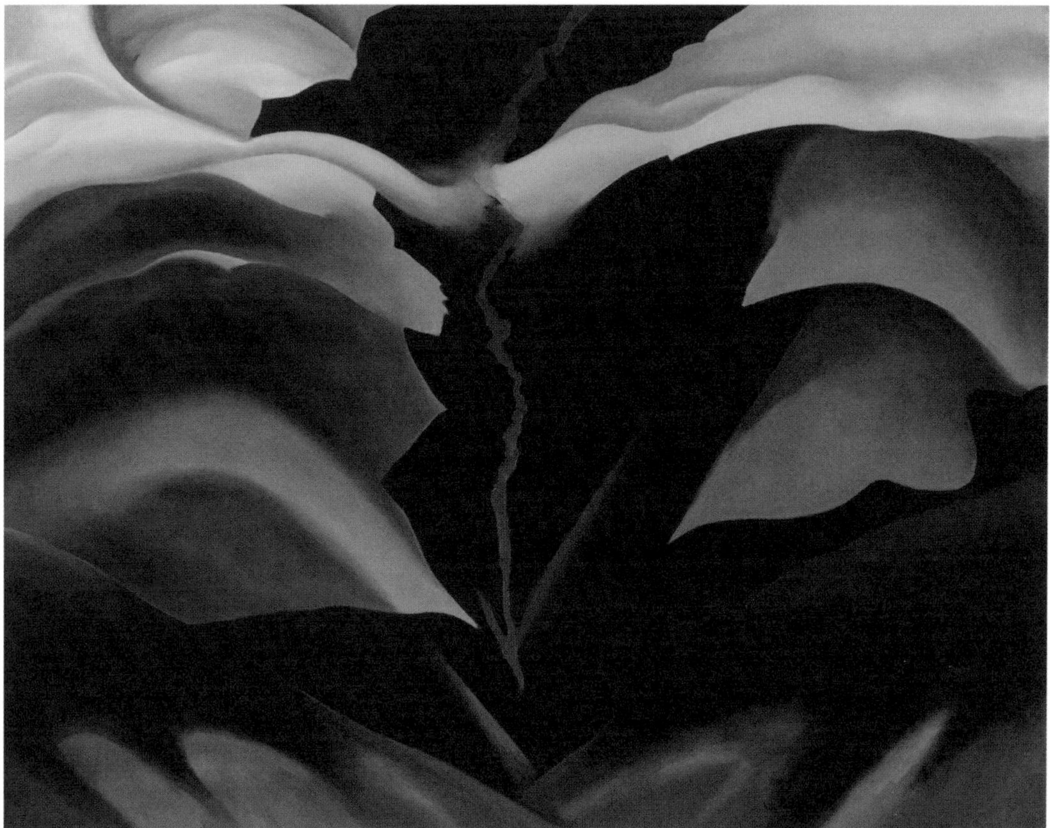

Above: Black Place II, Georgia O'Keeffe, 1944, oil on canvas.

Influential Modernist artist and celebrated painter Georgia O'Keeffe, (1887–1986) was best known for the wild beauty and abstractions of her large-format paintings of flowers, plant life and southwestern American landscapes. An ambitious, complex and singular individual, she endured an intense nervous breakdown in the 1930s which led to hospitalization and caused her to set aside her art for more than a year. In the jagged shadows and sky torn asunder of *Black Place II*, we can imagine the sorrows of the mental health challenges that had swept through her life.

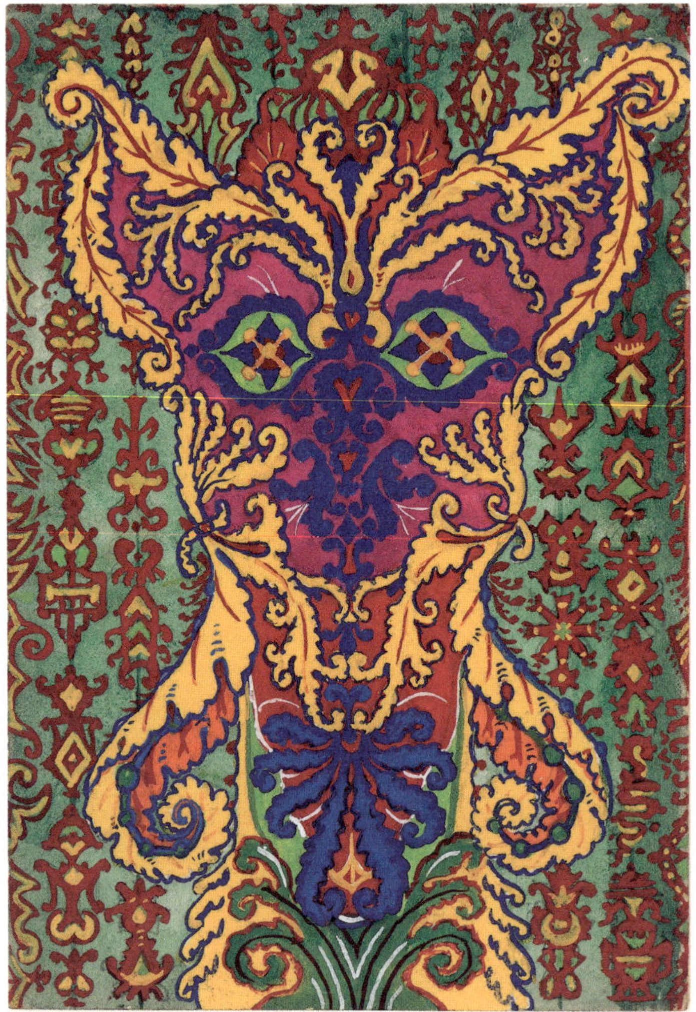

Above: A cat standing on its hind legs, Louis Wain, 1925/1939, gouache.

Louis Wain (1860 -1939) was an English artist whose wildly fanciful, kaleidoscopic drawings of anthropomorphized large-eyed cats grinning and winking, wining and dining, captured the Edwardian imagination. Later in life, he was confined to mental institutions and was alleged to have suffered from schizophrenia. While never officially diagnosed, many believe that he suffered from this condition and some have argued that his later drawings demonstrate his psychotic deterioration; the expressions of his cats seem to reflect the emotions felt by the artist, ranging from a sort of personified dismay to a full-blown, florid freak-out. Wain's intense personality, adroit observations and lifelong battle with mental illness coalesced in an iconic body of work that reflects the comedies, tragedies and absurdities of society - and continues to generate interest to this day.

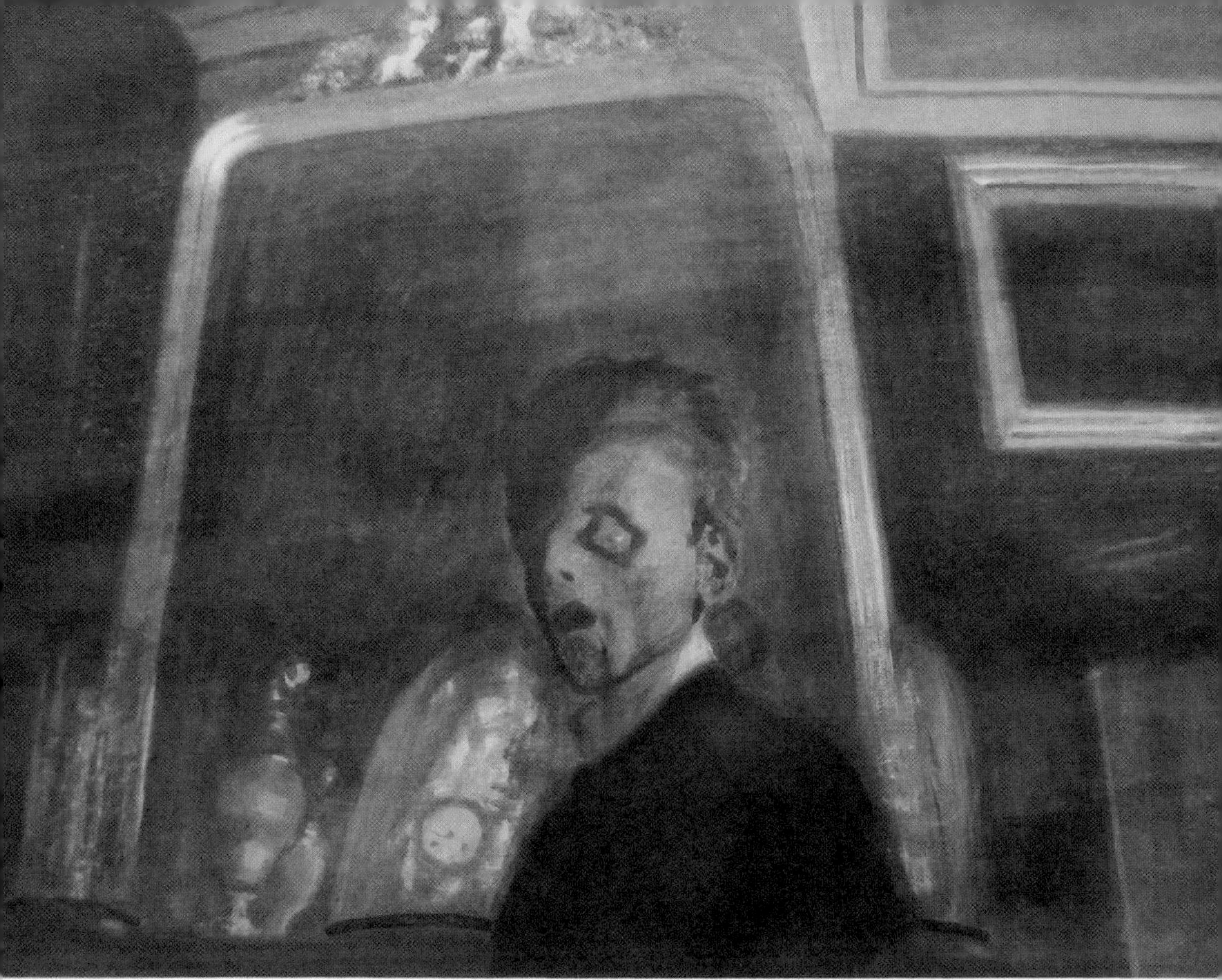

Above: Self-portrait in Front of a Mirror, Léon Spilliaert, 1908, Indian ink wash, brush, watercolour and coloured pencil on paper.

Filled with melancholy solitude, the mysterious atmospheric paintings of self-taught Belgian artist of nocturnes Léon Spilliaert (1881–1946) captured the diffused glow of streetlamps, the dampness of pavements, or moonlight over the dark, brooding sea. Due to his health problems, Spilliaert suffered from insomnia, and as a means of distraction from his sleeplessness, existential worries and physical ailments, he strolled through the empty streets and along the deserted promenade of his hometown late at night. Upon returning from these walks, he would create works from memory, in the dead of night, bringing to life the moody stillness of the town in the wee hours. Still living with his parents and continuing to suffer from ill health, these unnerving reflections suggest an unsteady and unsettled young man struggling with both his physical and mental well-being.

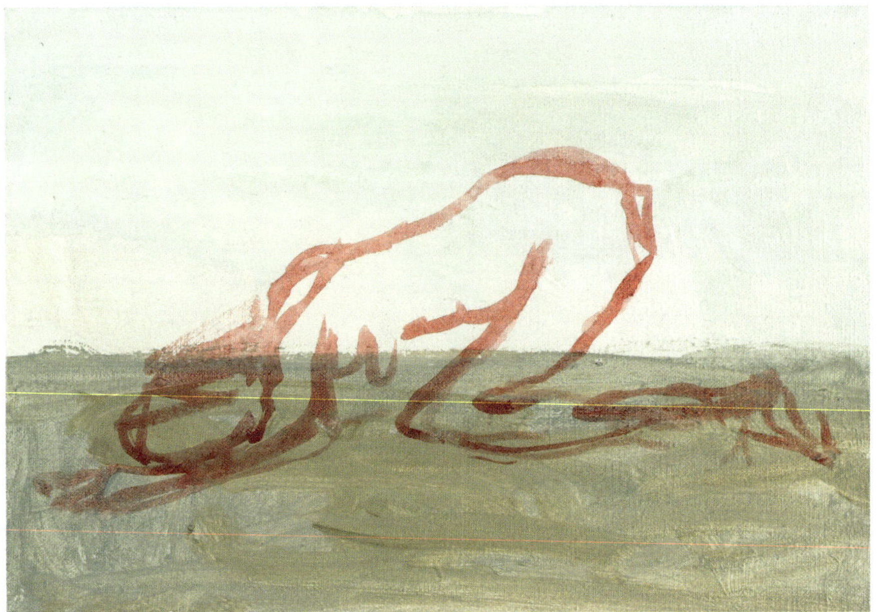

Above: Trying to Find You 1, Tracey Emin, 2007, acrylic on canvas.

Tracey Emin (b. 1963) is a British artist known for her intimate, confessional and boundary-pushing works that mine autobiographical details through a variety of media including painting, drawing, photography, video, sculpture and neon text. Emotional distress is a long-running theme in Emin's art; she cites Edvard Munch as an early inspiration for her expressive style of self-representation, a link that lies in a shared commitment to revealing unfiltered mental suffering - in Emin's case often linked to deeply traumatic experiences of depression and grief.

Opposite: Anxiety, Edvard Munch, 1894, oil on canvas.

Edvard Munch's youth was scored by tragedy: both his mother and favourite sister died of tuberculosis, another sister was diagnosed with mental illness, and the artist himself was often sick, subject to bouts of fever and bronchitis. 'I inherited two of mankind's most frightful enemies,' Munch later wrote, 'the heritage of consumption and insanity'. These anxieties suffused Munch's work throughout his early years, and he repeatedly returned to particular themes, reworking and repainting favourite motifs until old age. Less well known than his more famous iterations of *The Scream*, *Anxiety* presents viewers with a despairing sense of abstract horror, an eerie parade of not-quite-human faces whose expressions exude a feeling of subtle paranoia, discomfort and distrust, a collective desperation more sustained than the piercing angst experienced by the isolated individual in *The Scream*. The lasting influence of these works continues to powerfully resonate with viewers today - who among us can't relate to these distressing feelings at some point in our lives?

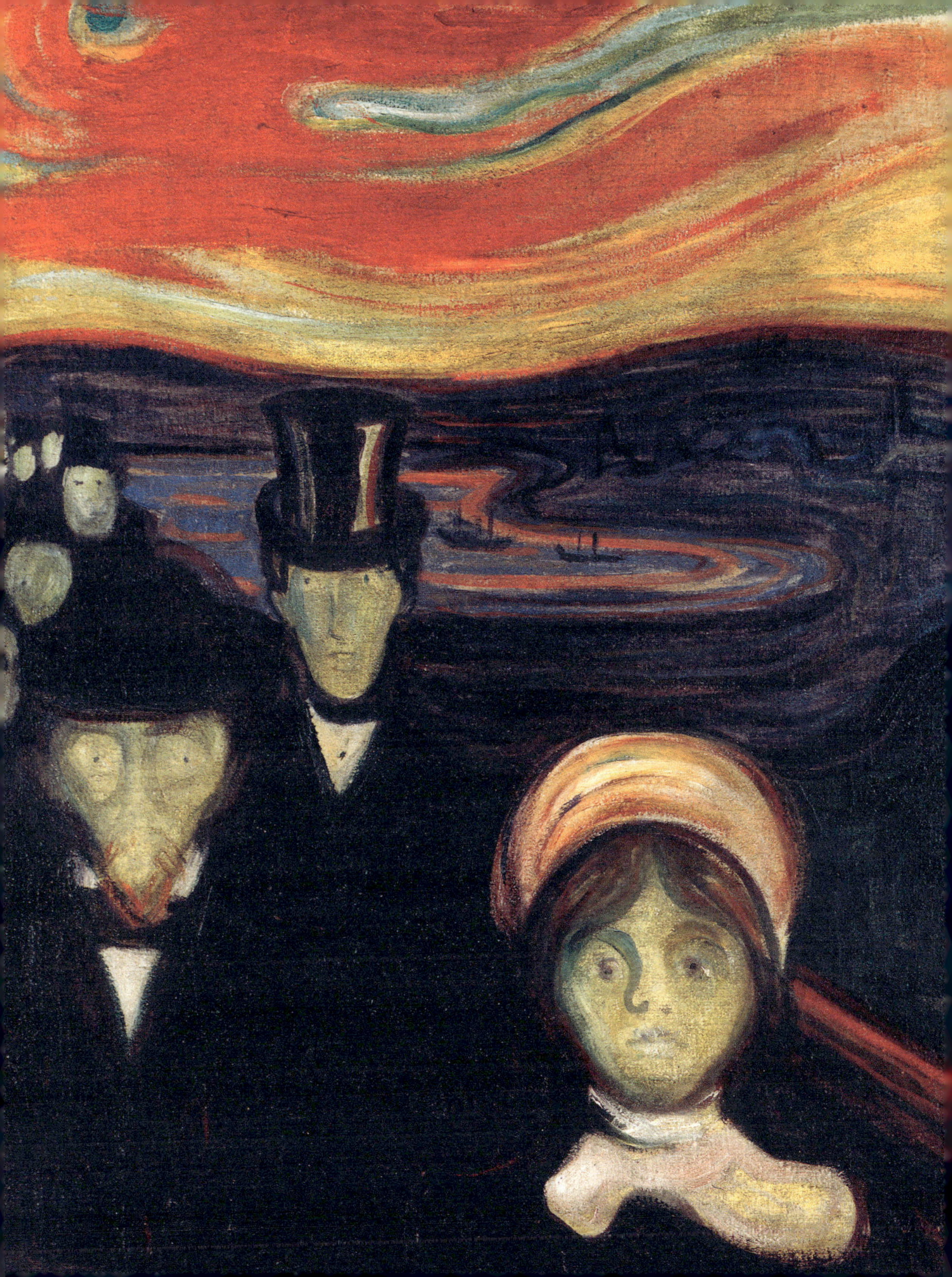

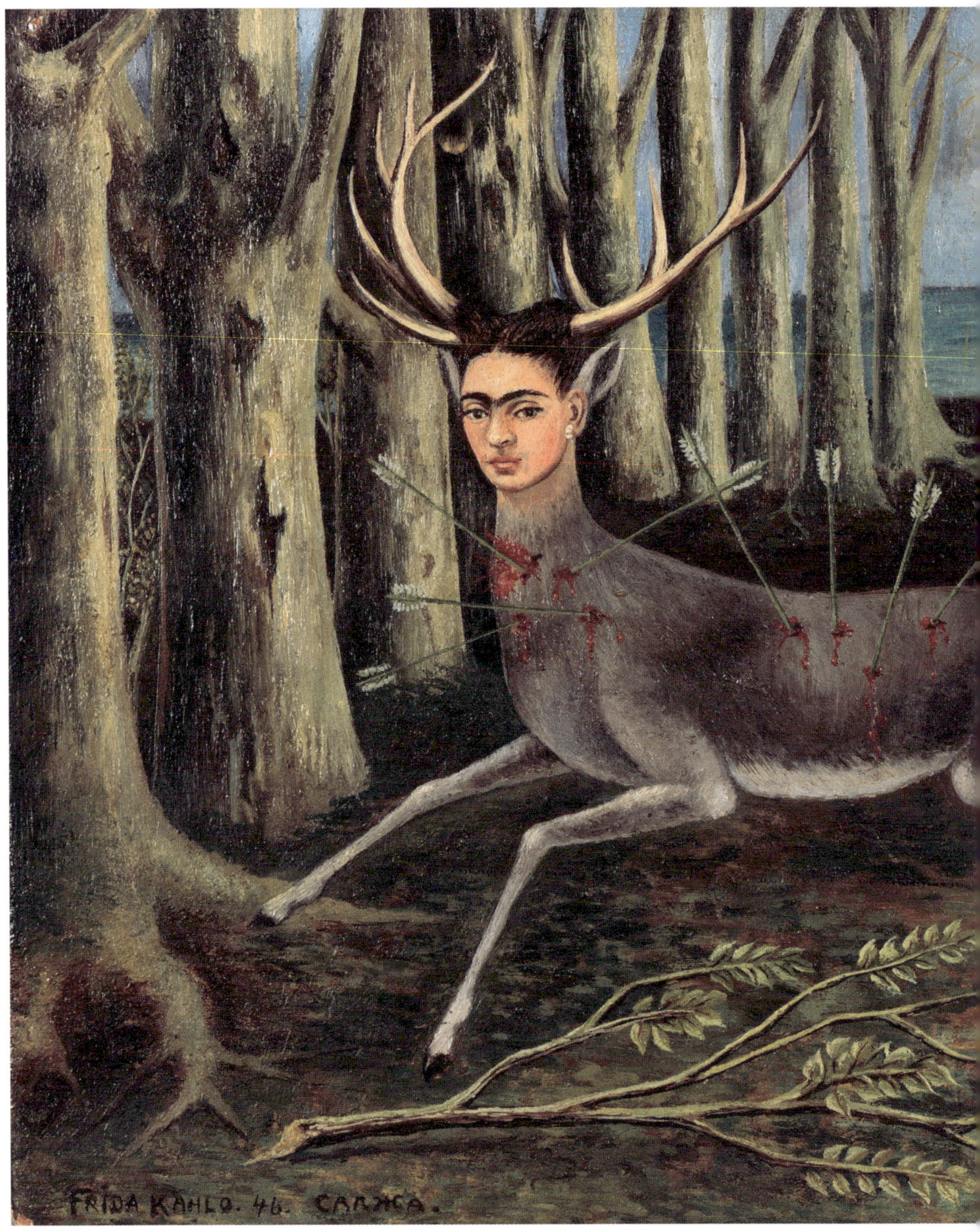
FRIDA KAHLO. 46. CARGA.

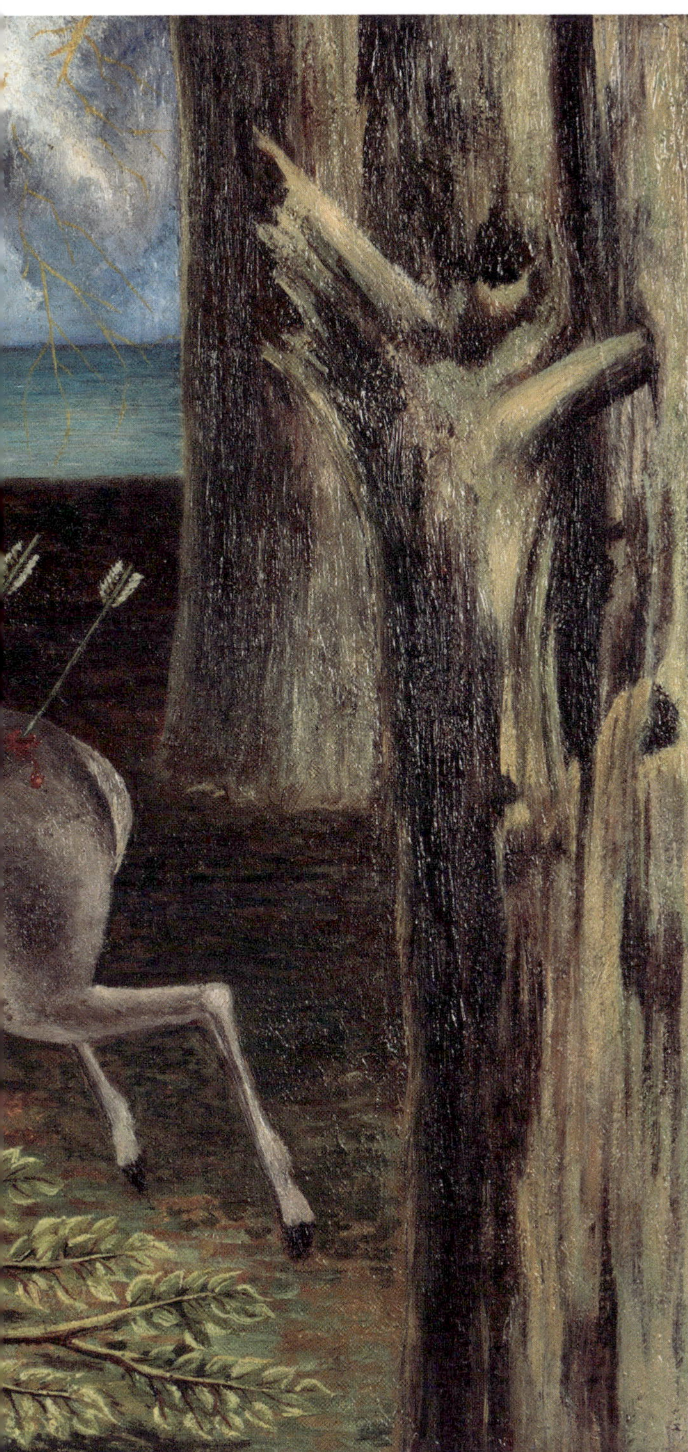

Left: The Wounded Deer, Frida Kahlo, 1946, oil on Masonite.

Feminist icon and one of Mexico's most well-known artists, Frida Kahlo (1907–54) was no stranger to suffering. She began painting in 1925, while recovering from a near-fatal bus accident that shattered her body and marked the beginning of lifelong physical agonies. Her entire life and her creativity were vastly influenced by chronic, severe illness, and her vivid, powerful body of work reflects this burden of pain, trauma and loss. She created haunting and stunningly original paintings that mingled elements of fantasy and folklore, using vibrant colours in a style that was influenced by indigenous cultures of Mexico as well as by European influences that include Realism, Symbolism and Surrealism. Many of her works are self-portraits that symbolically express her own pain. In these creations, Kahlo portrays herself time and again exploring and questioning herself and identity. Today Frida Kahlo ranks among the world's most renowned twentieth-century woman artists and her deeply and painfully personal paintings continue to fascinate and inspire art lovers around the world.

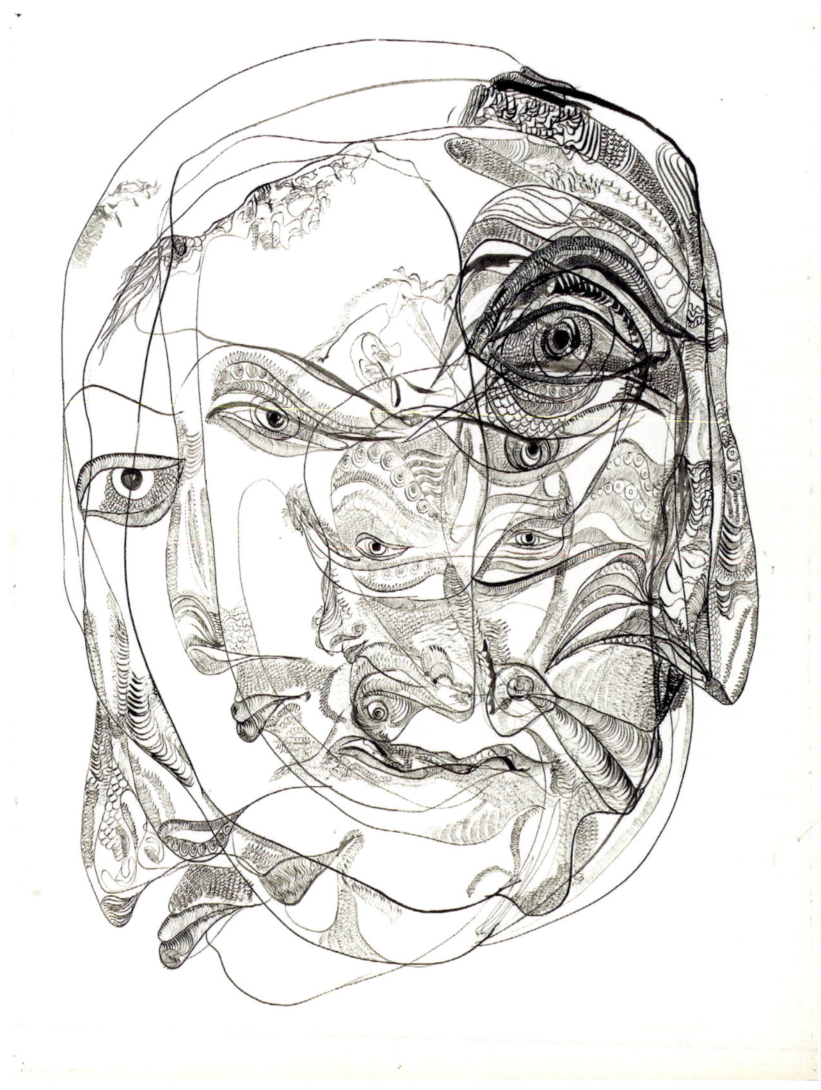

Above: Untitled, Unica Zürn, 1965, ink and gouache on paper.

Unica Zürn (1916–70) grew up surrounded by marvellous and unusual objects collected by her absent father, a cavalry officer whom she adored. Inspired perhaps in part by her father's gifts from afar and a longing to spend more time with him, Zürn developed a rich fantasy life and a vivid imagination. This is evidenced in her captivating, otherworldly drawings and shadowy mirages of fantastical creatures meticulously constructed out of finely rendered, obsessively repetitive shapes and lines. Also an accomplished author who wrote with cool detachment and even humour from the depths of her mental illness, which some believe to be schizophrenia, though others suggest she may have suffered from bipolar disorder with psychotic features, Zürn produced most of her oeuvre while involved with the German Surrealist, Hans Bellmer. During her time with him, Zürn began to experiment with 'automatic' drawings and anagrams as part of her long-held interest in hidden meanings and coincidences. On 19 October 1970, after a decade of mental crises, Zürn leapt to her death from the balcony of the Paris apartment she had shared with Bellmer.

Below: Materdolorsa, Aloïse Corbaz, 1922, pencil, ink and coloured pencils on postcard.

Aloïse Corbaz (1886–1964), after working as a governess in the entourage of Kaiser Wilhelm II, for whom she developed an intense – and imaginary – attachment, returned to Lausanne at the start of the First World War and soon exhibited signs of mental collapse. She was diagnosed in 1918 as schizophrenic and placed for the remainder of her life in the asylum La Rosière in Gimel, Switzerland. There, she began making art and eventually became known simply as Aloïse. Women of power and romance are the centre of Aloïse Corbaz's visual universe, and though she drew primarily with crayon and pencil, she would at times infuse works with stains from crushed floral petals and occasionally mix in toothpaste.

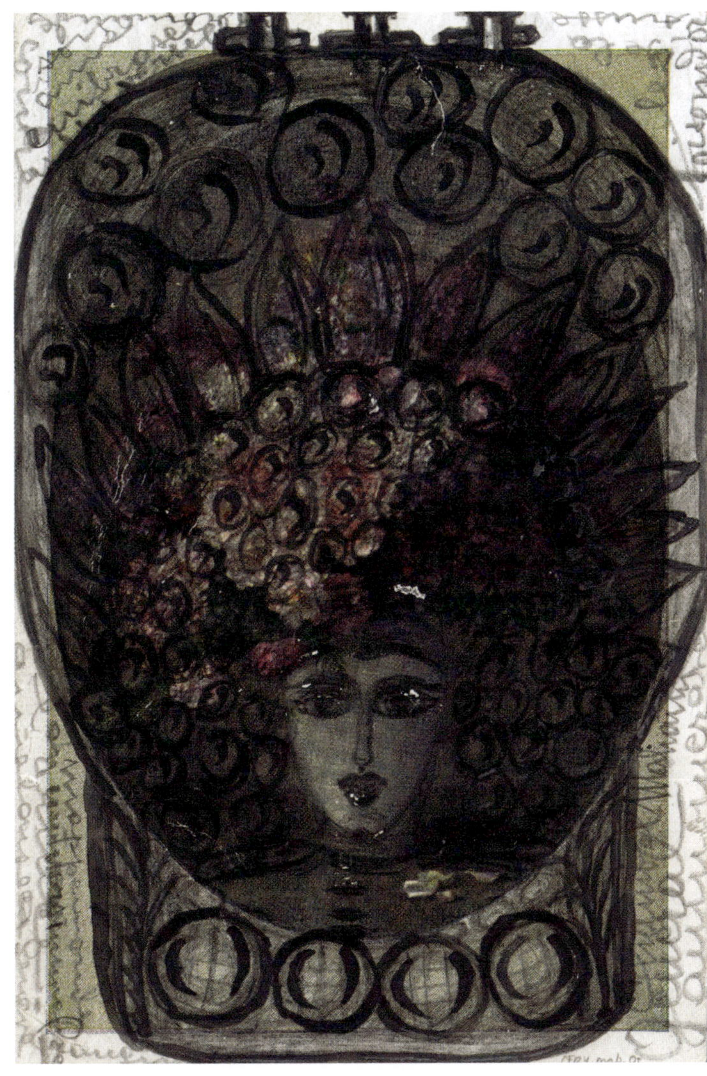

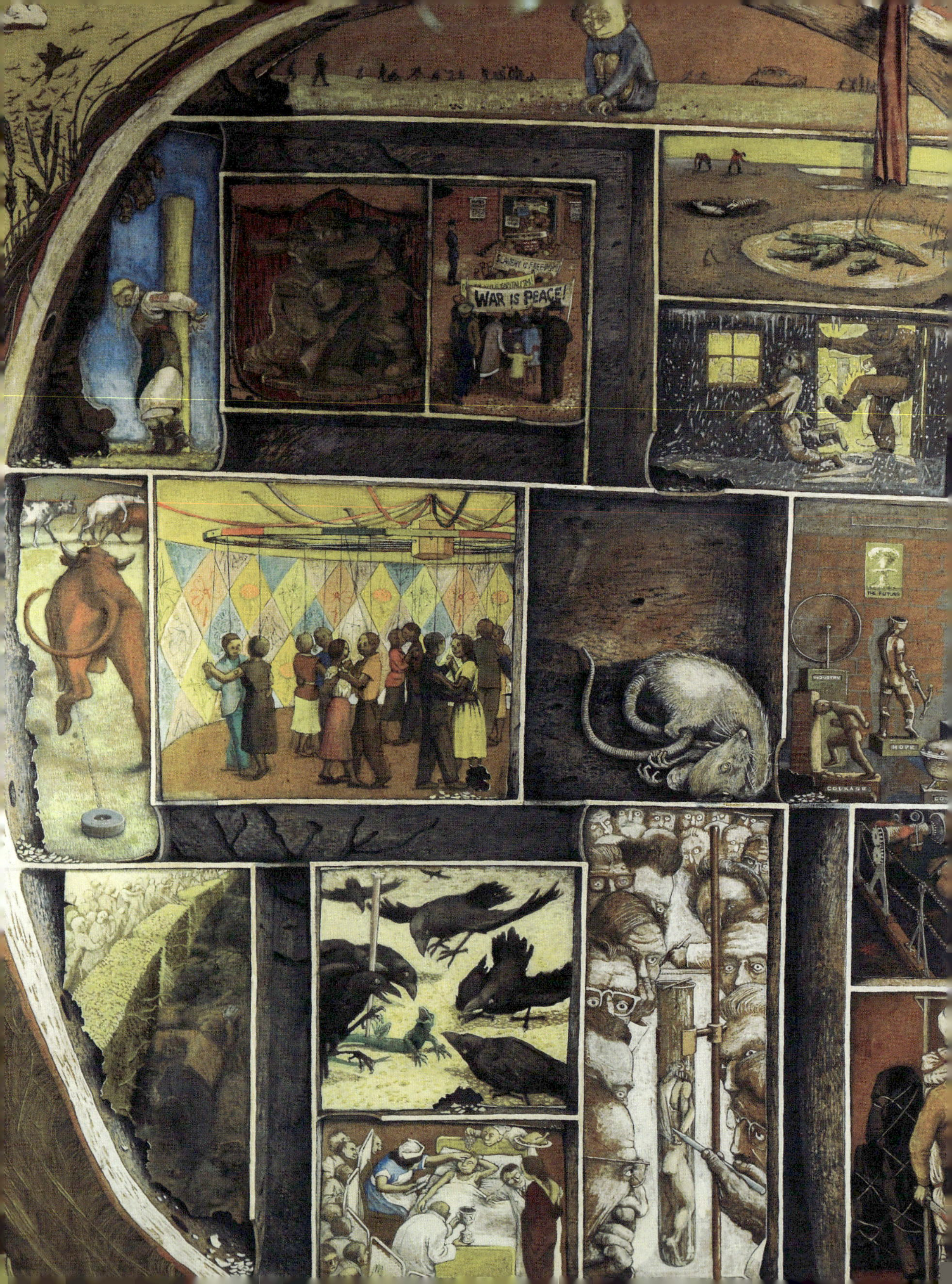
WAR IS PEACE!
THE FUTURE
INDUSTRY
HOPE
COURAGE

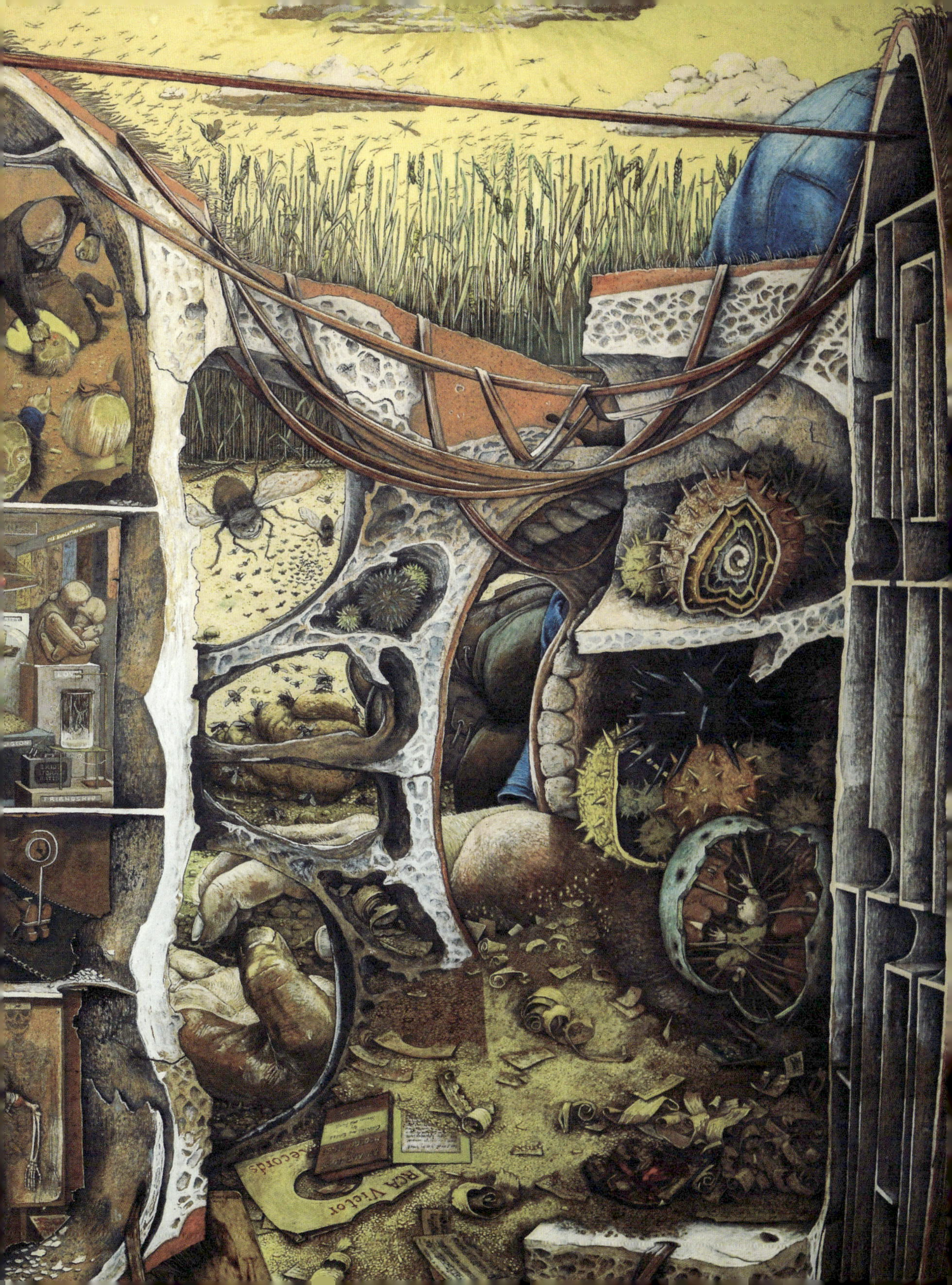
LOVE
FRIENDSHIP
RCA Victor
Records

Previous spread: The Maze, William Kurelek, 1953, gouache on board.

The art of William Kurelek (1927–77) navigated the harsh realities of Depression-era farm life while exploring the sources of the artist's debilitating mental suffering, and these nostalgic and apocalyptic works represent an unsettling and controversial record of global anxiety in the twentieth century. By the time of his death, he was one of the most commercially successful artists in Canada, whose paintings remain coveted by collectors many years after Kurelek's premature death. *The Maze* is a painting that Kurelek produced while a patient at the Maudsley Hospital in London. Professionals at Maudsley quickly recognized the gravity of Kurelek's suffering – although the precise nature of his illness remains unknown – and while there receiving treatment, he was also given a room to paint in. *The Maze*, described by the artist as 'a painting of the inside of my skull', can be interpreted as Kurelek's attempt to justify this privilege; as he wrote, 'I had to impress the hospital staff as being a worthwhile specimen to keep on'.

Opposite: Woman Leaving the Psychoanalyst, Remedios Varo, 1960, oil on canvas.

The canvases of Catalan Surrealist artist Remedios Varo (1908–63) are boldly enigmatic ciphers, notoriously elusive of solution, despite the abundance of magical keys and clues. Painted towards the end of her life, *Woman Leaving the Psychoanalyst* plays upon the pseudoscience of psychoanalysis, the initials of its three fathers inscribed on the portal behind the central figure, 'FJA' standing for Freud, Jung and Adler. In a dreary medieval courtyard above which heavy clouds linger, a green, cloaked figure drops a ghostly, disembodied head down a well without a trace of hesitation or compunction, and nary a backward glance. Painted towards the end of Varo's life, this, according to the artist, was 'the proper thing to do when leaving the psychoanalyst'.

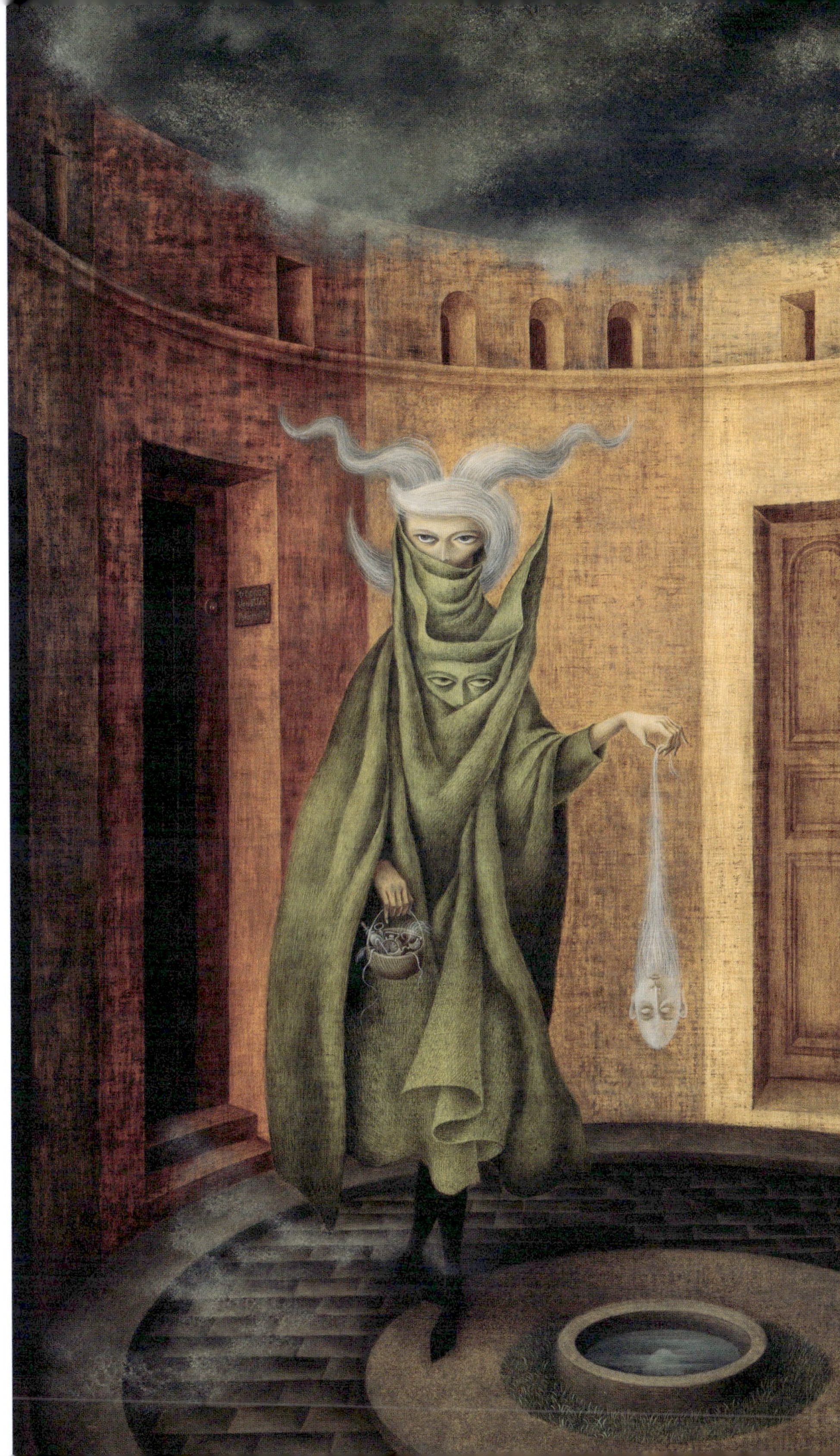

III

—

Whispers from the Void

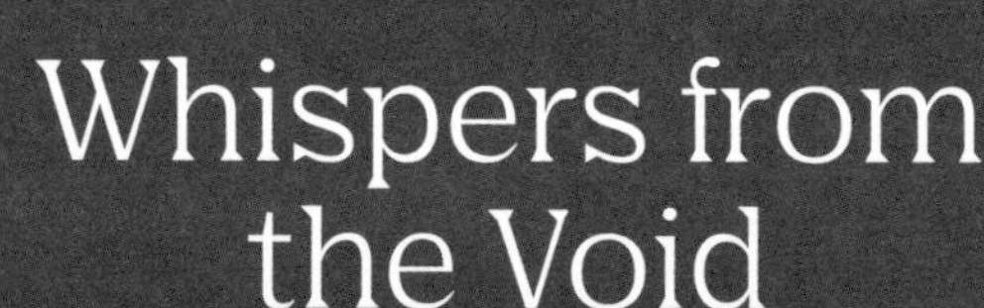

'I feel stupid and contagious. Here we are now, entertain us.'

What's the point?

In today's modern world, with its excesses of information and images of violence, trauma and injustices, you may catch yourself discontented and despairing. Things feel meaningless and shallow, you're alienated from nature, from others, and your own, authentic self. Nothing seems . . . worth it. These pervasive feelings of existential angst creep into your consciousness and create a gloomy, cynical inner monologue dripping in disdain for the human condition and leave you questioning the meaning of life.

Humans have long pondered on the nature of existence, and what it means to be a thinking, feeling, acting individual being in the face of a world that can often seem senseless and devoid of meaning. In these moments of schism and psychic numbing, understanding stalls, language fails and powerful, formless, unsettling questions arise. It's the disquietude and distress of experiencing this emptiness that manifests as existential anxiety – an ever-present, anxious dread that is always lurking, even beneath our happiness.

In the void of this uncertainty, how do we find our purpose, how can we make our own meaning? Creativity, as you might have guessed, is essential in this pursuit. Creativity is a persistent theme in Existentialist thought and may be required, as German philosopher Friedrich Nietzsche suggests, to become who we are, and who we may want to be. Artists are well acquainted with this demand for meaning and desire to express identity, and their work and practice is often a response to this human hunger for understanding. Using the creative process as an act of self-assertion, and an expression of freedom and authenticity, artists have for centuries generated works expressing this poignant anxiety about the fate of humanity. In the visual arts, Existentialism refers to the mood, thought and impulses perceived in the works rather than a distinctive and consistent style, but the analogues of Existentialism can be found in Surrealism and Expressionism. Existentialism provided abstract painters with a terminology that enabled them to assert the importance of their very personal expressions.

Existentialism was a powerful influence on post-war art in Europe, as artists, writers and thinkers struggled to reconcile with not only the physical devastation wrought by war, but with the trauma of its psychological repercussions as well.

This philosophical response was popularized amid these horrors by Jean-Paul Sartre whose treatise *Being and Nothingness* described the anxiety and meaningless of existence and the pursuit of authenticity in life, and found its themes of alienation and individual autonomy explored by artists such as Francis Bacon, Alberto Giacometti and Jean Dubuffet. Existentialism naturally influenced numerous mid-century artists' understanding of existence as an isolated solitary phenomenon in an absurd world and yet still afforded one the freedom for one to define oneself. Simone de Beauvoir said in 1965 that for these artists Existentialism seemed to 'authorize them to accept their transitory condition without renouncing a certain absolute, to face horror and absurdity while still retaining their human dignity'.

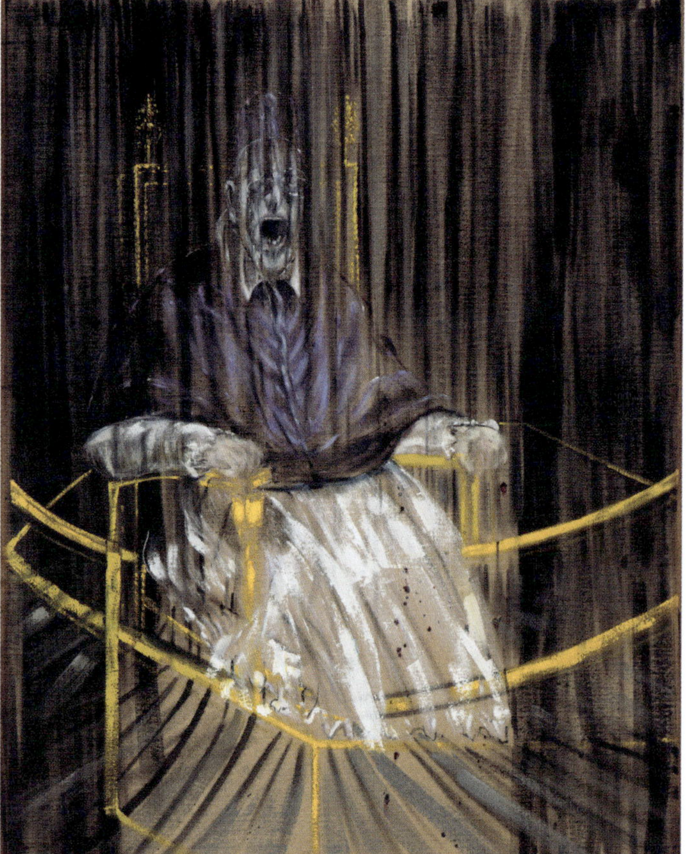

Left: Study After Velázquez's Portrait of Pope Innocent X, Francis Bacon, 1953, oil on canvas.

Many art historians and theorists consider Francis Bacon (1909–92) the quintessential Existentialist artist, and in viewing his 1953 *Study*, we can get a glimpse as to why. In this bizarre, garish scene, we see the tortured expression of a blood-spattered pope imprisoned upon a rather uncomfortable-looking throne. Though the paint strokes obfuscate the screams of the figure, we can certainly imagine them. Known for his theatricality, violence and claustrophobic environments, Bacon seems the most unforgiving and anguished of the Existential artists. He identified as a Nietzschean and atheist, and some contemporary critics saw the series as symbolic execution scenes, as if Bacon sought to enact Nietzsche's declaration that 'God is dead' by killing his mouthpiece on Earth.

Edvard Munch painted the delirium and the dread of existence, the feverish chaos of sickness, and the fearful way in which we may sense death although we properly cannot imagine it for ourselves. The wild and aggressive painting of the Paris-based German artist Wols is characteristic of the European abstract movement Art Informel and was claimed by Jean-Paul Sartre for Existentialism, writing that his work was a visualization of our 'universal horror of being-in-the-world', our fascination with the 'otherness' of worldly phenomena.

While Existentialists express diverging views about many topics, most can agree it is a philosophy that invites individuals to live life with creativity, and that Existentialist thinking encourages living life as a work of art. In the context of the twenty-first century, the legacies of these boundary-challenging artists continue to resonate with contemporary creators striving to make art that challenges our beliefs and our sense of reality and creates spaces for incongruencies to coexist – such as Karen Cronje, a South African artist who explores the intersection of human interaction and the environment and how our individual associations influence how we experience the same place.

'Embrace the pandemonium,' offers the ever-pragmatic Eleanor Shellstrop in the television series *The Good Place*, a piece of Existentialist theatre if ever there was one, and which through its narrative explores these philosophical themes of absurdity, alienation, the lack of meaning and purpose in life. And in embracing our creativity, we, hopeless, helpless humans with our disunited existences in this absurd universe, imbue our search for meaning *with* meaning, and we manage to live on in this weird, beautiful and dreadful world. To come full circle and paraphrase Friedrich Nietzsche, we have art in order not to die of life.

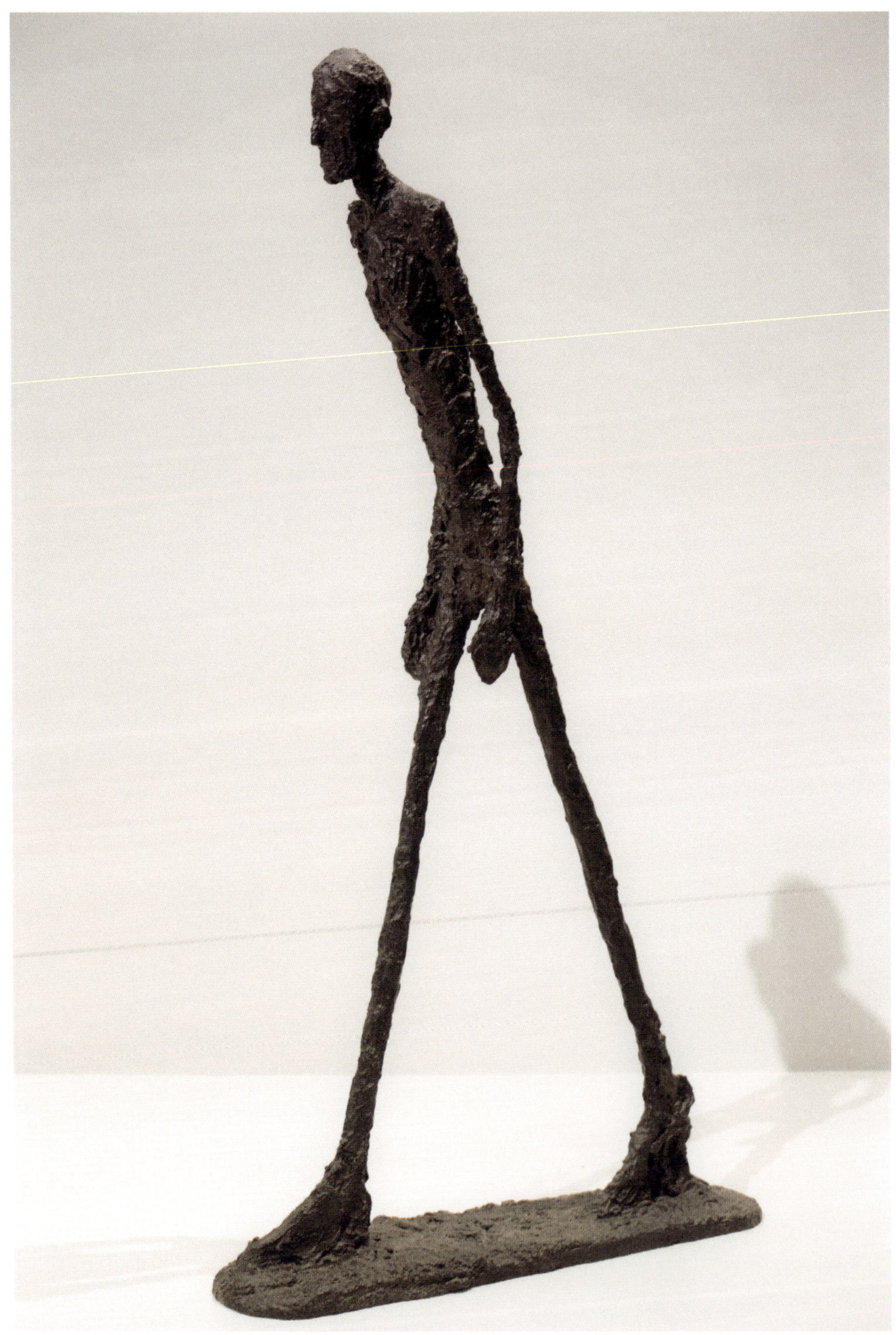

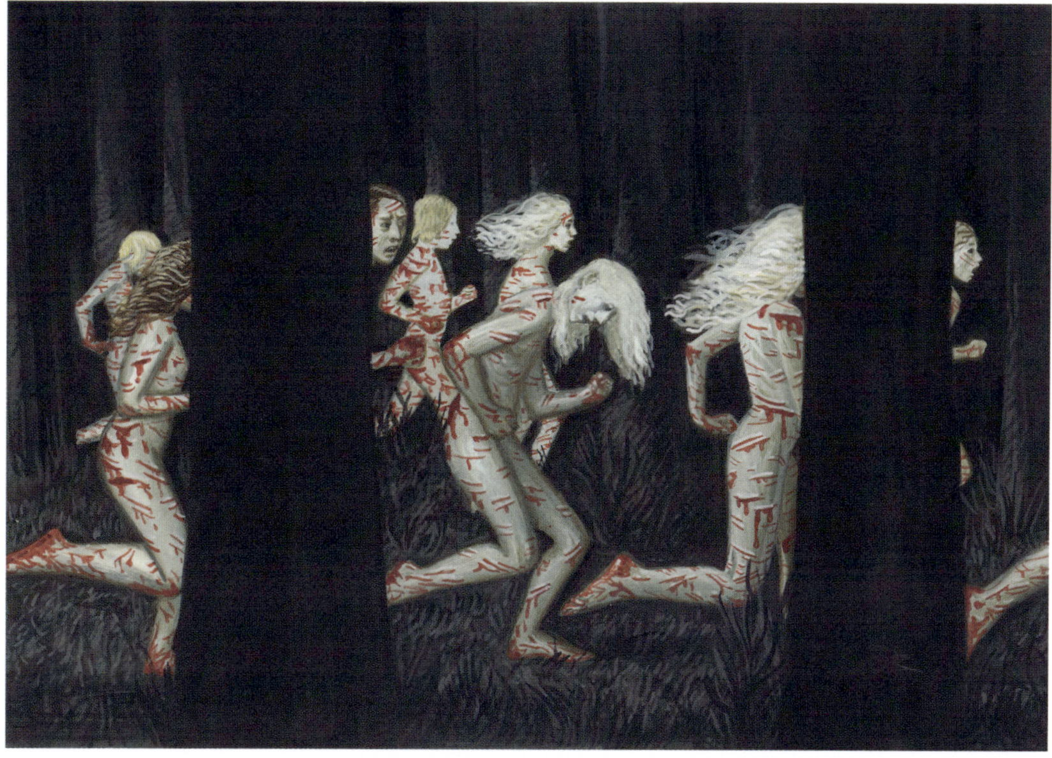

Opposite: Walking Man I, Alberto Giacometti, 1960, bronze sculpture.

Above: Bieg Chlosta, Aleksandra Waliszewska, 2010, gouache on paper.

Alberto Giacometti (1901–66) created fragile figures lost and exposed in wide open spaces, and is best known for his elongated, withered representations of the human form, including his 1960 sculpture *Walking Man I*, which in 2010 broke the record for a work of art sold at auction when it fetched 104.3 million US dollars. Giacometti's severe figures explored the psyche and the charged space occupied by a single person. Linked to Jean-Paul Sartre and Existentialism, they are seen as metaphors for the post-war experience of doubt and alienation.

Polish painter Aleksandra Waliszewska (b. 1976) creates some of your most brutal nightmares: morbid compositions exploring oppressive themes and dark, tortuous subject matter. Unfortunate events abound, and a trail of carnage, both physical and psychological, streaks gore-soaked and deep through Waliszewska's works. Whether random or ritualistic, the violence runs rampant, with characters who are either coming to brutal ends or are depicted engaging in the brutality themselves. Sometimes it is unclear as to who is the victim and who is the villain, and yet we can't look away. Waliszewska is flaying the face of the mundane and peeling back the layers to give us a peek at what lies beneath - attraction and repulsion.

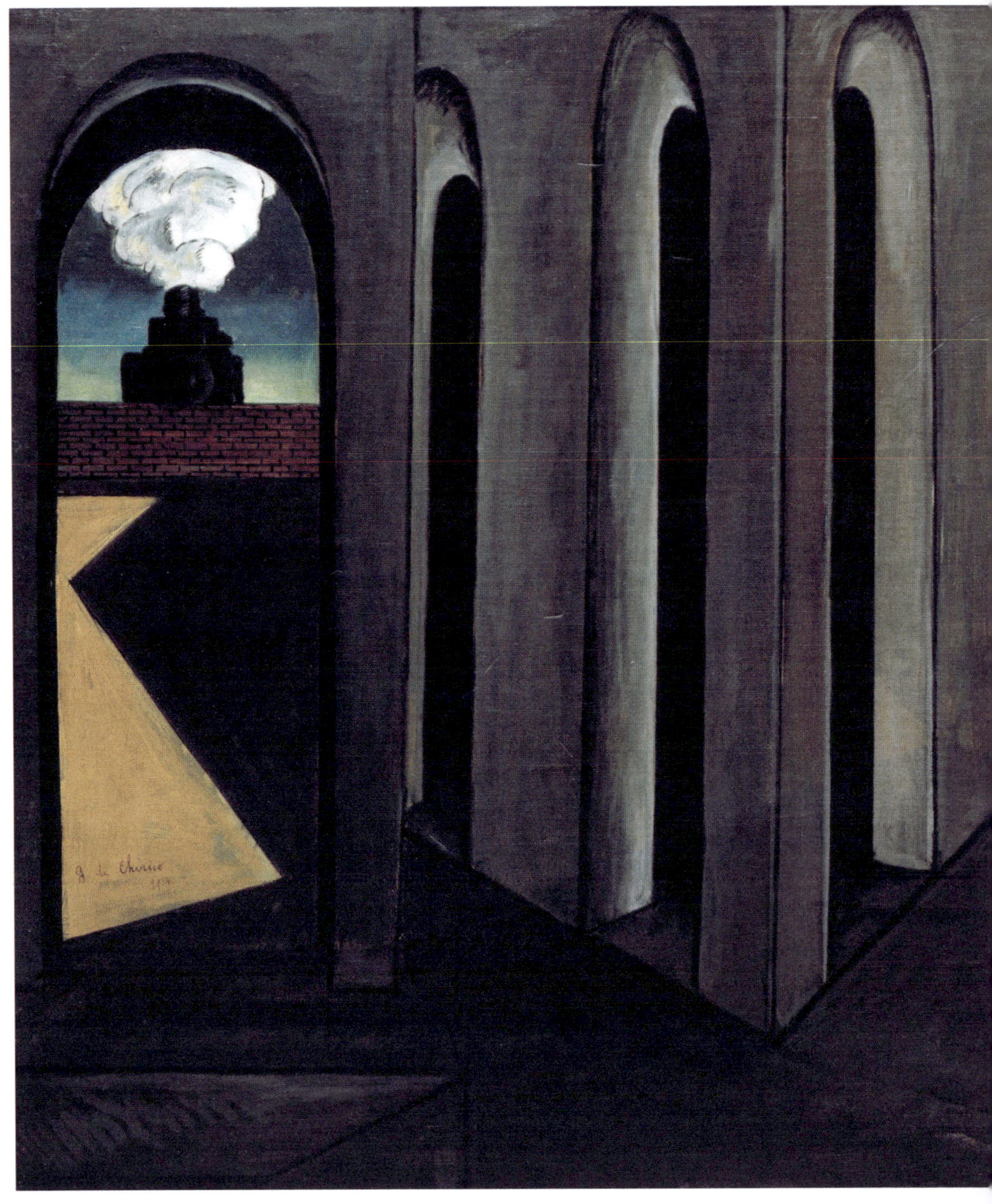

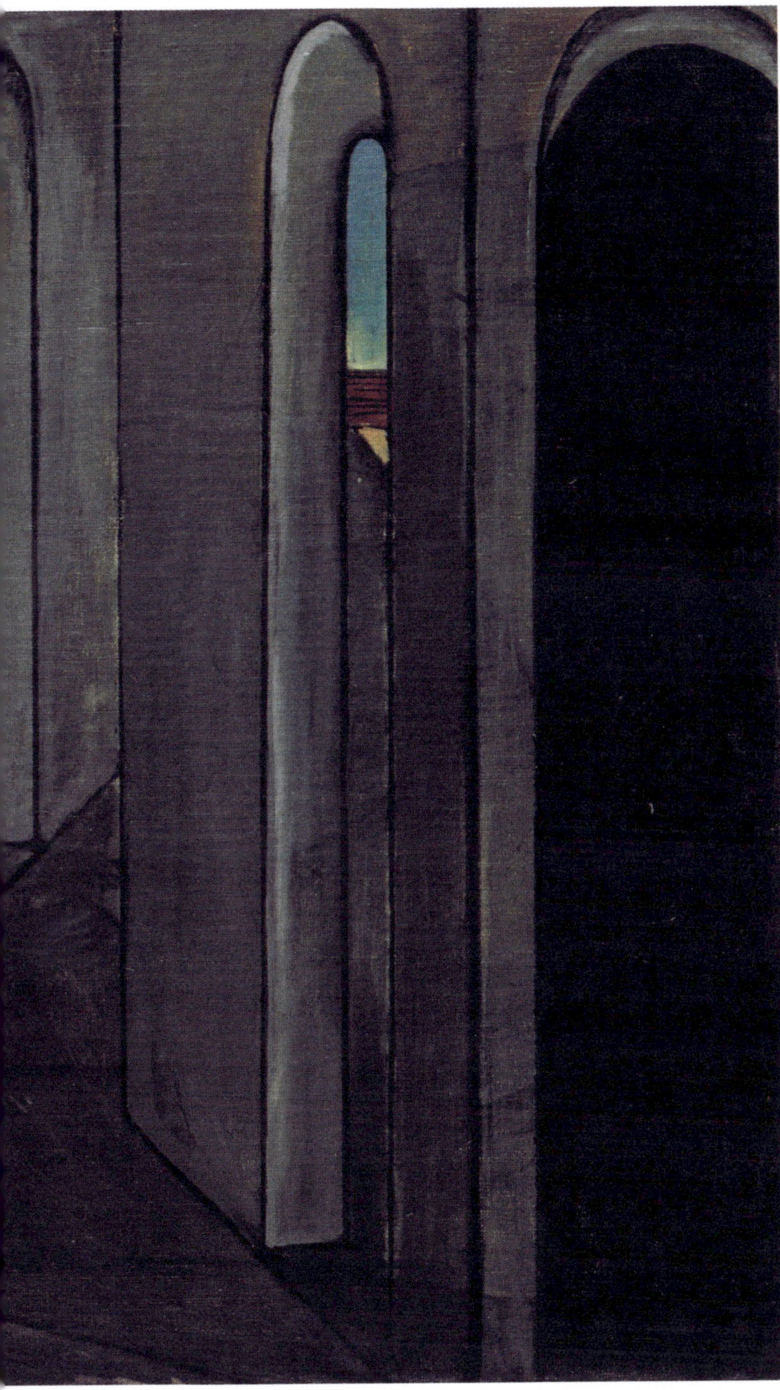

Left: The Anxious Journey, Giorgio de Chirico, 1913, oil on canvas.

The works of artist and writer Giorgio de Chirico (1888–1978) embody the contemplations of an artist profoundly concerned with dreams and questions of being, and include elements of Surrealism, Italian Futurism and mid-twentieth-century existential emptiness. In 2020, our world became the vague, eerie disorientation of a Chirico painting – empty streets and spaces where life in the foreground seemed to have stalled and the trappings of modern existence continued uninterrupted in the background. This sense of our lives in limbo while the world continued on without us was, to many of us, the 'new normal'.

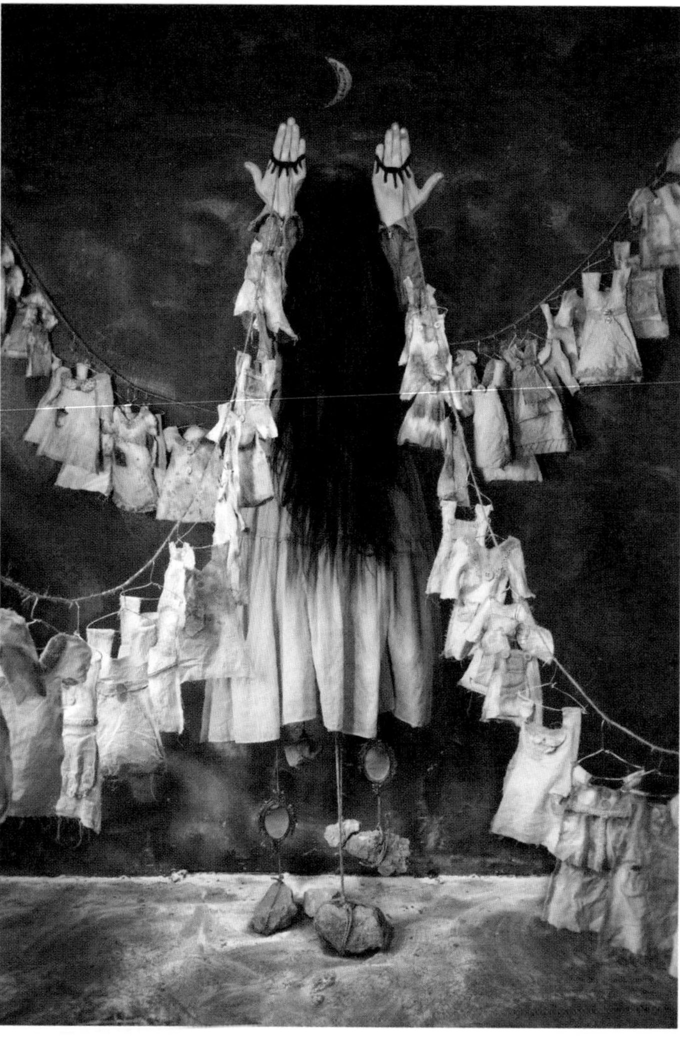

Left: Histories of She, Darla Teagarden, 2017, digital.

Profoundly resonant for those among us who view the world through a splinter of enchantment, Darla Teagarden's surreal photographic narratives walk a tremulous line between fable and reality. These feverish visions are deeply imbued with fragile secrets, intense emotion, and an eerie sense of urgency - an otherworldly plucking at the senses. Teagarden builds these vividly expressive vignettes from wood, paper, and plaster for images that also include handpicked vintage props, clothing and hand-drawn backgrounds. It is this tender, liminal space, rebuilt and reimagined many times over, in which most of her darkly cinematic images are created.

Opposite: Skull of a Skeleton with Burning Cigarette, Vincent van Gogh, 1885–86, oil on canvas.

This painting, rendered in sombre tones by Vincent van Gogh (1853-90), of a grinning skull with a lit cigarette clenched between its teeth, is a bit of a juvenile joke. The work is purported to have been a humorous analogy to artistry of the human form during the artist's studies and a satirical comment on conservative academic practices. Like Kierkegaard, Van Gogh believed that it was absurd for others to teach artistry to the artist and that one must develop art through one's own creativity and emotion. Quoted as denouncing his studies in Antwerp as boring and non-educational, Van Gogh grappled with existential questions during his twenties while working aimlessly as a picture dealer, schoolteacher, bookshop clerk and missionary. In the early 1880s, he committed himself to a life of art.

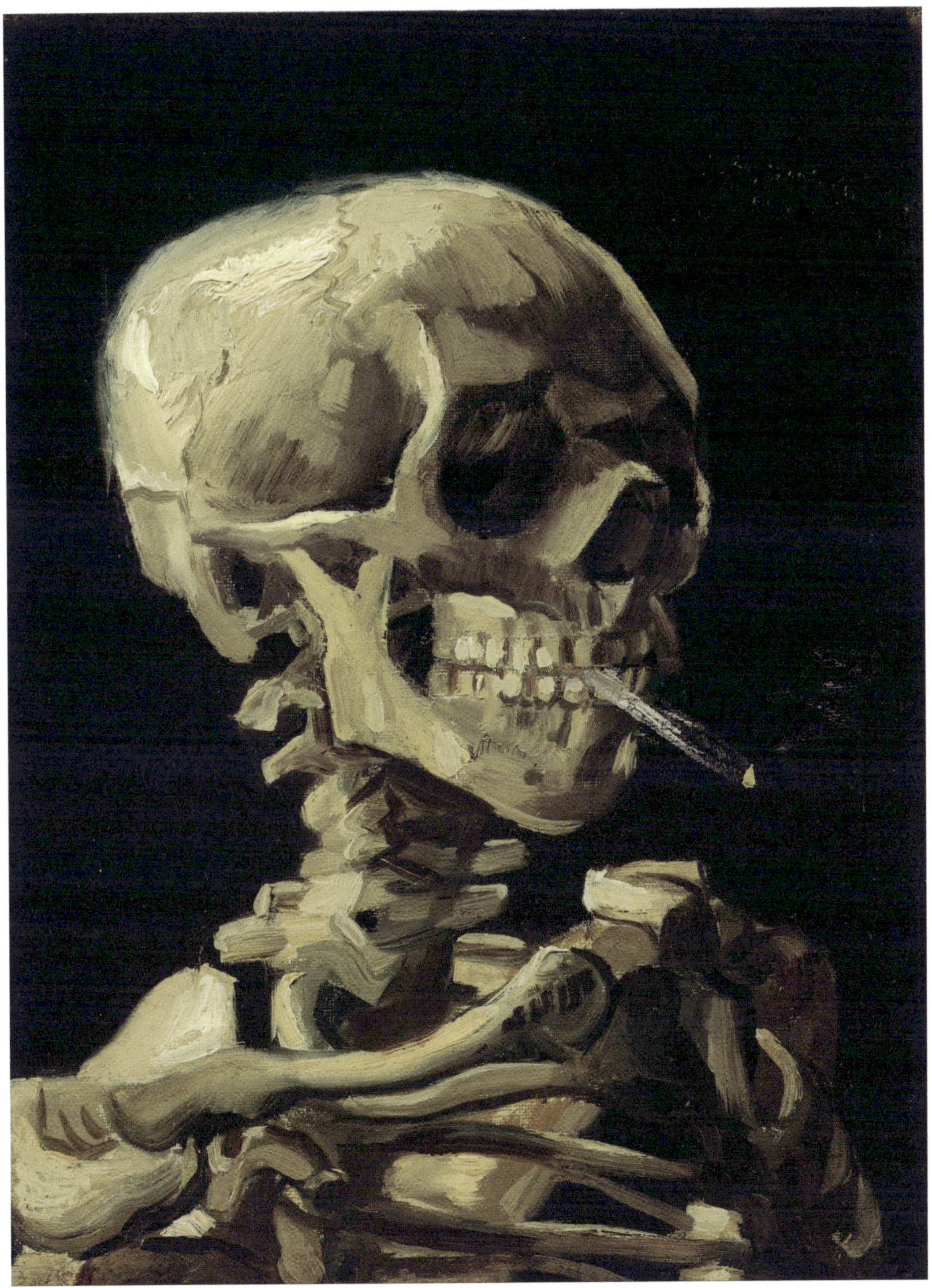

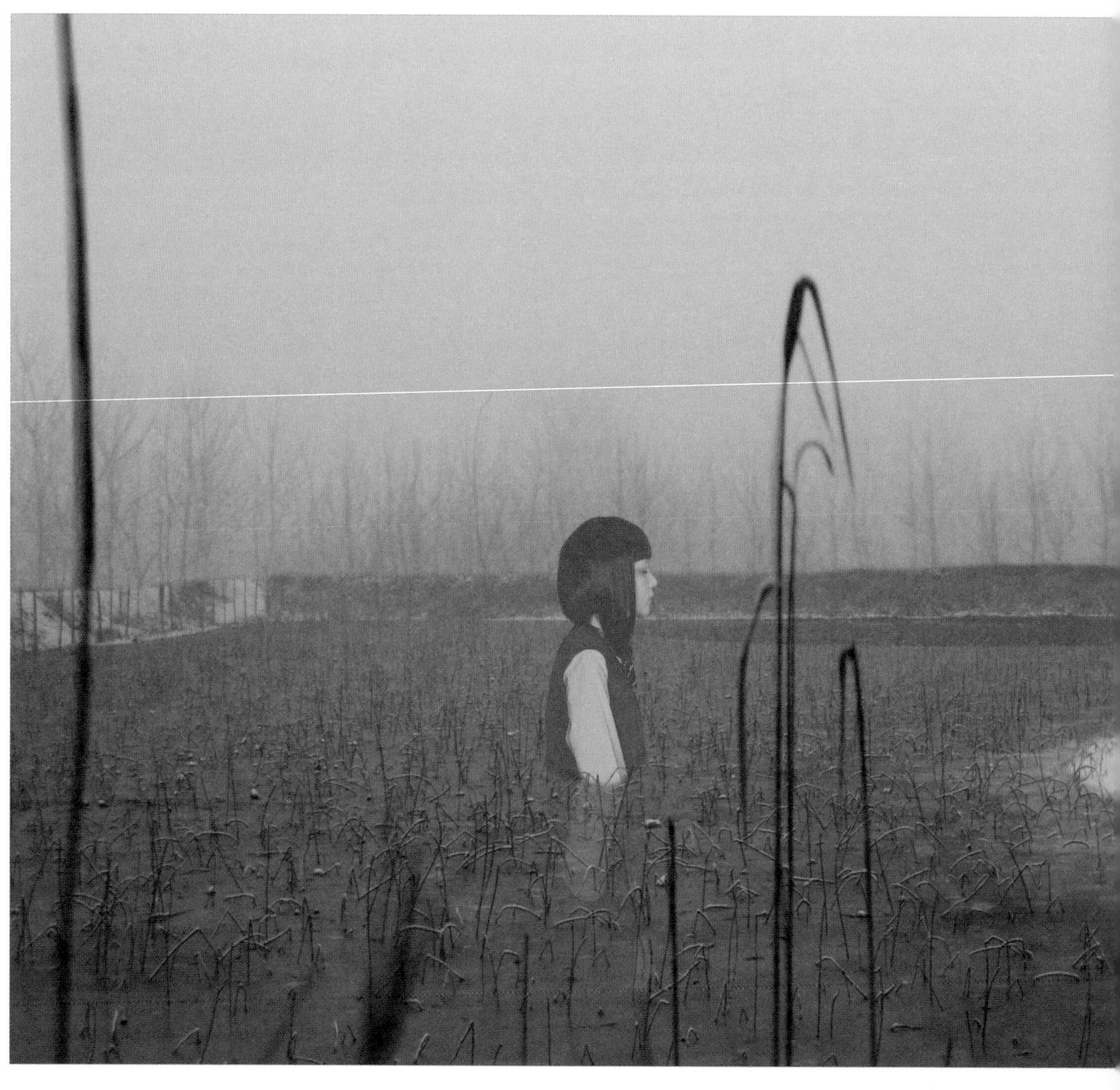

Above: Existential Emptiness No. 18, Cui Xiuwen, 2009, C-Print.

The series Existential Emptiness by Cui Xiuwen (b. 1970) is a reflection of the woman as individual in modern China. This body of work from one China's foremost female photographers shifts her focus from physical to spiritual in an exploration of the woman's psyche. Mostly monochromatic digital photographs, with a palette and format inspired by traditional Chinese ink painting, the scenes take place in the still landscape of the ice- and snow-covered mountains of Northern China - an ideal setting for exploring the mind and questions of beingness. The physical appearance of the doll - obvious joints, revealed ribcage bones and scarred womb - alludes to the violence of a woman's experiences and how they impress upon her spirit.

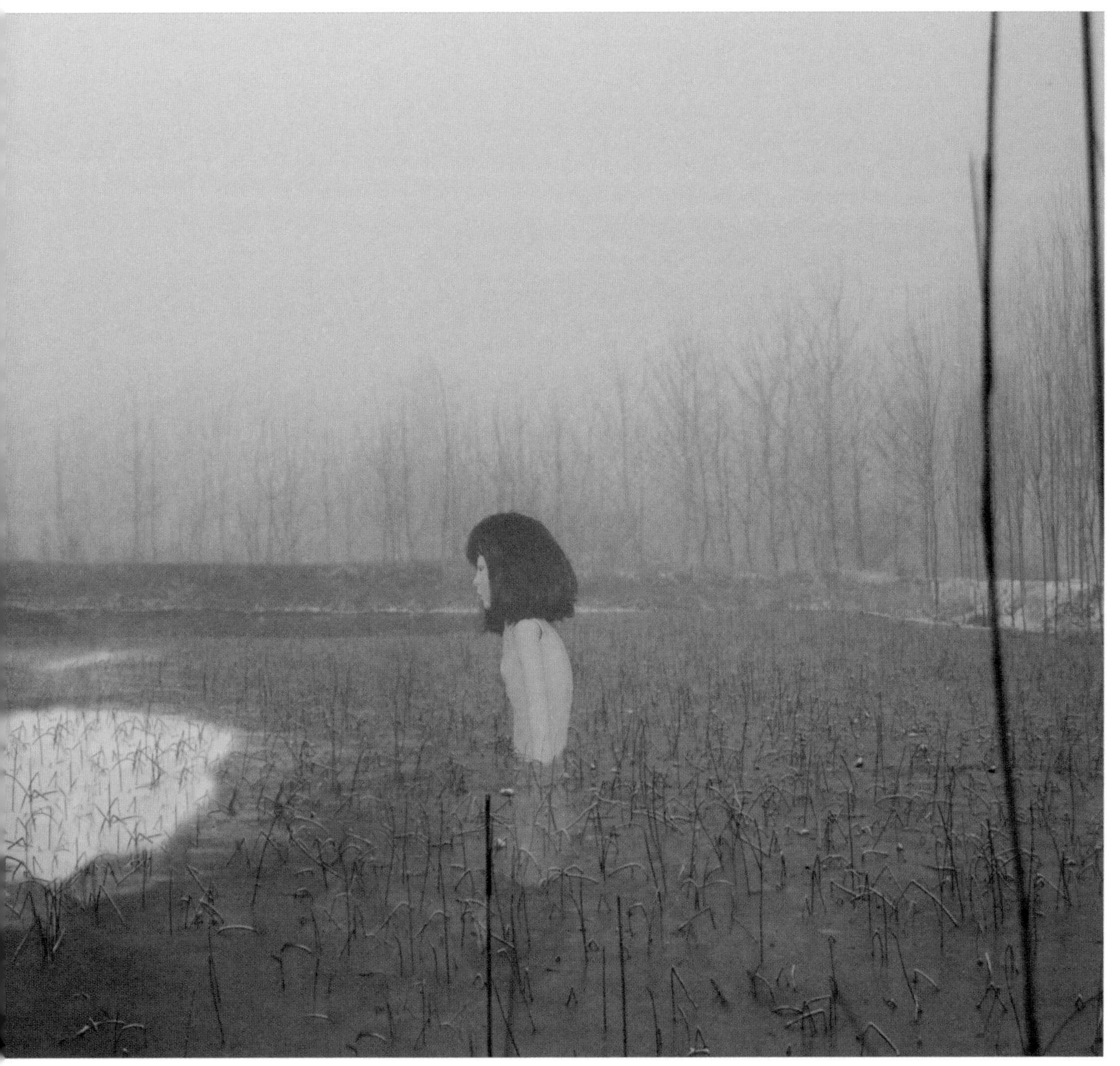

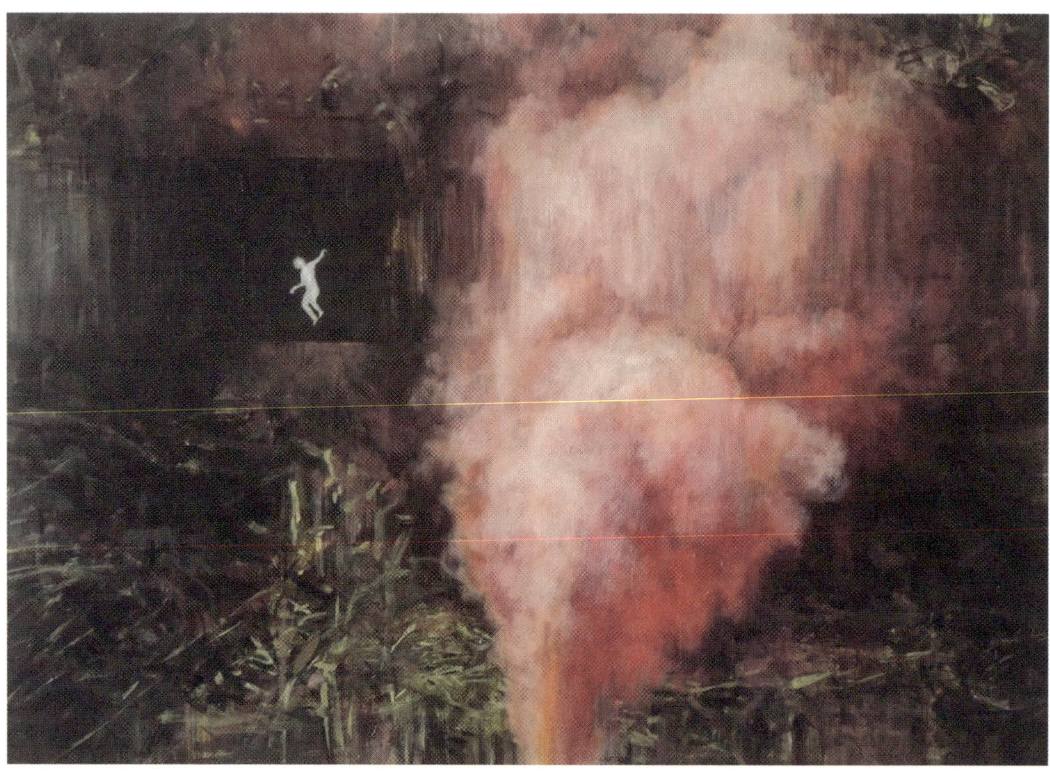

Above: Existential Crisis, Karen Cronje, 2016, oil on primed paper.

Karen Cronje (b. 1975) is a South African painter who lives and works in Cape Town. Cronje's work explores a range of ideas centring around the notion of a dystopian view of the contemporary world, and reflects ideas around landscape, memory and the intersection of human interaction and the environment. She explores her interest in the 'stuff' of landscape - patterns, textures - and how our individual memories, associations and viewpoint influence how we experience the same place.

Opposite: Self-Portrait, Stanisław Ignacy Witkiewicz, c. 1912, photograph.

Stanisław Ignacy Witkiewicz (1885–1939) or 'Witkacy', as he became known, is remembered in his homeland of Poland as an accomplished artist, aesthetician, novelist, pioneering dramatist and philosopher; his photographs are only one aspect of his art. An intense and troubled man who believed that Western culture was decadent, degenerate and undermined by the collapse of ethical and philosophical certainties, he used photography, perhaps more than other art forms, as a way to explore his existential anxiety. In Witkiewicz's haunting self-portrait, the artist's stoic face emerges from the depths of formless darkness, yet remains trapped behind a cracked pane of shattered glass.

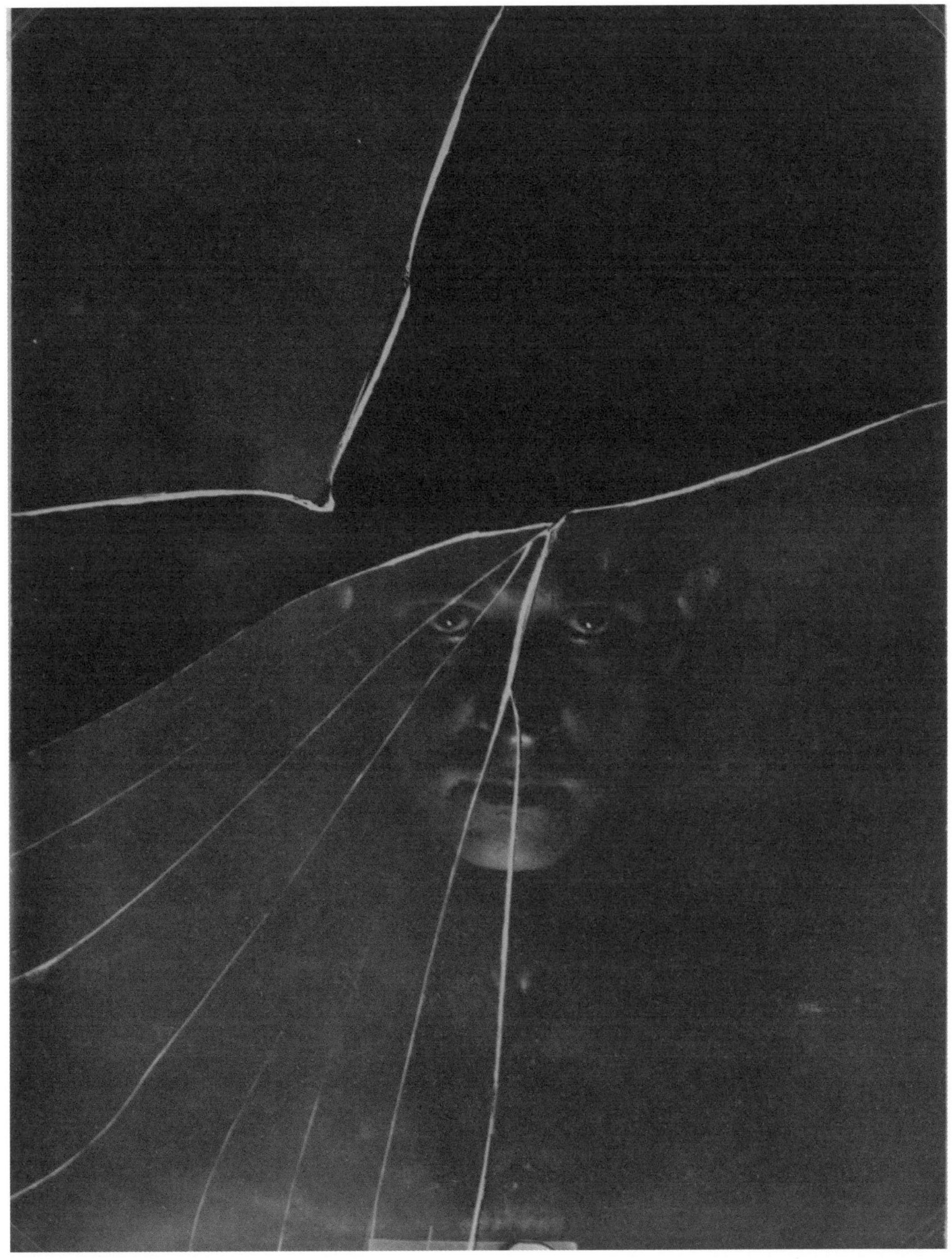

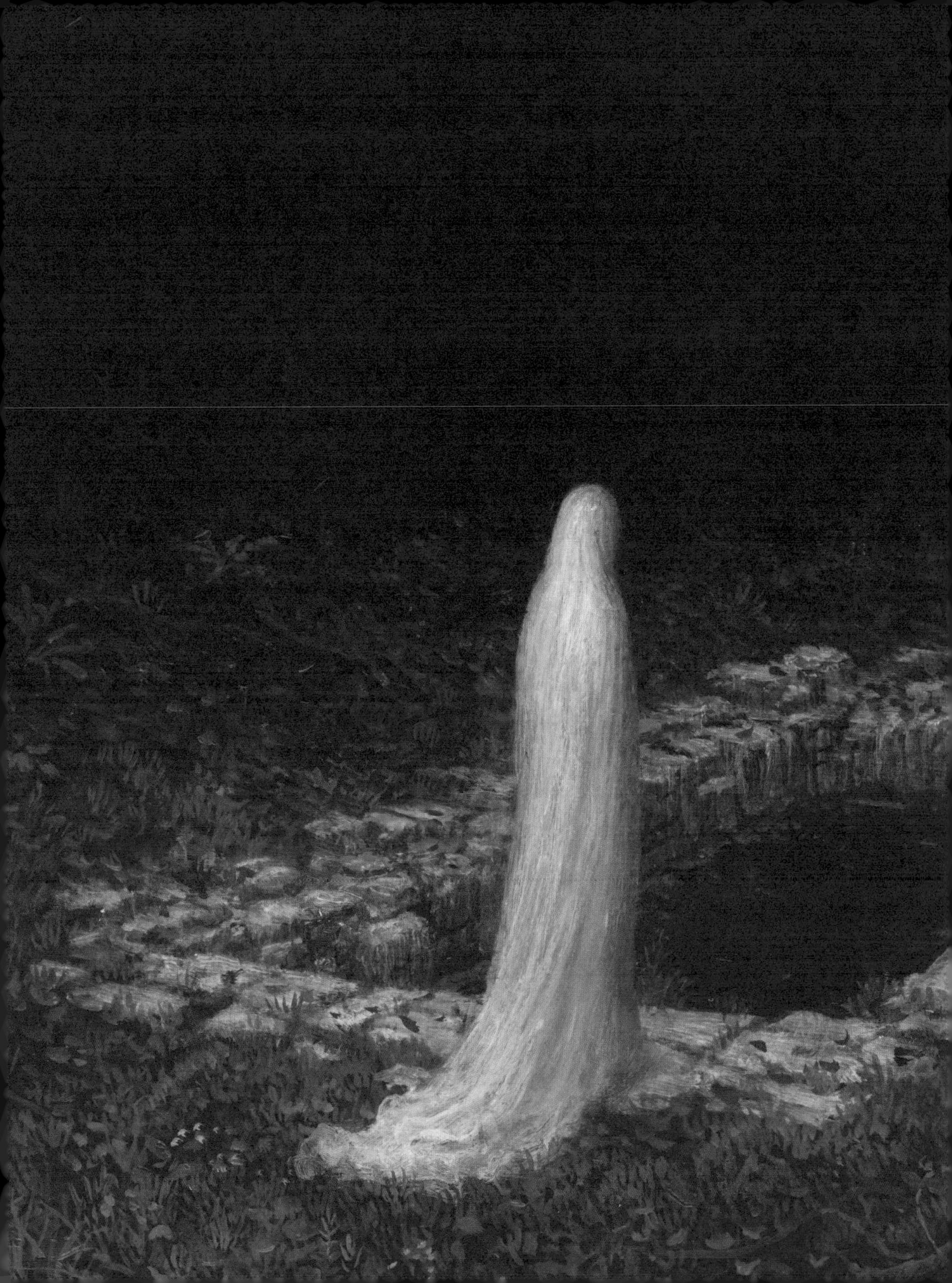

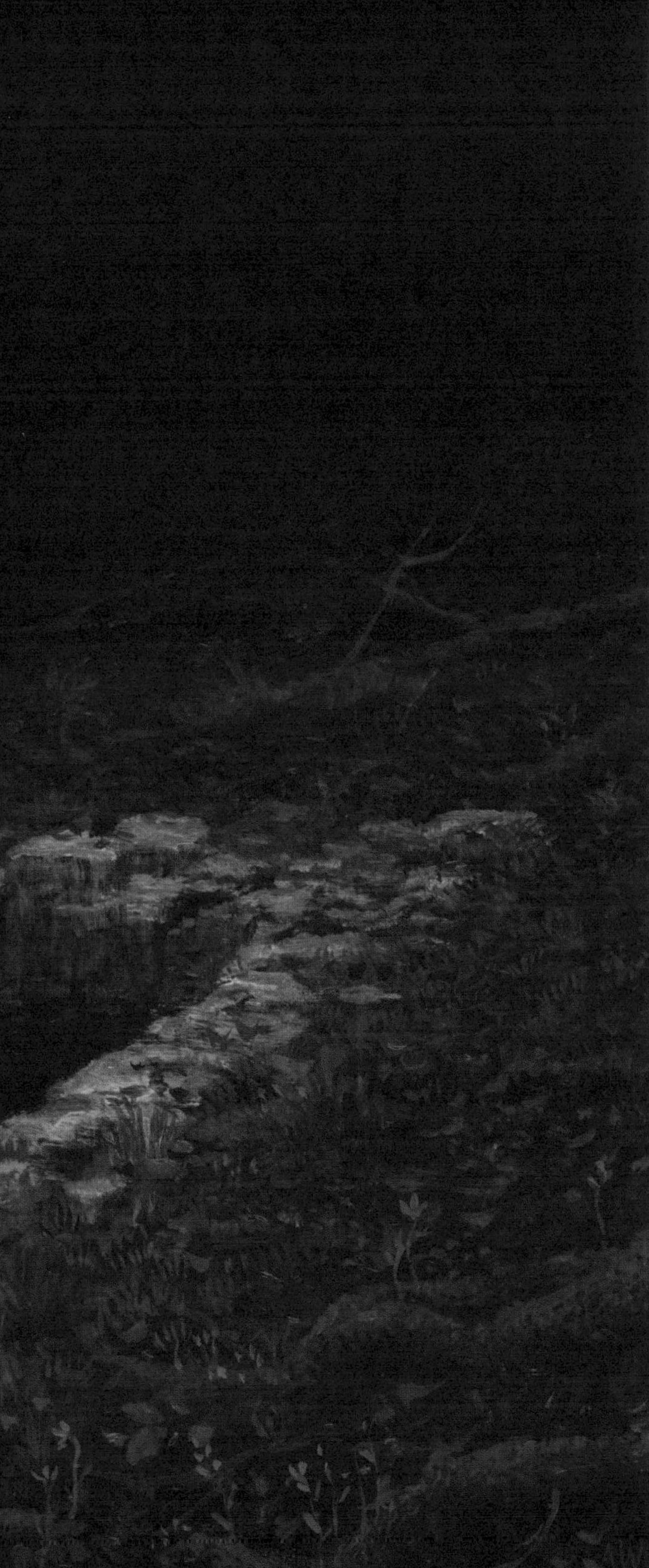

Left: The Pit, Aron Wiesenfeld, 2019, oil on panel.

The moody spaces of the contemporary works by American artist Aron Wiesenfeld (b. 1972) thrum quietly with moments of melancholy and a deep sense of loneliness. His scenes are of dim-lit liminality: sparse, shadowy landscapes outside of borders where the wilderness and urban converge and paths or portals often appear. We don't know whether the characters in them will take that road or make the leap beyond; they exist perpetually at the threshold of their own personal fable in the solitude of self-reflection as they s tare off into an enigmatic abyss.

PART TWO

—

The Human Condition

'What would your good do if evil didn't exist, and what would the earth look like if all the shadows disappeared?'

– MIKHAIL BULGAKOV

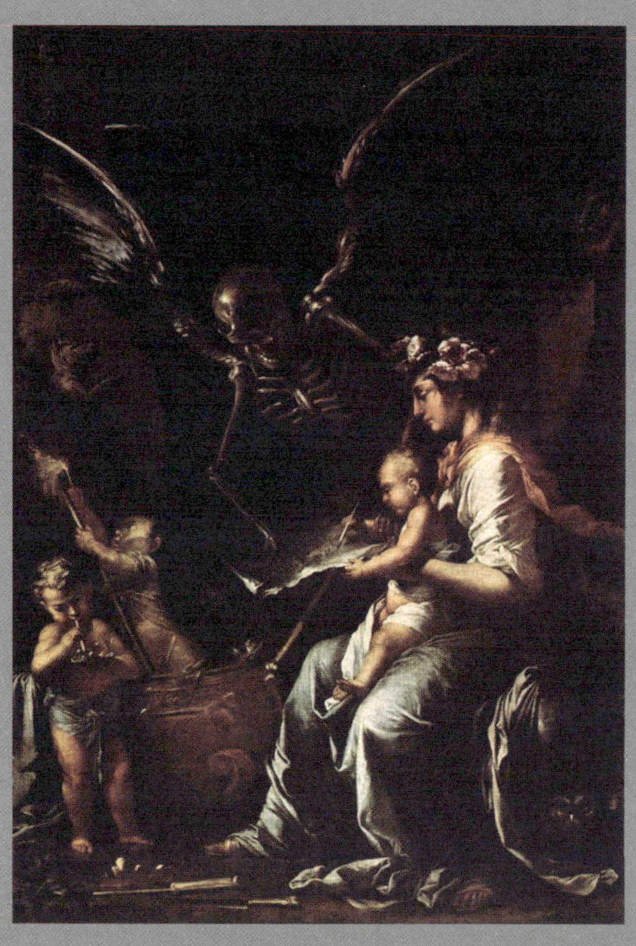

Humans are fallible and tremendously flawed – from the literal flesh of our hearts, decaying slowly over the course of our lifetimes, to the metaphorical battles of good and evil waged within those hearts. Anger, jealousy, vengeance. Sickness and disease. Violence and conflict. Grief, loss and, perhaps most powerful of all, death. Delving into these depths of the darker side of the human condition is an often painful and inevitably messy undertaking, and in peeking at humanity's fragile underbelly, we're unfortunately not going to like what we'll see. But if we want to understand and fully appreciate who we are and the world around us, we must confront and come to terms with all aspects of our wildly beautiful and terrible human hearts.

Just as all of life's excitement and joy is found in art, so too can we glimpse all of life's potential darkness. Within the sordid treasure chest of art history's greatest masterpieces, we can unearth all the horror and sadness pertaining to existence and life's most difficult – and darkest – questions. Why is there so much suffering in the world? Why are we such a violent and destructive species? Is it natural – rational even – to fear death? How do we live in this troubled world and make meaningful lives in the face of darkness, doom and despair? We can look to the canvas to see each and every one of these questions writ large.

And if our internal battles with morality and philosophy weren't enough to contend with, there's the reality of our physical bodies breaking down, bit by bit, day by day. Artworks inspired by or reflecting upon sickness and disease can provide *both* a refuge from the intense emotions associated with illness, as well as insight into our understanding of the human body and related themes of health, care and connection. Perhaps in witnessing these visions of corporeal distress we can begin to access new pathways of compassion and empathy, and in transformative or emancipatory ways, we can challenge and redefine what society expects from our bodies.

Ah, but those wily, yet utterly predictable human bodies. No matter how well we take care of them, they've all got an expiry date. Artists have forever found terror, beauty and awe in the concept of death, and painting scenes depicting or reflecting upon the dead and dying, or scenes of grief and loss, is a powerful way for them to examine and reckon with their mortality. And gazing upon this art is one way for us to

Opposite: Human Frailty, Salvator Rosa, c.1656, oil on canvas.

acknowledge our own mortality as well. It's no surprise that something so imminent, and yet so profoundly unknown, has been represented in such a variety of creative ways throughout history – and continues to unnerve and intrigue us today.

We're good people, right? We do the right thing, don't we? We probably don't consider ourselves evil, and in a similar vein, it's likely that, just as we believed when we were children, many of us are still quite confident that we're going to live forever. But the truth is we're all capable of hurtful behaviour and destructive acts, every one of our bodies is destined to fail us at some point – and there's no other way to say it friends – we're born to die.

So what do we do? Stay open and receptive. Though the following works of art reflect the less popular, more unpleasant and problematic aspects of the human experience, let them into that human heart of yours, if for nothing else, the potent emotional response it will evoke. File it away, let your subconscious deconstruct and decode it over time. Just look. That's it. We can't turn away from the ugliness, violence, suffering and death. It's all part of who we are – and we're all human, aren't we?

Opposite: Vanitas, Matthias Withoos, c. seventeenth-century, oil on canvas.

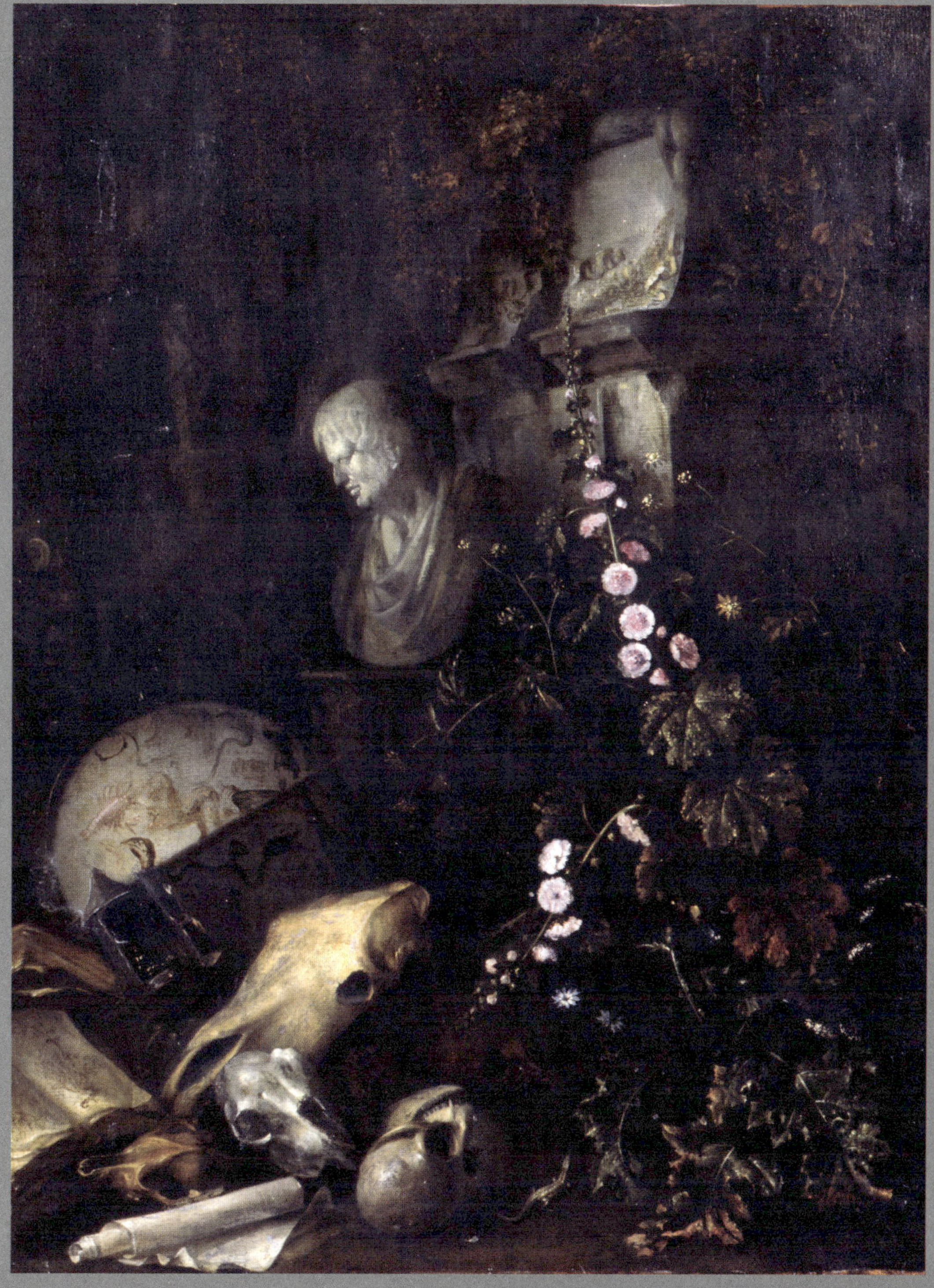

IV

—

Ailments & Afflictions

'Art is a wound turned into light.'

– GEORGES BRAQUE

What does it mean to be human? To inhabit a mortal body with all of its corporeal limitations, susceptible to what at times feels like our flesh betraying or failing us? To suffer pain, to face illness, to fight and sometimes succumb, to disease? As living, feeling beings, these ailments and afflictions affect us both psychologically and emotionally, and so it is only natural that the torments of illness and suffering have been the subject of artists for centuries.

Vincent van Gogh, who feverishly painted hundreds of masterpieces alive with rich colours and exhilarating brushstrokes, suffered from seizures which doctors believed to be caused by temporal lobe epilepsy. Frida Kahlo lived with chronic pain caused by a severe bus accident in her youth, and navigated this agony through her lush, expressive self-portraiture. Illness and physical debilitation have been the subject of countless works of art throughout history. Sometimes artists actually portray particular illnesses and at other times they are influenced or inspired by their respective conditions.

How have artists given the concept of disease, and the more personal experience of illness, concrete form through art? In gazing at representations of the sick or those with disabilities do we become more empathetic to the pain of others? How can these works speak to inequities in accessing care, and alternatively, how can they give a voice to the sick? And what happens when artists take something scientifically objective and turn it into a work that could be viewed subjectively or be used as propaganda?

Some of the most terrifying and prolific images of illness were created by artists in the Middle Ages and Renaissance. In Pieter Bruegel the Elder's *The Triumph of Death* (c. 1562), we witness an army of scythe-wielding skeletons sweeping through a coastal farming village, wreaking havoc on the peasants and illustrating the breadth of suffering caused by the plague. From the Renaissance onwards, we start to see artists reliably depicting signs of disease or illness, as characteristics of their sitters, creating records of the different pathologies of the body and aiding in the development of studies in anatomy. Some of these representations of illness and the unwell body stand at the intersection of art and medicine. Renowned for the naturalism of his works, Giovanni Battista Moroni carefully depicts a prominent goitre in his 1557 portrait of Abbess

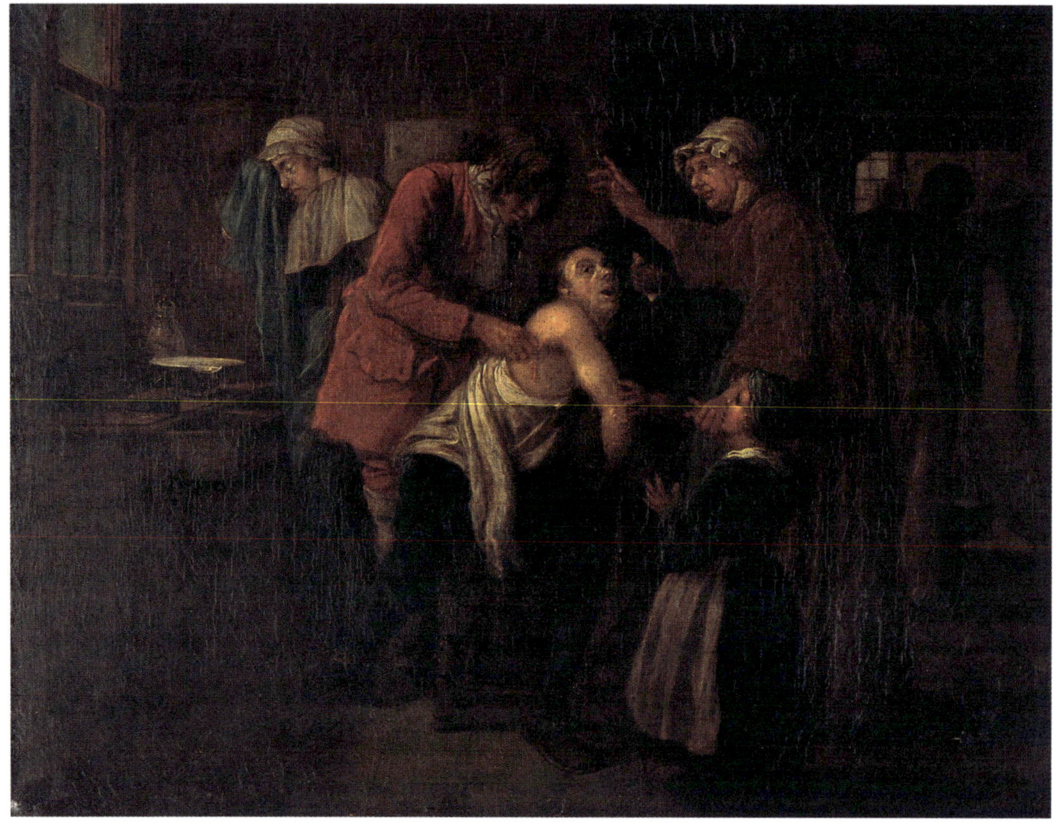

Above: A Surgical Operation, Jan Josef Horemans, 1720–29, oil on canvas.

The works of Jan Josef Horemans (1682-1759) frequently depict vivid moments in private houses, inns and courtyards - in this instance a surgeon's house where a patient has come for treatment. While the surgeon heads up the case, his apprentice has begun the manual treatment of an aggrieved-looking patient with an incision just below the armpit. Could they be lancing the bubo (the infected, enlarged lymph nodes) of bubonic plague? Nearby awaits a fretful woman, who may be either a distressed relative of the injured man or the next patient agonizing over her own condition, now that she's observed the sort of medical care she is about to receive.

Lucrezia Agliardi Vertova. Researchers uncovered two of the earliest known depictions of breast cancer in paintings dating back to the 1500s: *The Night*, painted by Michele di Ridolfo del Ghirlandaio, and *The Allegory of Fortitude*, depicted by Maso da San Friano.

In the nineteenth century we find more sympathetic and touching depictions intended to affect our emotions and raise awareness. Artists like Edvard Munch had personal connections to people who had tuberculosis and created very emotional pieces reflecting these relationships. With a series of paintings, lithographs and etchings, Edvard Munch depicted his older sister Sophie on her deathbed, suffering from the late stages of tuberculosis. In Alice Neel's 1940 painting *TB Harlem*, she paints a man named Carlos Negrón, who is suffering from advanced tuberculosis, and who had been 'treated' with the procedures of the time. These works depict personal connections, creating emotional pieces reflecting relationships. Later in the twentieth and twenty-first centuries HIV/AIDS awareness campaigns were and continue to be vital in educating people about the disease, preventing the disease and fighting against stigma. Artists and activists such as Keith Haring, Jean-Michel Basquiat and others delivered socio-political messages through their artworks as well as profound expressions of longing and loss.

Illness, pain and suffering can be isolating feelings to live with, and from the outside, we can struggle to make sense of that suffering when it is happening to someone else. Art can be a refuge from those intense emotions associated with illness as well as an insightful method with which to explore understandings of illness. 'To make the private into something public is an action that has terrific ramifications,' wrote artist David Wojnarowicz, who was thirty-seven when he died from AIDS-related complications. And is there anything that feels more intensely private than our aches, our agonies, our afflictions? Taken as a whole, the representation of disease in art shows how people have sought explanation through religion, through study and treatments, through personal experiences and raising awareness. Providing an environment for people to think about the embodied human experience is one of the extraordinary roles that this often gloomy art plays throughout the course of history as we continue exploring how artists engage with pain, medicine, biological science and disease.

Right: Cholera in Paris, François-Nicolas Chifflart, 1865, etching with drypoint on laid paper.

The free-spirited, independent-thinking French painter, engraver and illustrator François-Nicolas Chifflart (1825–1901) was an artist who in the initial years of his vocation was torn between his rigorous academic training and a desire to embrace more romantic subject matter. Encouraged by poet and novelist Victor Hugo, Chifflart launched his new career as an illustrator with works for Hugo's *Toilers of the Sea* (1866), and a new edition of *The Hunchback of Notre Dame*. In this horrific romance of this allegorical scene, Chifflart presents a dramatic contrast between the placid city of Paris and the whirling, spectral cloud of death which hovers over it during a cholera epidemic in 1865.

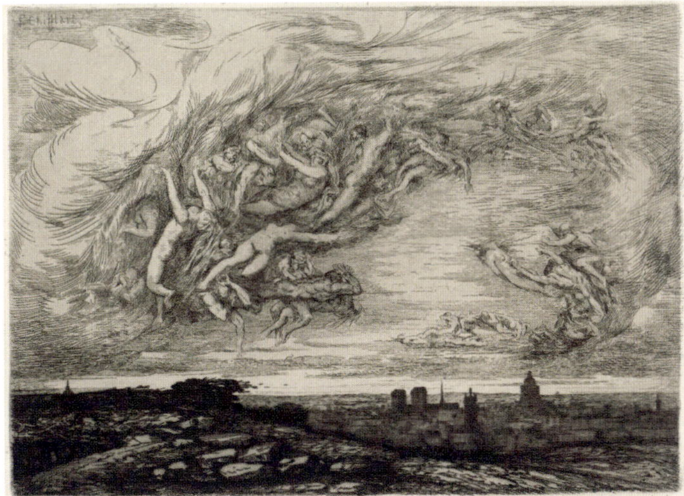

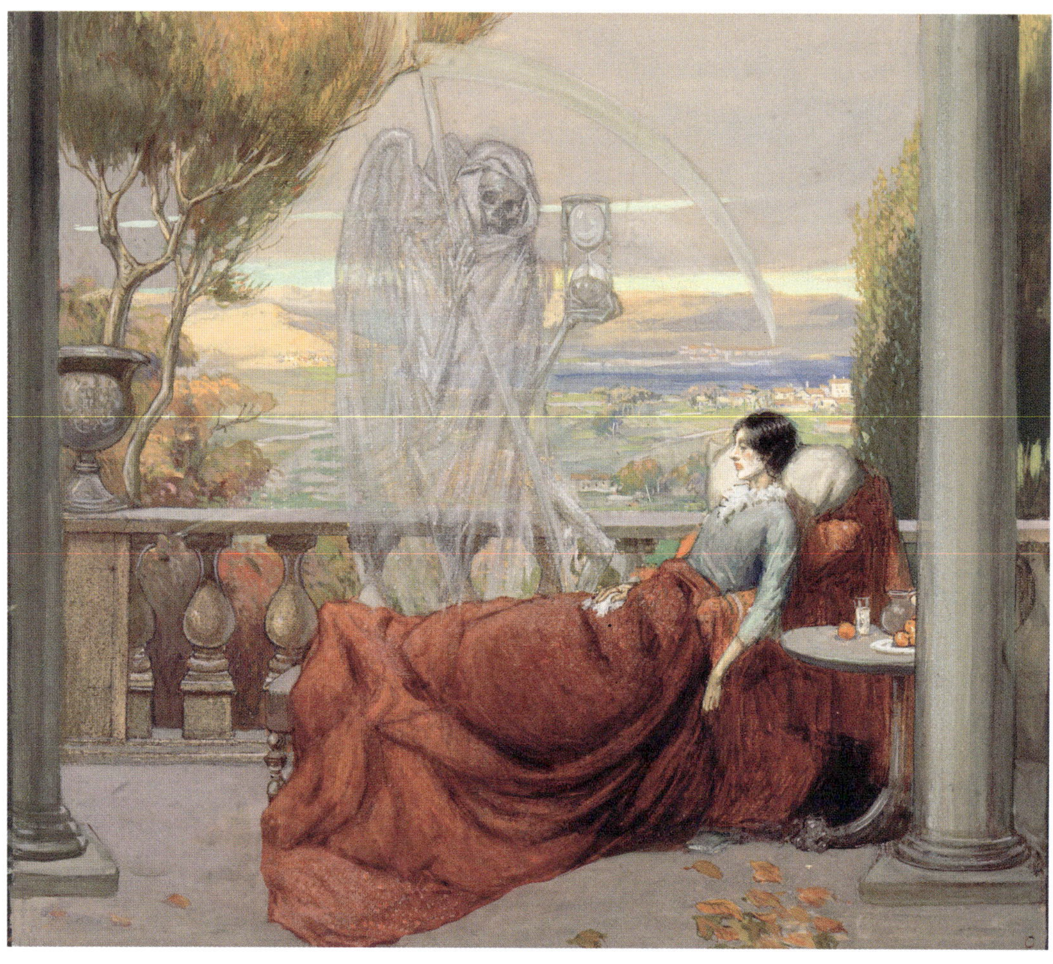

Above: A sickly young woman sits covered up on a balcony; death (a ghostly skeleton clutching a scythe and an hourglass) is standing next to her; representing tuberculosis, Richard Tenant Cooper, c. 1912, watercolour.

The works of Paris-trained artist Richard Tenant Cooper (1885–1957) are as beautiful as they are dramatic and disturbing and owe much to the Decadent movement, both aesthetically with its excess and delight in perversion (we might call it 'a bit extra' today) and thematically with their depiction of fear of disease, in particular sexually transmitted disease and the trend of depicting women as temptresses encouraging sins of uncleanliness and sexual indulgence. An official war artist, Cooper created symbolic paintings depicting death and disease – tuberculosis, syphilis, breast cancer and diphtheria to name a few – after returning from the First World War before moving to commercial work.

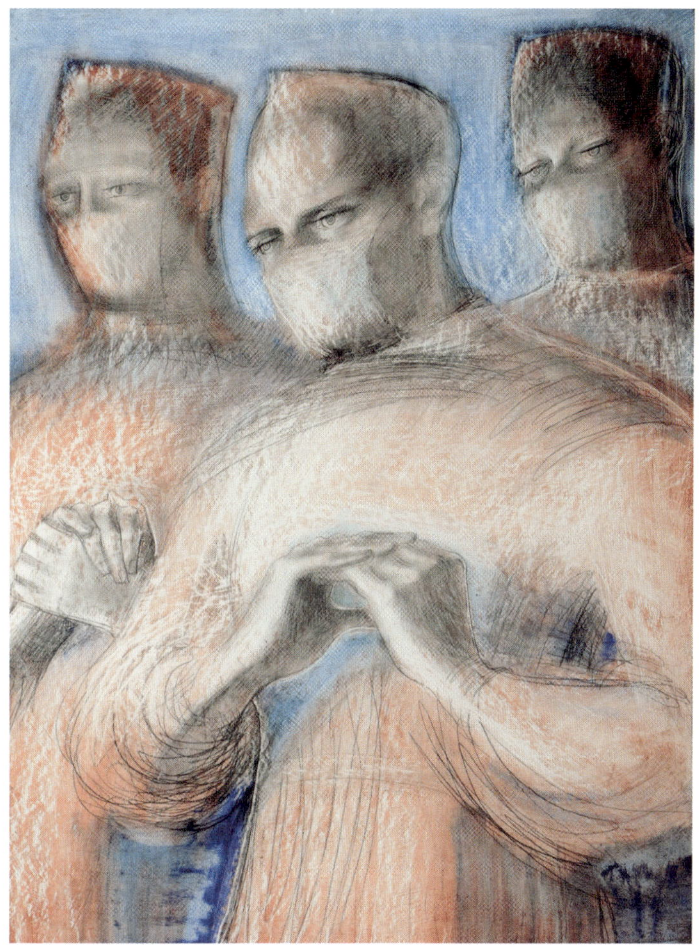

Above: Skiagram, Barbara Hepworth, 1949, pencil and oil on gesso-prepared board.

Primarily a sculptor, Barbara Hepworth (1903–75) called her drawings 'surrogate sculptures'. Some of her most prominent and stimulating drawings were depictions of surgery created during a pivotal time for her career. Hepworth came to the subject matter when one of her children was diagnosed with osteomyelitis and she was invited, by the orthopaedic surgeon, to sketch his operations. For two years, Hepworth watched various surgeries, describing in letters, how some days she would spend up to ten hours observing in the operating theatre – resulting in a series of almost a hundred hospital drawings. Thanks to this experience, the artist revealed that she believed there to be 'a close affinity between the work and approach both of physicians and surgeons, and painters and sculptors', both of whom seek 'to restore and to maintain the beauty and grace of the human mind and body'.

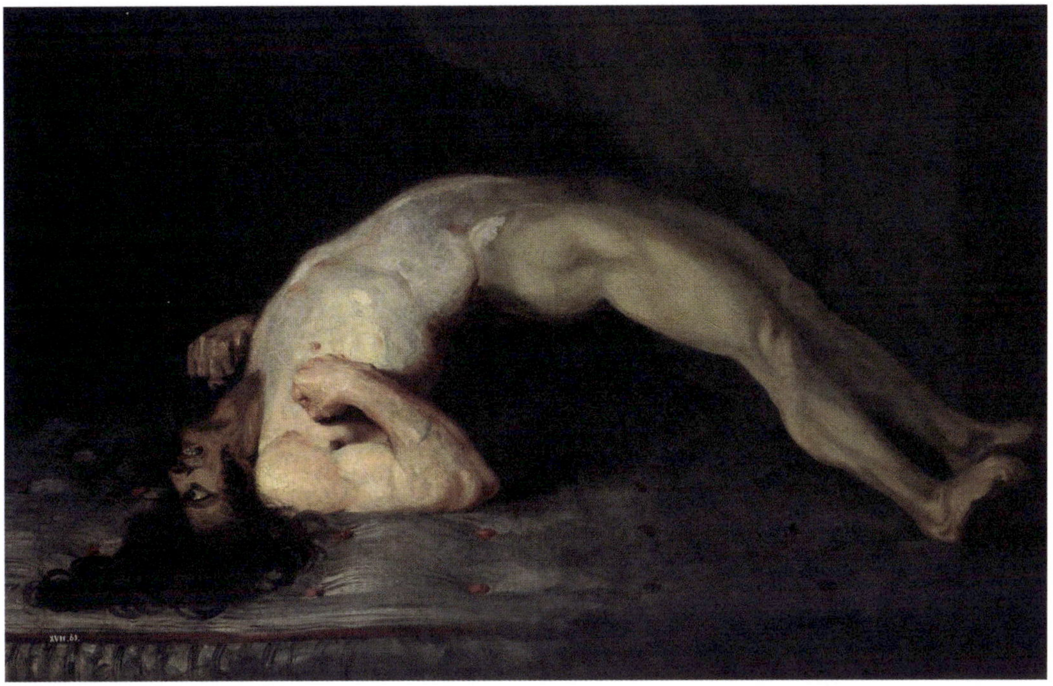

Opposite: Sickness, Rodney Dickson, 1988, oil on canvas.

Rodney Dickson (b. 1956) grew up in Northern Ireland during the troubled years of civil disorder that engulfed that country. Having drawn and painted since childhood, he reacted to his early experience by considering the futility and hypocrisy of war through art. The artist is best known for his large, thickly executed oil paintings, which have a physical presence so visceral that they confuse, question and blur the line between what is abstract and what is real. Some of these paintings appear as though they were executed very quickly, but most were painted, scraped over and painted again. In *Sickness*, we see a grim, dimly lit narrow room, almost subterranean in nature, that perfectly captures the misery of being alone and unwell.

Above: Opisthotonus in a patient suffering from tetanus, Sir Charles Bell, 1809, oil on canvas.

Sir Charles Bell (1774–1842) was a Scottish surgeon and anatomist (also a physiologist, neurologist, artist and philosophical theologian – he had quite the career), who also possessed, according to one friend '. . . a little too much ambition . . . and . . . a small degree of misanthropy, particularly towards persons of your own profession'. In other words, apparently the good doctor's behaviour and character sometimes got in the way of his career. Bell published a series of anatomical works based on his own drawings; in *Opisthotonus in a patient suffering from tetanus,* we observe a state of severe hyperextension in which an individual's head, neck and spinal column enter into a 'bridging' or 'arching' position. This extreme arched pose is an extrapyramidal effect and is caused by spasm of the axial muscles along the spinal column.

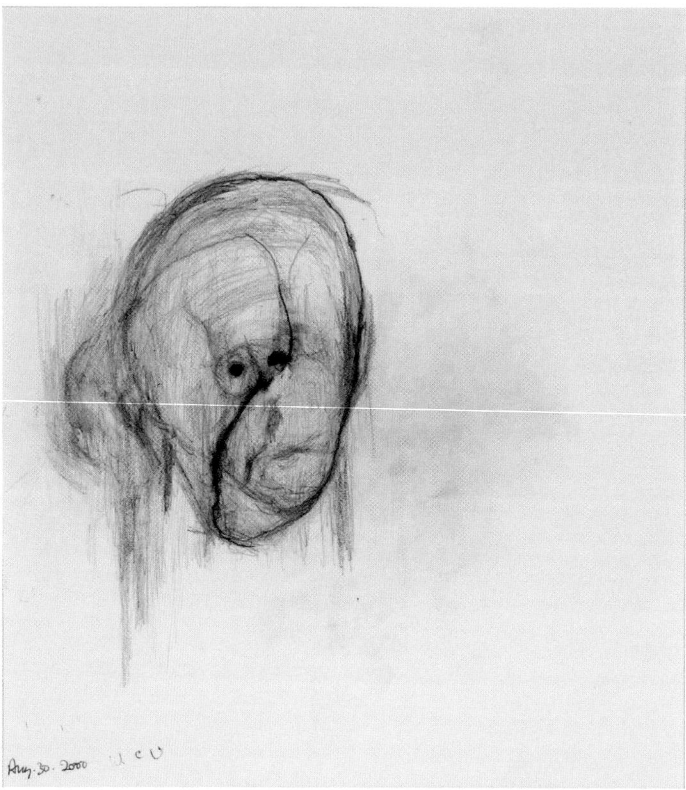

Left: Head I, 2000, William Utermohlen, 2000, pencil on paper.

UK-based artist William Utermohlen (1933–2007) was diagnosed as suffering from Alzheimer's disease in 1995 and died in 2007. His last works, the Late Pictures 1990–2000, documenting the gradual decay of his mind, serve as a rare glimpse of the inner life of a patient suffering from Alzheimer's disease. With a technique increasingly affected by the symptoms of dementia as they unfold, the images show the gradual modification of his perception of the world, both of his external environment and of his psychic universe. Through them we share his terrible feeling of dereliction, progressive isolation and loss of self-control.

Opposite: Toshima Tomiyo Who Stayed with Her Leper Husband, Tomozō, Tsukioka Yoshitoshi, 1875, woodblock print.

Tsukioka Yoshitoshi (1839–92) is widely recognized as the last great master of the ukiyo-e genre of woodblock printing and painting. He is also regarded as one of the form's greatest innovators. His career spanned two eras – the last years of the Edo period in Japan, and the first years of modern Japan following the Meiji Restoration. Although the artist was interested in new things from the rest of the world, over time he became increasingly concerned with the loss of many aspects of traditional Japanese culture, among them traditional woodblock printing. Created for Yoshitoshi's Postal News series, *Toshima Tomiyo Who Stayed with Her Leper Husband, Tomozō* illustrates an 'honourable' wife compassionately tending to her leprosy-stricken husband. There was considerable stigma and shame attached to leprosy in Japanese culture, where, according to Buddhist lore, the disease was believed to result from wrongdoings committed in past lives.

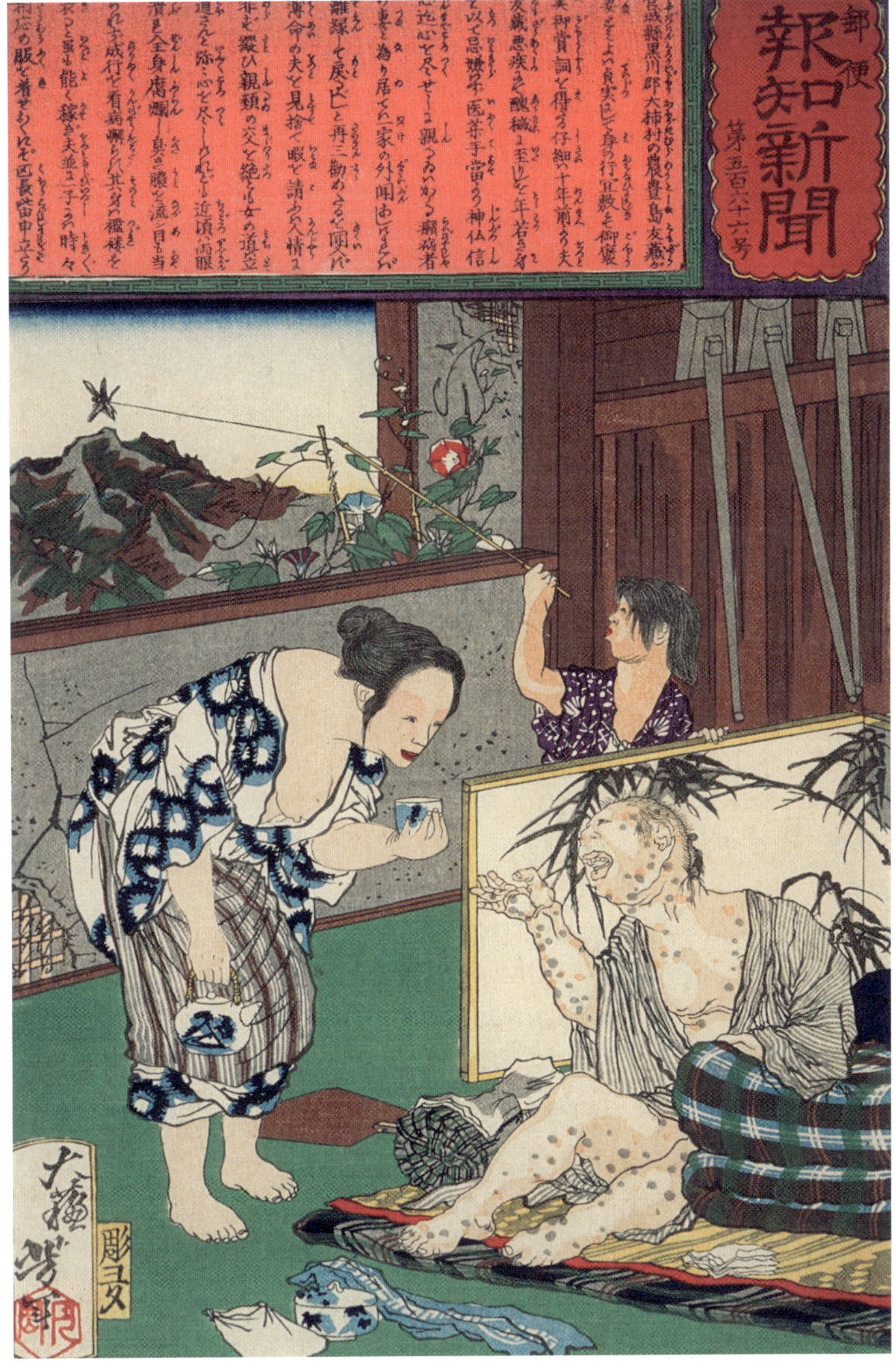

郵便報知新聞
第五百六十六号

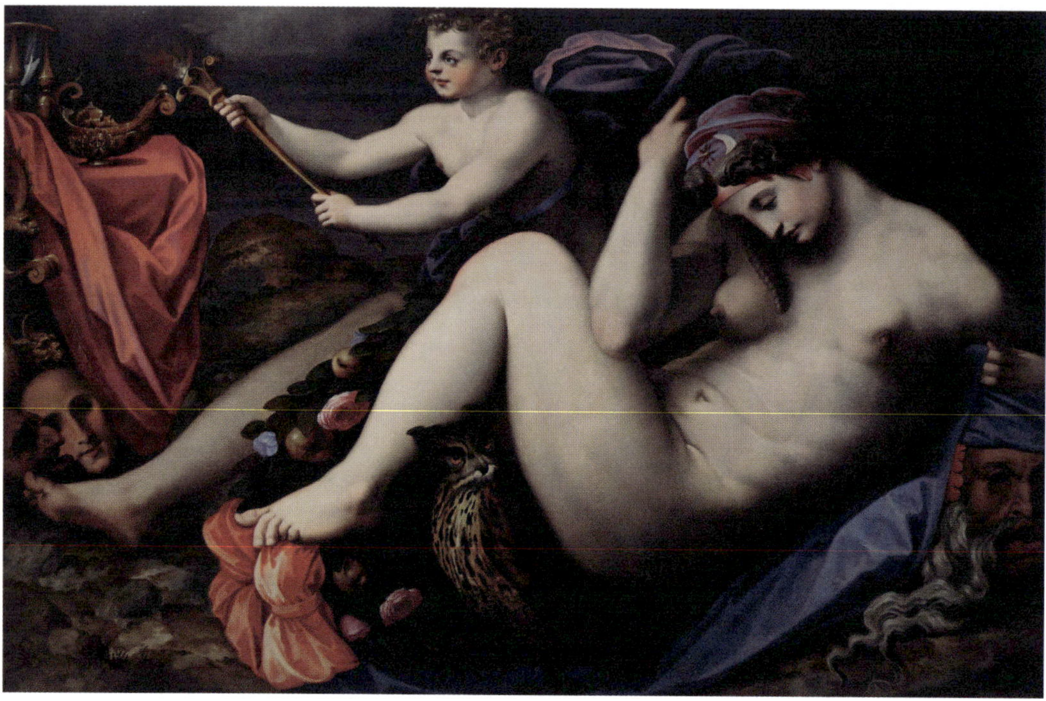

Above: The Night, Michele di Rodolfo del Ghirlandaio (Michele Tosini), 1555–65, oil on canvas.

Recent studies show that cancer is not a modern disease as once thought. Signs of the disease were found in the oil panel transposition of Michelangelo's statue *The Night*, painted by Michele di Rodolfo del Ghirlandaio (1503-77, also known as Michele Tosini), in the sixteenth century. A nude woman reclines uncomfortably, ideal in neither pose nor body, at least by classical Greek standards. We blame the beauty industry for unreasonable standards, but it sure goes back much further than that! Her breasts are unsymmetrical, the left appearing smaller than the right and showing signs of nipple retraction. According to the authors of these studies, this is suggestive that she had the disease. The nightmarish ambience of the painting suggests an encroaching darkness and the model's countenance seems to agree.

Opposite: The Funeral, George Grosz, c. 1917–18, oil on canvas.

German Expressionist artist George Grosz (1893-1959) became famous for his satirical drawings and paintings of Berlin in the 1920s. *The Funeral* melds together aspects of both Futurism and Cubism in order to illustrate an urban city funeral procession as a hellish landscape populated by obscure and grotesque attendants, and displays the bleakness, cynicism and disquiet that pervaded the times. The recurrent theme of disease and an ever-mounting death toll finds expression in this apocalyptic and deeply pessimistic painting.

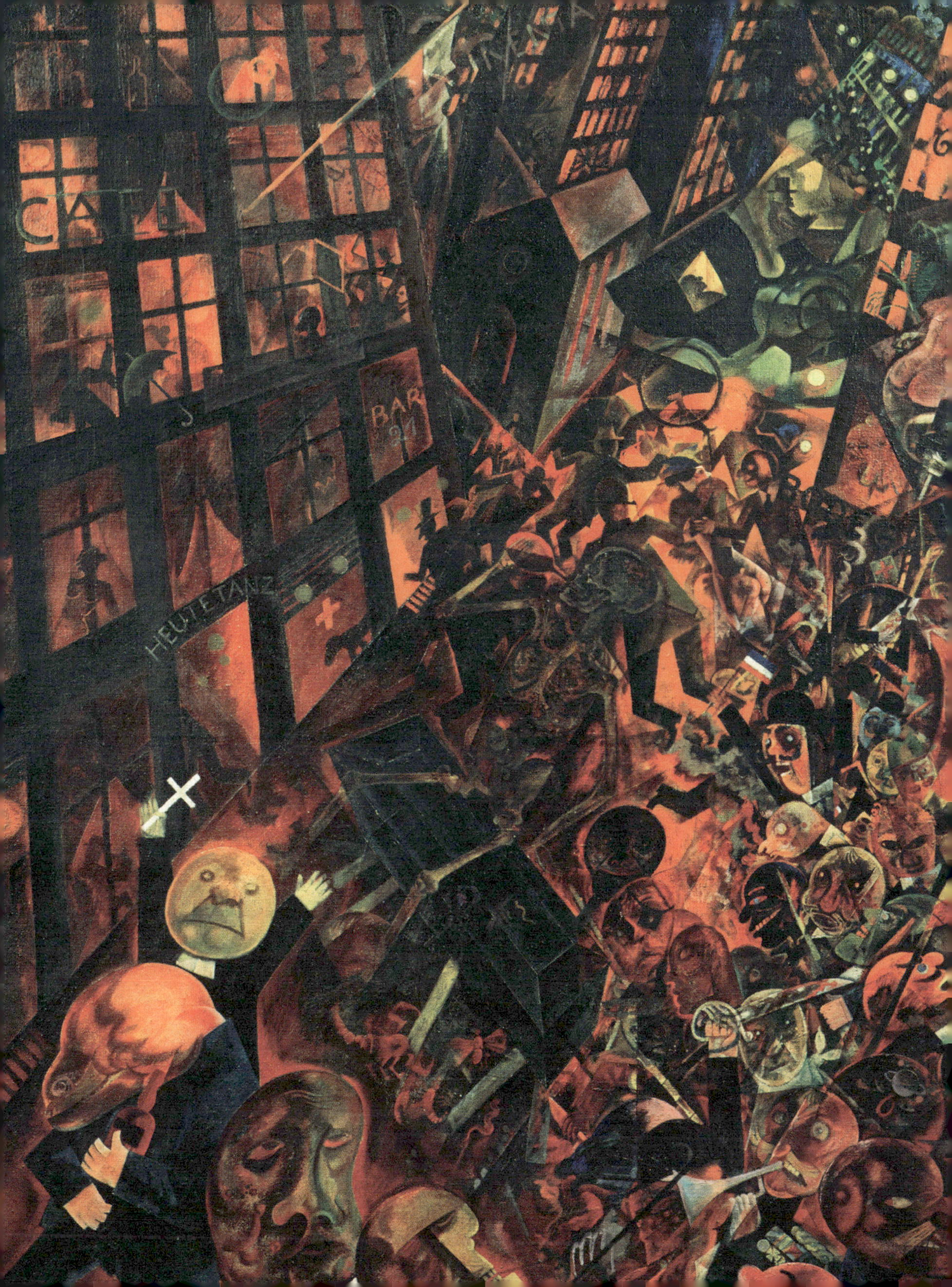
CAFE
BAR
HEUTETANZ

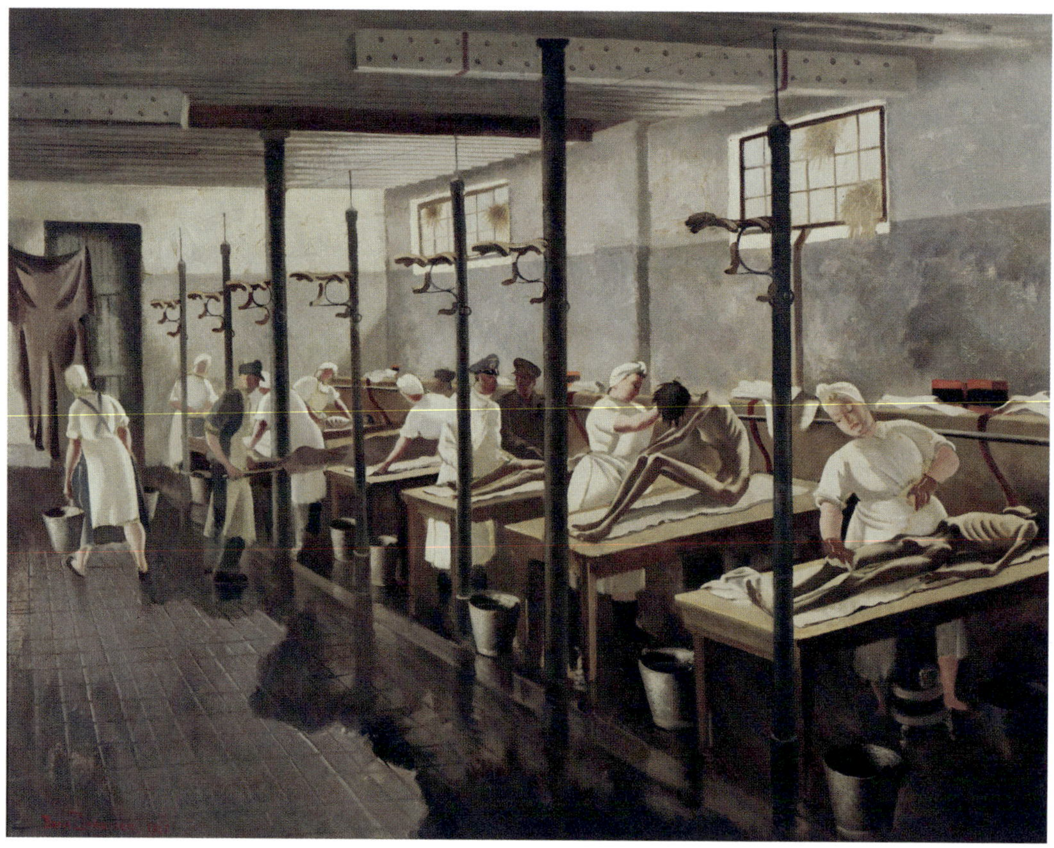

Above: Human Laundry, Belsen April 1945, Doris Zinkeisen, 1945, oil on canvas.

Doris Zinkeisen (1898–1991) was a painter, commercial artist and theatre designer. Her artistic career started out in a much more fashionable and 'posh' place than where it would eventually take her. Well known for her society and equestrian portraiture, and for scenes reflecting the lifestyle of the upper class at the time, she was commissioned by the British Red Cross and St John Joint War Organisation to record their work in northwest Europe and was one of the few women war artists to be sent overseas. Her work as a war artist included three days at the Bergen-Belsen concentration camp in April 1945, immediately after its liberation. One of a group of works produced by Zinkeisen during this time, this one shows the 'human laundry' which consisted of about twenty beds in a stable where German nurses and captured soldiers cut the hair of the inmates, bathed them and applied anti-louse powder before they were transferred to an improvised hospital run by the Red Cross.

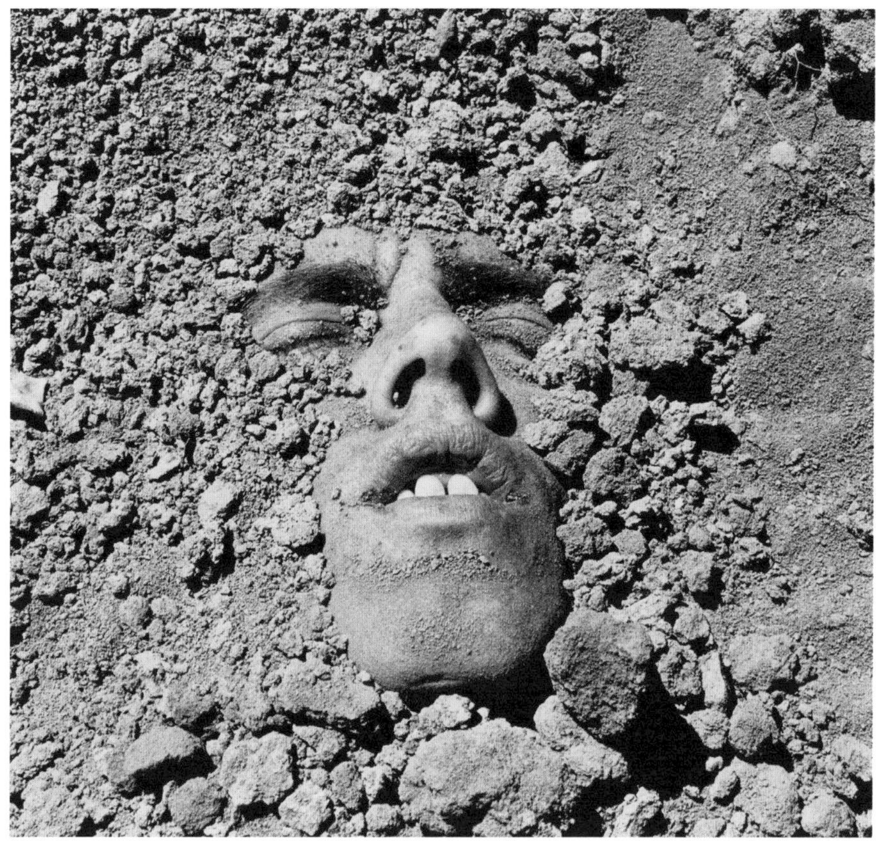

Above: Untitled (Face in Dirt), David Wojnarowicz, 1990, gelatin silver print.

David Wojnarowicz (1954–92) created a body of work that spanned photography, painting, music, film, sculpture, writing and activism. Wojnarowicz saw the outsider as his true subject. Queer and later diagnosed as HIV-positive, he became an impassioned advocate for people with AIDS when an ever-increasing number of friends, lovers and strangers were dying due to what he perceived as government inaction.

This photograph was taken in late May 1991 at Chaco Canyon in New Mexico while Wojnarowicz and his friend Marion Scemama took a road trip around the American Southwest. Cynthia Carr, Wojnarowicz's biographer, describes how the photograph came to be: 'He had been there before and knew exactly where he wanted to stage this. "We're going to dig a hole," he told her, "and I'm going to lie down."'

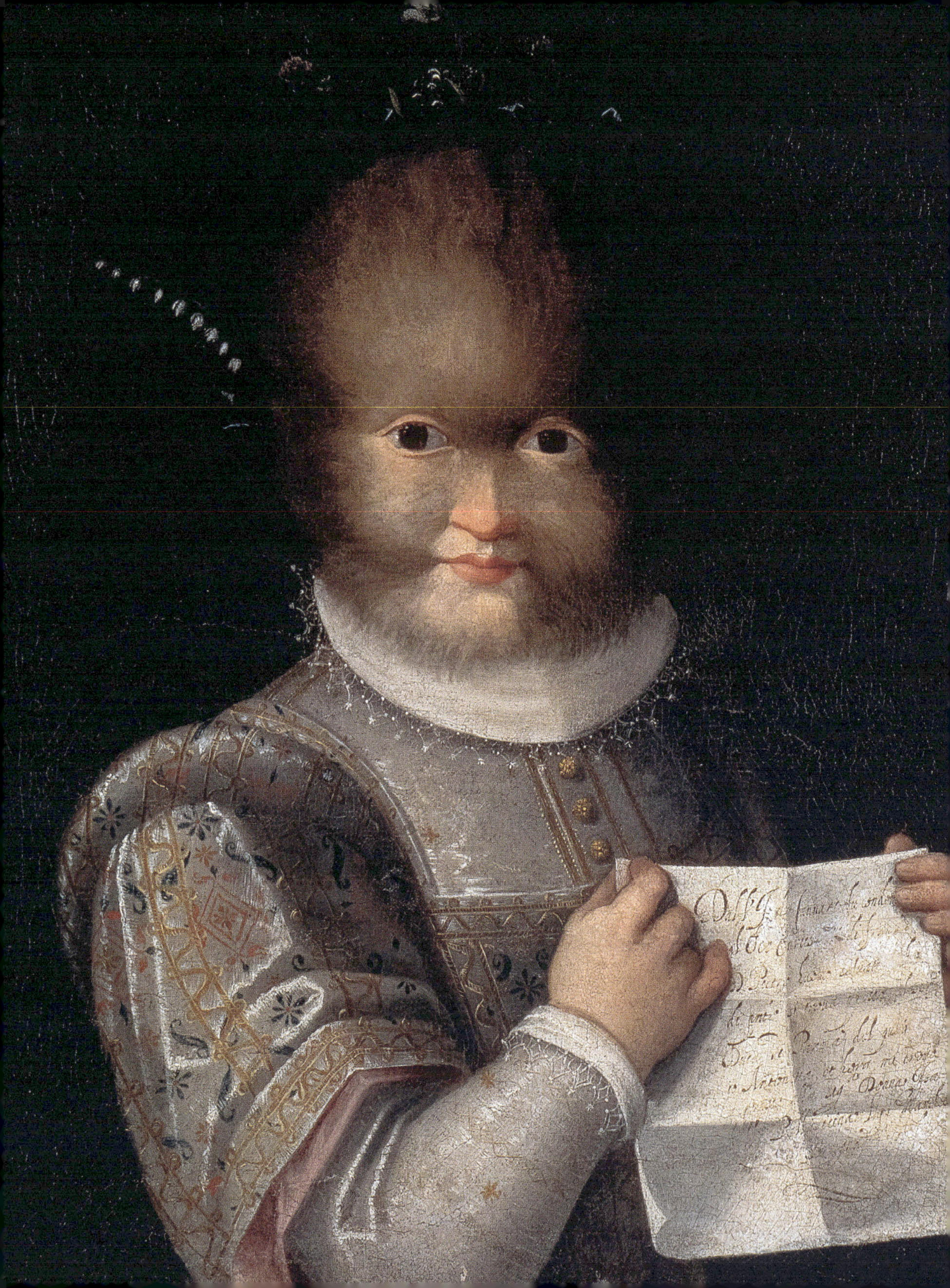

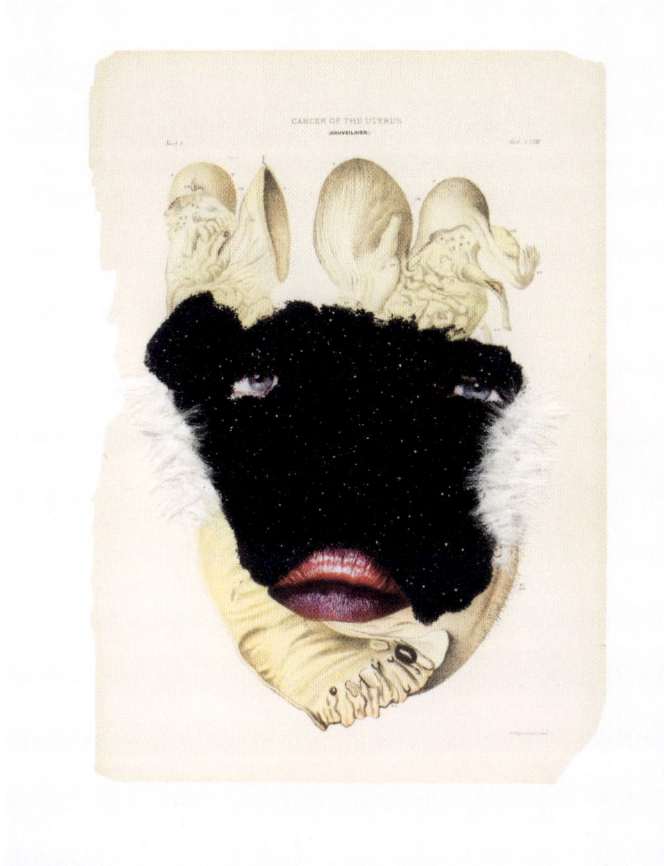

Left: Cancer of the Uterus, Wangechi Mutu, 2006, glitter, fur, collage on digital print.

Contemporary Kenyan artist Wangechi Mutu (b. 1972) trained as both a sculptor and anthropologist and is noted for work encompassing gender, race, art history and personal identity. Creating complex collages that appear both ancient and from a science fiction future, Mutu's work features recurring mysterious motifs such as masked women and snake-like tendrils. Her pastiche-like practice combines a variety of source material and textures to explore consumerism and excess. In *Cancer of the Uterus*, her subject is both glamorous and ominous, a goddess born from a medical pathology diagram, facial features cut from a magazine, fur and a heavy application of black glitter to create an eerily distorted face – the dazzling material alludes to the illegal diamond trade in Africa.

Opposite: Portrait of Antonietta Gonzalez, Lavinia Fontana, 1583, oil on canvas.

Lavinia Fontana (1552–1614) was a Bolognese Mannerist painter best known for her successful portraiture, but who also worked in the genres of mythology and religious painting. She is regarded as the first woman career artist in Western Europe as she relied on commissions for her income, and is also thought to be the first woman artist to paint female nudes – but this is a hotly contested topic among art historians. Antonietta Gonzalez, as well as her father, two sisters and other family members, had hypertrichosis, a rare genetic condition characterized by excessive hair growth on a person's body. It is suggested that Lavinia Fontana met young Antonietta and her family in Parma, and in this tender portrait Antonietta seems to be less than ten years old. She's dressed in a court dress and showing a handwritten note where she explains a little of her personal history.

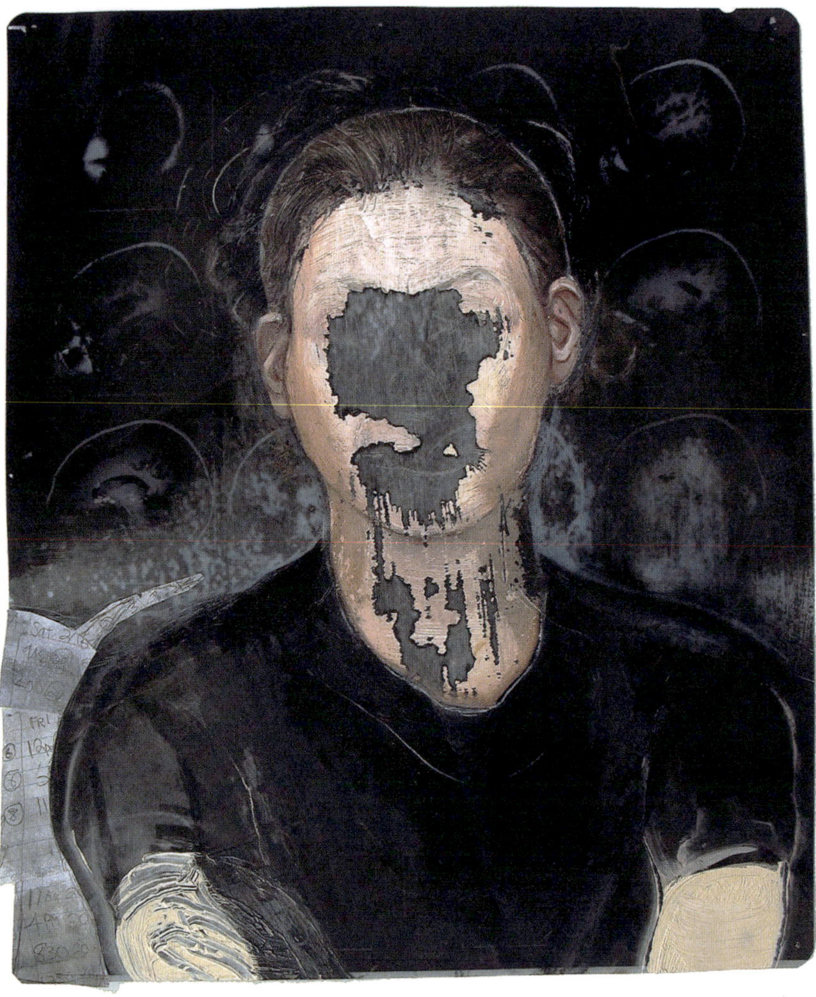

Above: Erasure, Susan Gofstein, 2003, oil and collage on MRI scan.

In Susan Gofstein's Resonance series, she illustrates the sentiment that, while pain is universal, it is also a solitary truth that is frustratingly subjective and resistant to language. To live in pain is to live in isolation. About the work, she notes, 'In the fall of 2000, I developed severe chronic facial pain. This domination of pain obliterated all sense of an inner self. "Resonance" began as an effort to structure and distance myself from an overwhelming existence.' In the works in the series, the MRI grids of the brain document both the origin of pain and the concept of a self, their altered surfaces - painted over, scratched, collaged - is wrought with struggle.

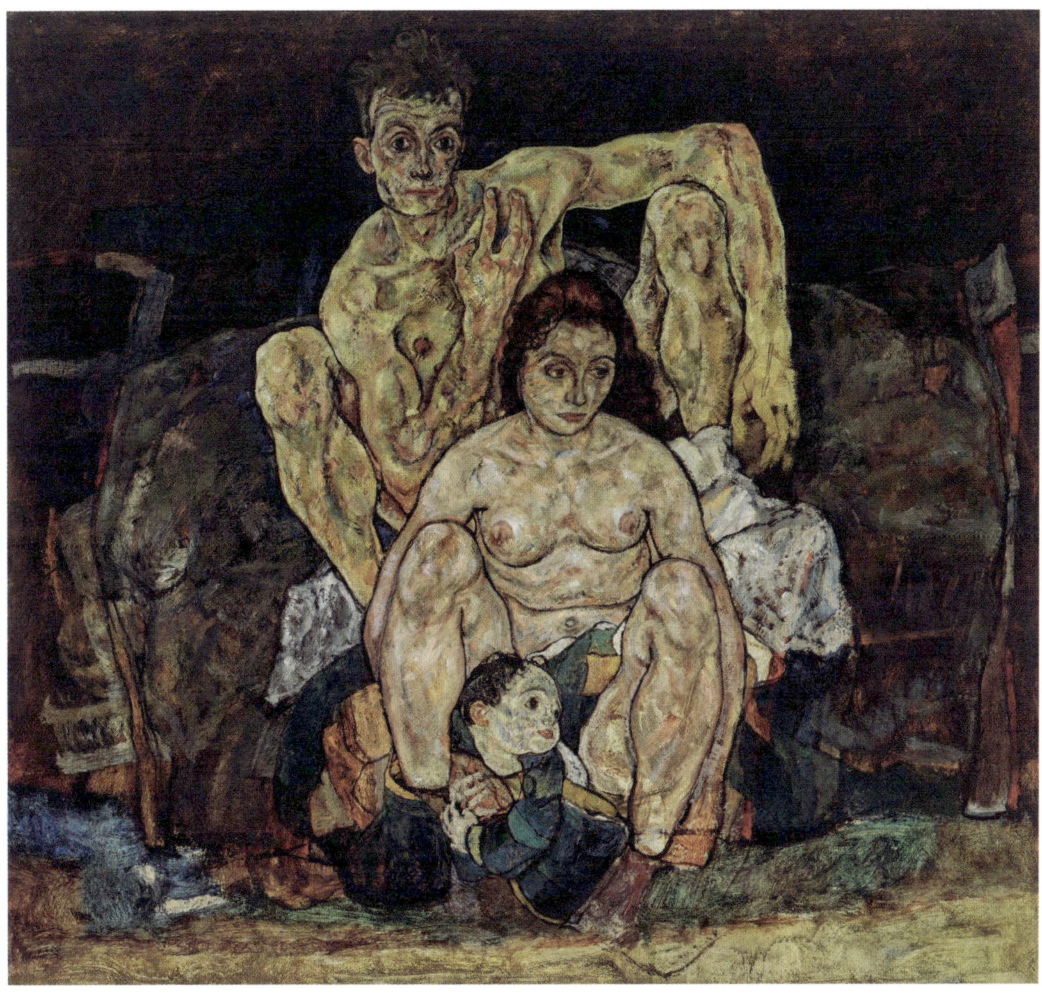

Above: *The Family*, Egon Schiele, 1918, oil on canvas.

During his tragically brief career, Egon Schiele (1890–1918) defined a distinct place for himself in twentieth-century art with his beguiling, Expressionistic figurative portraiture. In 1918, Egon Schiele began working on a painting that was to become his last painting: *The Family* (initially titled 'Squatting Couple'). This was meant to be a portrait of himself, his wife and their future child. Perhaps the sombre tone and quiet sadness permeating the canvas reflects a presentiment of doom: before he could finish the piece, his pregnant wife died of the Spanish Flu. Tragically, the child did not survive, and Schiele himself died of the same disease only a mere three days later.

V

Depravity & Destruction

'I represent to you all the sins you never had the courage to commit.'

– OSCAR WILDE, *THE PICTURE OF DORIAN GRAY*

This is a chapter about bad behaviour depicted in the visual arts. The misconduct shown runs the gamut from, say, a mild bout of petty professional jealousy through biblical sins to the atrocities of war – and as there is seemingly no end to the human capacity for depravity, destruction and devastation, there is sadly no shortage of art reflecting that back to us.

Filippo Tommaso Emilio Marinetti, Italian poet, editor, art theorist and founder of the Futurist movement, as well as the Fascist Manifesto, declared that 'Art, in fact, can be nothing but violence, cruelty, and injustice.' This is an edict which also glorified war and encouraged us to burn down all of our museums and libraries. No, thank you! Of course, violence and cruelty is *not* all that art is or should be . . . but there is a lot of it to be found in the art we consume. Rather than decry the perpetually bloodthirsty state of the world and vilify the artists who might be inspired by violence, vengeance and general human deviance, let us instead examine these works more closely – along with the world as it was when they were created, the motivations of the artists who coaxed them to bloody life, and focus on what can be learned from these creations.

Lust, gluttony, greed, sloth, wrath, envy and pride is quite the rollcall to separate the saints from the sinners. Sin is a concept as universal as it is personal, with a laser-focus on human frailty. Most people will do something they regret at some point, but the gravity of their 'sin' and the way it is dealt with very much depends on country, time and socio-cultural context. This ethical struggle between vice and virtue has always been fertile territory for the artistic imagination. Religious teachings were often used as a way to depict the tragic consequences of succumbing to the sin of wrath and anger. Peter Paul Rubens's emotionally charged canvases often referenced these aspects of Christian history, such as *Cain Slaying Abel* (1608). Greed for money and excessive love of food and drink seem to have been particularly attractive to artists. Both feature regularly in depictions of the sins by Hieronymus Bosch and others. For a time, artists were rather preoccupied with portraying human fallibility in their work, but as society became more secular, these allegorical representations became less fashionable.

'It is harder to imagine heaven than hell,' writes Darren Oldridge in *The Devil: A Very Short Introduction*. It is little wonder, then, that the imagery of hell has inspired countless artists.

Drawn from ancient myth, scripture and literature, the concept of hell and the corrupt souls occupying that infernal space has evolved and endured as a powerful metaphor in the Western collective cultural imagination, even as belief in hell as a physical place has declined.

Corruption exists the world over: in politics, in law, in business, in the environment, and even in education. Displayed through art, and protest art in particular, it presents an interesting form of communication. Sometimes it is easier to see what is wrong in the world – in that artwork makes the viewer question the society they live in – rather than read about it or have it reported to us.

Morality and art are sometimes connected in ways that transcend the canvas. Art that provokes and disturbs and that stirs up beliefs, values and morals, may cause controversies over artistic freedom or how society evaluates art. The artist's purpose is to express, regardless of how the subject matter may be interpreted. Does this freedom in interpretation mean that neither the artist nor society is responsible for their actions?

This author, for one, feels very different things when gazing between Goya's canvas depicting googly-eyed Saturn gulping down his son and Sirani's portrayal of Timoclea Killing Her Rapist. And what of us? The viewer? Without a doubt, there is a voyeuristic impulse towards gazing upon these horrors, and artists throughout history have exploited our gruesome interest in misdeeds. We, the observers, have a part to play in this push-and-pull creation and consumption. Could it be that artists are merely fulfilling a demand?

The underpinnings of human cruelty and wickedness hinge on motivations that the greatest works of art – whether created in response to combat, mass killings and sexual assault, or quieter offences – can aid our understanding in ways that logic and reason, ideology and analysis cannot. It can be a boon and a balm to seek meaning and clarity in art when the burden of that which is unfathomable and unspeakable becomes too great to find it anywhere else.

Right: Lucretia, or the Nude Murderess, Otto Müller, c. 1903, oil on canvas.

Otto Müller (1874–1930) was a German painter and printmaker of the Die Brücke expressionist movement. Known for his landscape painting, populated by the elongated figures of female nudes, Müller is typically noted as one of the most lyrical of German expressionist painters, and his work is thought to be less anguished and more balanced than other Die Brücke painters. The life-sized nude dominating this portrait is most likely his wife at the time, Maschka. She looks pretty anguished to me; I'm not sure I agree with those guys.

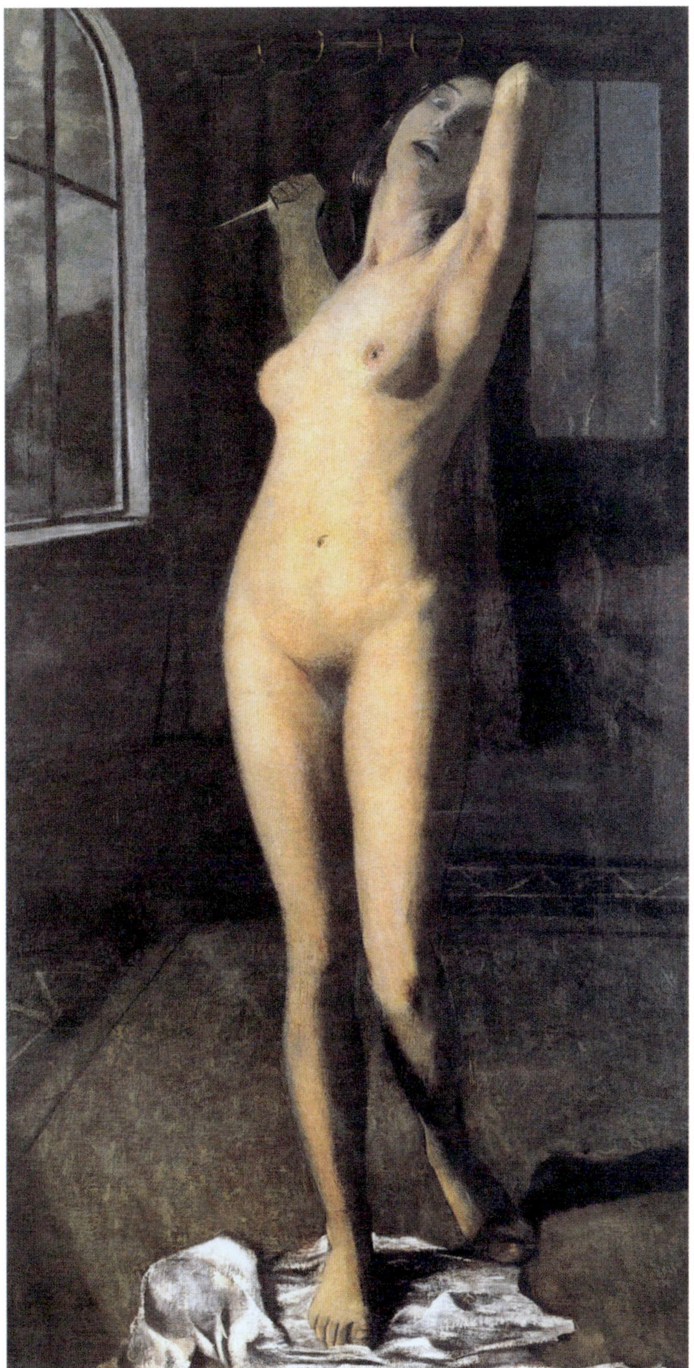

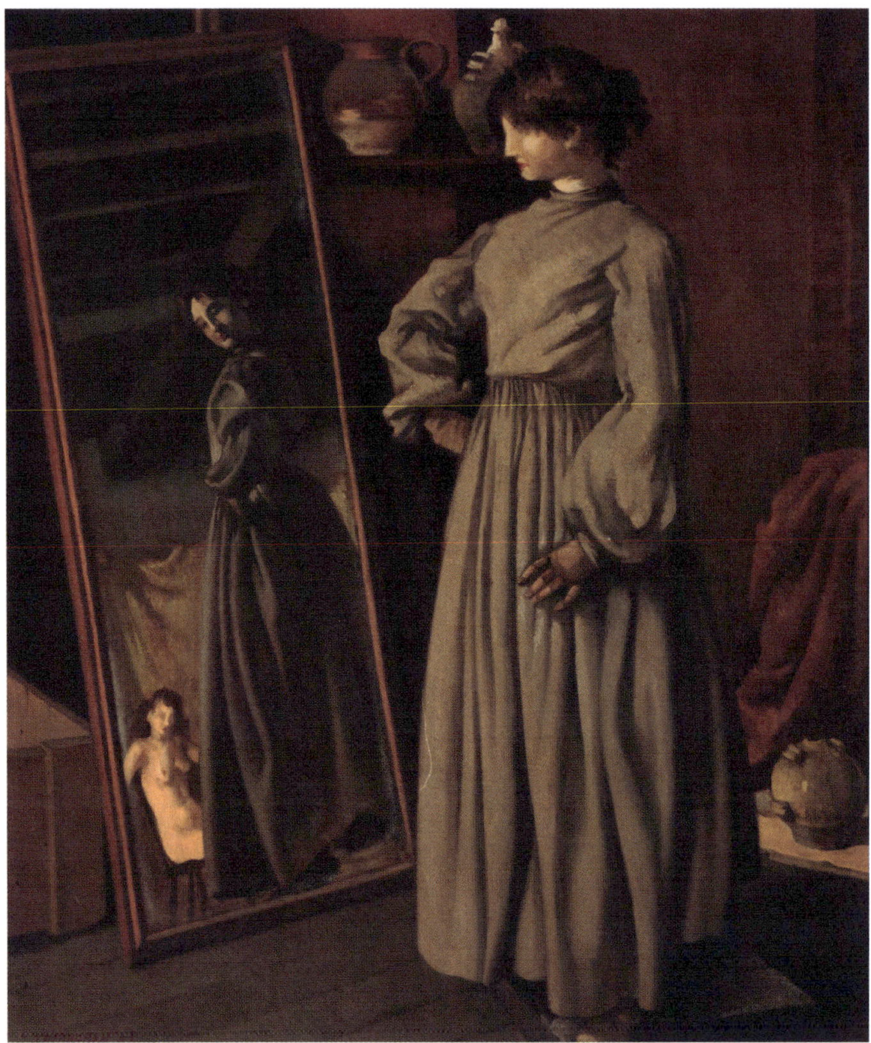

Above: Professional Jealousy, Joanne Pemberton-Longman, 1947, oil on canvas.

Joanne Pemberton-Longman (1918–73) studied at the Byam Shaw School of Art and went on to exhibit widely with various academies, institutes and societies of the day, winning a silver medal at the Salon Paris in 1961. In this curious scene, a mannequin gazes at her reflection in a mirror with a live nude seated in the background; from the painting's title, I wonder who is jealous of whom. The plaster model longing for life? The warm-blooded model yearning for the perfect posture, untiring limbs and flawless visage of the dummy? Or perhaps it is the one we don't see at all, creating the picture that unfolds on the canvas in a series of muted brushstrokes, admiring the two beauties in front of her, painting with glum envy that which she does not see mirrored in herself?

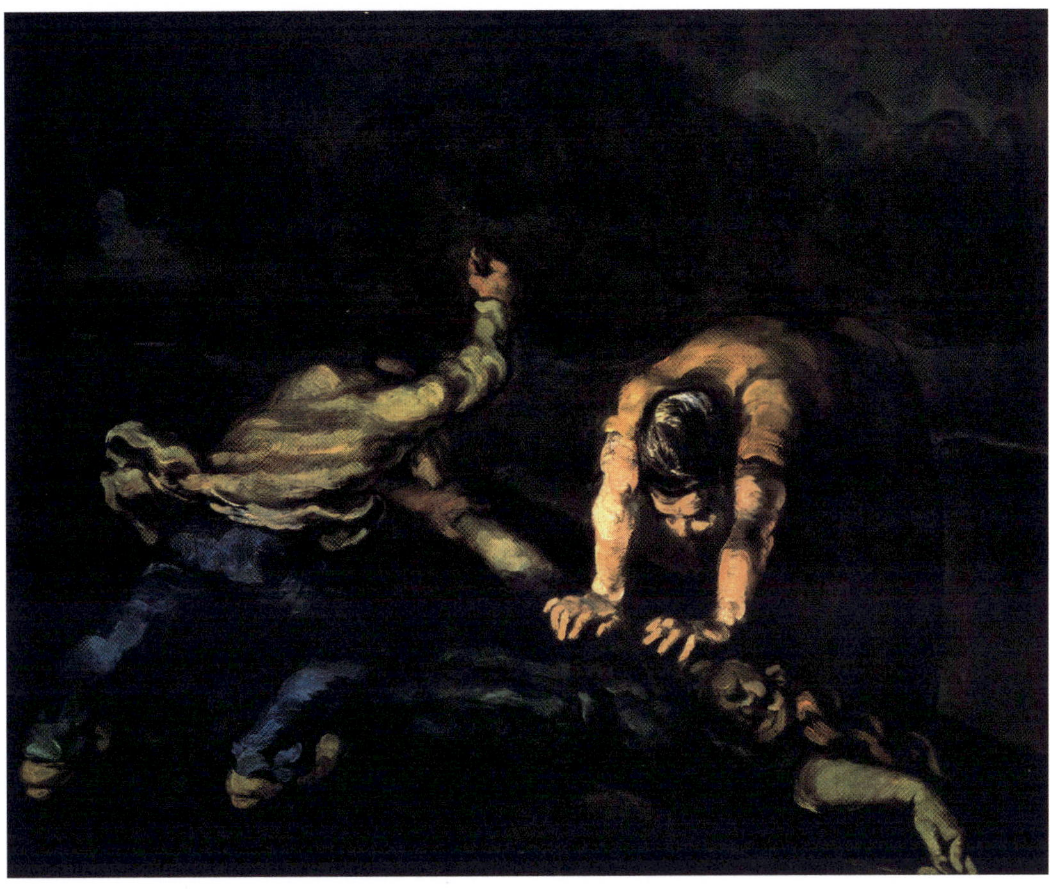

Above: The Murder, Paul Cézanne, 1868, oil on canvas.

Before Paul Cézanne (1839–1906) painted the hazy brilliance of his Post-Impressionist landscapes and peaceful fruit bowls using a refined palette, his works were imbued with the dark drama of the classical masters. In this nightmarish scene of *The Murder*, one of his earlier paintings, we witness with horror as the murderer lifts his hand to give the final strike while his collaborator is using all the force in her body to keep the victim down. While the expressions on the assailants, faces remain hidden from us, the victim's face is distorted in extreme pain and fear. Much like many are today, Cézanne was apparently fascinated by crime stories, or 'putrid literature' as the critics of the day called it. It is suggested that *The Murder* was inspired by the grisly 1867 novel *Thérèse Raquin* written by his childhood friend Emile Zola.

Right: Oedipus Cursing His Son Polynices, Henry Fuseli, 1786, oil on canvas.

Swiss painter Henry Fuseli (1741–1825) began his career in England as a history painter whose Expressionistic style was composed of a unique blend of influences – German Romanticism, the monumental vision of Michelangelo, and the physical and psychological exaggerations of the sixteenth-century Italian Mannerists. Fuseli's own pessimism and fascination with the extremes of human passion are evident in this emotionally charged scene of a mythical family feud from Sophocles' *Oedipus at Colonus*. The tragedy of the father's curse is played out through the extreme gestures and contortions of the four figures. Polynices, head twisted away from his body, has come to ask his father's support in overthrowing his brother Eteocles. Enraged at his son's request, Oedipus points in reproach and imposes his dreadful curse, that each son would die at the hands of the other. Ismene, in despair, kneels at her father's knee. Antigone is highlighted above the terrible drama as she reaches out to protect her brother with one hand and restrain Oedipus with the other. Her heroic gesture, as with much else in this particular family's history, is futile.

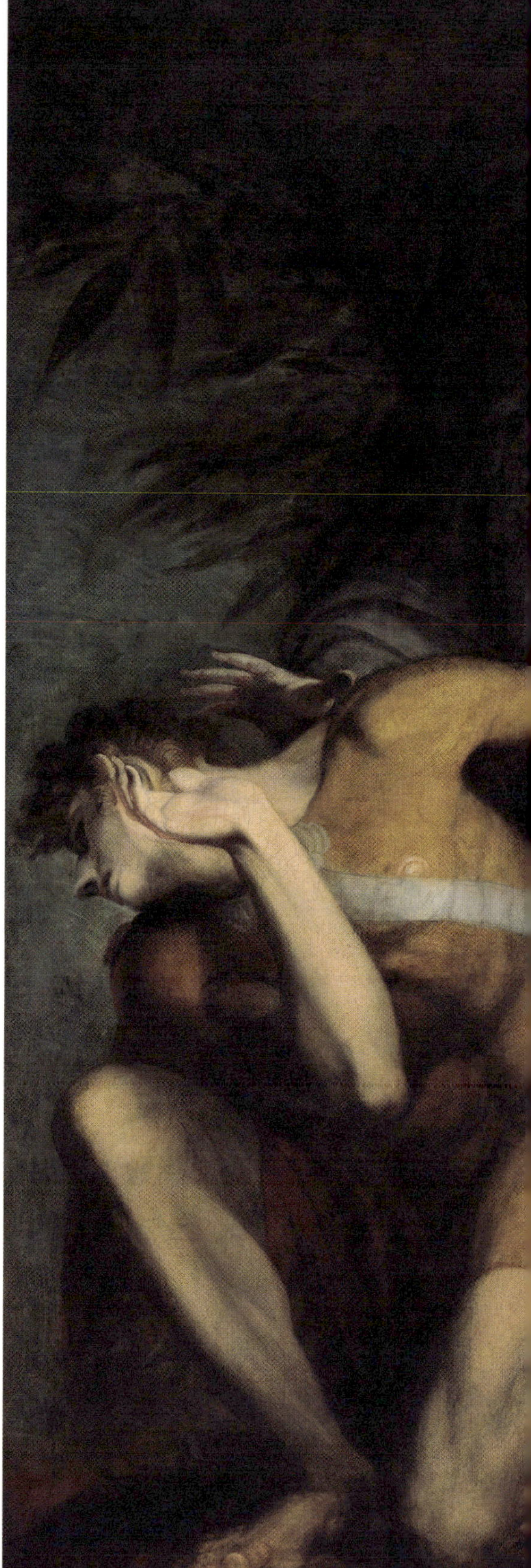

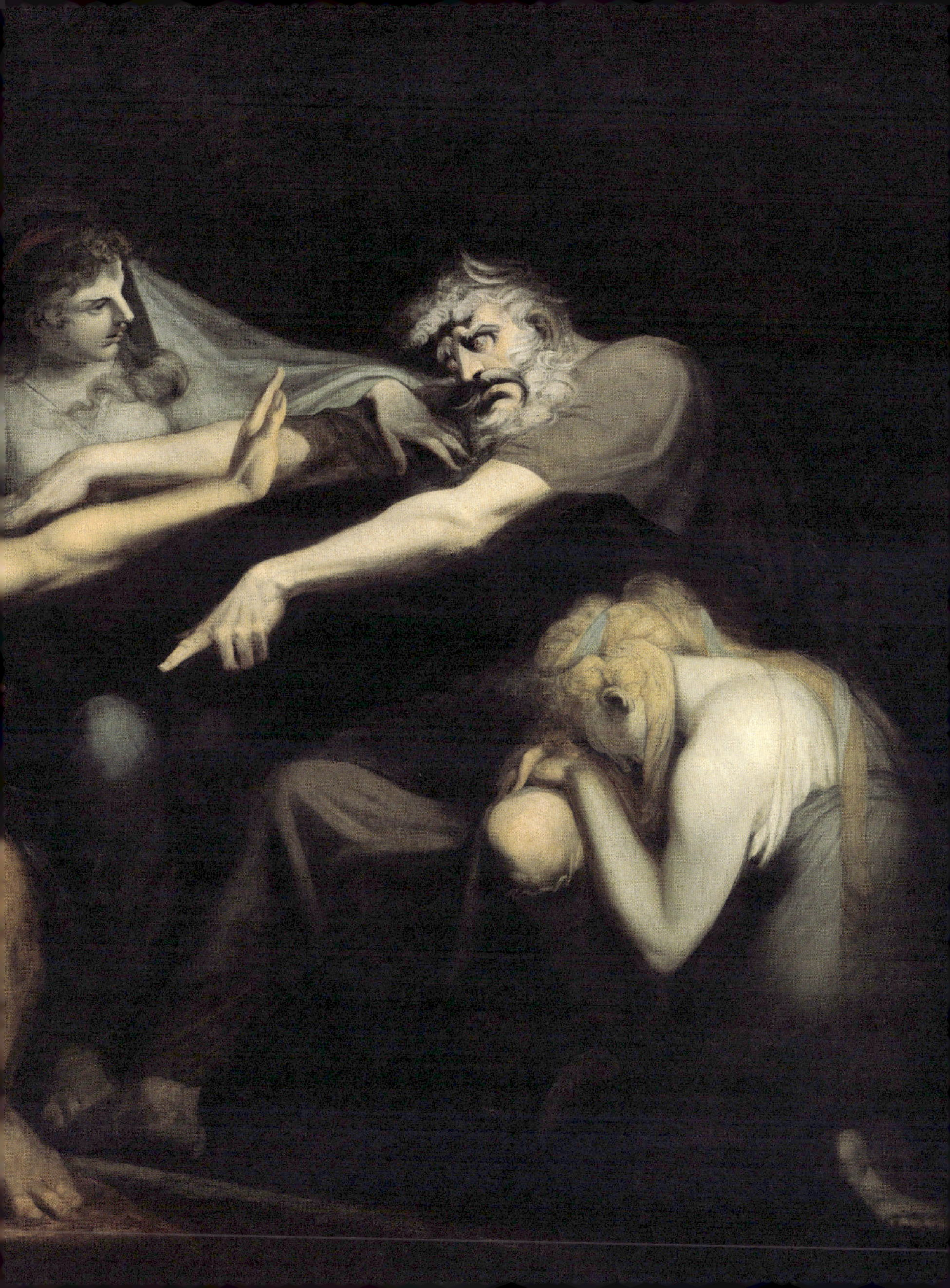

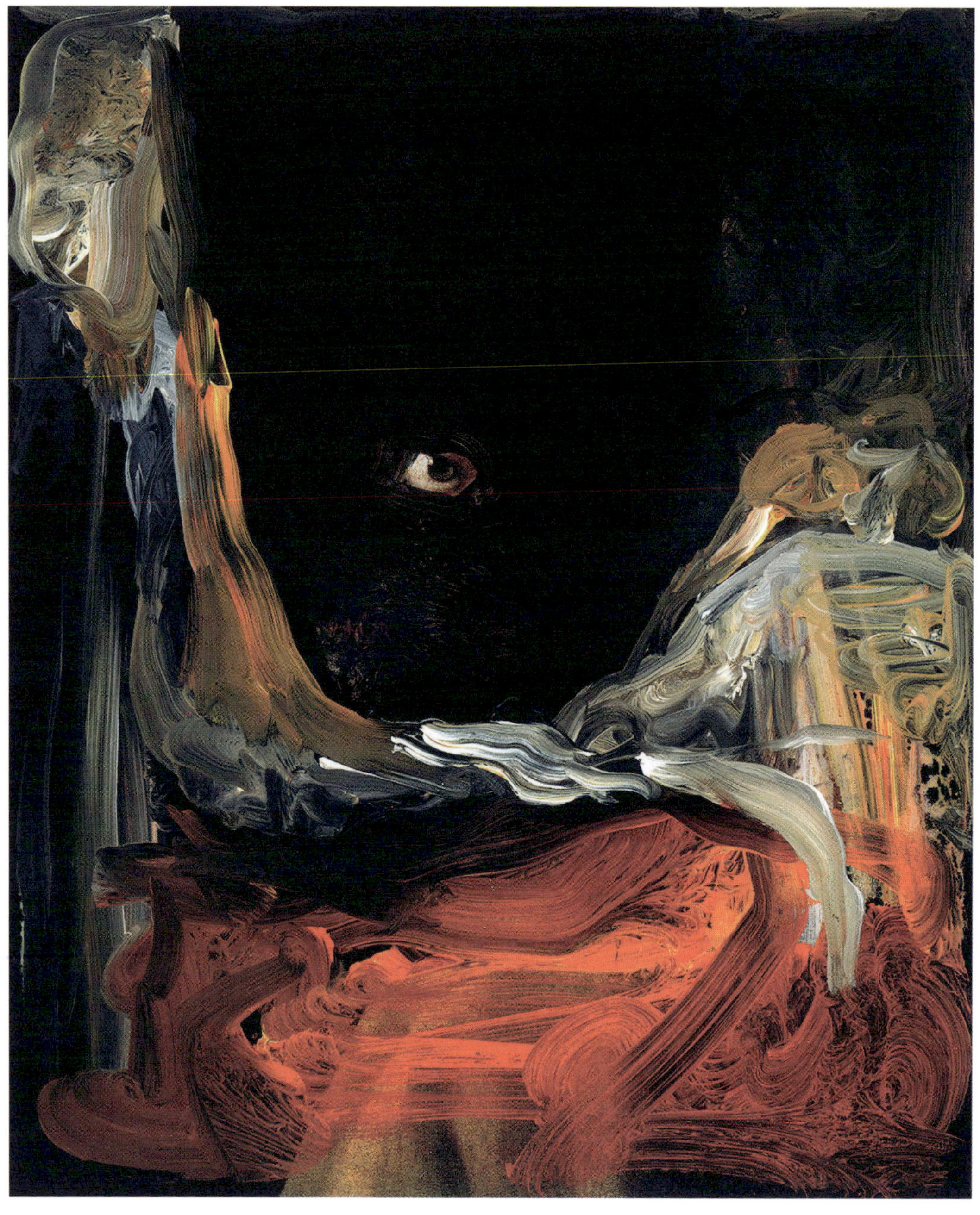

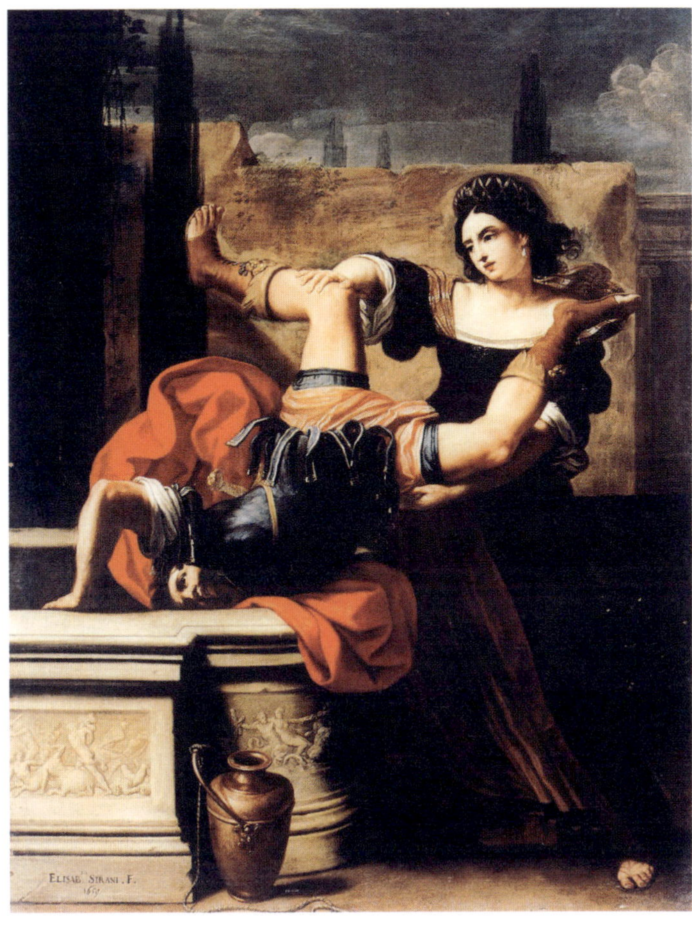

Opposite: Untitled, Joseba Eskubi, 2012, mixed media.

The abstract paintings of artist Joseba Eskubi (b. 1967), contrasting intense colours and darkness, are teeming with biomorphic forms and convulsive, contradictory shapes, and melting blobs that seem to ooze with sentient life at the same time as they are rotting in a grotesque and beautiful state of suspended decay. These amorphous creatures contain entire universes fraught with the murkier aspects of the human condition: secrets, movements and metamorphoses, a bubbling sludge overflowing with tensions from an entirely human-imagined abyss.

Above: Timoclea Killing Her Rapist, Elisabetta Sirani, 1659, oil on canvas.

Italian Baroque artist Elisabetta Sirani (1638–65), a significant and influential artist of the Bolognese School of painting, was thought of as one of the most learned, innovative and successful artists of the period. An independent painter by the age of nineteen, Sirani ran her family's workshop. When her father became incapacitated by gout, she supported her parents, three siblings and herself entirely through her art. Sirani advocated for both women painters and women subjects during her short life and opened a painting school where she trained many women, including her younger sisters. Her righteous championing of women and their stories is powerfully demonstrated in *Timoclea Killing Her Rapist*, wherein Sirani quite literally gives us the patriarchy turned on its head – Thebes resident Timoclea, after being raped by the captain of the Thracian forces, tossed the assailant into a well in her garden (where he had followed her after having the gall to ask her for money after he had assaulting her) and resolutely rained heavy rocks down on his head until her rapist was dead.

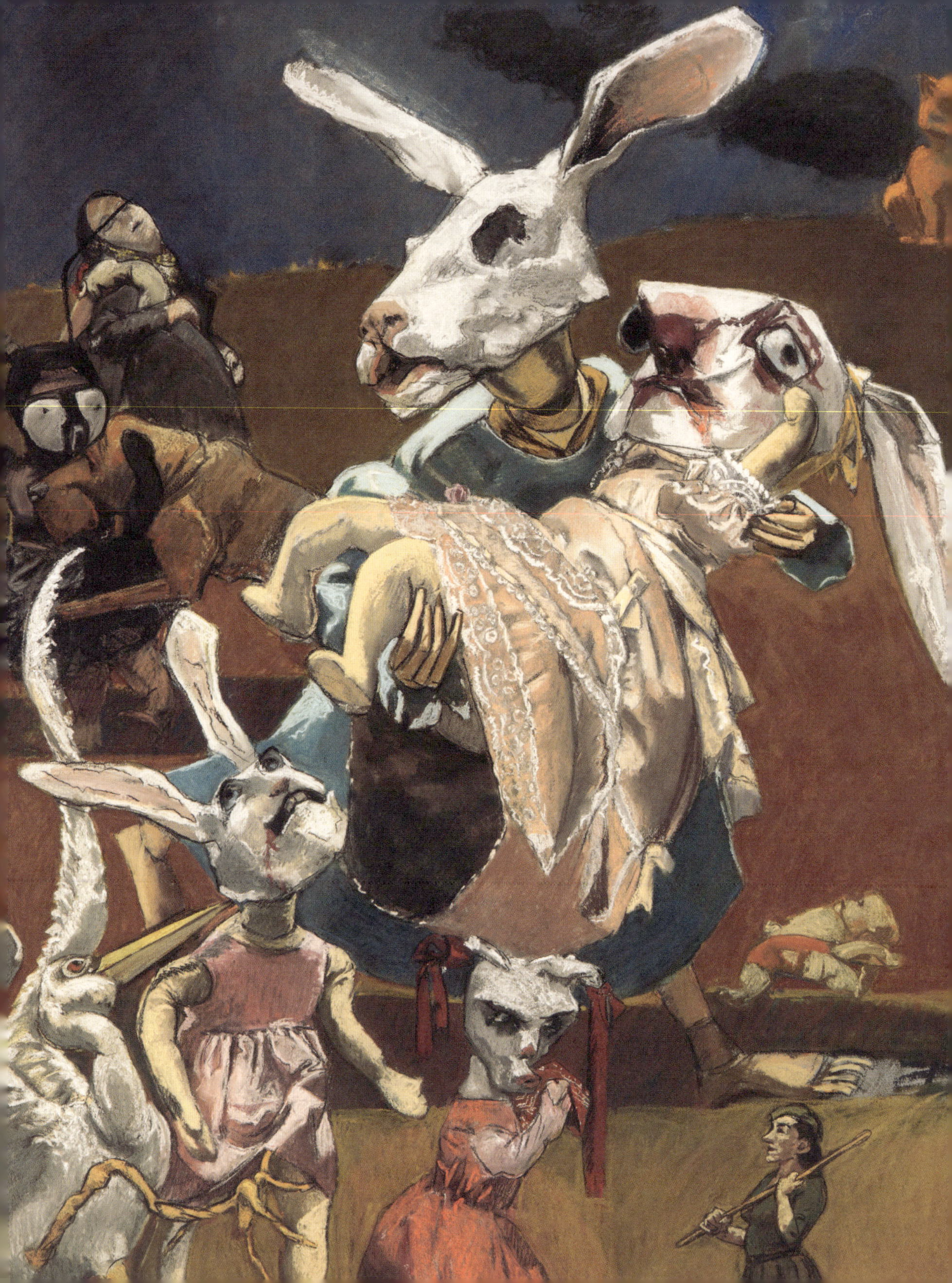

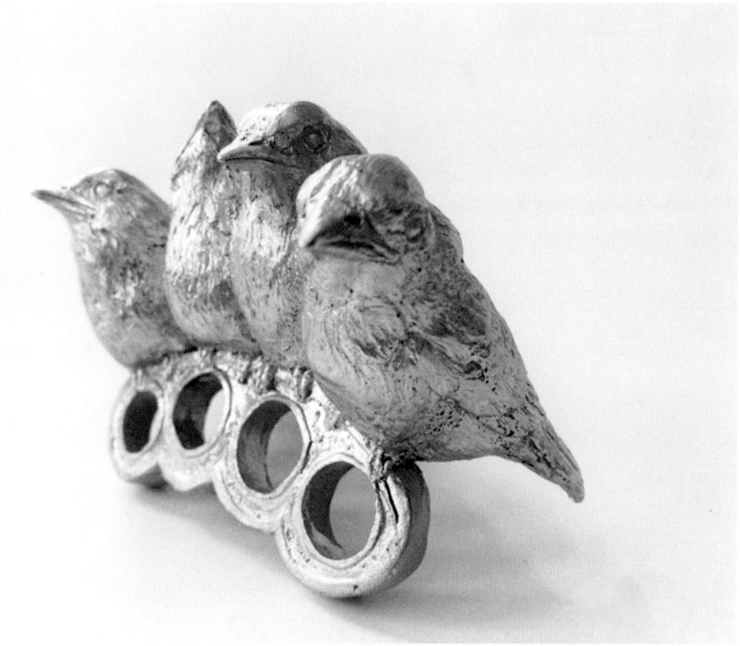

Opposite: War, Paula Rego, 2003, pastel on paper on aluminium.

This portrayal of war and suffering with bloodied rabbit marionettes centre stage by Portuguese-born British artist Paula Rego (b. 1935) was a response to a press photograph published in the early stages of the Iraq War. The photograph featured a screaming girl in a white dress running from an explosion, while a woman and a baby remain stationary behind her. Compositions combining animal heads and masks, young girls and children's toys, all of which appear in *War*, recur throughout Rego's work, which often invokes the imagery of fairy tales with sinister or gothic overtones and plays on viewers' notions of innocence.

Above: This Will Hurt Me More Than It Hurts You, Darla Jackson, 2021, polyurethane resin.

The work of contemporary sculptor Darla Jackson (b. 1981) is an exploration of human emotions, feelings translated through recognizable visual objects and combined with other elements to create symbolic dualities. The end result is a familiarity revealing some compelling and insightful peculiarities. This four-bird knuckleduster, an implement of fairy-tale violence both cute and intimidating, offers ideas of protection and self-defence that are so often needed yet usually suspiciously absent in portrayals of women in popular culture. According to the artist, the title, *This Will Hurt Me More Than It Hurts You*, is a reference to the fact that women are often criticized for standing up for themselves.

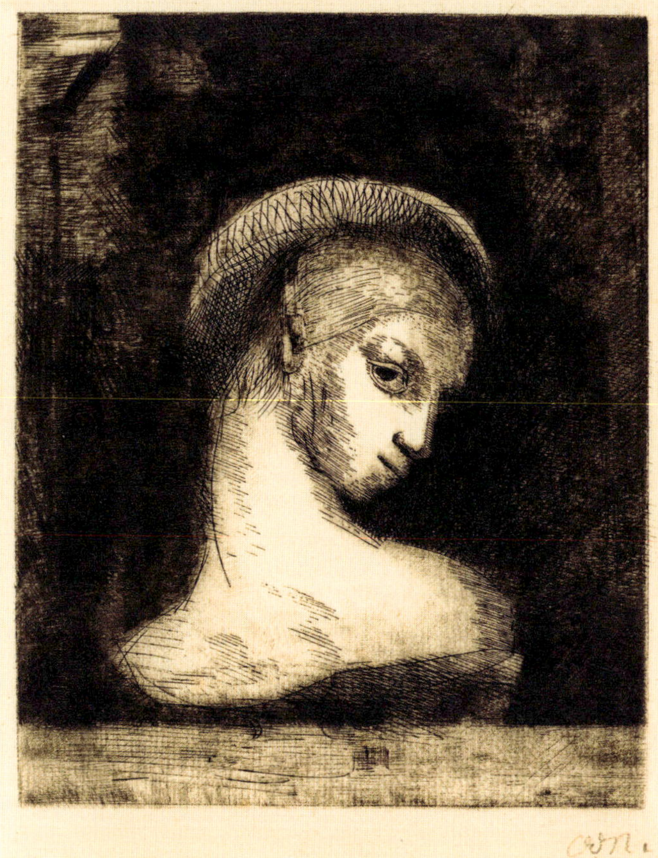

Left: Perversité (Perversity), Odilon Redon, 1891, etching and drypoint print.

Highly influential among the late nineteenth-century French avant-garde circle and noted for his singular and intriguing artistic style evoking a mysterious world of melancholic fantasy, Odilon Redon (1840–1916) created imaginative scenes which were frequently explorations in light and darkness. In *Perversity,* a face emerges from murky shadows and twists languidly over one shoulder with a indefinable yet decidedly decadent expression that nonetheless evokes profound unease. You don't really want to know what's on this figure's mind. Or . . . do you?

Opposite: Saturn Devouring His Son, Francisco Goya, c. 1819–23, mixed method on mural transferred to canvas.

The mural paintings that decorated the house known as La Quinta del Sordo, where master-of-horror Spanish painter Francisco Goya (1746–1828) lived, have come to be known as the Black Paintings, because he used so many sombre pigments and blacks in them, and also because of their morbid subject matter. One of the images he placed in the interior of the living room, dealing with his haunting fears of death, was the unspeakably cruel and horrifying image of the Titan Saturn devouring one of his sons. This mythological god could be the personification of such a human feeling as the fear of losing one's power, but also many of the interpretations of *Saturn Devouring His Son* are focused on the artist's inner conflicts between old and young age, as well as the disturbing relationship with his own son and the metaphor of the revolution eating its children.

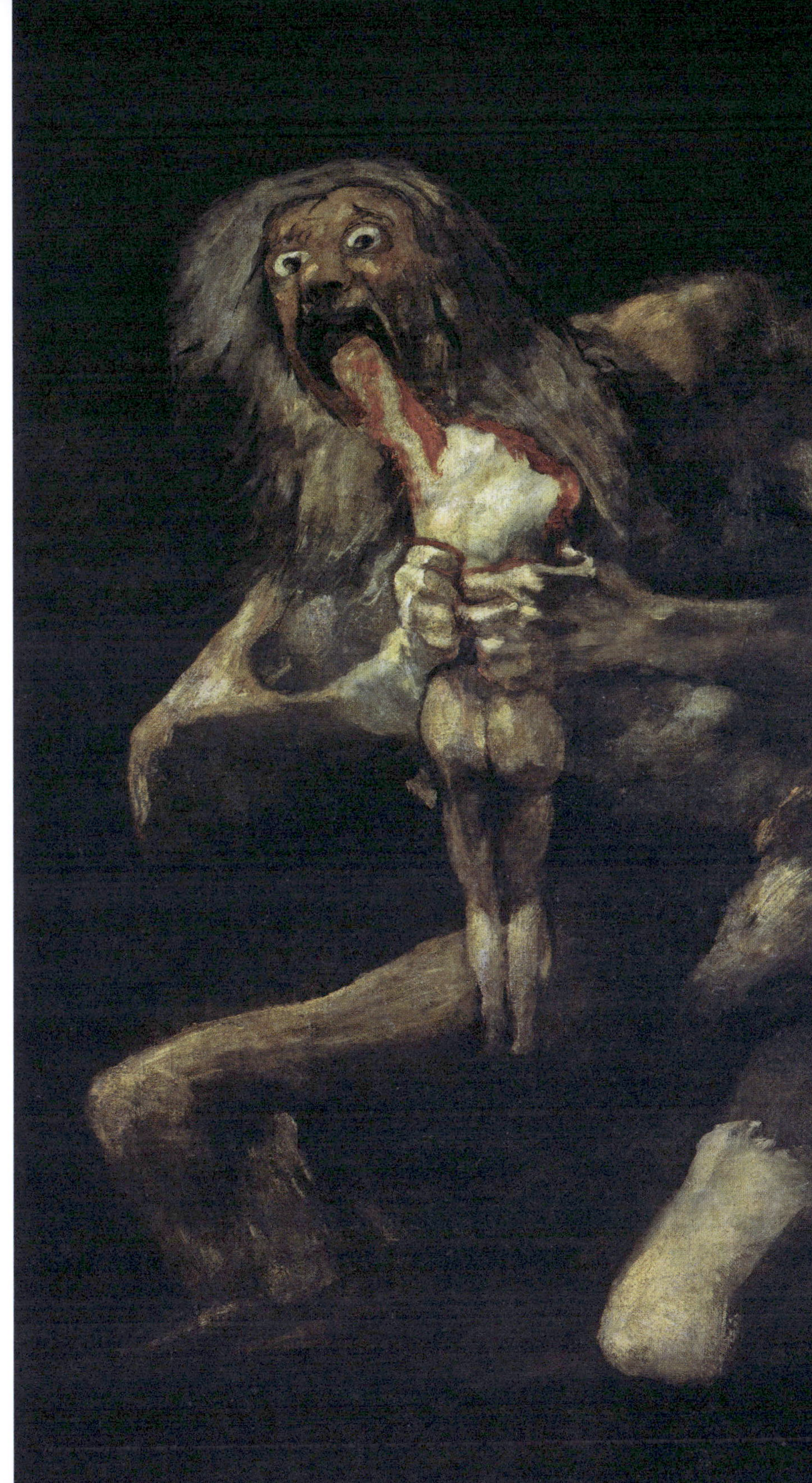

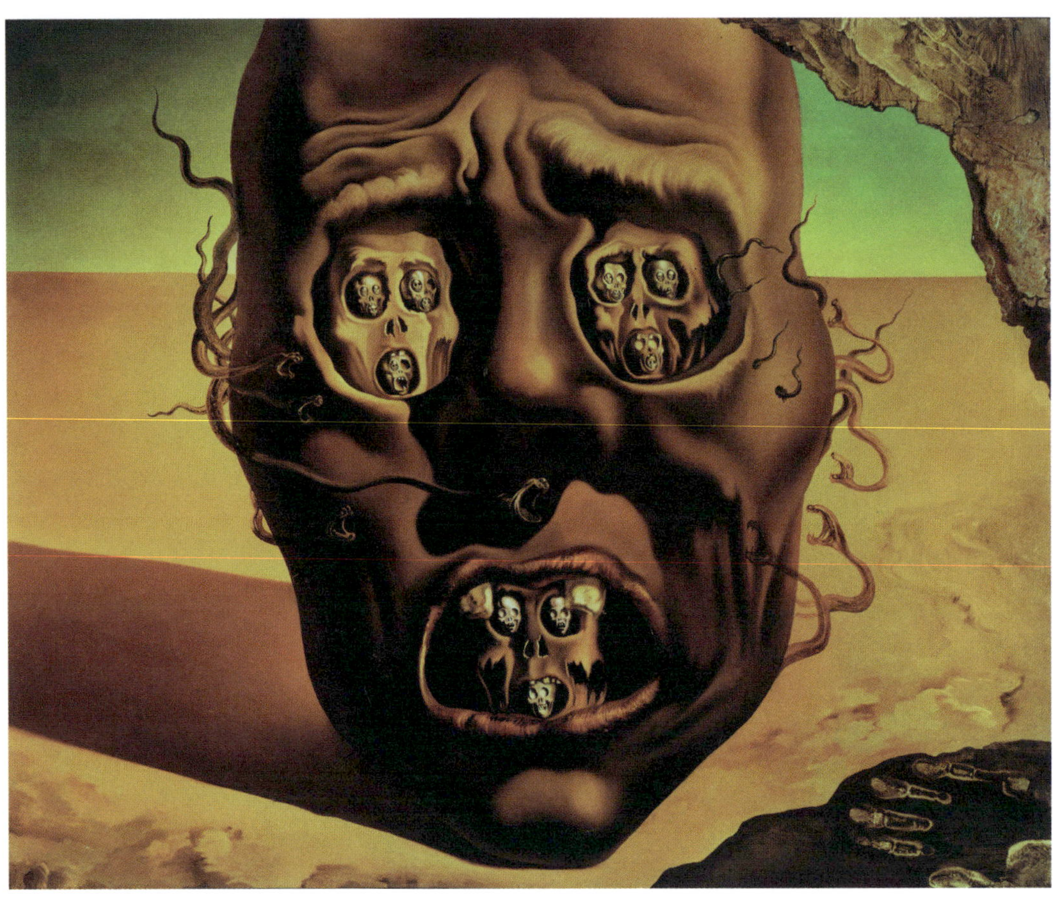

Above: The Face of War, Salvador Dalí, 1940, oil on canvas.

The Face of War, by world-renowned Surrealist artist Salvador Dalí (1904–89), is a surreal vision of the trauma and horror of war and is frequently interpreted as premonition of the Second World War, as it was painted in the period after the Spanish Civil War and just before war breaks out in Spain again. The focus of this Surrealist painting is a disembodied face hovering against a barren desert landscape, with identical faces filling mouth and eye holes. Within the optical illusion, skulls are multiplying in the face holes to infinity thus illustrating feelings of the eternal continuity of death and horror. Surrounding the face are serpents creeping around the empty and abandoned landscape. The emptiness and pessimism of this painting reveals the real sentiments of people exhausted by the never-ending destruction of war in Europe.

Right: Victim, Gustave Moreau, unknown date, oil on canvas.

The works of French Symbolist artist Gustave Moreau (1826–98) often focused on biblical and mythological figures, narratives overwhelmed with beauty and the sublime, wrought with the artist's distinct sense of phantasmagorical theatricality. In *Victim*, we behold an accusing figure whose dark fury and wrath is nearly vibrating off the canvas. One knows not what mystery lies within this wordless recrimination, what sins or slights were visited upon the injured party – one can only hope that they are not the culprit at the end of that resolute finger.

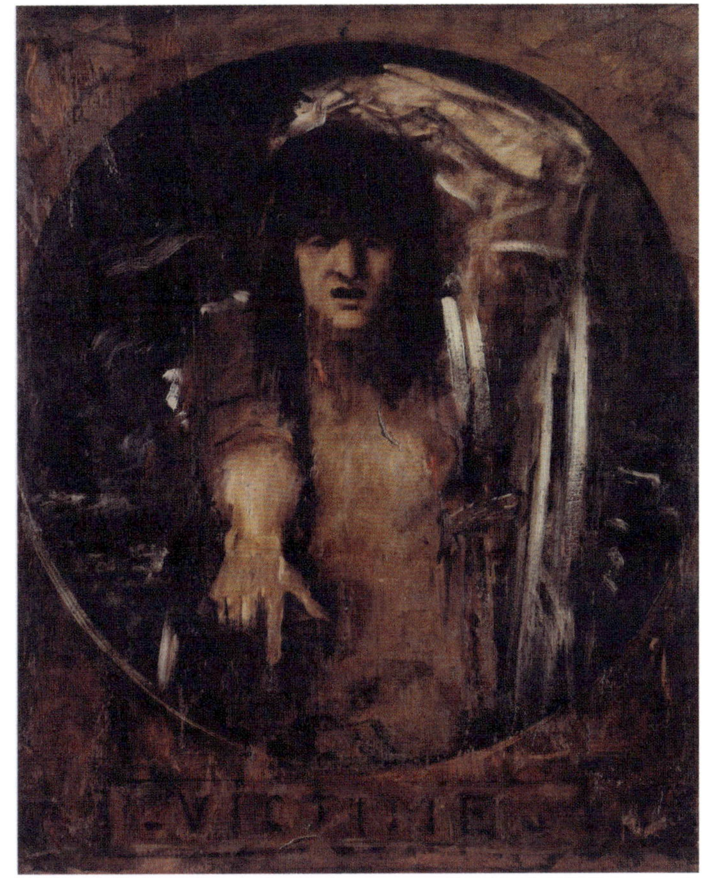

Following spread: Romans during the Decadence, Thomas Couture, 1847, oil on canvas.

Academic painter Thomas Couture (1815–79) was best known for his portraits and historical genre pictures, such as *Romans during the Decadence* (1847), which created a sensation at the Salon of 1847. Combining soft, eighteenthth-century colouring and the rigid pomposity of nineteenth-century classicism in this work concerning a debauched ruling class abandoning themselves to vice, Couture appeared to his contemporaries to have succeeded in combining Antiquity and the present (along with creating an allegorical criticism of the government in nineteenth-century France.)

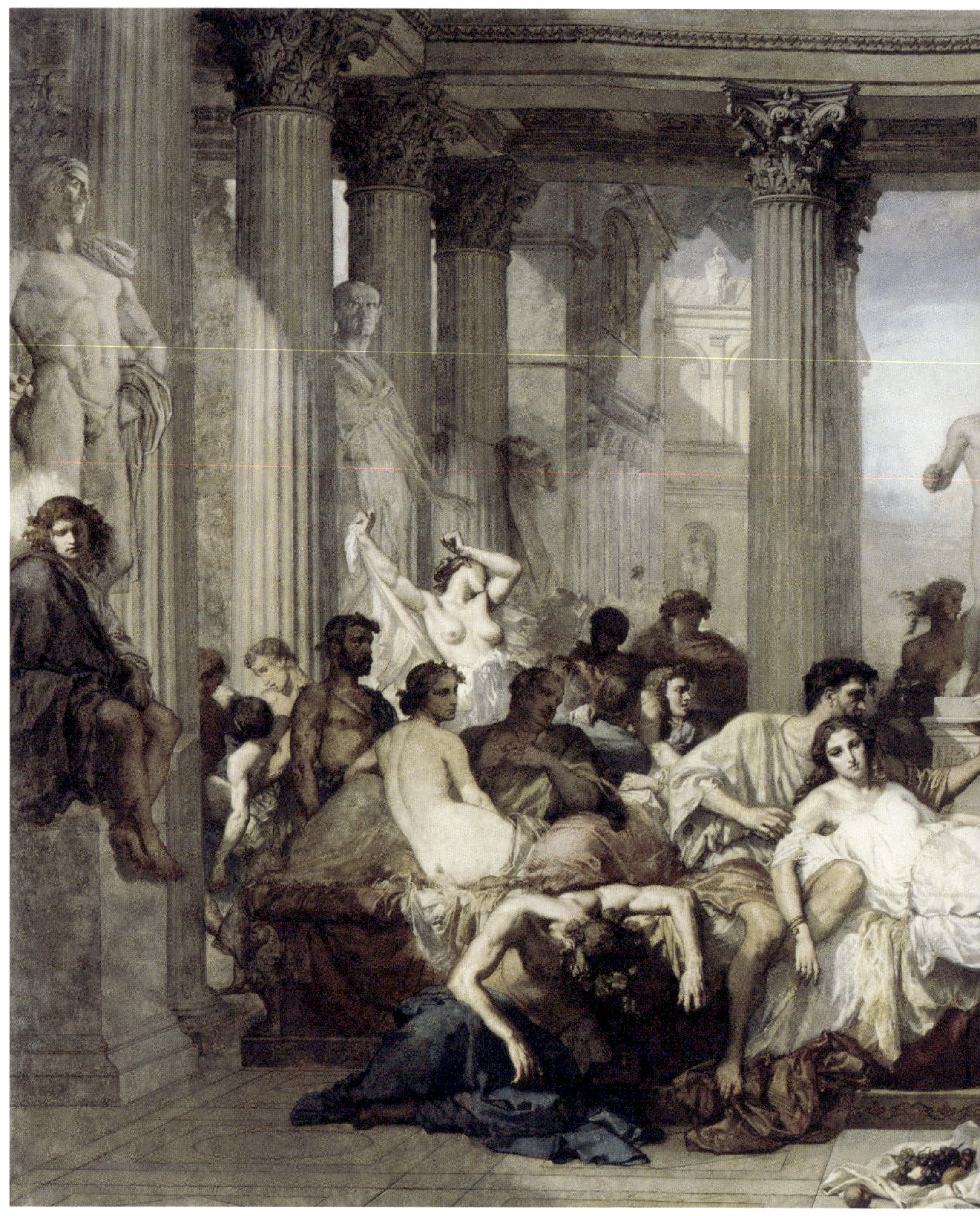

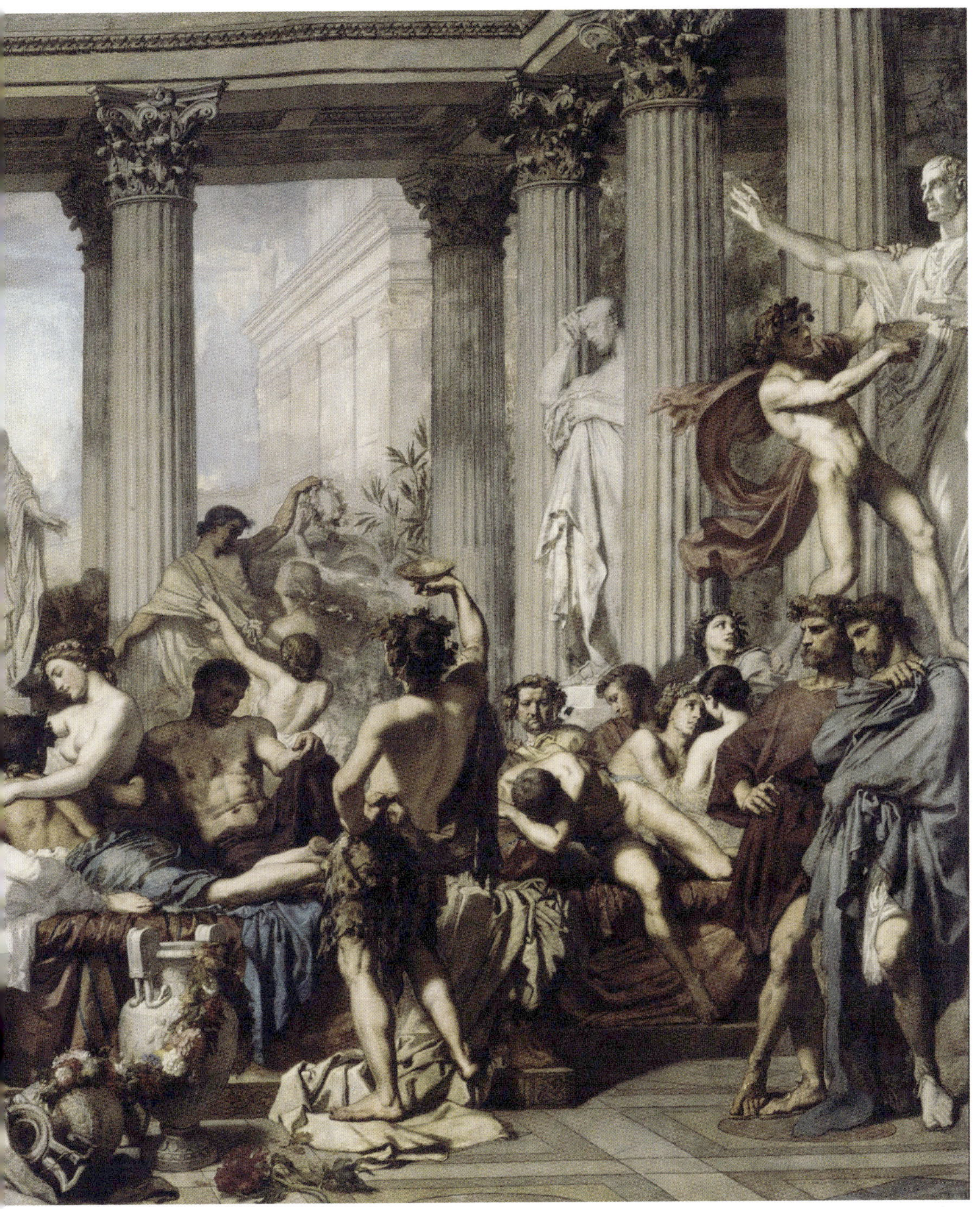

VI

Matters of Mortality

'Dying / Is an art, like everything else.'

– SYLVIA PLATH, 'LADY LAZARUS'

In your grim fancies and imaginings, I'm fairly sure that notions of dark-themed art don't get more morbid and miserable than envisioning the macabre-minded artist who appears to be alarmingly obsessed with death: artists whose lightless canvases are strewn with skulls both screaming and silent, the rot and decay of the flayed corpse, ornate coffins, lonely gravestones and grim reapers gone wild. But please do not be alarmed! This fascination with death and mortality is a common theme woven in and out of many artists' work, and it's not always as obvious as the imagery above suggests. There may even be a painting or two among your favourites wrought with such subtlety that you might not even have realized the artist's intent was to grapple with mortality.

There is but one certainty in life, and that is that none of us will be here forever . . . and furthermore, unless you are a time traveller or a psychic or playing a character in that subgenre of horror film where you learn your death date, we don't know when our time is up. No mortal knows with certainty when the thread of life will be snipped short; when, thus untethered, we will shuffle forever from this plane of existence. And in the mystery of this uncertainty lies one of the most pervasive themes in art history. This fascination is so prevalent, universal and relatable I sometimes wonder why we consider it to be a 'dark preoccupation'. We've all been there. We're all headed there.

Almost every culture formulates its own ideas, however formless and hazy, as to what happens to the individual after death, from the Christian geographies of heaven and hell in Michelangelo's *The Last Judgment* (1536–41) and Botticelli's *The Abyss of Hell* (c. 1485) to the Buddhist beliefs in reincarnation and the cycles of life, death and rebirth as seen in the Tibetan Wheel of Rebirth, to the famous Egyptian Book of the Dead, a perfect example of the work of art created for the sole purpose of helping the soul pass to the other side. Likewise, every culture has rituals and traditions surrounding death, concerning the treatment of the body, the preparation of the grave and mourning.

Down through the ages, particularly in times of strife, people were encouraged to ponder death and its meaning. Artworks created during times of plague, for example, reminded even the most powerful that their life was fragile, temporary and provisional. These *memento mori*, a phrase that translates to 'remember that you will die', may seem ghoulish to some, but were designed to remind the viewer of the shortness and fragility of human life. For centuries, artists have explored the concepts of *memento mori* in a number of unique ways, developing a common language of expressive visual symbolism over time. *Vanitas* was a popular theme in the art of still lifes of sixteenth- and seventeenth-century Flanders and Netherlands, utilizing the still-life form to evoke the fleeting quality of life and the vanity of living. Modern artists continue to explore these themes, communicating that the things of this world – pleasures, money, beauty, power – are not everlasting.

The early twentieth century saw swift changes on industrial, economic, social and cultural levels which provided a basis for new artistic movements, and with the tremendous scale of death and destruction resulting from the greatest war the world had ever seen, art increasingly became abstracted. Avant-garde ideas challenged traditional art history and these Expressionistic approaches to art-making changed the representation of death in art. Death no longer required such obvious symbolism. A field of crows? Death. A canvas painted completely black? Death. We know it when we see it, don't we? The manner in which contemporary artists negotiate death moves beyond the actual spectacle of death. In work by artists such as Damien Hirst and Shirin Neshat we observe how mortality brings us face to face with profound ethical and even political issues, to include powerful memorial work for communities experiencing vast devastation.

Death is an inherent and imminent part of life and, despite humanity's prodigious advancements, we still don't boast the science for immortality – though I maintain that the creation and appreciation of art is certainly the next best thing. For the present: the next time you find yourself confronted with the shocking imagery of a skull with hollow eyes and a grinning visage, take a moment to accept your fear, recognize the universal human experience being shared in the moment, mentally pat that skull on the head and acknowledge your kinship, and say, It's OK, friend. I'm right behind you.

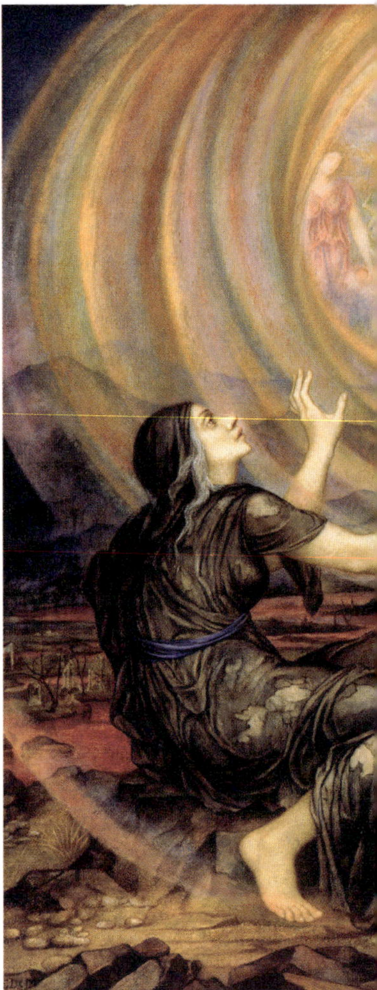

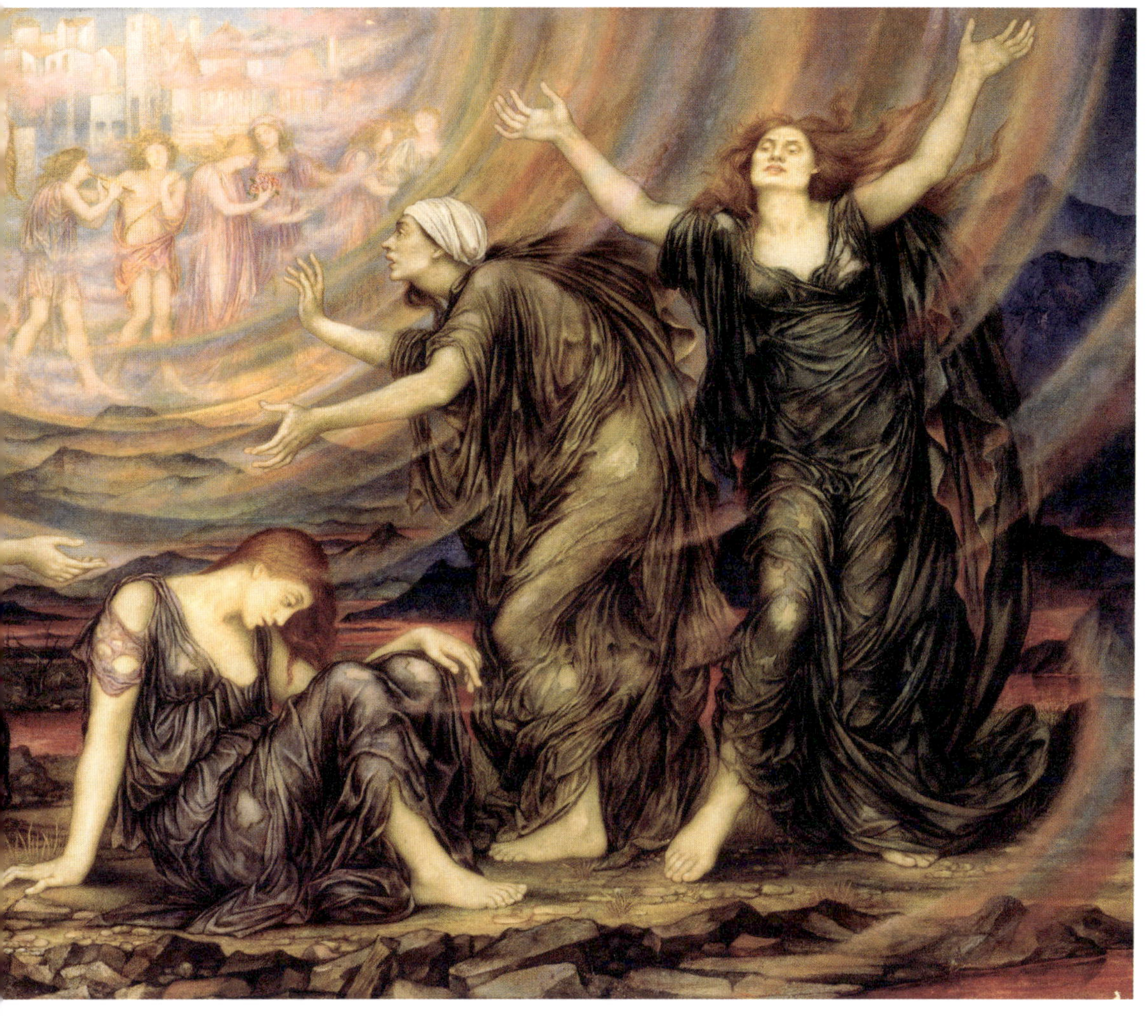

Opposite: The Mourners, Evelyn De Morgan, c. 1915, oil on canvas.

The Mourners by Evelyn De Morgan (1855-1919) is one in a series of symbolic pictures of war subjects inspired by the artist's distress over the First World War. The horrors of the war and its enormous death toll this brought had a profound effect on de Morgan and her artwork, typically reflective of the artist's penchant for allegorical or symbolic subjects. In this work wrought in sombre shades amid a barren landscape, lamenting figures in ragged robes, with arms raised in despair and grief, gaze towards a vision in a striking vortex of golden light. An original label on the reverse reads: 'The unhappy people, in their misery, are haunted by a vision of past happiness.'

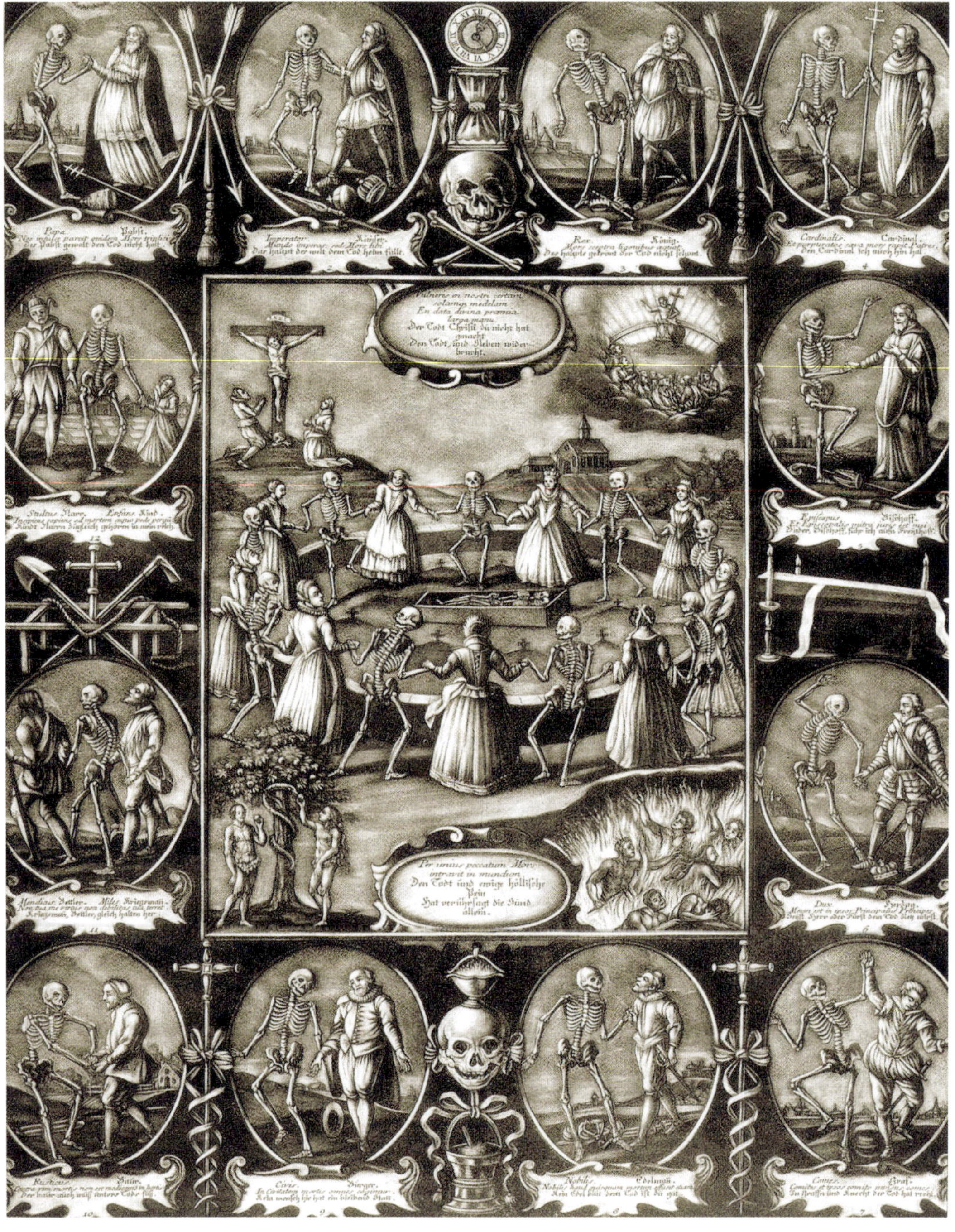
Papa.
Imperator.
Rex. König.
Cardinalis.
Vulnera en nostri certam
solamq medelam
En data divina praemia
larga manu
Den Todt Christi du nicht hat
gmacht
Den Todt, und Leben wider-
bracht.
Per unius peccatum Mors
intravit in mundum
Den Todt und ewige höllische
Pein
Hat verursacht die Sünd
allein.
Dux.
Comes.
Nobilis.
Civis.
Rusticus.

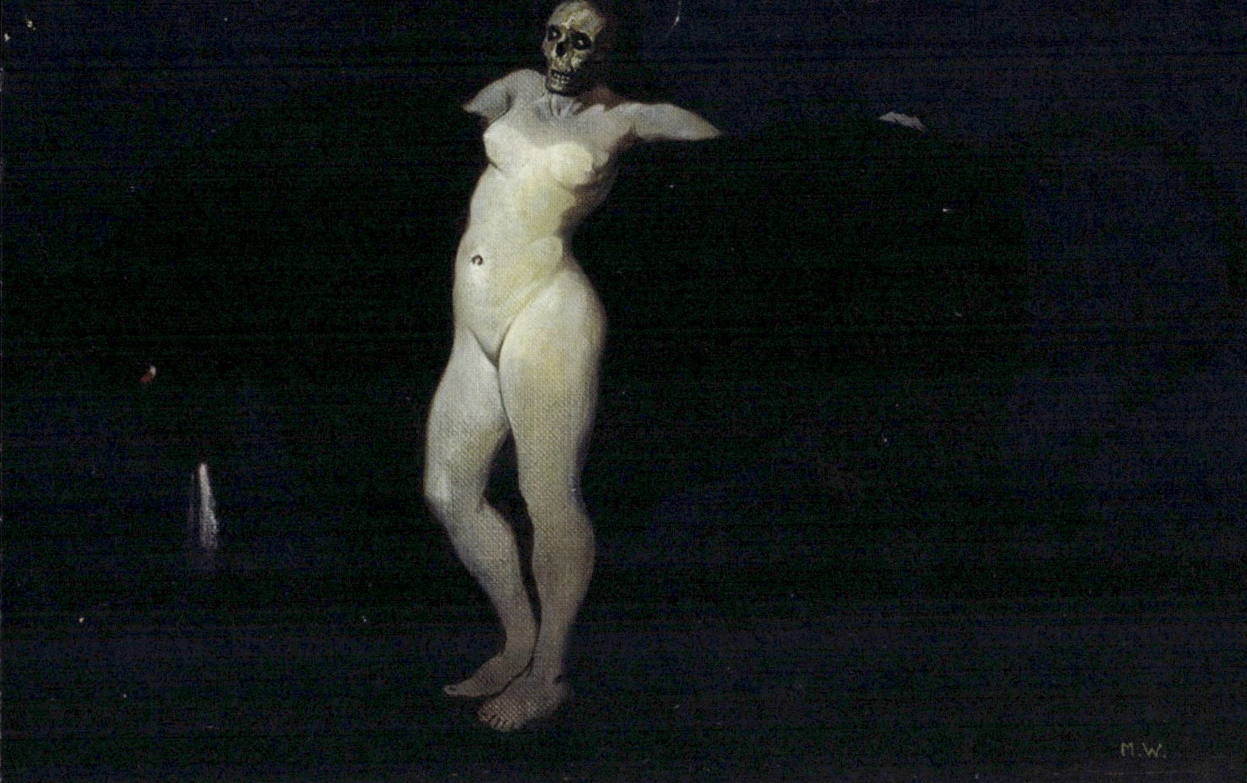

Opposite: Danse Macabre, Johann Elias Ridinger, mid-eighteenth century, mezzotint.

Above: Śmierć każdego ułagodzi (Death Appeases Everyone), Marian Wawrzeniecki, 1898, oil on canvas.

In *Danse Macabre* by German painter and engraver Johann Elias Ridinger (1698–1767), nine women from a variety of social backgrounds gather in order to dance with the dead around two skeletons in a coffin. The entire economy of salvation is depicted, from the Fall, through the crucifixion, to Heaven and Hell. This artistic genre of allegory of the Late Middle Ages is a comment on the universality of death: no matter one's station in life, the *Danse Macabre* unites all. This is a theme which has proved remarkably adaptable over the centuries; some artists have taken the whole Dance of Death and set it in their own time, while others have taken a traditional episode from the Dance of Death and have treated it in their idiosyncratic style.

Warsaw-born Polish painter, art historian and archaeologist Marian Wawrzeniecki (1863–1943) was influenced by Slavic culture and French and German Symbolism. He painted fairy-tale motifs in the context of the archetypes of the human psyche and much of his output was governed by the prospect of death, which threatens every person with ruthless cruelty.

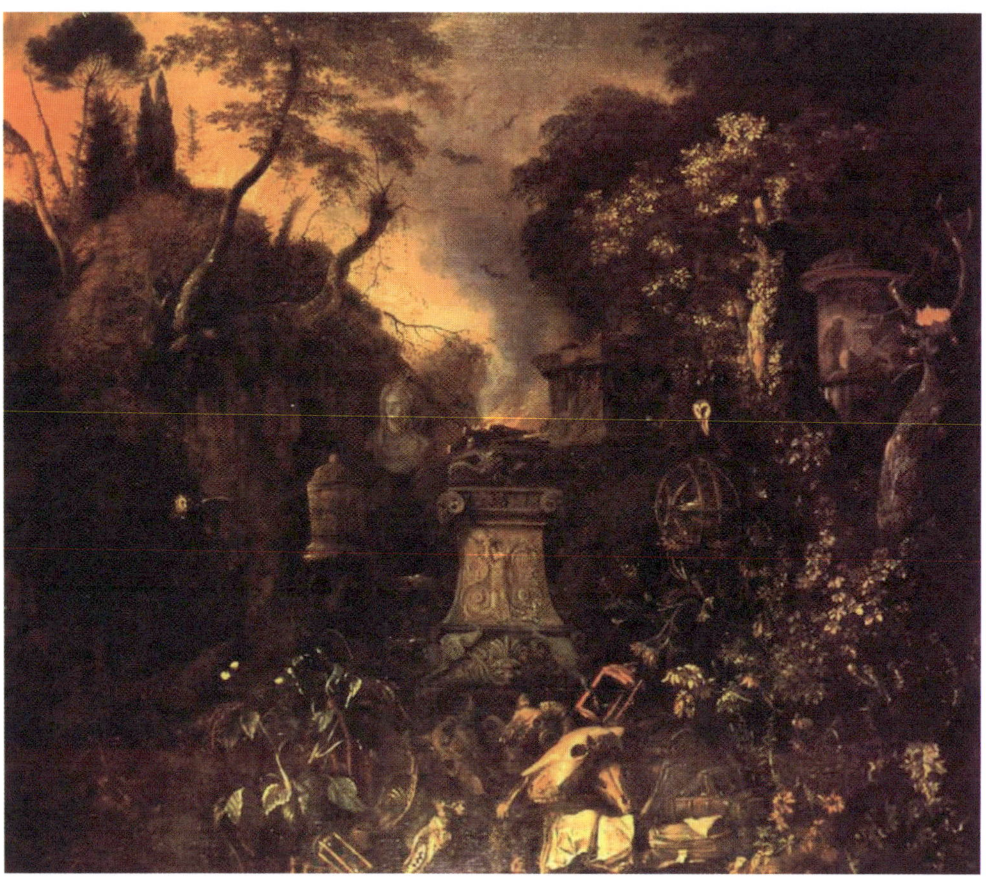

Above: Landscape with a Graveyard by Night,
Matthias Withoos,
c. seventeenth century, oil on canvas.

Matthias Withoos (1627–1703) was a Dutch painter of city scenes and gloomy wildlife tableaux, many of which incorporate vanitas motifs and which are notable for their close-ups of the mysterious flora and fauna enlivening dark forest undergrowth. In this melancholic graveside scene bathed in dusk's dramatic lighting, we sense in the tangled ivy and weathered stone that time is indeed marching on, as unseen below, the dead slumber on.

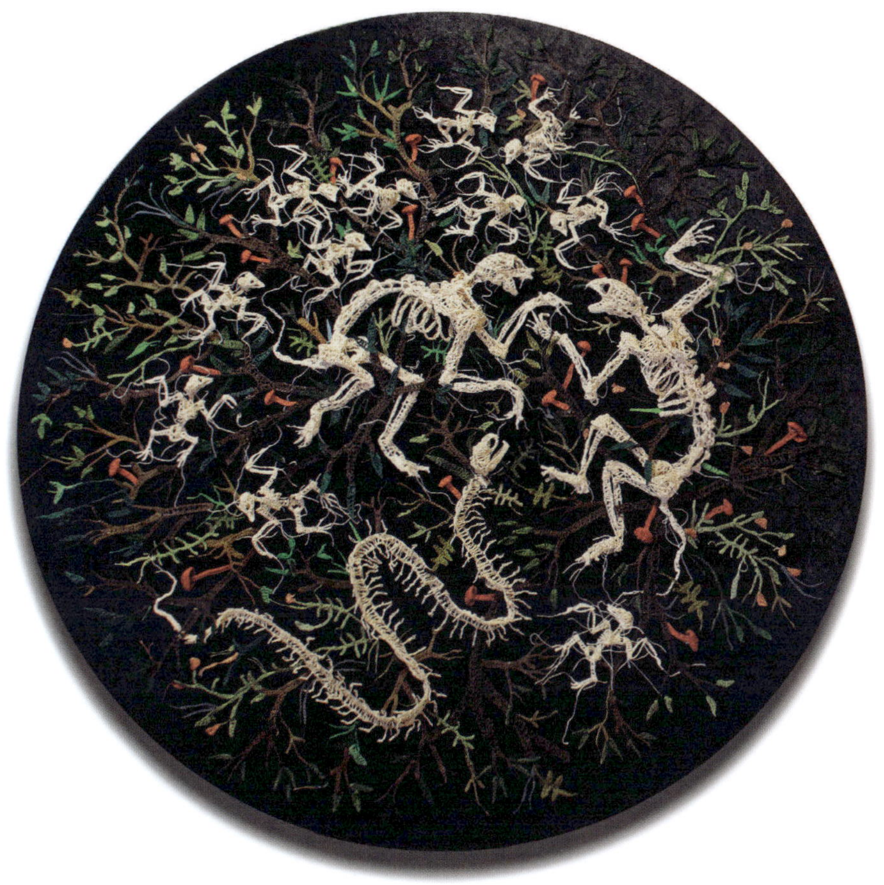

Above: Cold Soil Kettle, Caitlin McCormack, 2020, crocheted cotton string, glue, foraged pigments, steel pins, velvet.

Caitlin MacCormack creates work of sombre delicacy, ghostly skeletal remains tenderly chained with fragile lace, via cotton, glue and a quickly flashing crochet hook. By utilizing media and practices inherited from departed relatives, the artist aims to generate emblems of a diminishing bloodline, representative of both the persistence of memory and the significance of cloth and thread in the realm of human experience.

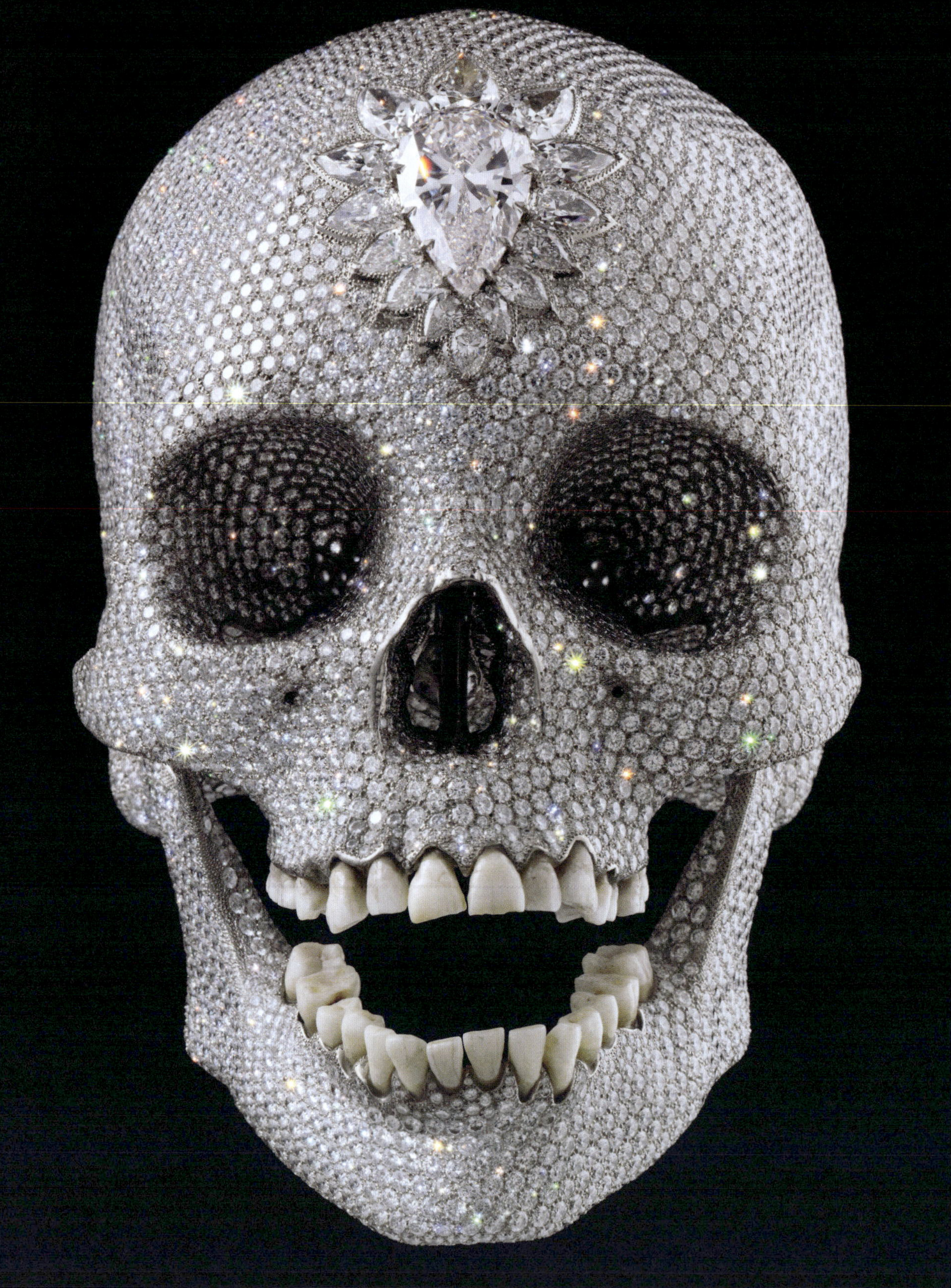

Right: Vanitas Still Life, Jan van Kessel the Elder, c. 1665–70, oil on copper.

A versatile artist who practised in many genres, Jan van Kessel (1626-79) specialized in small-scale pictures of subjects culled from the natural world, including studies of animals and insects both living and dead, still lifes of fruit, bouquets and garlands, marine and paradise landscapes, allegorical compositions and genre scenes. His brightly coloured, minutely detailed paintings on panel or copper were highly prized by connoisseurs and collectors. Vanitas, the loose category of artwork that illustrates the transience of life, the futility of pleasure and the certainty of death - often featuring conspicuous allegory in the form of dusty skulls, decaying flowers and the dwindling sands of hourglasses - offered an artful pretext to paint still-lifes of opulent objects behind a veneer of morality.

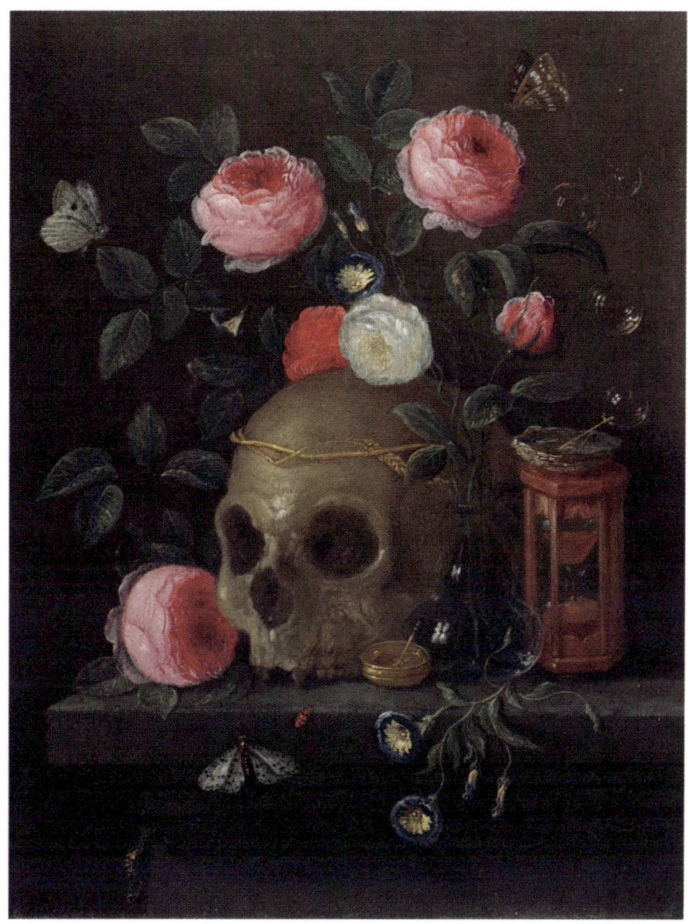

Opposite: For the Love of God, Damien Hirst, 2007, platinum, diamond and human teeth.

In 2007, Damien Hirst (b. 1965) made headlines with a work consisting of 8,601 of the world's finest diamonds encrusting the platinum cast of a human skull from the mid-1800s, complete with the skull's original real human teeth - titled *For the Love of God*, apparently in response to a question posed by the artist's mother ('For the love of God, what are you going to do next?'). Hirst's fascination with skulls began at a young age. At sixteen, the artist began visiting the anatomy department of Leeds Medical School to draw the cadavers. '[Death is] just something that inspires me, not something that pulls me down,' Hirst once explained. 'And every day your relationship with death changes.' Since it was first exhibited in 2007, *For the Love of God* has become one of the most widely recognized works of contemporary art. It represents the artist's continued interest in mortality and notions of value.

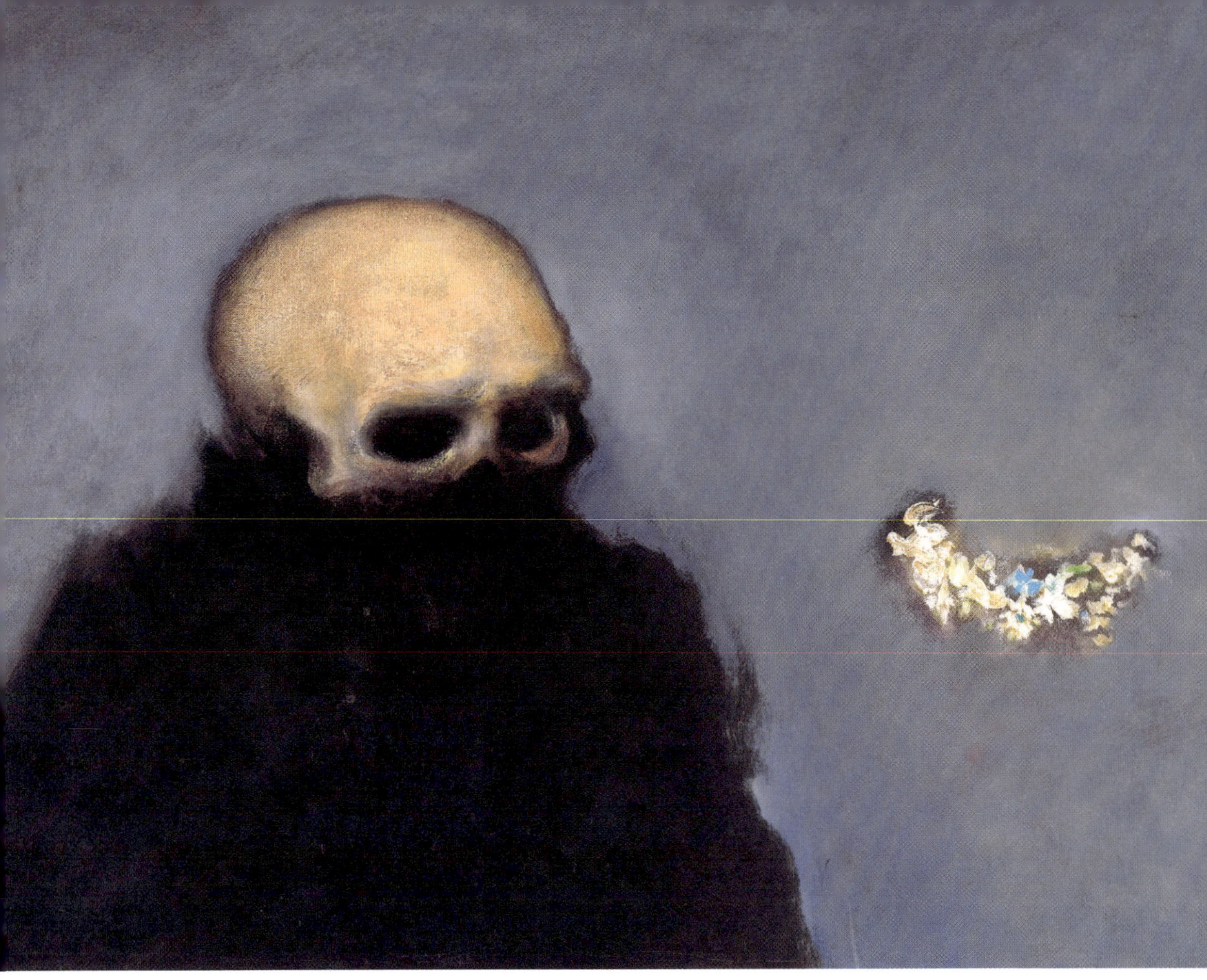

Above: Memento Mori, Walter Kuhlman, 1973–74, oil on canvas.

US painter, printmaker and teacher, Walter Kuhlman (1918–2009) was a noted figure in the post-war Bay Area Abstract Expressionist movement based in San Francisco. He practised an abstract style of ragged forms and discordant colours that evolved into a softer but equally enigmatic figurative manner with symbolist undertones. The image of the human skull has appeared in several of Kuhlman's paintings. Here, a hunched skull-headed figure stares at a floating flower garland: death yearning for life.

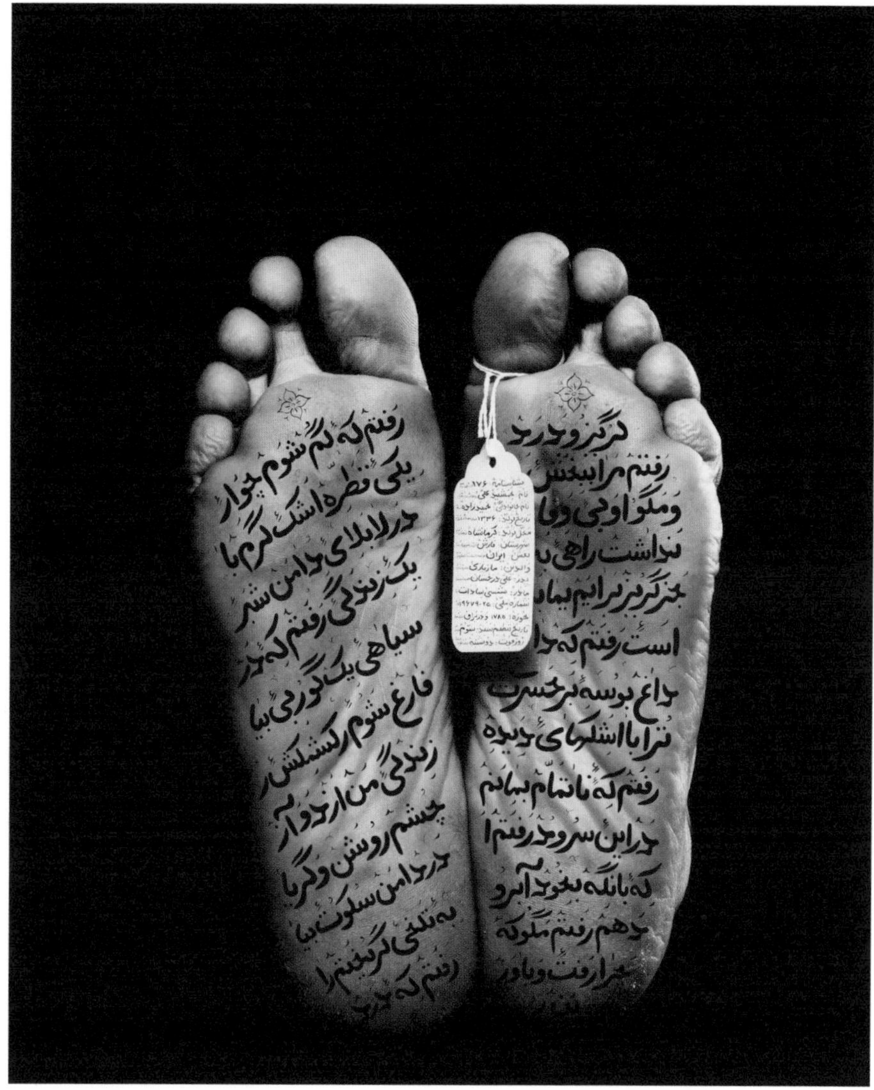

Above: Rahim (Our House Is on Fire), Shirin Neshat, 2013, ink on digital chromogenic print.

Shirin Neshat (b. 1957) is a contemporary Iranian visual artist best known for her work in photography, video and film. Neshat's series Our House Is on Fire stems from the death and destruction she saw in Cairo, including the corpses of 'young men and women and little children with tags on their feet', when she travelled there to work in 2012. Like many of Neshat's works, this series consists of portraits and details of hands and feet, capturing emotions that are at once individual and universal and exploring how people deal with pain on both a personal and national level.

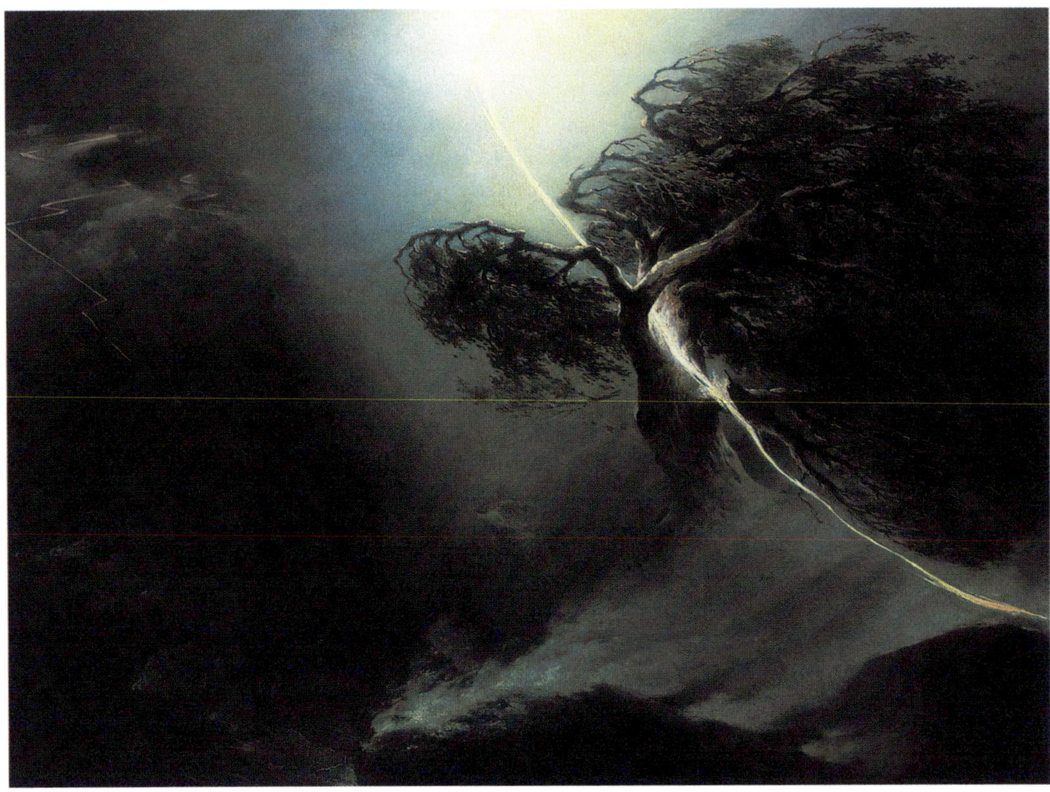

Above: Oak Fractured by Lightning, Maxim Vorobiev, 1842, oil on canvas.

Russian Romantic landscape painter Maxim Vorobiev (1787–1855) specialized in picturesque seascapes and peaceful countryside views, as well as architectural monuments and war scenes. The staggering loss depicted in *Oak Fractured by Lightning* is markedly different. An allegory on his wife's death, this emotionally charged vision captures the shock and anguish of losing a loved one. A bright bolt of opalescent lightning streaks down from the gloom of stormy skies, shattering an old oak tree in two – it is perhaps the perfect metaphor to express the howling desolation and heart-wrenching pain of the sudden death of someone you love.

Opposite: Grief, Oskar Zwintscher, 1898, oil on canvas.

Those who have suffered a terrible loss know well the crushing feelings of despair that suffuse all of the colourless days that follow. In this work of the German artist Oskar Zwintscher (1870–1916), he eerily captures the unyielding and overwhelming emotional weight under which the bereaved suffer. Death is rendered a bit-player behind the massive, lightless stone, faceted with myriad aspects of grief's crushing gravity, relentlessly pressed upon the one who is left behind.

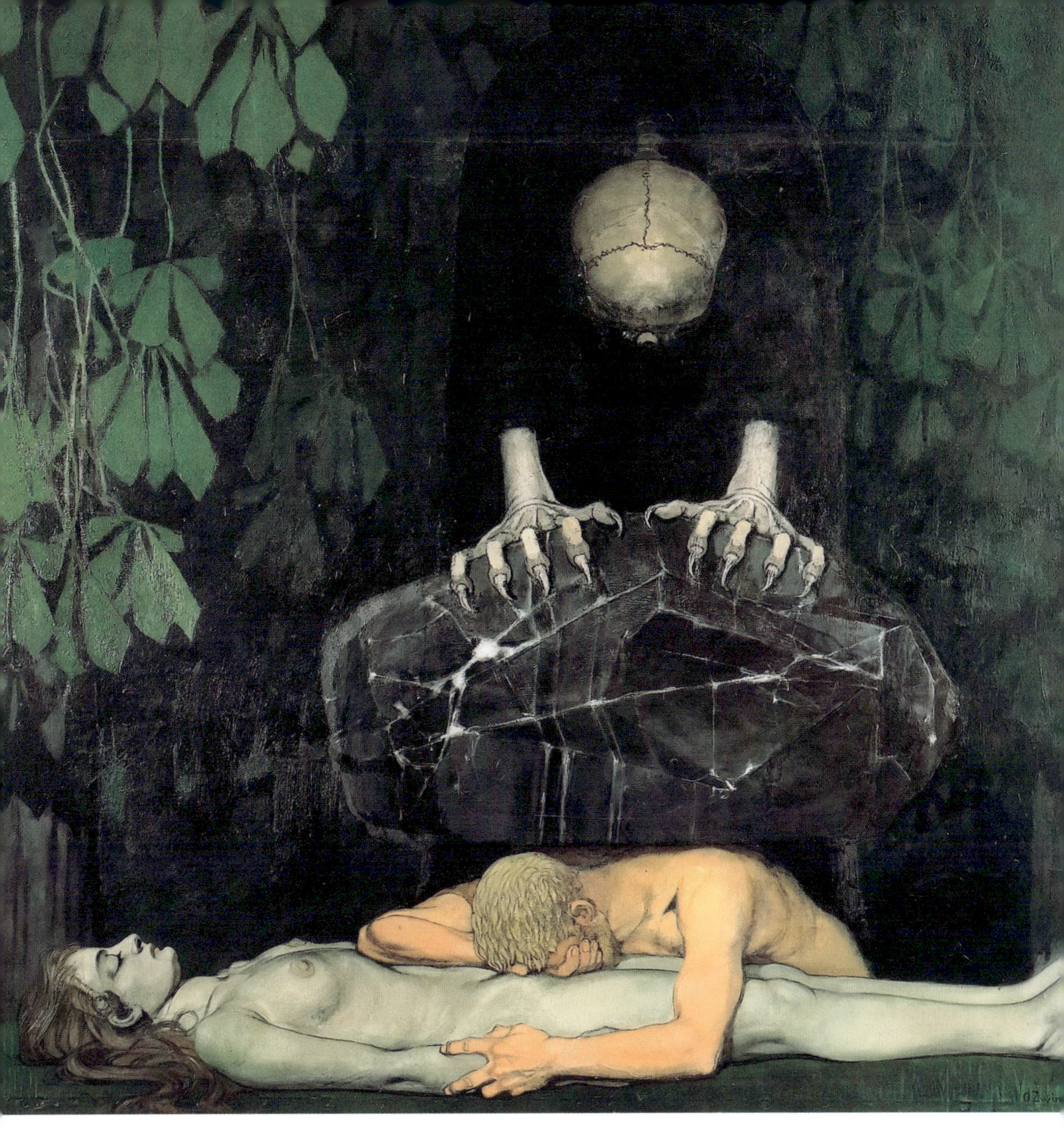

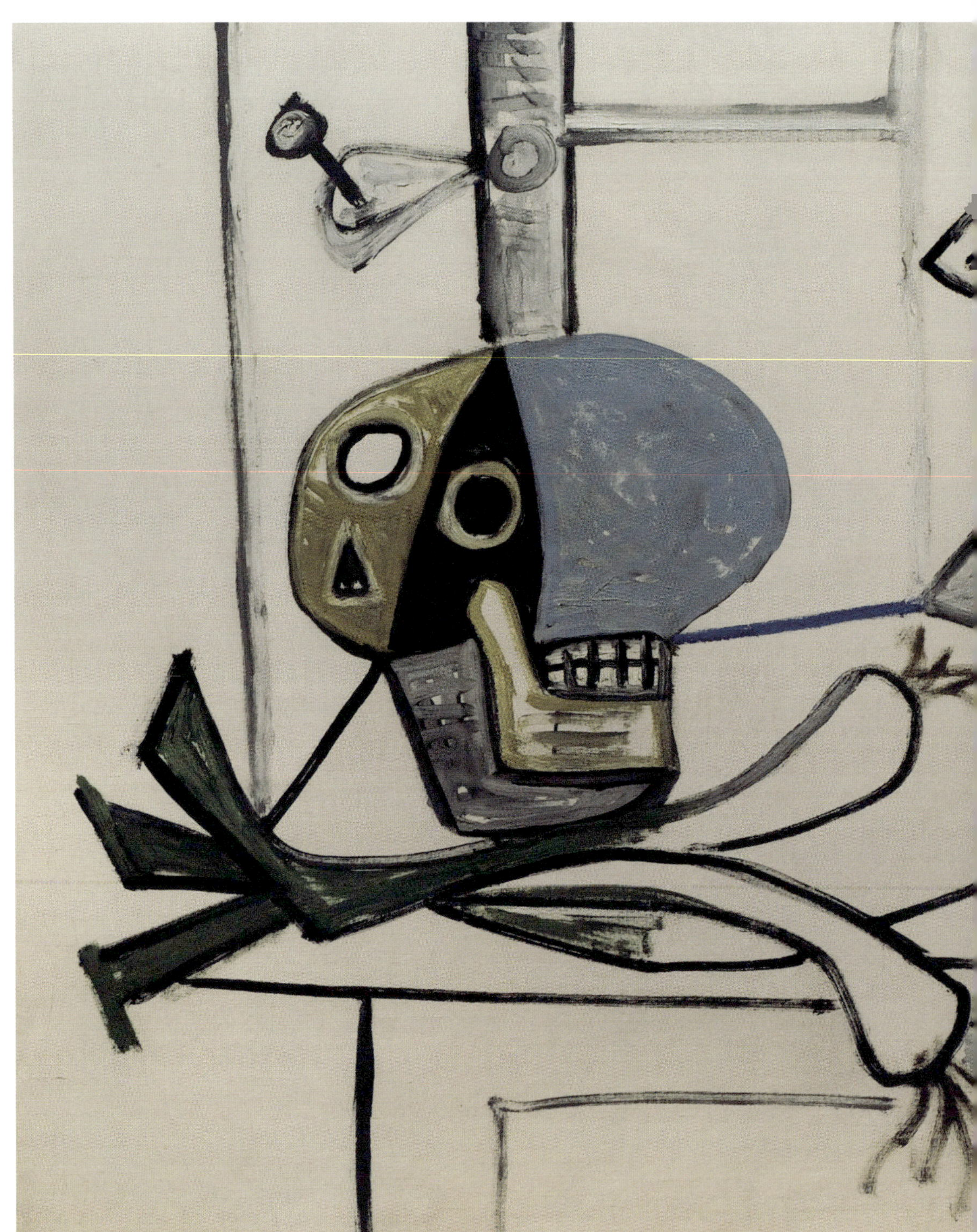

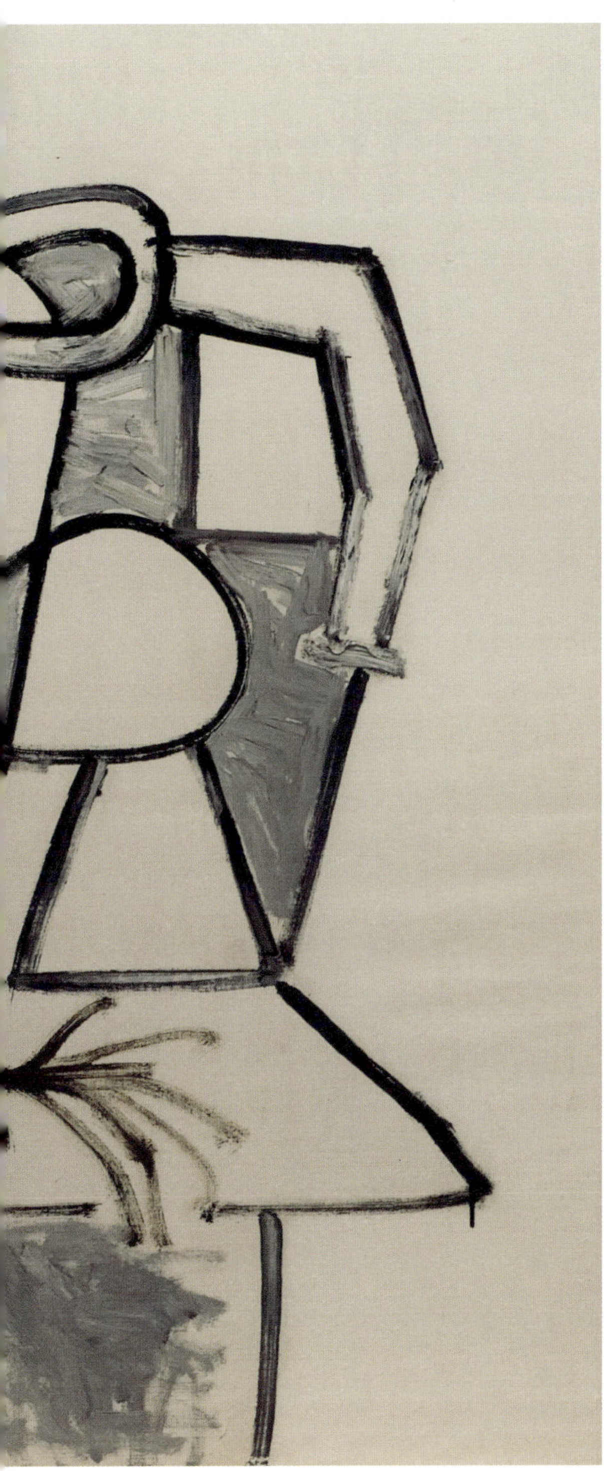

Left: Still Life with Skull, Leeks and Pitcher, Pablo Picasso, 1945, oil on canvas.

Painted by Spanish artist Pablo Picasso (1881–1973), in distinctive Cubist style, *Still Life with Skull, Leeks and Pitcher* draws on the centuries-old artistic traditions of *memento mori* and vanitas – revealing the transience of life and inevitability of death by placing ordinary, everyday vegetables and household objects alongside a symbol of mortality, such as the ubiquitous skull. Critics believe that Picasso was particularly preoccupied by this type of still-life art in the wake of the Second World War, during which so many people lost their lives. Like seventeenth-century vanitas paintings, Picasso's artwork invites viewers to think about where death fits into our daily existence. It reminds us that life goes on, but death is never far behind: a clear metaphor for life in Occupied France where death, once a remote abstraction, sharply came into focus.

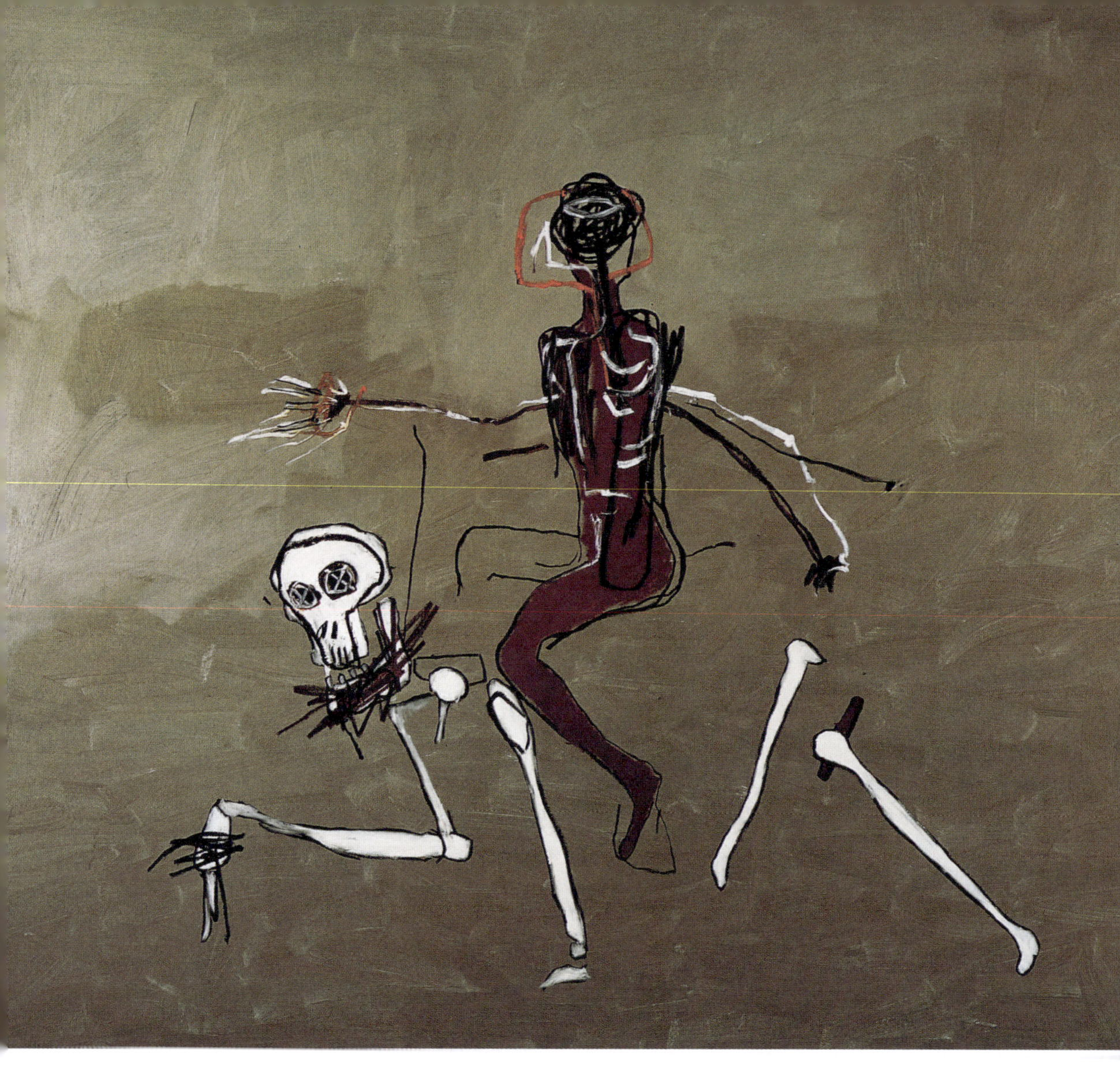

Above: Riding With Death,
Jean-Michel Basquiat, 1988,
acrylic, crayon on canvas.

Jean-Michel Basquiat (1960–88) was an African-American artist who reinvigorated the New York art scene of the 1980s with his Neo-Expressionist paintings and drawings. *Riding with Death* came towards the end of Basquiat's life and features some common themes which ran through most of his career. It is an example of how the artist combined inspiration wherein Basquiat connects to his Afro-Caribbean background, while also using influence from European art. *Riding with Death* is one of the last paintings Jean-Michel Basquiat painted before his death in 1988. This fact, coupled with its disturbing imagery, suggests it represents his opinion on the state of the world.

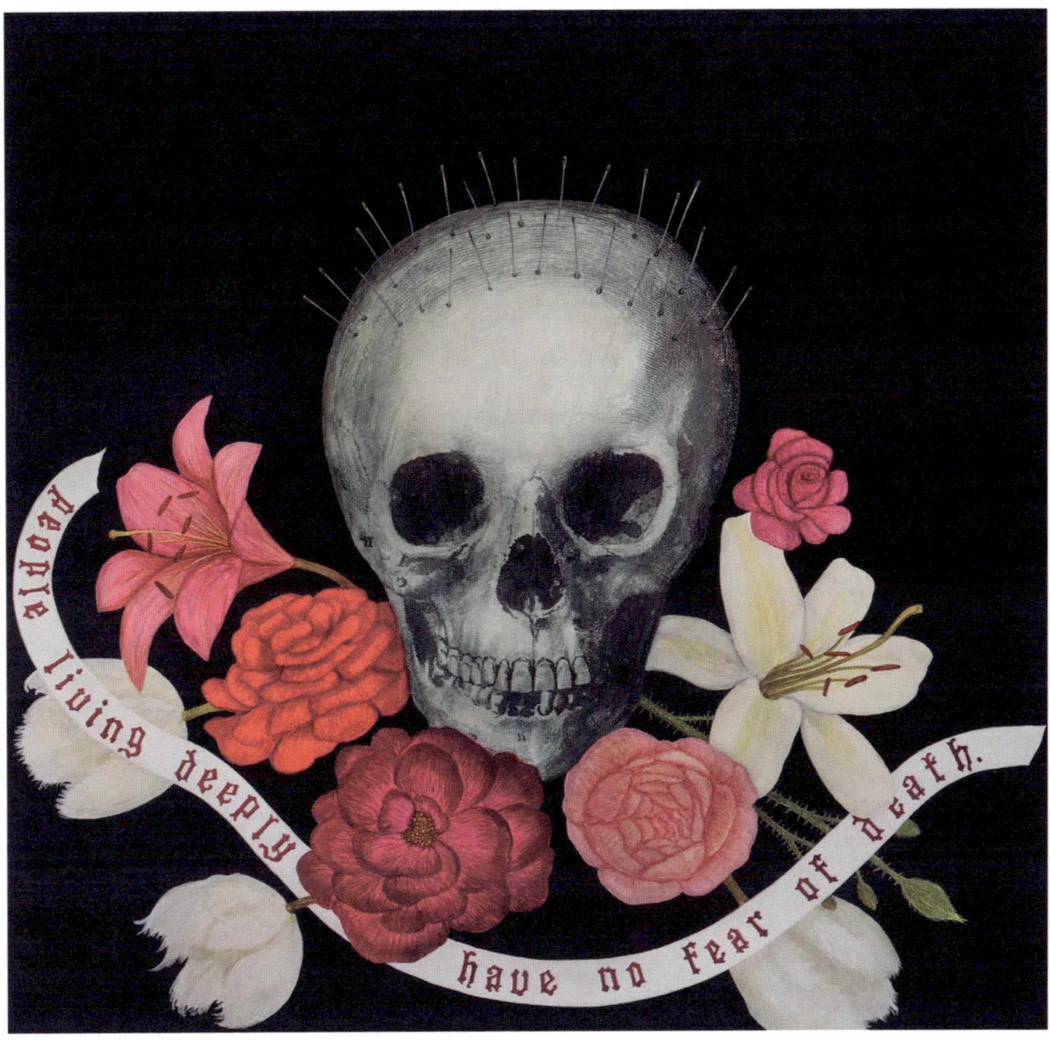

Above: No Fear, Susan Jamison, 2012, egg tempera on panel.

Contemporary artist Susan Jamison's delicate iconography spans several media, including painting, drawing, textile-based sculpture and installation. However, she is best known for the lush, luminous imagery of her intricate egg tempera paintings, steeped in ritualistic and mythological associations. In *No Fear*, a needle-pricked skull surrounded by flowers reminds us via a swirling banner that 'people living deeply have no fear of death'.

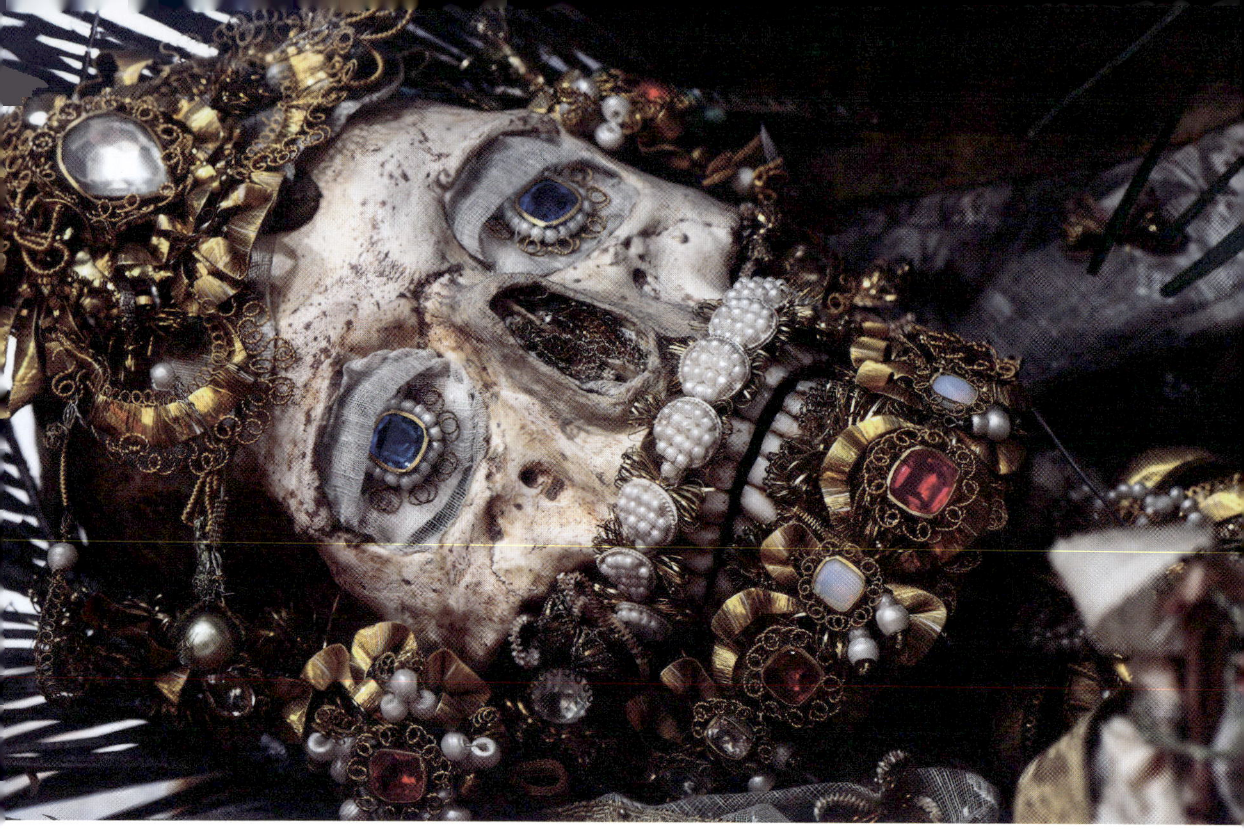

Above: St Valerius, Paul Koudounaris, 2013, digital pigment print on pearlescent paper.

Paul Koudounaris is an author and photographer from Los Angeles whose publications in the field of charnel house and ossuary research have made him a well-known figure in the field of macabre art and art history. For his series Heavenly Bodies, Koudounaris was able to gain unprecedented access to various religious institutions and it reveals an intriguing visual history of the veneration in European churches and monasteries of bejewelled and decorated skeletons.

Opposite: Gathering My Ghosts, Rebecca Reeves, 2016, miniature mirrors, thread, metal rods and glass cloche.

Mixed media artist Rebecca Reeves' work is intricate and enthralling, delicately wrought with thin black thread and fraught with powerful, piercing themes of family and loss. Some pieces work to contain and preserve their contents - poignant heirlooms or other meaningful objects - while others encapsulate their interior in a suffocating struggle of sorrow and grief.

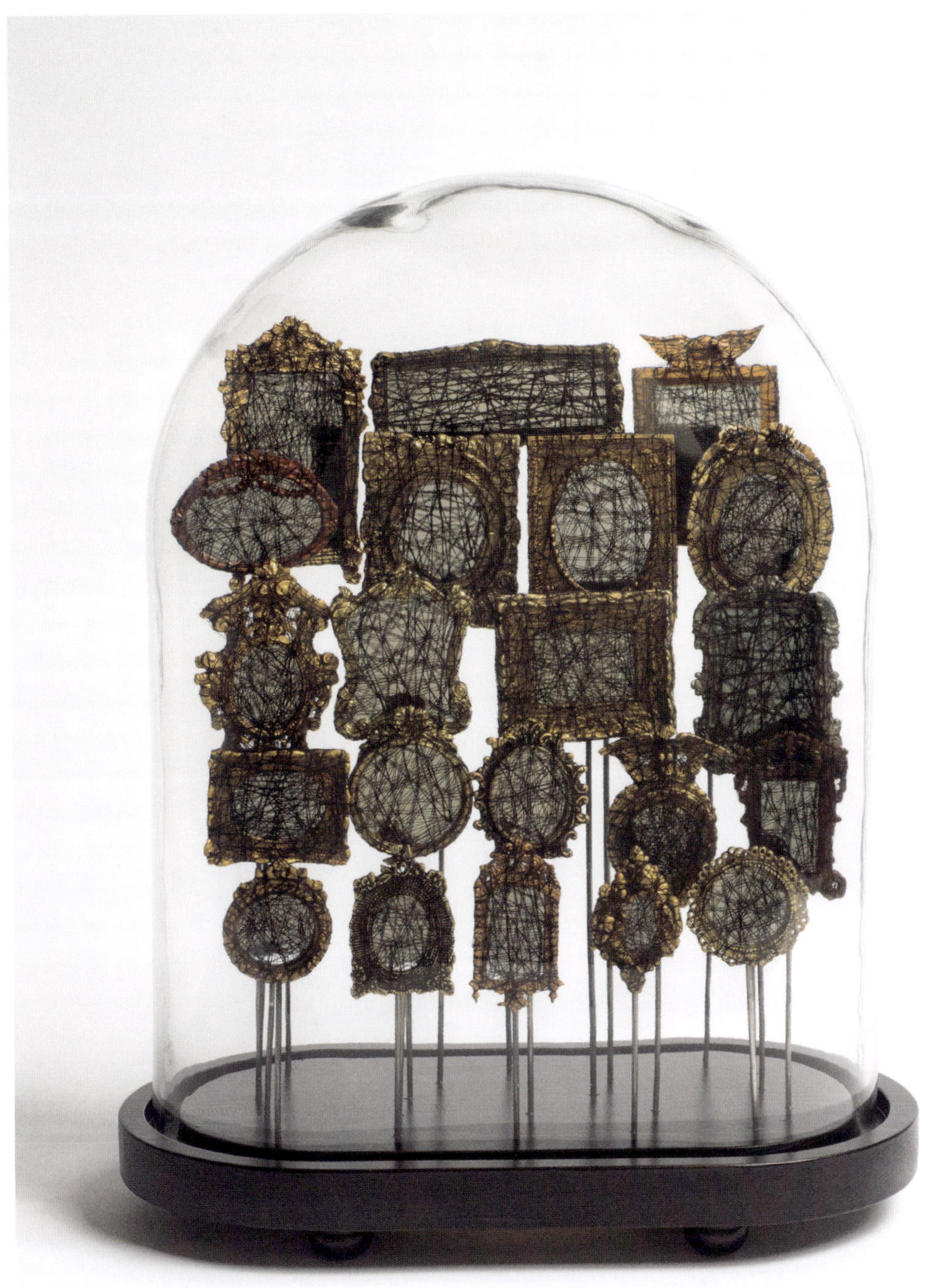

PART THREE

—

The World Around Us

'All I know is a door into the dark'

– SEAMUS HEANEY

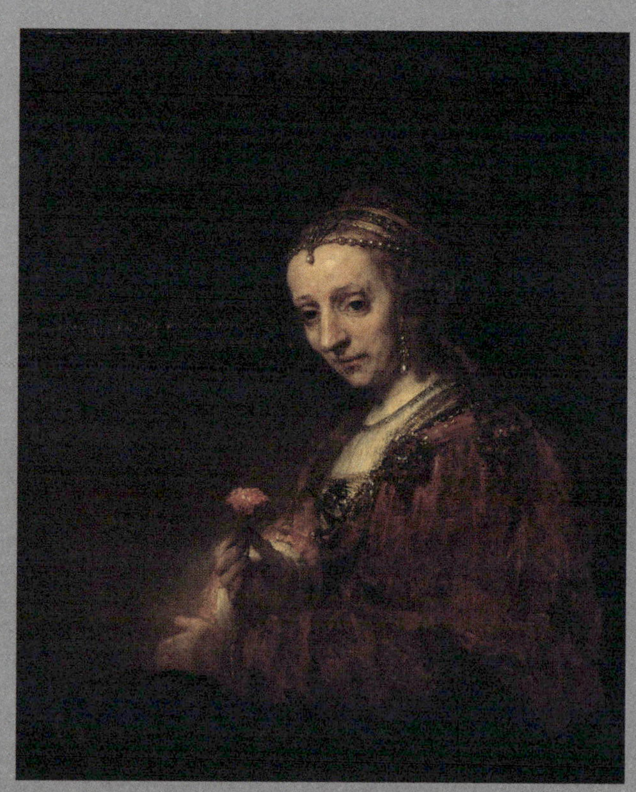

A storm-shadowed, misty coastline whispers mysterious secrets. A glowing-eyed owl glares balefully from the branches of a crooked pine, a looming threat in the night. The dreadful allure of skeletal ruins, remnants of bygone eras ravaged by time . . . or the creeping, tenacious greenery bringing a strange, strangling life back to these ravaged places. The eerie aesthetics of these haunting scenarios at first glance appear to be the set of a horror film but peek closer and you'll see an artist's signature in the corner of these canvases. Much like those scary films, we almost don't want to know what lies in the murky brushstrokes of those twisted thickets or the charcoal renderings of those crumbling pillars – but oh, how our gazes return to these perilous, mesmerizing artworks time and again.

Nature in both its noble and humble aspects fascinates artists and viewers alike, and art and nature have always gone hand in hand. The natural world is a constant source of inspiration the world over, and we find solace and delight in its beauty: from representations of animal and plant life to landscapes and still life, humans have explored their reverence for, affinity towards, dependence on and isolation from nature through various means of artistic expression. Art involving nature may reflect the splendour of the natural world around us, observe scientific phenomena, or open our minds to philosophical ideas about our own enduring connection to nature and beyond. Of course, art is never a mere replication of reality. Every rendering of the natural world is, ultimately, translated through the filter of our own interests, values and desires.

As vast as the changing face of our planet, as minute as a seed struggling forth from the wormy soil, for centuries artists have gazed into the churning darkness of nature and conceived of new ways of seeing and thinking about the world and our place in it. Plucking at the immeasurable and the unfathomable edges of creation, many artists interpret and reimagine the earthly realms we inhabit and the life these spaces give host to, through a shadowy lens of the savage and the sublime. Sometimes these artists focus on the natural decay of our world, or parasitical relationships necessary for survival and growth. Other artists aim to incite a conversation about the inevitable effects of the existence of humans on the environment. And what our minds cannot know, the imagination fills in the empty spaces: for thousands of years, artists everywhere – sometimes

Opposite: Woman with a Pink, Rembrandt, early 1660s, oil on canvas.

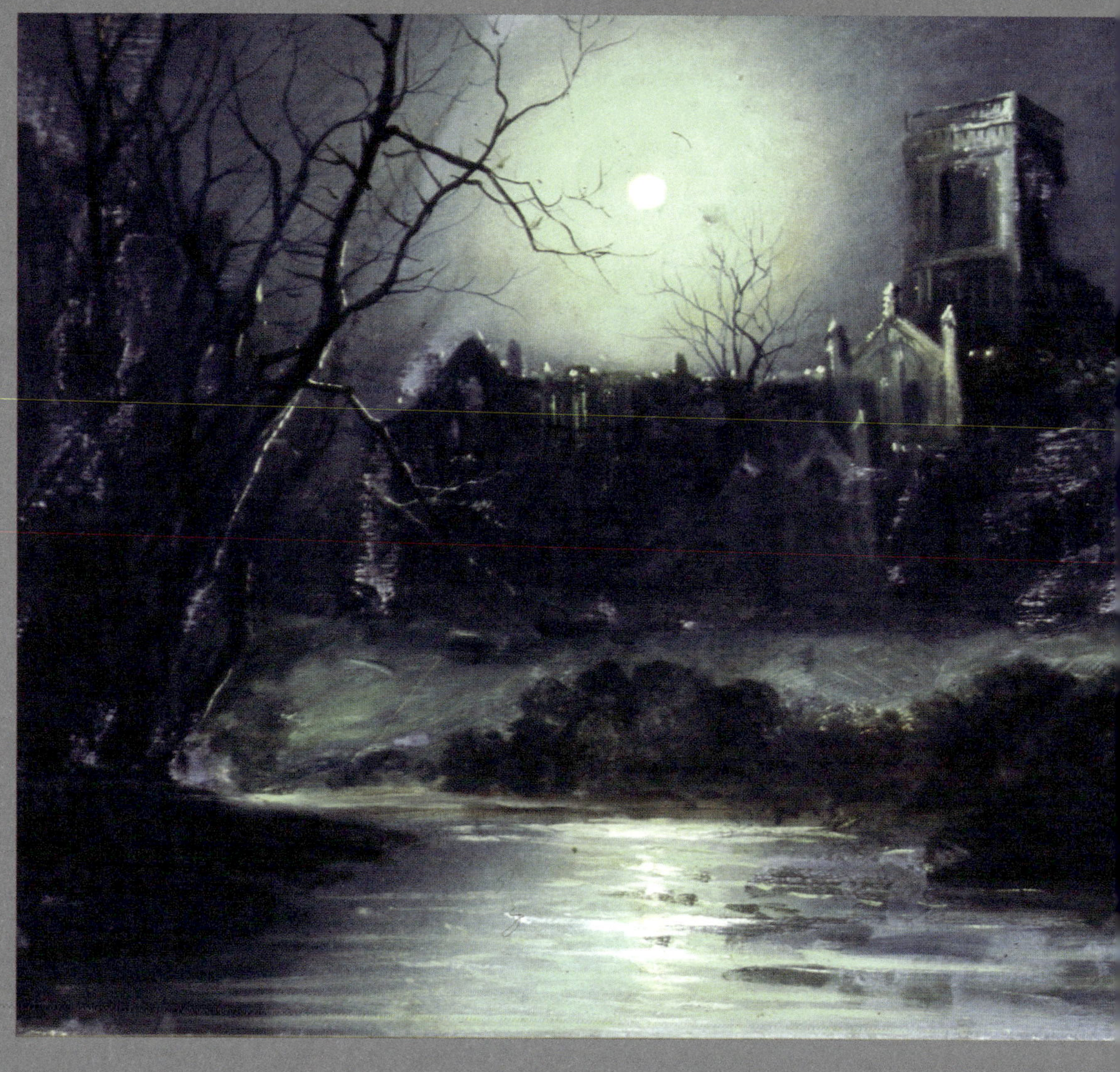

Above: Kirkstall Abbey by Moonlight, Walter Linsley Meegan, c. 1880–99, oil on canvas.

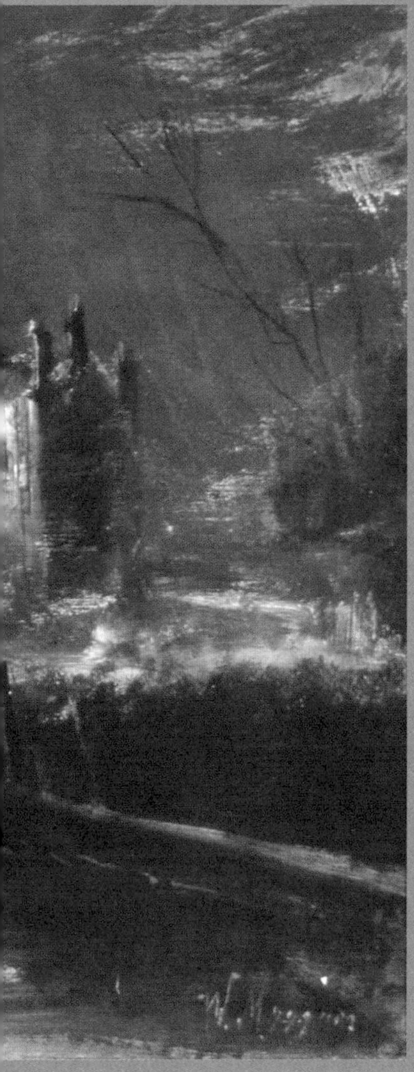

inspired by living animals or even fossils – have summoned from the bizarre realms of dreams and imagination fearsome mythic creatures, and then rendered them in paint and chalk and stone. By exploring these images, we can learn more about the different cultures that created them and more about the ways that we as humans move through the world, and then perhaps how to become better stewards of the world we live in.

When next presented with visions of a sinister vista, or forbidding flora or fauna, take a moment to lose yourself in its variations of twilight, interpret the patterns in the tall, spectral grasses, search for the secrets concealed in the glittering eyes and scrabbling claws of the forest floor. Commune with the colour and form of the full moon's lonely presence above a still, midnight sea. Nature, much like life itself, is both breathtaking and brutal, as fearsome as it is fascinating – and its darkness is just as interesting and immersive as the light.

VII

—

Darkness in Bloom

'And my hands pick flowers,
And my soul doesn't know it.'

– FERNANDO PESSOA

There are few things as miraculous and exquisitely life-affirming as the first flowers of spring. After a miserable winter of ice and snow and darkness, long after you have forgotten what damp earth and nature feel like, your snowdrops and daffodils arrive in their vivid, fragrant glory, brimming with a wistful perfume and vibrant palette, to bring it all back again. Your senses are rekindled, and life feels grand. Winter didn't last forever, after all.

Plant-lovers and nature enthusiasts possess an inherent appreciation for beauty. We marvel at the fragile, verdant curve of a fern, the unexpected colours and textures revealed in the heart of a crimson rose bud, a glistening drop of morning dew atop a plump, inky nightshade berry. Whether artfully arranging flowers to welcome guests, admiring a gnarled cypress tree in a local park, or observing seedlings tracking the sun, the contemplation of plants is a visually captivating and emotionally engaging activity, adding a wealth of meaning to our lives.

The aesthetics of the natural world and its wealth of growing things have always held a place in the visual arts; over the centuries, creatives have been drawn to their expressive qualities, revealing their rich symbolism and tracing their varying meanings in images ranging widely in subject and purpose – from devotional images of saints and scenes from the scriptures, to portraits and still lifes, in subjects from secular history and mythology. Depending on the context, a single flower can represent rebirth or decay, faithlessness or devotion, fondness or ill-will – or perhaps nothing more than a pile of wilted petals.

Botanical symbolism has its origins in myth and stories of antiquity, where plants are often metaphors for virtue and vice. In classical mythology, human beings are transformed into plants as a reward or punishment, as in the story of Narcissus, the vain youth who fell in love with his own reflection and was changed into a flower that bears his name. The Bible and the Apocrypha contain many references to trees, fruits and flowers in moralizing parables, from the 'apples' of Genesis and the 'bitter herbs' of Passover to the New Testament's 'lilies of the field'. Plant symbolism was also found in medieval herbals describing the natural properties of plants, the method for their cultivation and their use in cooking and in medicine. These properties usually hinted at a moral interpretation: the poisonous hemlock

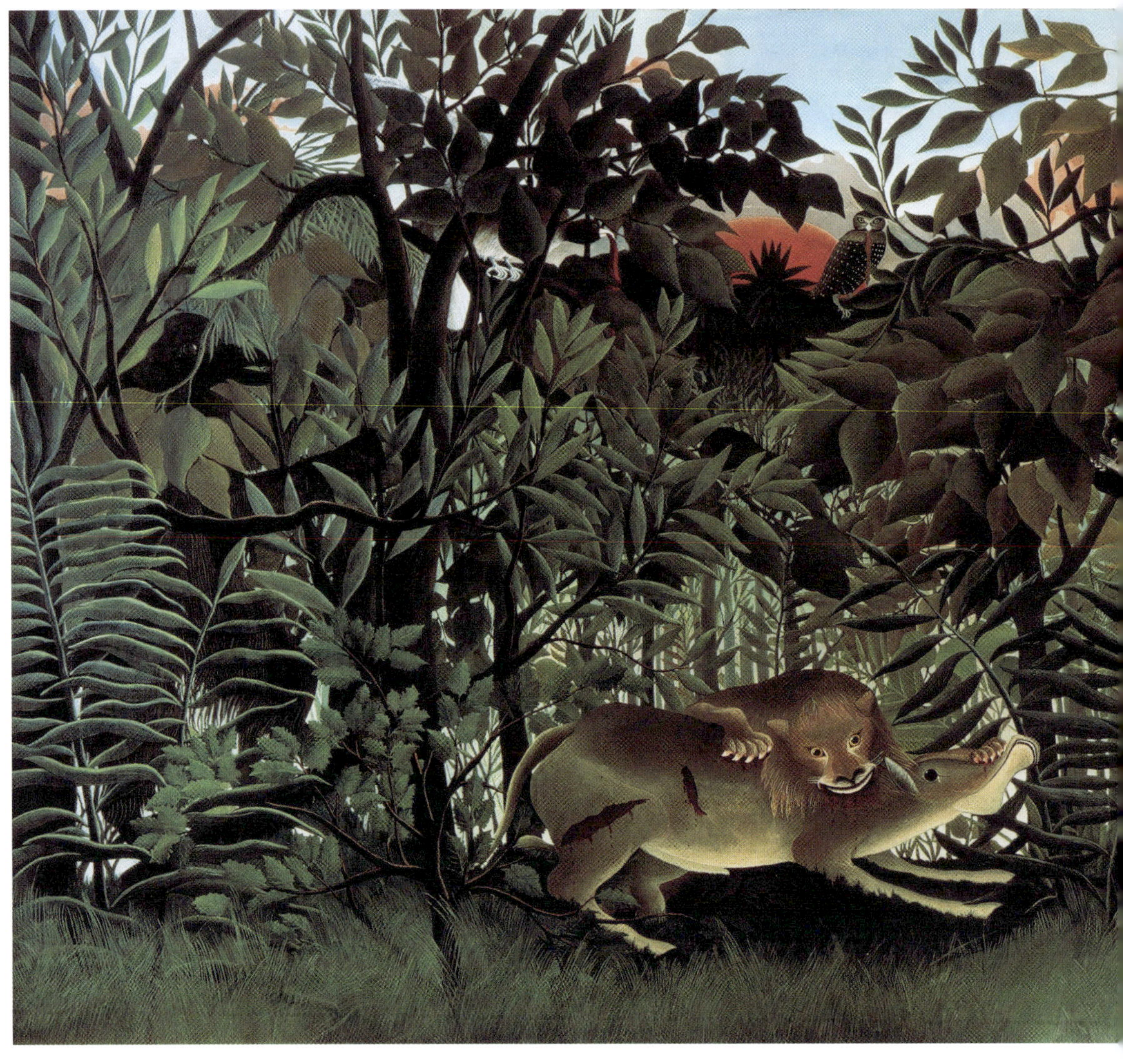

Above: *Le lion, ayant faim, se jette sur l'antilope* (The Hungry Lion Throws Itself on the Antelope), Henri Rousseau, 1898–1905, oil on canvas.

Though many of the works by the Post-impressionist French painter Henri Rousseau (1844–1910) are tranquil in nature, *The Hungry Lion Throws Itself on the Antelope* depicts a scene of dangersome blood-minded business in the midst of thick green foliage illuminated by a deep red setting sun. Though the title hints at some of what is going on in this lush jungle scene, it doesn't immediately reveal the whole story . . . one piece being that this jungle was painted by an individual who had never even seen a jungle! It is said that Rousseau based the central pair of animals on a diorama of stuffed animals at the Paris Muséum national d'histoire naturelle. In the foreground, a lion bites deeply into the neck of an antelope, while a nearby owl holds a strip of flesh from the dying animal in its beak. A leopard glares from the right while a darkened ape-like creature, hidden in the leaves, lurks to the left. This fantastical scene of Rousseau's internally cobbled-together jungle, despite its distinct lack of fangs and other pertinent pieces of the predatory anatomy, does indeed present a real sense of threat at every turn.

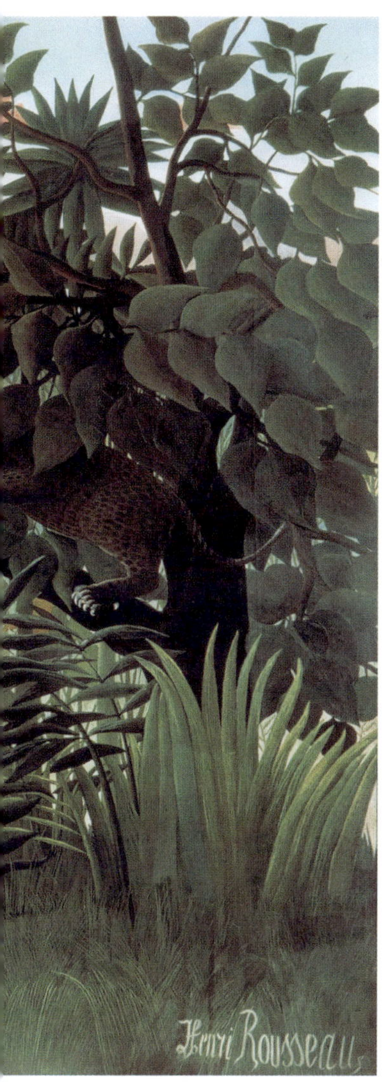

represented evil and death, while the clover, with its three leaves, was a symbol of the Holy Trinity, and so on.

During the industrial revolution, botanical symbolism moved away from religious references, which were eschewed in favour of images of plants and animals as savage entities. In the nineteenth century artists began to contrast human culture as a civilizing force against flora and fauna as wild, backward and untameable. One instance of this is the Post-Impressionist painter Henri Rousseau's *The Hungry Lion Throws Itself on the Antelope*. Not only does the ensuing violence appal us but the complete indifference of the lush, surrounding forest, and the unruffled apathy of the onlooking wildlife leaves the viewer feeling unsettled.

The appearance of plants in art is impacted by evolving values, as well. As we become more and more aware of environmental concerns, we are forced to reckon with the violence we do to each other, as well as the Earth. Consequently, artists have been responding to the urgent concerns of the precarious position we find our planet in, as seen in Sonia Rentsch's Harm Less series, which depicts a number of weapons made from organic materials, a commentary on the human predilection to manipulate our environment through technology to suit our desires. Such works, despite their bloody connotations, can evoke sadness, or outrage, which may lead to a weird sense of empathy, and perhaps a vague, feeling of connection with other living beings.

It is clear enough that with colourful petals and irresistible scents, flowers have a defined purpose: for luring insects to their pollen to ensure reproduction and, ultimately, survival. But why do humans find flowering plants pleasing to gaze upon? Some scientists contend that we are drawn to them due to their proximity to fruit and sustenance, while others suggest that harmonious colours, soft curves and blossoms offer a type of objective beauty. Whether we find meaning and value in their nutritional implications or their lovely appearance, the seeds of their personal, cultural and religious significance have long been planted in people's minds. As history has proven, the power of their beauty, whether symbolizing good or evil, illustrating peace or violence, defies categorization – but also helps us question and better understand the changing nature of human culture.

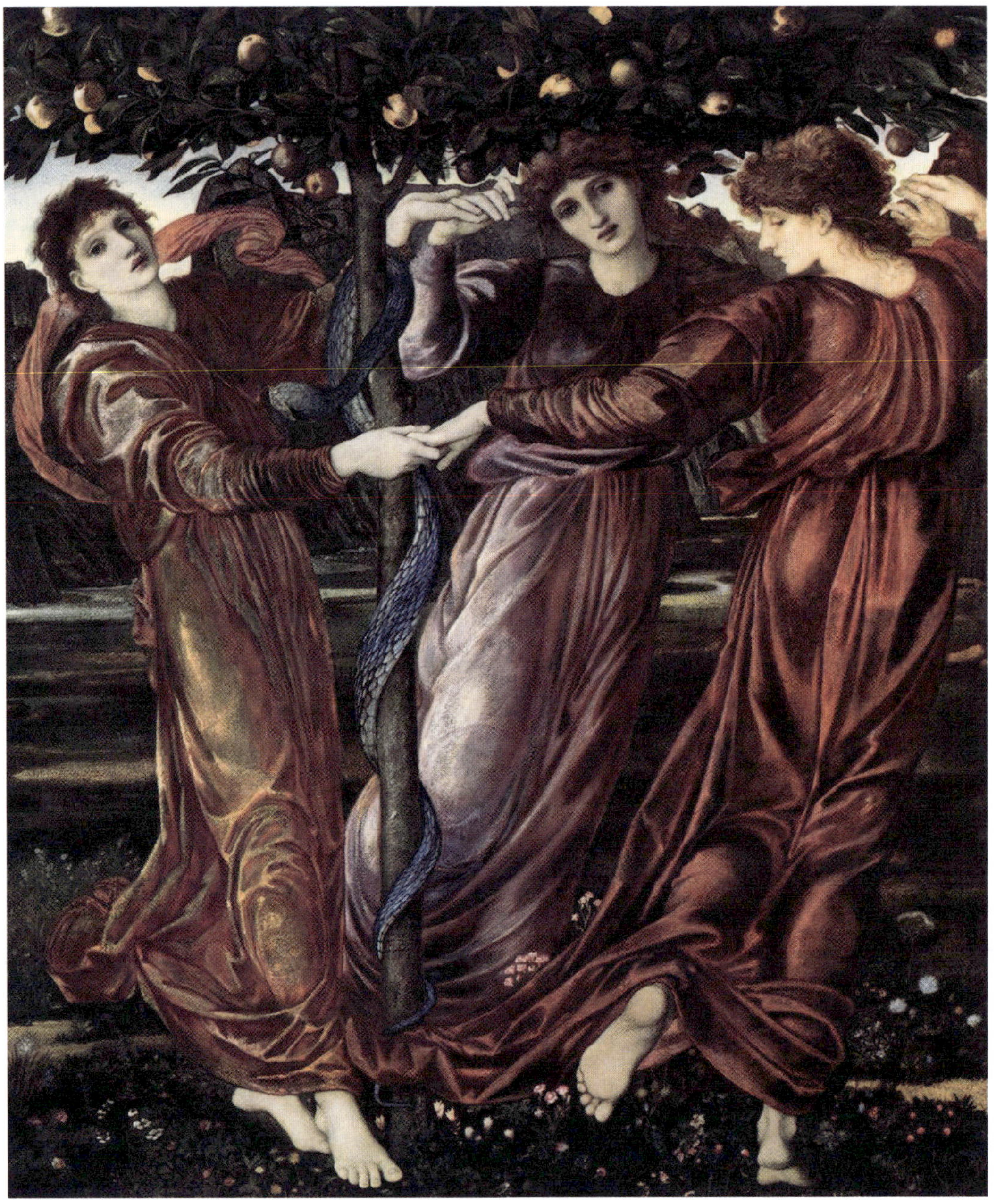

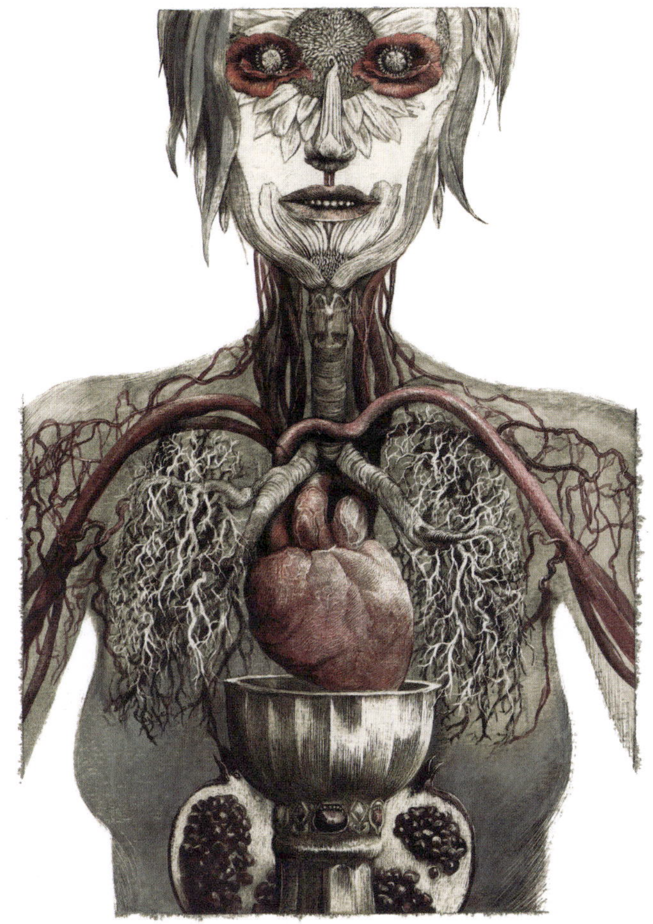

Right: Rappaccini's Daughter, Santiago Caruso, 2015, ink and scratch over cardboard, ballpoint pen on paper.

The works of Argentinian-born Santiago Caruso (b. 1982) are grounded in Symbolist aesthetics and reveal a unique vision of the world with regard to the unconscious and the ghosts we've buried. Through these revelations, the artist invites us to contemplate the beautiful and the frightening, as well as the repressed or things forgotten in the shadows. In *Rappaccini's Daughter* we are treated to a spectral X-ray in which the subject's innards are veined with strange fruit and flowers, inspired by Nathaniel Hawthorne's story in which Rappaccini, scholar-scientist in Padua, grows only poisonous plants in his lush garden. His lovely daughter, Beatrice, has been nurtured on poison and is sustained by her father's toxic plants.

Opposite: The Garden of Hesperides, Edward Burne-Jones, c. 1869, oil on canvas.

English Pre-Raphaelite painter Edward Burne-Jones (1833–98) was captivated with the classical world and is famous for his sumptuous, dreamlike depictions of myths, legends and fairy tales drawing on ancient sources, stories and symbolism. In this canvas, we peek in on Greek mythology's Garden of the Hesperides, a tranquil place of perpetual rosy twilight, situated on the slopes of Mount Atlas, the sunset edge of all lands. A tree of golden apples grew in these mythical grounds, tended to by the daughters of Hesperus the evening star, and watched over by a dragon that never slept. In the myth of the Judgement of Paris, it was from the Garden that Eris, Goddess of Discord, obtained the Apple of Discord, which led to the Trojan War.

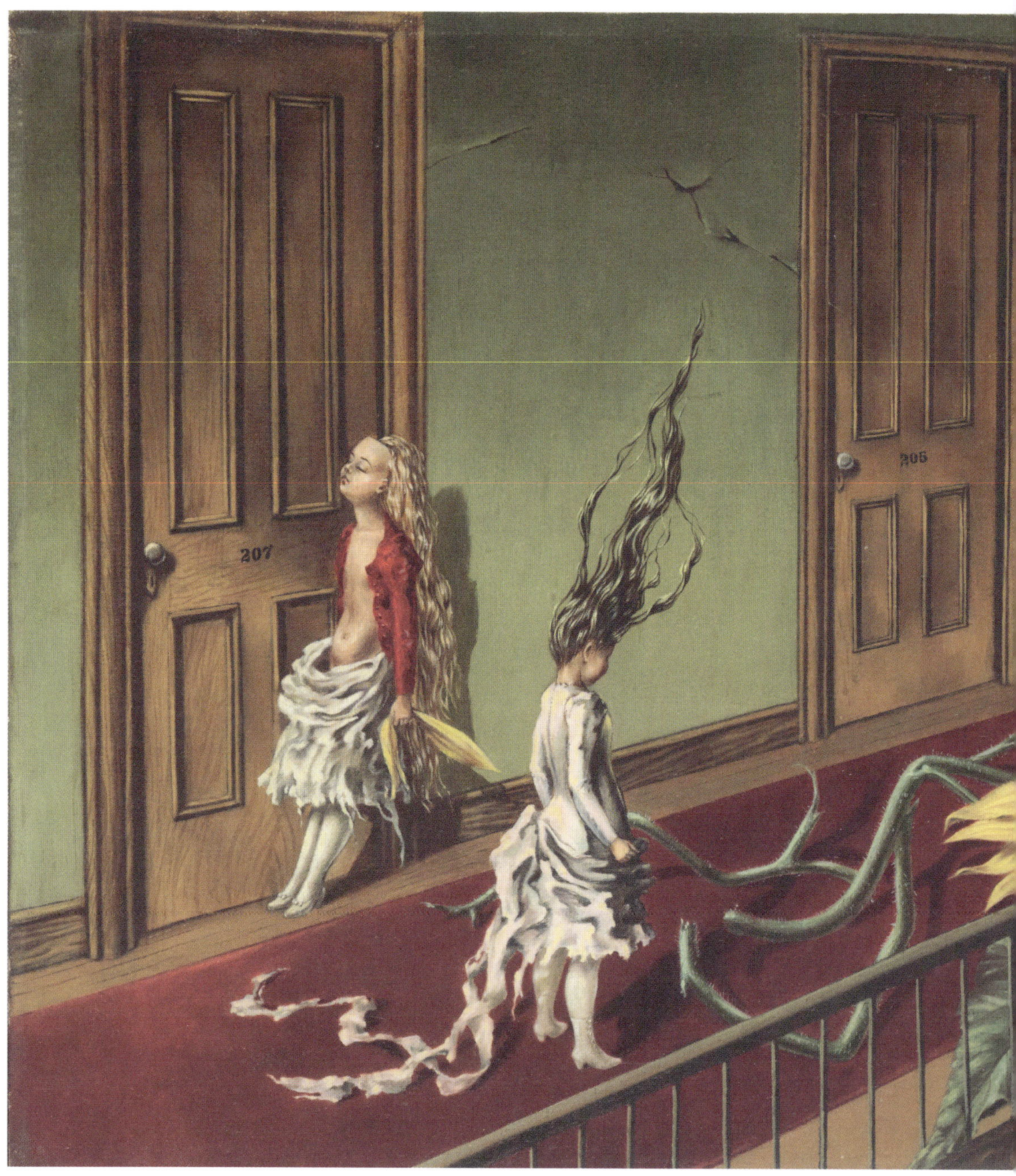
207
205

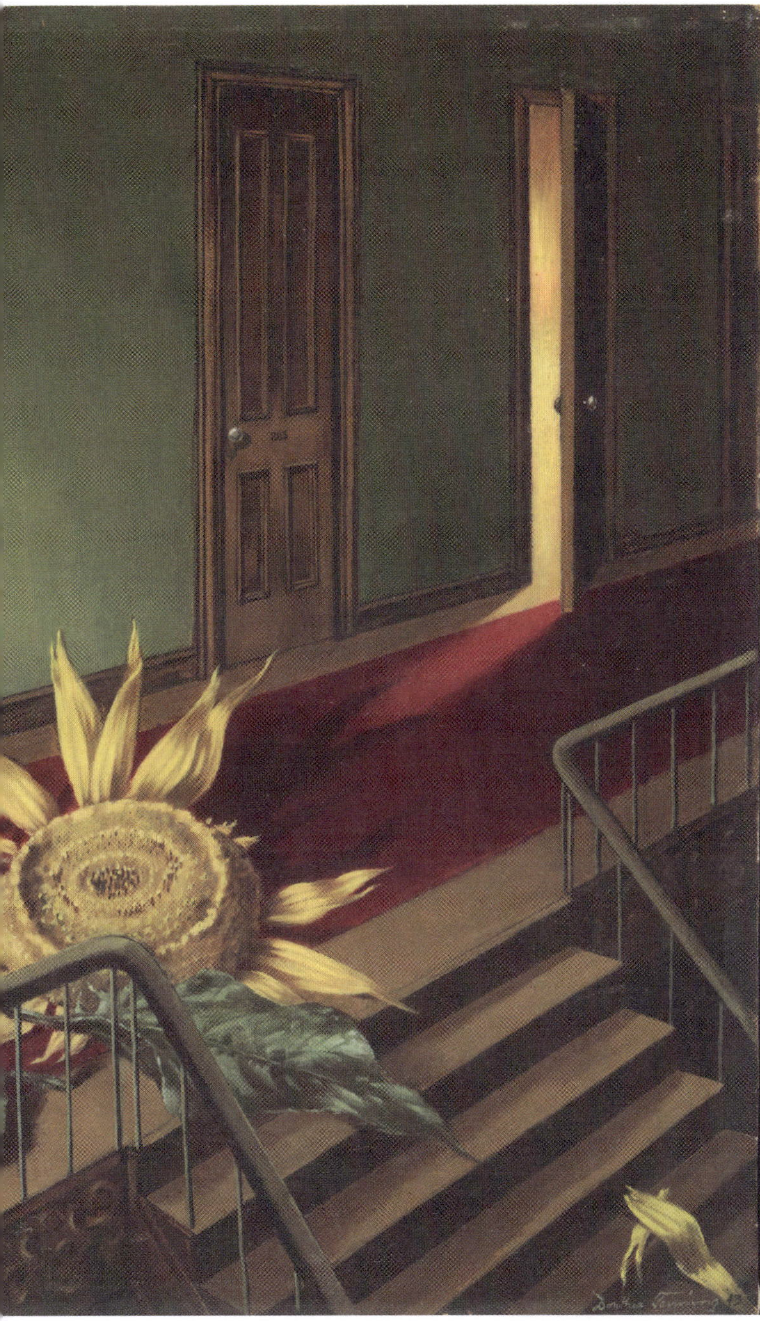

Left: Eine Kleine Nachtmusik, Dorothea Tanning, 1943, oil on canvas.

Dorothea Tanning (1910–2012) was an American painter and *Eine Kleine Nachtmusik* is one of the best known of her early paintings. We observe a hotel corridor where lying on the landing there is a giant sunflower and pieces of its torn stem strewn about. Fallen petals tumble down the stairs; one is clutched in the hand of a dishevelled girl, while the other girl in the hallway looks to be in a state of aggressive magical energy, and the tattered clothing worn by both suggests that there has been some sort of struggle or encounter with powerful forces. Tanning has said: 'It's about confrontation. Everyone believes he/she is his/her drama. While they don't always have giant sunflowers (most aggressive of flowers) to contend with, there are always stairways, hallways, even very private theatres where the suffocations and the finalities are being played out, the blood red carpet or cruel yellows, the attacker, the delighted victim . . .'

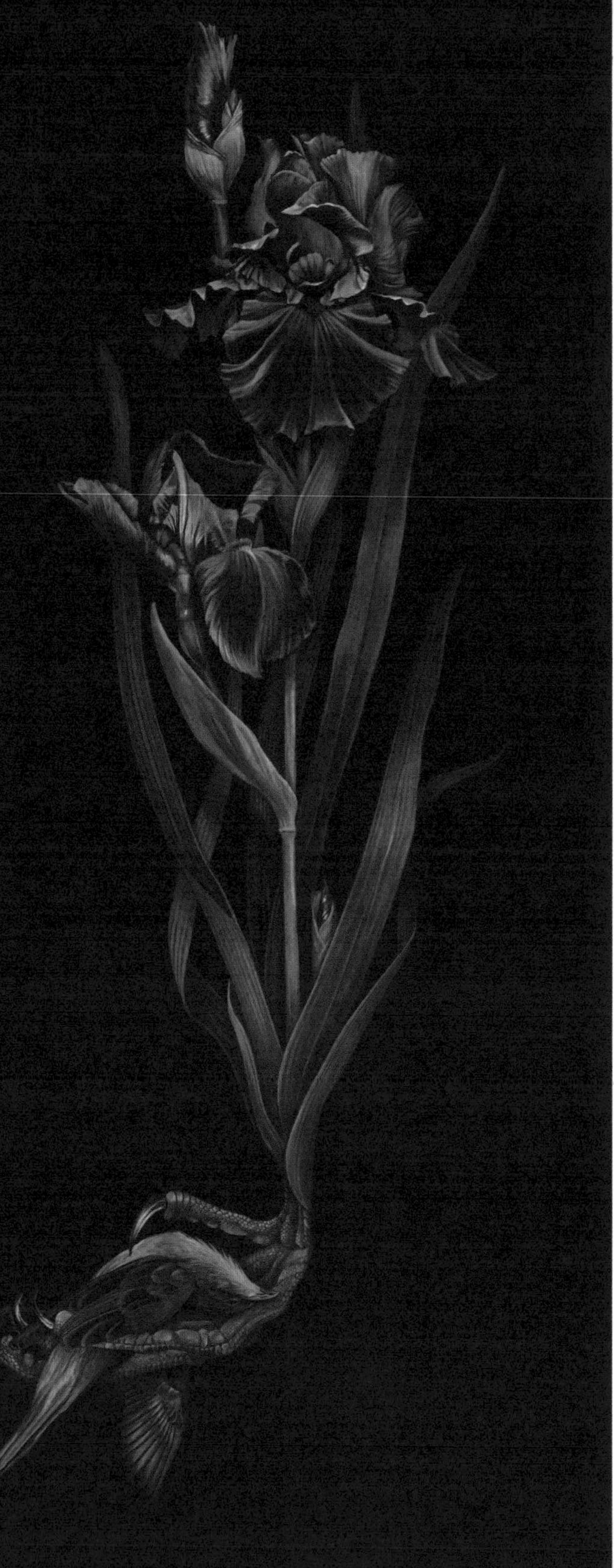

Left: How to Hold, Chris Mrozik, 2018, acrylic on paper.

An American artist who has spent the majority of their life observing the natural world and the various relationships within it, Chris Mrozik (b. 1986) parses these quiet complexities through their drawings and paintings: lush, liminal intricacies that unite flora and fauna in haunting hybrid forms. In Mrozik's own words, 'I think art speaks in ways that words cannot and there is power in both metaphor and image; that there are vague but intense places of emotion and intention that need more room and less definition so that we can exist as the overflowing, messy beings that we are.'

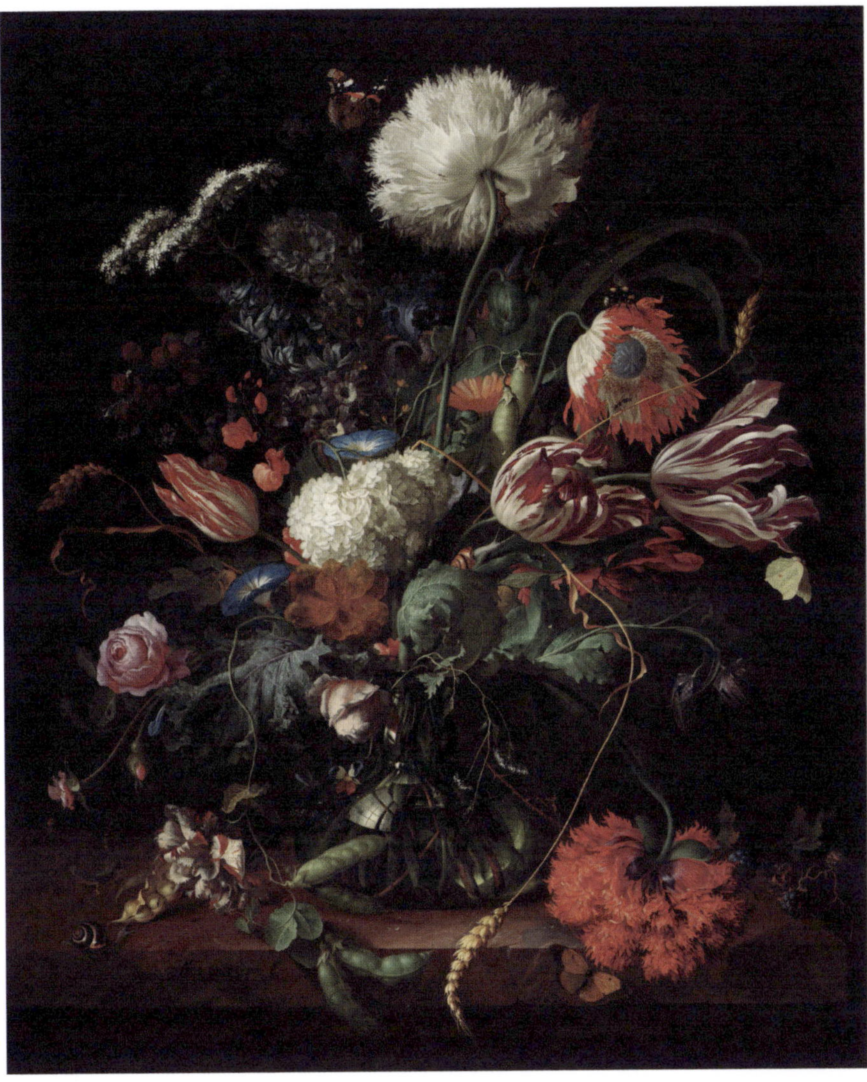

Above: Vase of Flowers, Jan Davidsz. de Heem, 1660, oil on canvas.

Utrecht-born Jan Davidsz. de Heem (1606–84) specialized in virtuosic floral still life compositions that were delightedly collected by aristocrats and wealthy merchants alike. Dutch artists worked in a variety of still life traditions that ranged from banquet pieces to paintings focused solely on fruit, shells, books or flowers, and De Heem is noted to have been one of the most gifted, versatile and influential among them of them. In this elaborate yet restrained floral explosion we can delight in his realistic depiction and myriad details of tulip petals, bent and drooping ears of wheat, and tiny, short-lived insects. De Heem chose many of these elements because of their symbolic meanings; the transient beauty of flowers, for example, was commonly used metaphorically to remind the viewer of the temporality of life. The bugs and snails that climb about the blossoms were understood allegorically to represent forces that help hasten the demise of temporal beauty.

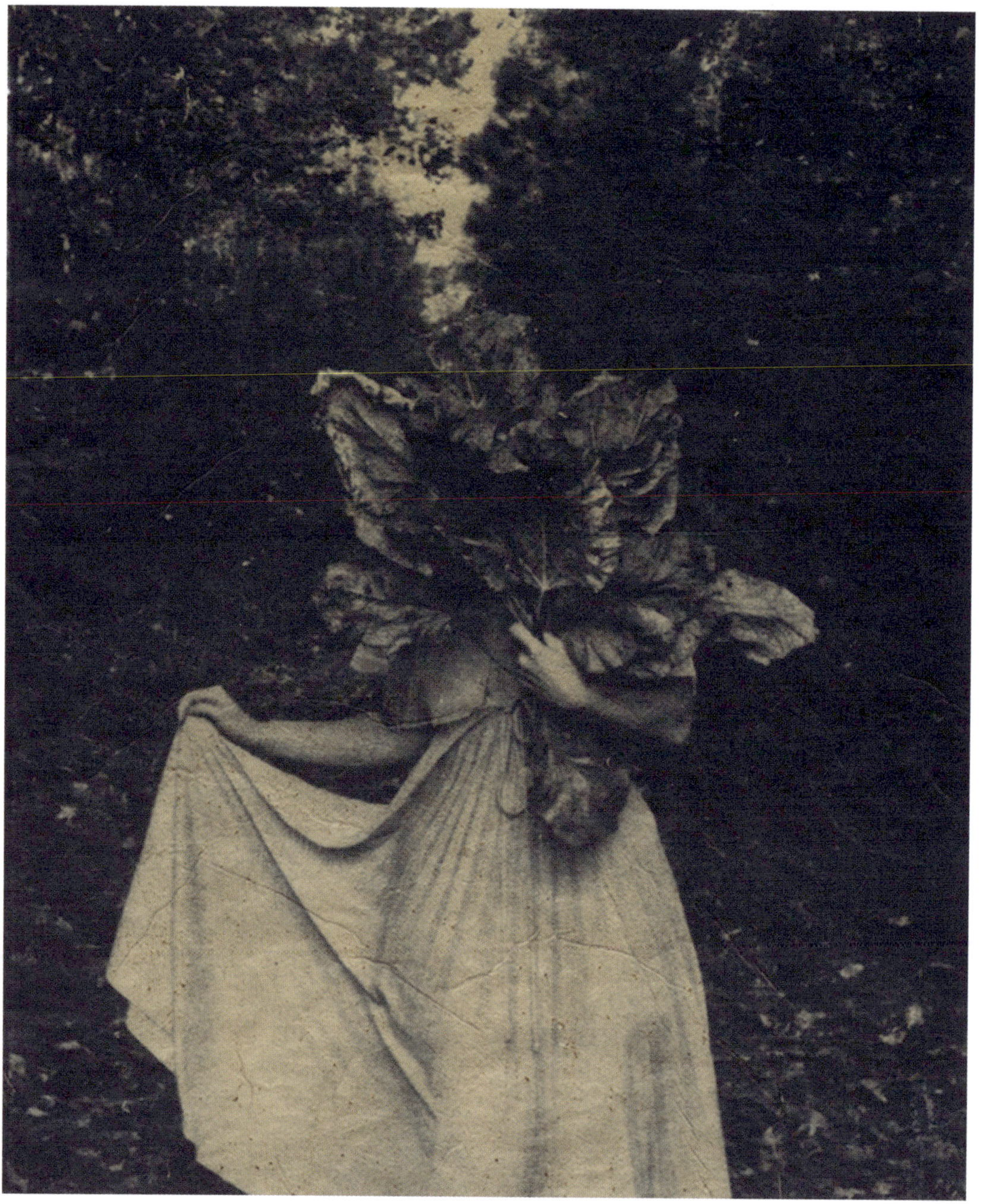

Right: Menarca, Marco Mazzoni, 2016, coloured pencils.

Contemporary Italian artist Marco Mazzoni (b. 1982) weaves a world steeped in the cycles of nature, saturated in secrets and metaphor - intricate works of chiaroscuro overlapping light and dark for an intense and profound glow. Inspired by the matriarchal culture of Sardinia, and based heavily in Italian folklore pertaining to the ancient art of healing, Mazzoni depicts female herbalists and midwives from the sixteenth to eighteenth centuries, often framing their faces with the medicinal plants of their profession. The women's vision obscured, their identities anonymous, the artist says he consciously does not depict the eyes, so the viewer doesn't consider the artwork a portrait, but instead a still life where all elements have equal importance.

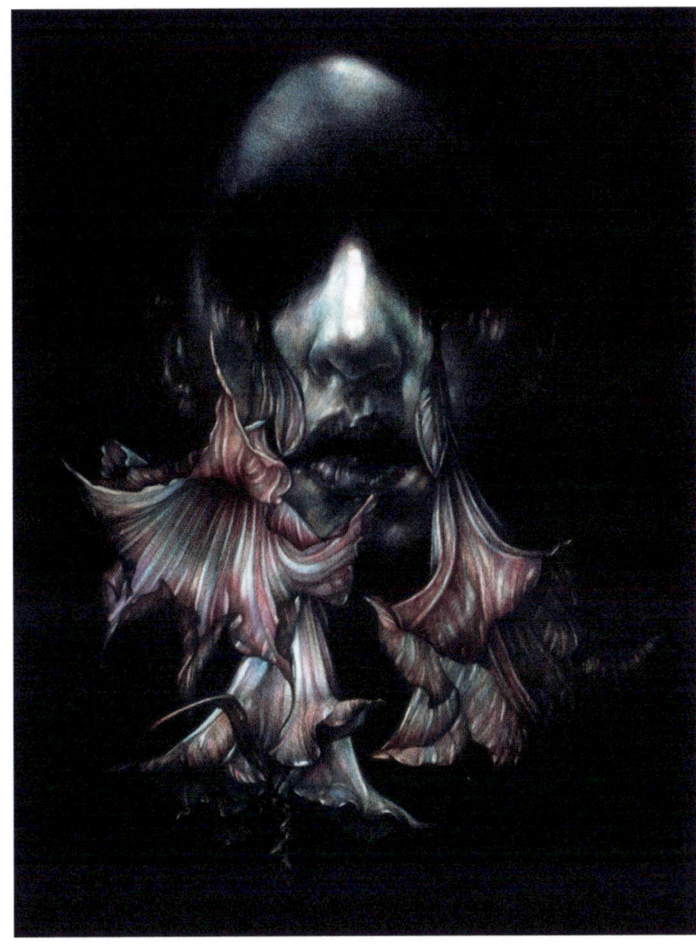

Opposite: La Llrona, Jaime Johnson Aelavanthara, 2014–17, cyanotype.

American fine art photographer Jaime (Johnson) Aelavanthara explores themes of the human condition and our interconnectedness with nature in her works. She uses a cyanotype process which shifts focus from potentially colourful landscapes and figures to patterns, textures and the relationships of forms within the images. Tea-staining the prints dulls the blue and adds an earthy warmth and, paradoxically, a strange otherworldliness. Printing on Japanese Kitakata paper, which is prone to ripping, tearing and wrinkling, reflects the deterioration of nature and gives the prints a feeling of fragility. Her works, frequently framed within the narrative of the American South, reflect upon our relationship with the natural environment, a contrast of both beauty and decay, life and death.

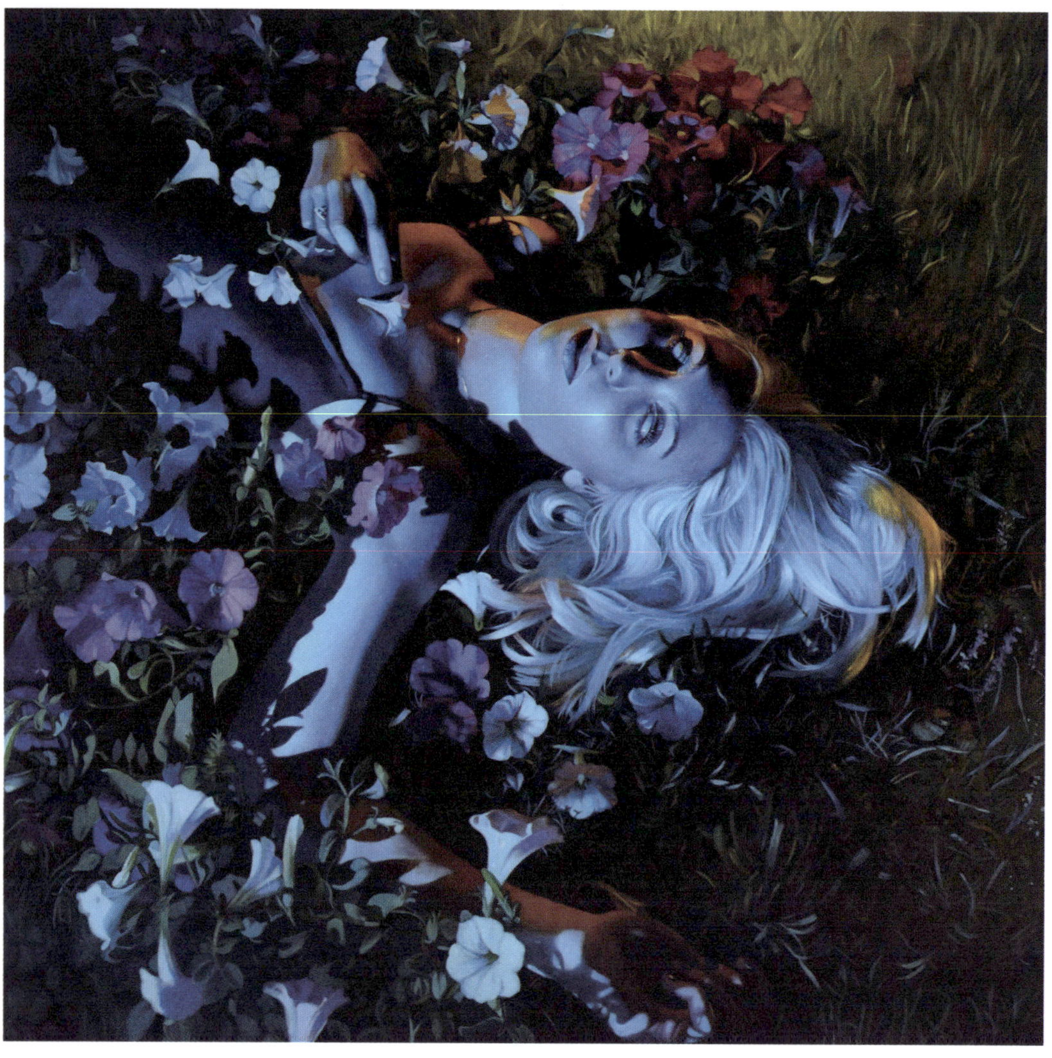

Above: Twilight, Rachael Bridge, 2020, oil on panel.

Contemporary artist Rachael Bridge brings a singular perspective to traditional portraiture. Saturated in palettes somehow both electric-technicolour and sunless-sombre (how the heck does she do that?) and shrouded in shadow, her subjects appear to vanish into the murmuring whispers of a dark and deeply personal wonderland. Vespertine mysteries teem behind their luminous, milky gaze, but far from loveless and hollow, these otherworldly eyes offer a glimpse into the complexities of the human psyche, the very real-world themes of anxiety, isolation, dread and despair.

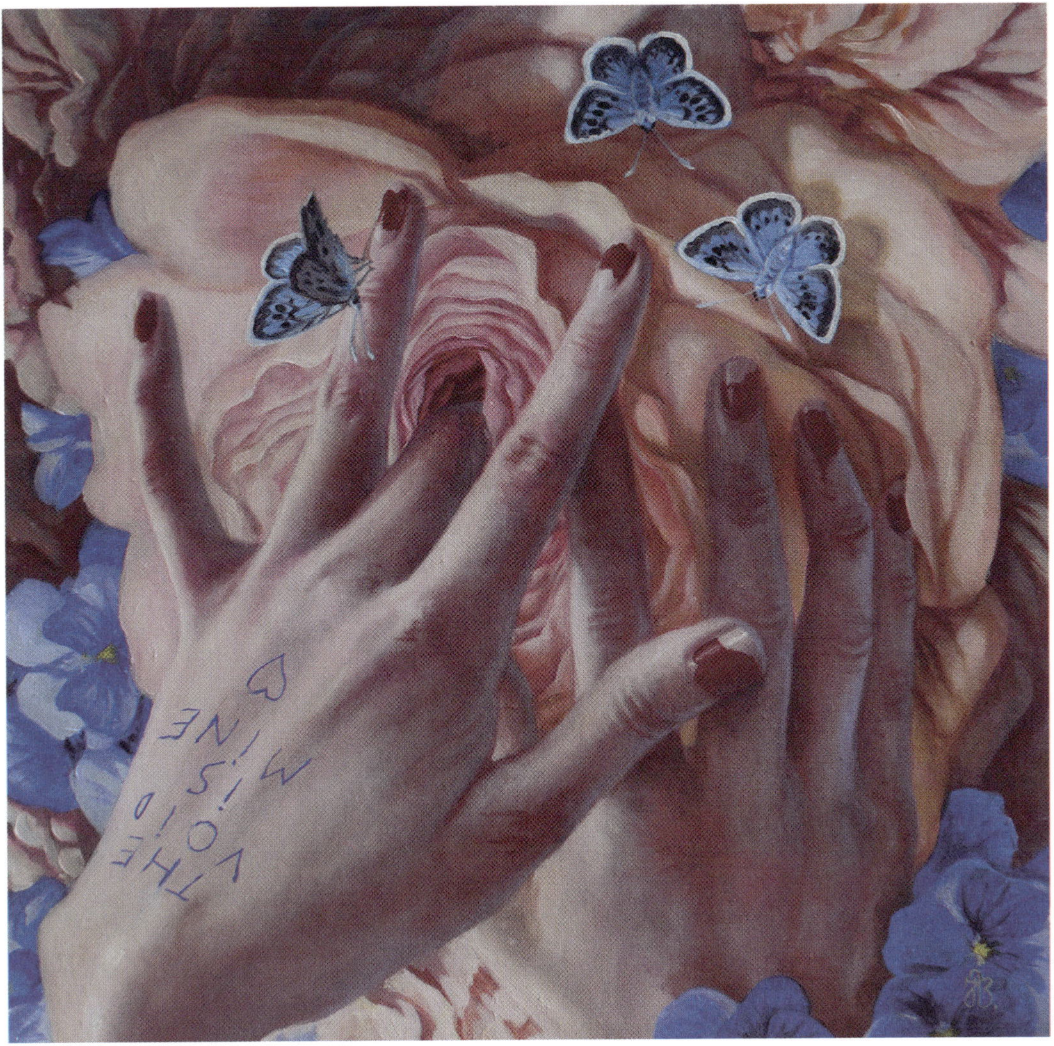

Above: The Void/Flowers of Life, Jana Brike, 2016, oil on canvas.

The main focus of the work of contemporary artist Jana Brike (b. 1980) is the state of a human soul and transcendence of the human condition, the growing up that we experience over the course of our lives, and self-discovery along the way. Engaging with themes of exploration, innocence, curiosity, vulnerability and love, these evocative pieces allow us to observe an intimate world of what she describes as a 'poetic visual autobiography', brimming with intuitive personal symbolic expression. These dreamscapes often show human figures in playful and unselfconscious discovery of the world around them. These acts are symbolic of the continual exploration and growth we all do throughout our lives and the process of transformation of the dark and heavy parts of our lives into lightness and joy.

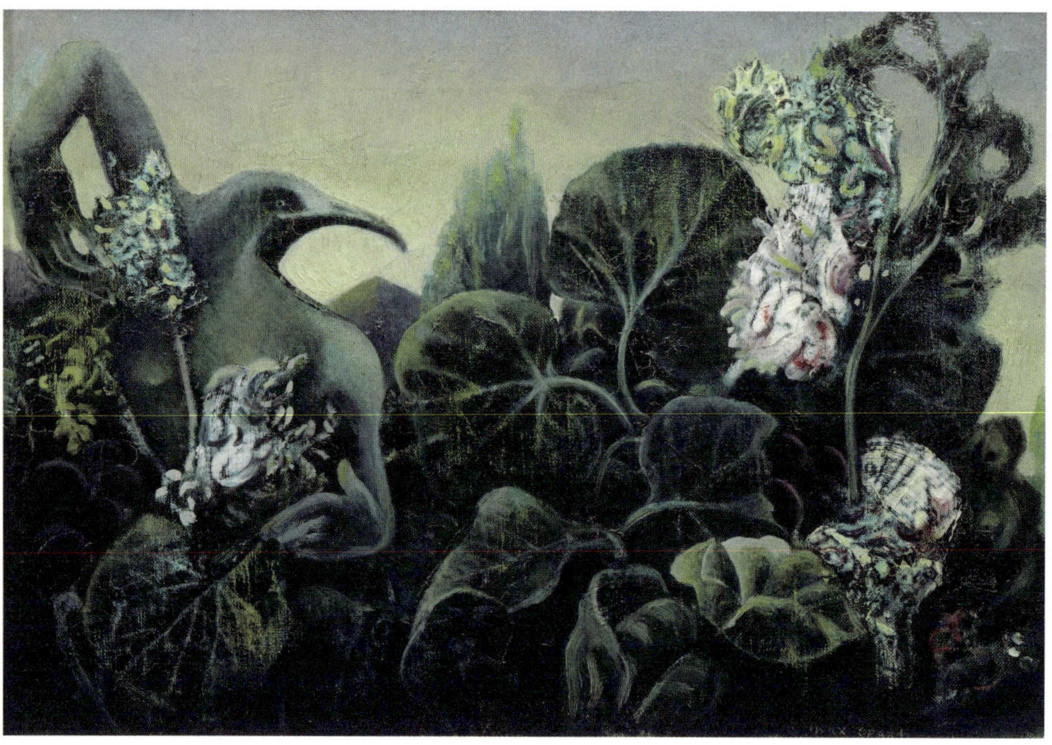

Above: Nature in the Morning, Max Ernst, 1936, oil on canvas.

In recollections of his childhood, German Surrealist provocateur Max Ernst (1891–1976) recounted his fear of and fascination with the forest that surrounded his home, referring to it with a feeling of 'delight and oppression' and what the Romantics called 'emotion in the face of Nature'. Conceiving of an invisible realm at work in the natural world, in this scene of pursuit a phantom anthropomorphic bird creature plunges through a shadowy, jungle-like thicket. In this forest scene we can stealthily observe both nature and its dark sides if we view this single-minded creature as the artist's ego, relentlessly chasing down inspiration.

Opposite: Suiseke, Agostino Arrivabene, 2017, oil on wood.

An Italian painter of rarefied decadence, dreams and ancient symbologies, Agostino Arrivabene (b. 1967) produces his fantastical surrealist works from the solitude of his seventeenth-century house located just outside Milan. Lensed with the eye of an artist who observes reality with a sideways glance, wrought in a parallel language are inscrutable representations of things half-familiar, in a realm that has no time, boundaries or laws of physics - and that's just where these paintings begin. In hues of lapis lazuli, indigo, cinnabar and madder, and dragon's blood, the beings inhabiting these worlds have met its gods, experienced sublimity and indescribable mystery, and come away changed - morphing, melting, growing, radiating strangeness. The agonies and ecstasies of becoming something both beautiful and terrible. Something extraordinary.

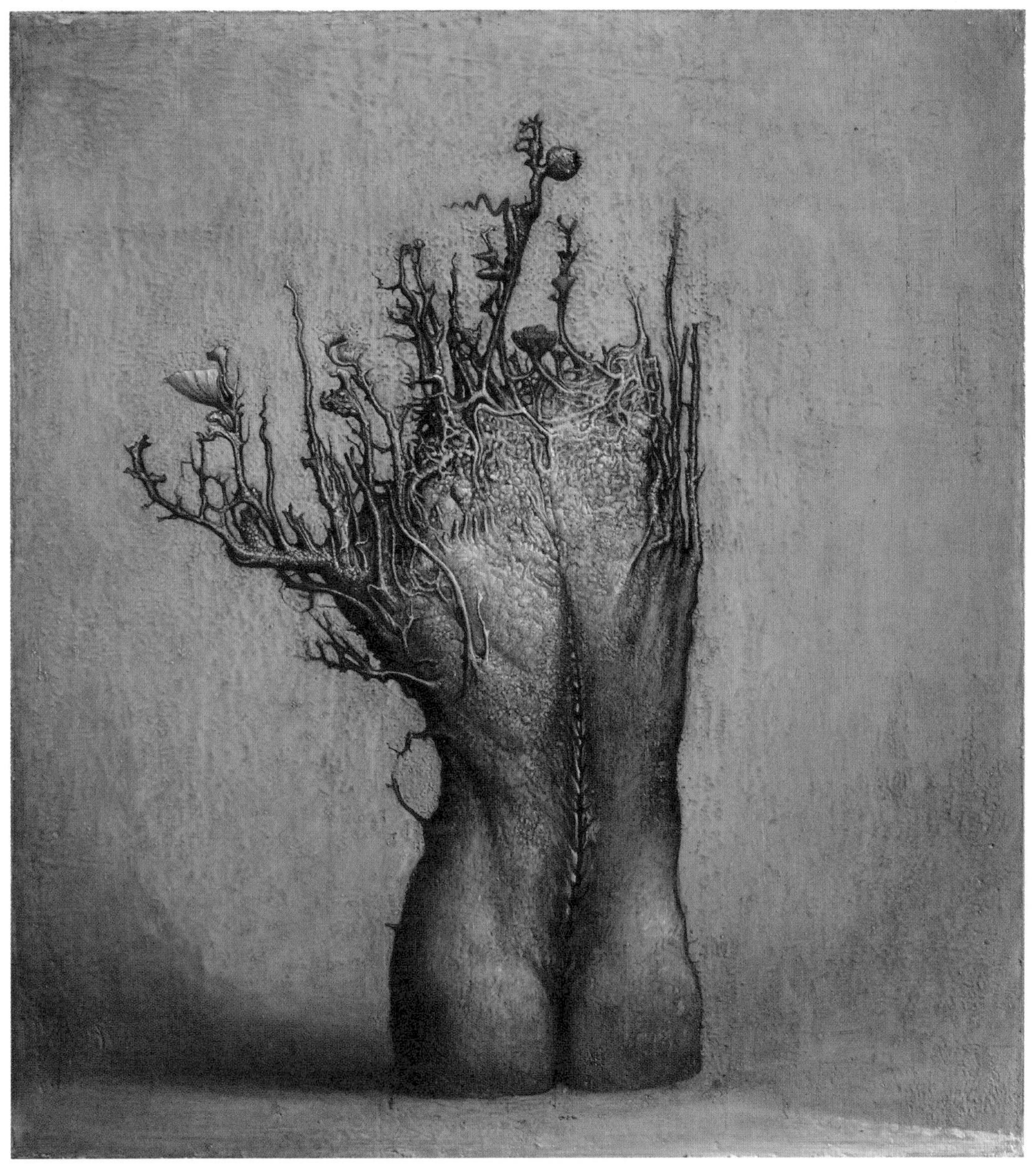

VIII

—

Where the Wild Things Are

‘Listen to them, the children of the night.
What music they make!’

– BRAM STOKER, DRACULA

Rendered in ochre and oxides and seen by torchlight, the beautifully haunting prehistoric art in the famous decorated Lascaux caves reveals profound treasures of art history within the darkness of its chambers. 'Nothing stays still. Shadows nestle in the cavities; a flicker of light across pale protruding rock turns a hoof or raises a head. One shape recedes as another emerges, and everything lingers in the imagination,' writes author Jane Brox, in *Brilliant: The Evolution of Artificial Light*, about the 15,000–17,000-year-old paintings. The caverns, decorated with some 600 painted and drawn animals and symbols and nearly 1,500 engravings and created by our distant ancestors, contain very few depictions of humans.

But this is hardly a surprise. As anyone who has ever watched a cartoon or read a children's storybook knows, animals, whether the violent sort lurking in the shadows eager for the chance to gobble us up, or the benevolent kind who offer advice and teach us life lessons, have always been an integral component of human storytelling. From ancient folk tales and myths, animals have been used to embody and appraise human behaviour to both represent human traits and critique the world we humans live within. They stand in for humans in fables and take the place of people in morality tales. They scare us into behaving or they inspire us to be brave. In fact, the personification of animals is so common that most of us inherently accept animals as representative symbols for human behaviour and interaction.

Artists have ascribed meaning to animals both real and imagined since classical antiquity. In the twelfth century, medieval scholars created vibrant compendia of beasts. A bestiary was an illustrated guide that offered both history lessons and moral associations for a wide variety of creatures, the tales of which became so familiar that they often fled the pages to appear in all manner of artworks, ranging from stained glass to tapestries. In the seventeenth century, scenes illustrating the spectacle of dramatic life-and-death struggles between man and beast were popular, such as the somewhat gruesome still lifes of Frans Snyders, or Peter Paul Rubens' *Hippopotamus and Crocodile Hunt*, 1616. (Rubens had never even seen a hippopotamus when he painted this!) In the eighteenth century, artists honoured the beauty and majestic power of animals, such as peacocks and monkeys, in their natural habitats. Nineteenth-century

Victorian artists painted poignant images of their livestock and domestic pets. Twentieth-century artists like Pablo Picasso, Franz Marc and Frida Kahlo explored animals across a range of art movements and artistic styles, and artists today continue the tradition of relating our human stories through wings and whiskers, stealthy padding feet and eyes that see in the dark.

Spiders, snakes and bats, oh my! Though some cultures might see these as auspicious animals, many others view these creatures as bad luck, ill omens or unequivocally evil. Whether or not we believe it's true, we have all heard that black cats are associated with bad luck and, in the Christian faith, Satan is commonly depicted as a goat, or other creature with cloven hooves. Owls have had a place in folklore and mythology since time immemorial and are both feared and venerated for their associations with death and magic (though they're really only a problem if you're a small rodent). These connections with darkness, mystery and nocturnal malfeasance are a rich source of inspiration for the artistic imagination.

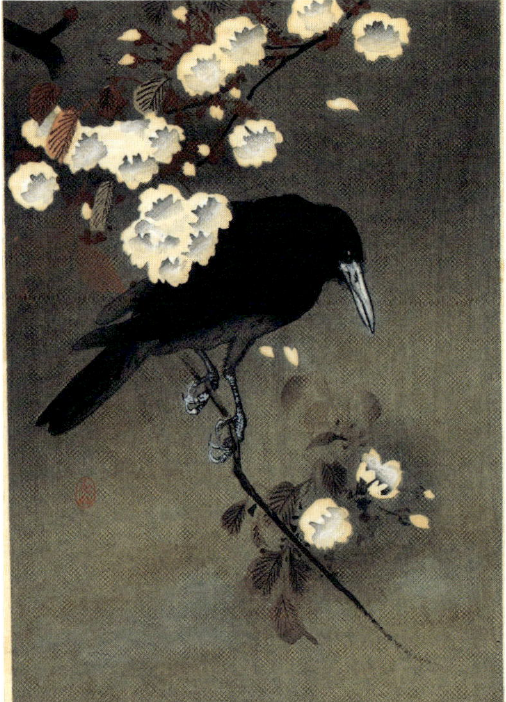

Left: Crow and Blossom, Ohara Koson, c. 1910, woodblock print.

Ohara Koson (1877–1945) was a prolific Japanese painter and woodblock print designer of the late nineteenth and early twentieth centuries, whose career commenced at a time when the Ukiyo-e print tradition was dying out and the shin hanga ('new print') movement had not yet begun. Famous as a master of kachō-e (bird-and-flower) designs, his crows, cranes and camellias captured an elegant sense of stillness and quietude and were depicted with palpable reverence and meticulous care, and his designs featuring these daring and highly intelligent birds remain in great demand.

Right: Armida, Francesco Montelatici known as Cecco Bravo, c. 1650, oil on canvas.

Known for religious genre, figure easel painting and fresco church decoration, Francesco Montelatici Cecco Bravo (1600–61) was apparently also known for his violent temperament. I'm not exactly suggesting that the artist's aggressive nature is reflected in the intensely passionate subject matter and tempestuous brushstrokes of this work, but I'm not . . . not saying that either, I suppose. In this scene, the beautiful princess Armida, abandoned by the crusader Rinado, has fallen into despair and fury. Having called upon all the spirits to accompany her, she then joins the Egyptian ranks to exact her revenge. She is flanked by a bizarre and grotesque variety of animals, dragons, serpents and demons and other fantastical apparitions, all prepared to show that Rinado a very bad time, upon their mistress's command.

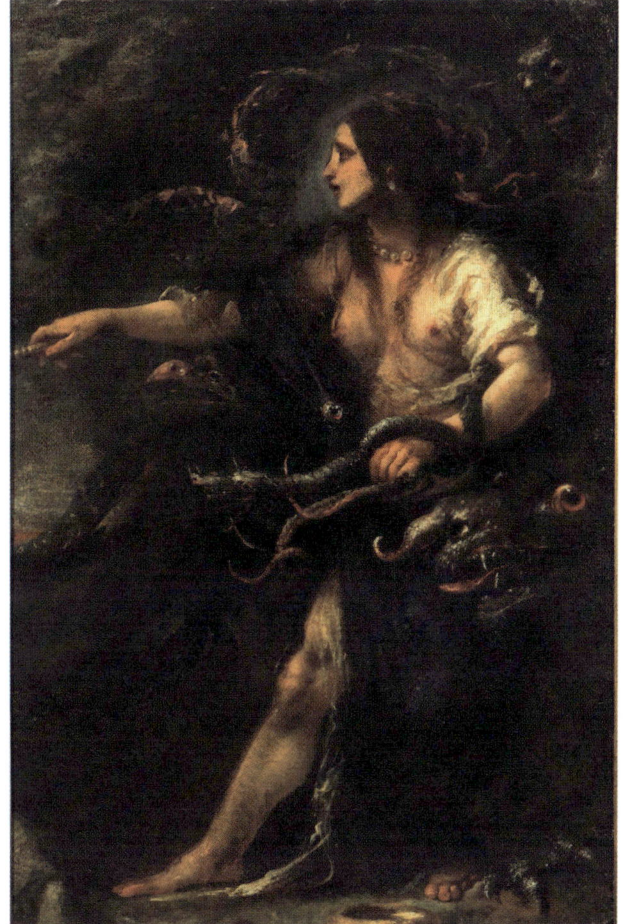

From ferocious creatures of myth to the very real animals right in our backyards, from snarling wolves to hissing snakes and smiling spiders, art history is brimming (and buzzing and bleating and bellowing) with a veritable menagerie of creatures, both mythical and mundane and, of course, malevolent too. Or, to quote hoary old Van Helsing edifying us from within the pages of *Dracula*, 'the meaner things . . . the rat, and the owl, and the bat, the moth, and the fox'. Though we no longer paint our stories within the gloom and murk of lightless caves, these creatures great and small, wild, wondrous or wicked, continue their tradition of delighting and disturbing us, charming us and terrorizing us – and in the spark of that feral clamour, illuminating humankind's greatest hopes, fears and dreams.

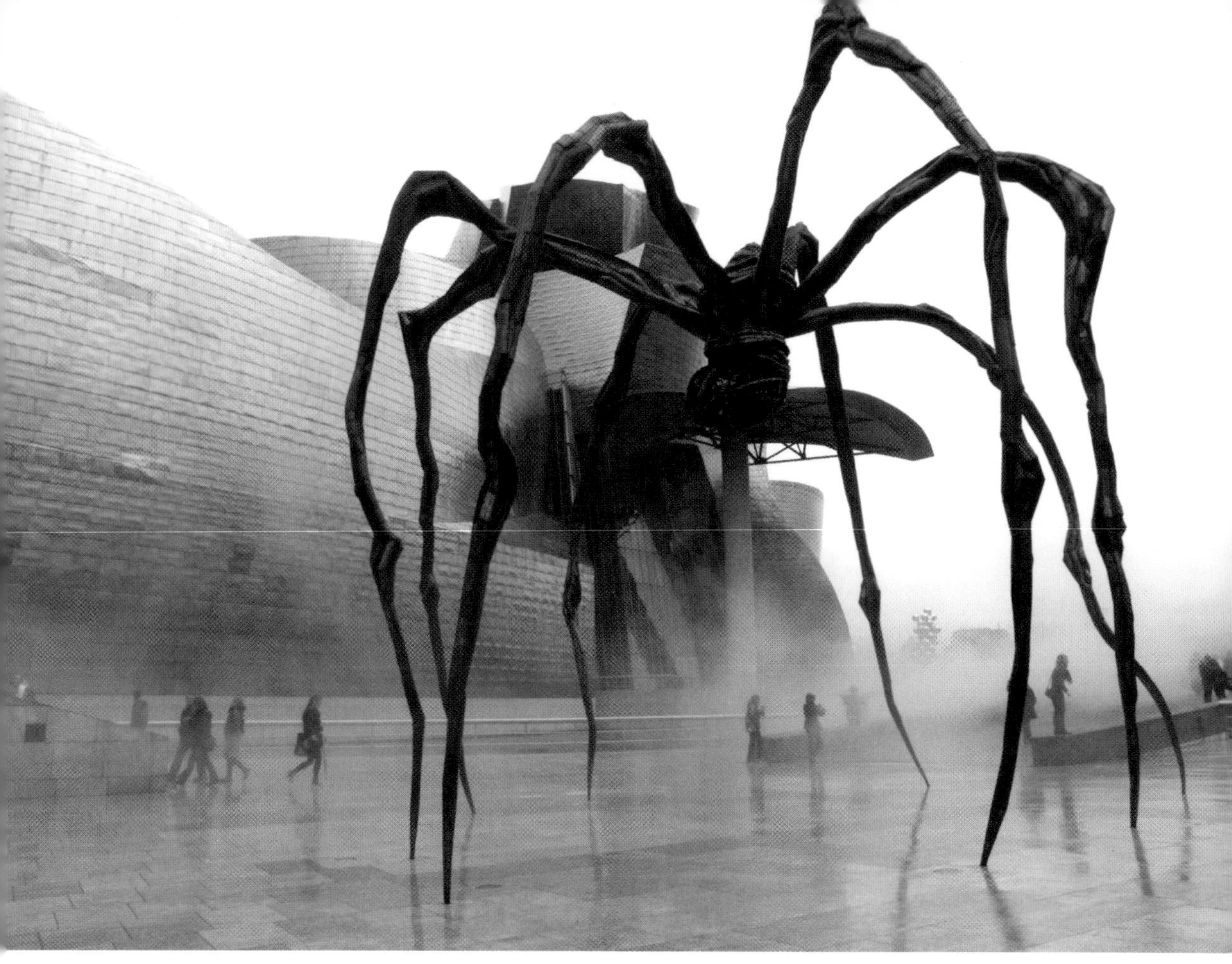

Above: *Maman*, Louise Bourgeois, 1999, bronze, marble and stainless steel.

With a highly successful artistic career and a vast oeuvre spanning over six decades, French-American artist Louise Bourgeois (1911–2010) today is recognized as one of the most influential female artists of modern and contemporary art, who passionately plumbed the depths of human emotion. Supported on eight slender, rickety legs and more than thirty feet high, *Maman* is a larger-than-life steel spider from your most arachnophobic dreams, casting a powerful physical and emotional shadow. So massive that it can only be installed outdoors, this sculpture is one of the most ambitious undertakings in the long career of Louise Bourgeois.

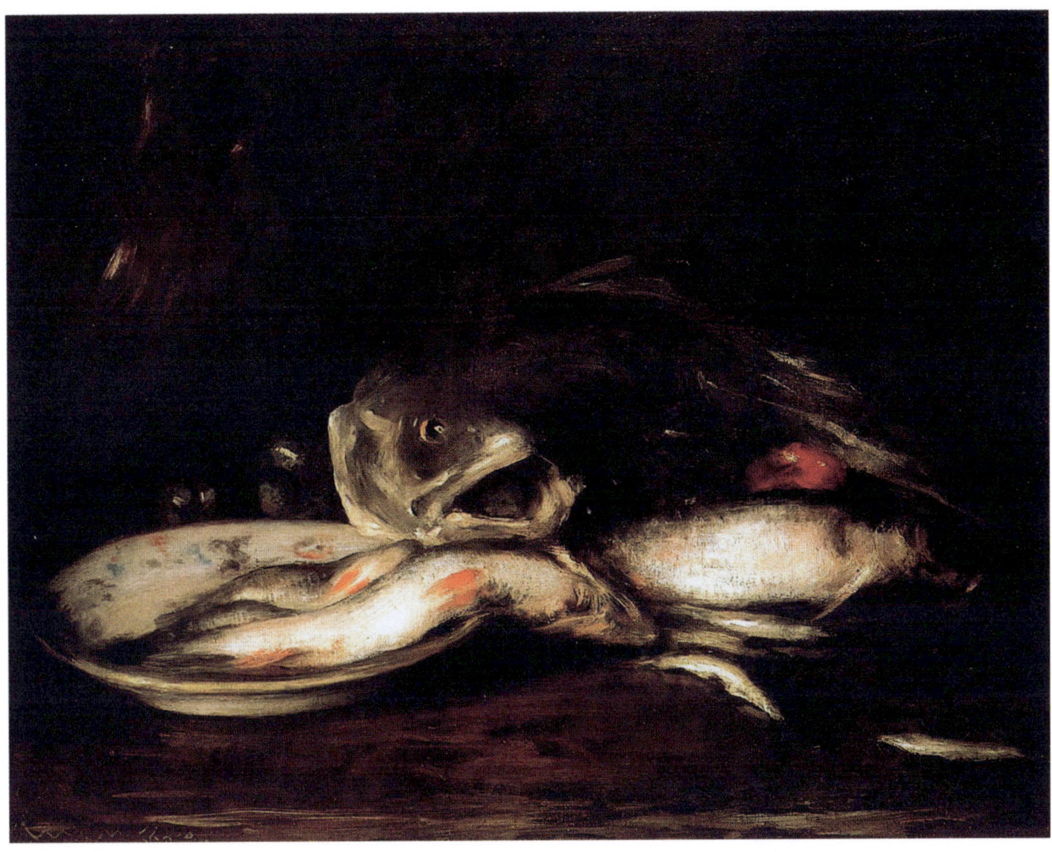

Above: Still Life With Fish, William Merritt Chase, 1915, oil on canvas.

As we consider the masterful *Still Life With Fish* by American artist William Merritt Chase (1849–1916), we easily reach the conclusion that, while most people don't wish to sit down and stare at a platter of dead fish, you can't deny the talent it requires to take up a brush and render a portrait of them so lifelike it looks like they might leap right off the table and flap their way back out to sea in a rush of scales, silver and trailing sea water. And created with such speed, too! Apparently, Chase often painted fish during class demonstrations at his New York School of Art, where the students described how he went to the fish market, bought it, painted it and returned the fish before it went bad. Georgia O'Keeffe, Edward Hopper and George Bellows, all very different artists, studied under Chase and likely saw the charisma and confidence of these sure, stunning brushstrokes firsthand.

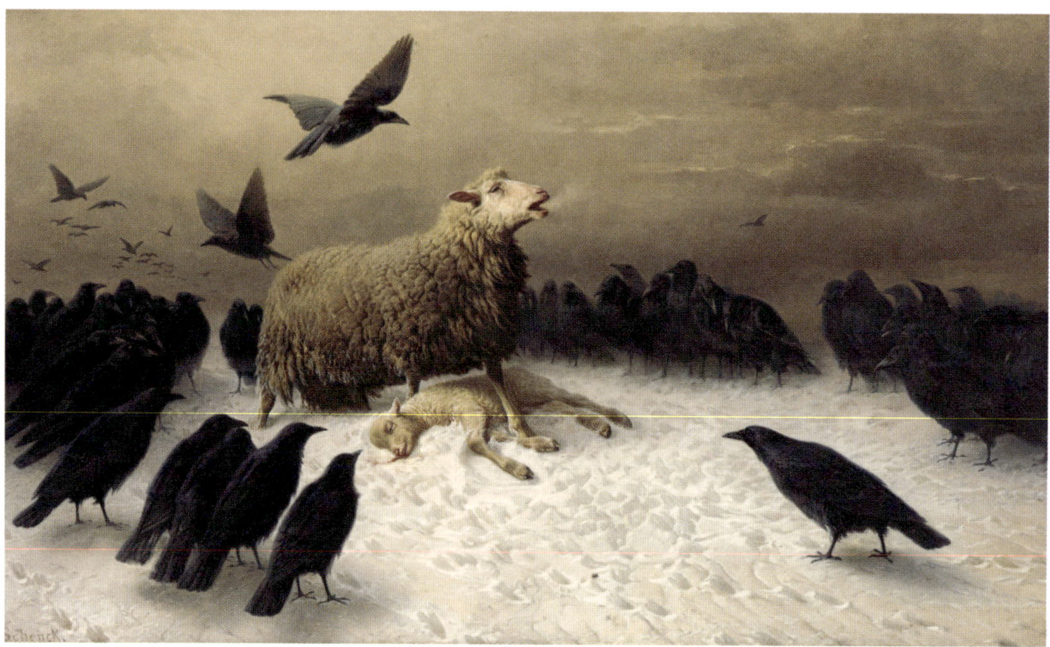

Above: Anguish, August Friedrich Schenck, 1878, oil on canvas.

Despite the fact that little is known of the Danish artist August Friedrich Schenck (1828–1901), his painting *Anguish* remains incredibly popular to this day. Thought of as 'schmaltzy' by some and 'heart-rending' by others, this depiction of a ewe bleating in grief, standing protectively over her deceased lamb in the snow, while a murder of crows swarms portentously around her under dull grey cloudy winter sky never fails to evoke a response. It has been suggested that the work may have taken inspiration from the 1872 book *The Expression of the Emotions in Man and Animals*, in which Charles Darwin argued that emotions have biological origins, and that animals experience similar emotions to humans. It has also been interpreted as a commentary on the cruelty of society, represented by the crowd of opportunistic crows.

Opposite: L'Araignée souriante (The Smiling Spider), Odilon Redon, 1881, charcoal on paper.

Known for his unique blend of artistic naturalism and symbolic subject matter, Odilon Redon (1840–1916) was highly influential among the late-nineteenth-century French avant-garde circle. Working in charcoal, pastel, oil and lithography, Redon created mysterious, imaginative scenes that, while often based in the supernatural, were nonetheless executed in a highly representational manner. Influenced by the provocative decadence of the poetry of Charles Baudelaire, the artist was also fascinated with the natural sciences, and studied anatomy, osteology and microscopic life. Many of his monsters were based on observation but were reborn and embellished by the artist's imagination. It is the recognition of our humanity in these strange hybrid beasties – the friendly, toothy grin and capering legs on a fuzzy spider – that makes them so enchanting and horrid at the same time.

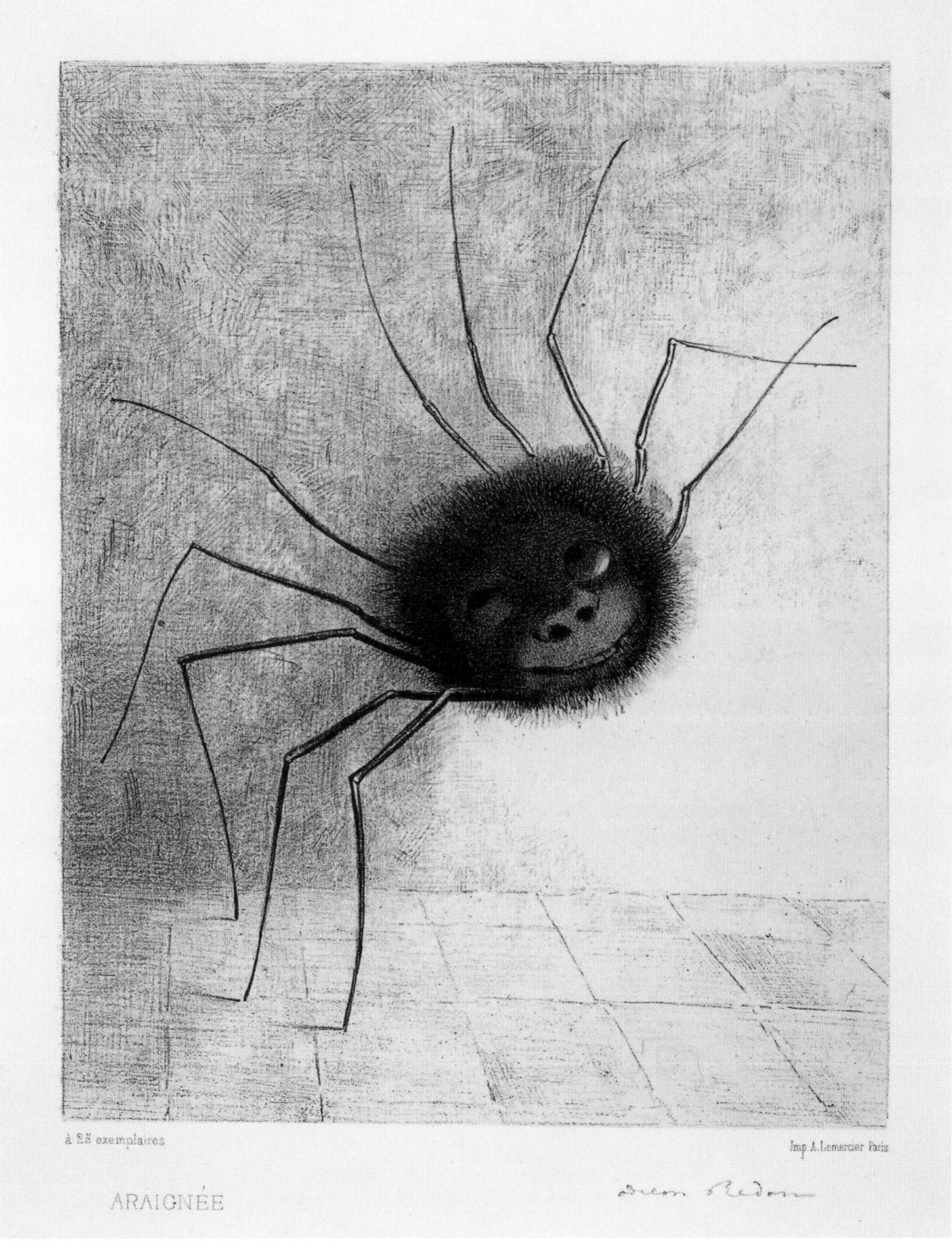
à 25 exemplaires
Imp A. Lemercier Paris
ARAIGNÉE

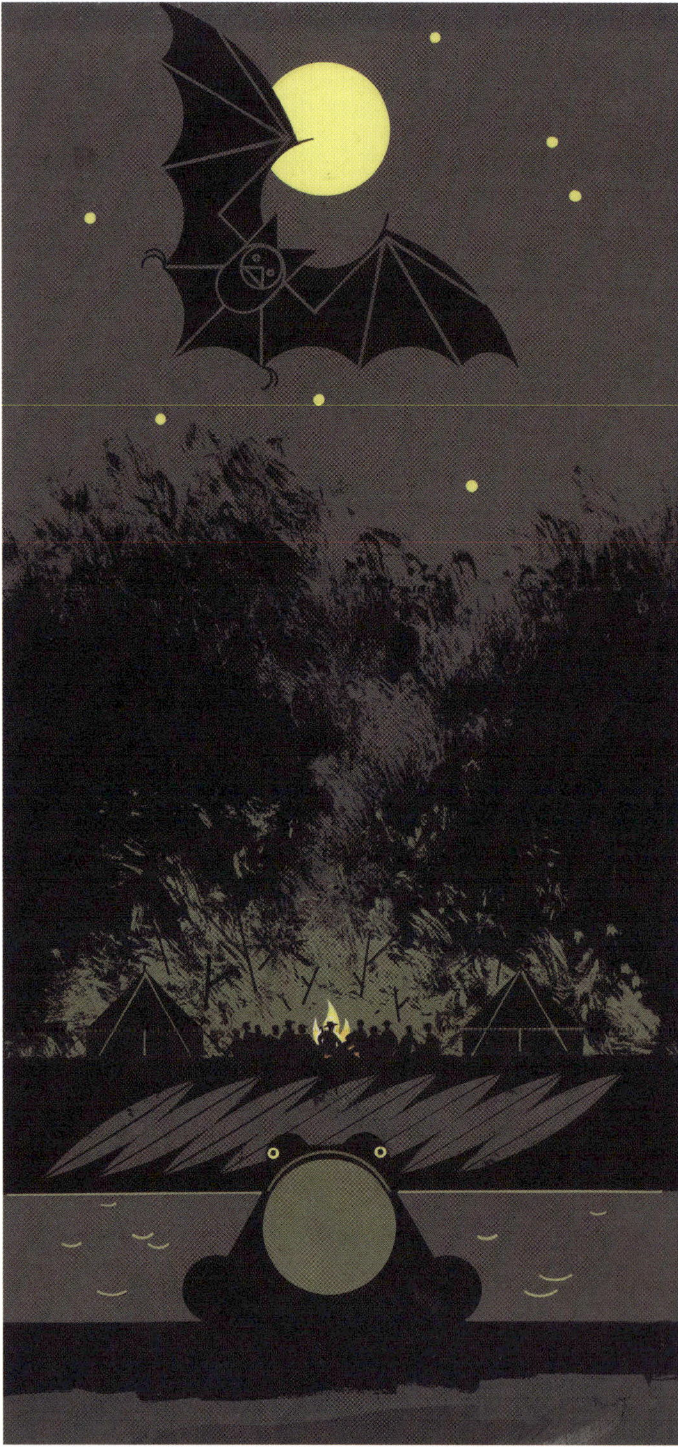

Left: Bat, Bullfrog, and Bonfire, Charley Harper, 1968, lithograph.

Celebrated American Modernist artist Charley Harper (1922–2007) was beloved for his playful, stylized wildlife prints, posters and book illustrations. Vivid, whimsical, and immediately recognizable, Harper's works were large expanses of vibrant colour and jaunty shapes, blurring fine art and graphic design. Inspired by his love for the beauty and simplicity of nature, Harper revealed the unique aspects of his subjects through his unassuming, minimalist approach. His art was often laced with levity and gentle wit; even eerie nocturnal scenes of bats and frogs loitering in the midnight glooms become a playful nighttime meditation in fascinating shapes and frolicsome behaviour! An artist as well as a conservationist (and perhaps a comedian at heart), Harper believed that humour made it easier to encourage changes in our attitudes and awareness of environmental concerns.

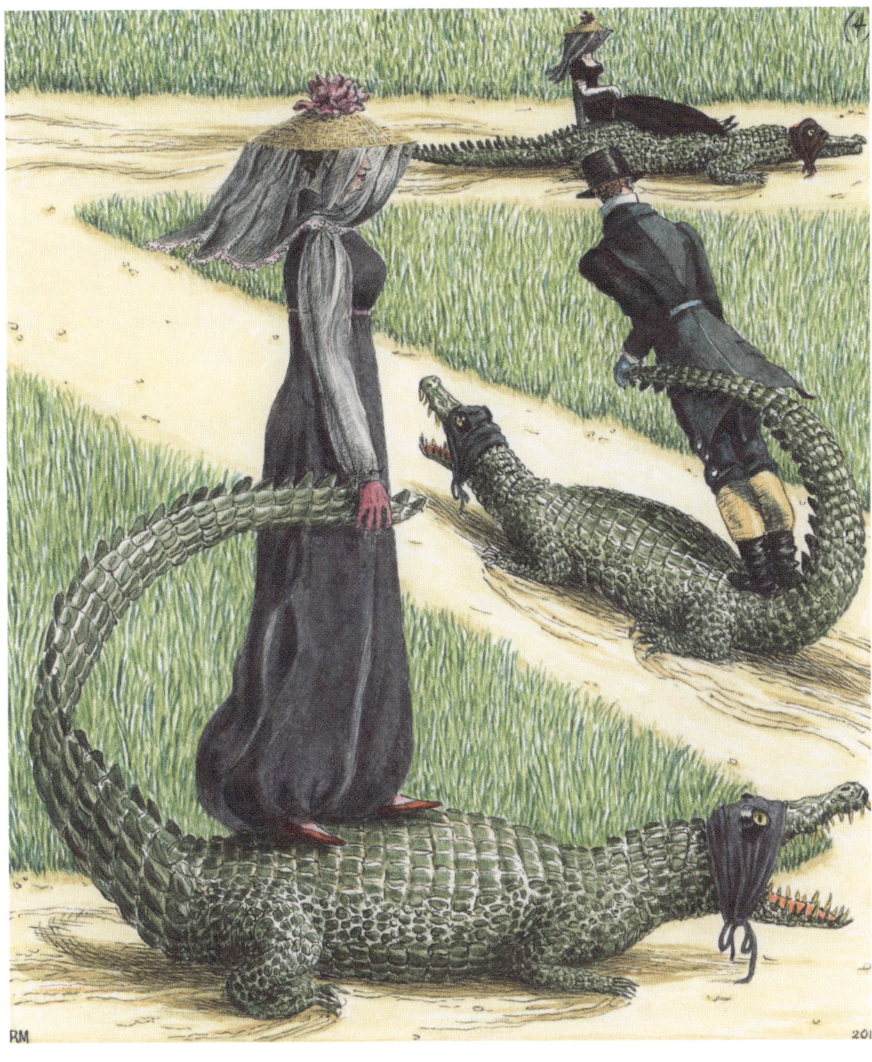

Above: 4, 2015, from Fountains & Alligators, Ruth Marten, 2015, nineteenth-century engraving with ink and watercolour additions.

Ruth Marten (b. 1949) is a native New Yorker, and the works from her Fountains & Alligators series are a delightful mix of sombre, sly and surreal. Engaging with eighteenth- and nineteenth-century prints and illustrations, the artist works with Indian ink and watercolours, deftly altering the images with delicate enhancements, and surprises us by subverting their original intention or meaning. These additions create bizarre disconnects and weird new worlds of strangeness; in this illustration we observe some gloomy Victorians, ostensibly in mourning attire, tootling along a path with their pet alligators. Many people online have infamously adopted this particular image as proof of 'how people in southern Florida get around town'. As the artist has noted herself, 'Once you drape an alligator shawl around a lady's shoulders . . . any and all interpretations are welcome.'

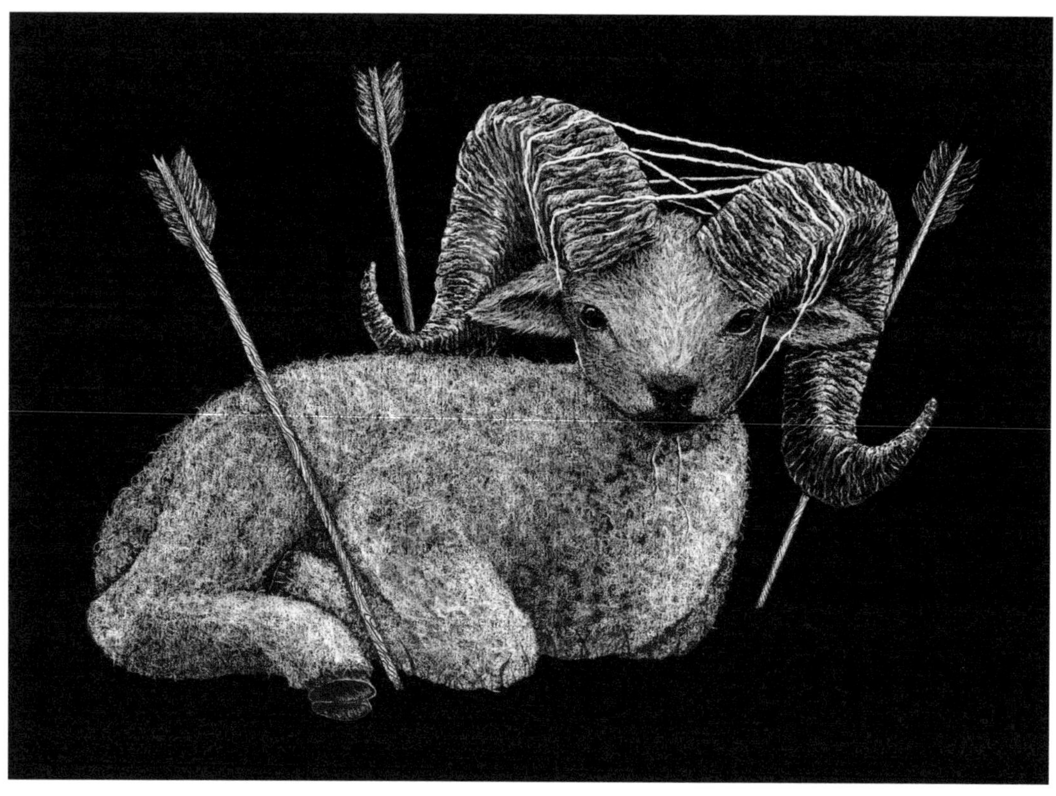

Above: Rot from the Inside Out, Dylan Garrett Smith, 2016, ashes, chalk-lead and ink on black cotton rag paper.

Foxes stalking the darkness, padding through a thicket of thorns. Shadowy snakes snarled in somnolent repose. A skull cupped tenderly, a candle's flame snuffed. Rendered in ash, chalk-lead, and ink on black cotton rag, the funereal monochrome visions of artist and printmaker Dylan Garrett Smith reflect the artist's views regarding our relationships with the natural world. Combining ecological and occult concepts with existential fears and anarchism, Smith stresses the importance of the cycle of birth, bloom, and decay and the ultimate triumph of nature in the end–whatever that 'end' might be.

Opposite: Botanica Reliquaire, Frances Pelzman, 2014, photographic process with mixed media.

Frances Pelzman creates emotive works using her own relics, botanical items and personal mementos. These works interpret the staggering beauty of the natural world and the enchanted landscape of the inner world. Phlox, zinnia, mums, viburnum berries, callicarpa, milkweed, bacopa, coreopsis, impatiens, hydrangea, coral berry, aster, goldenrod - every type of botanical and natura finds a home under the delicate touch of this former punk/street photographer-turned flower photographer.

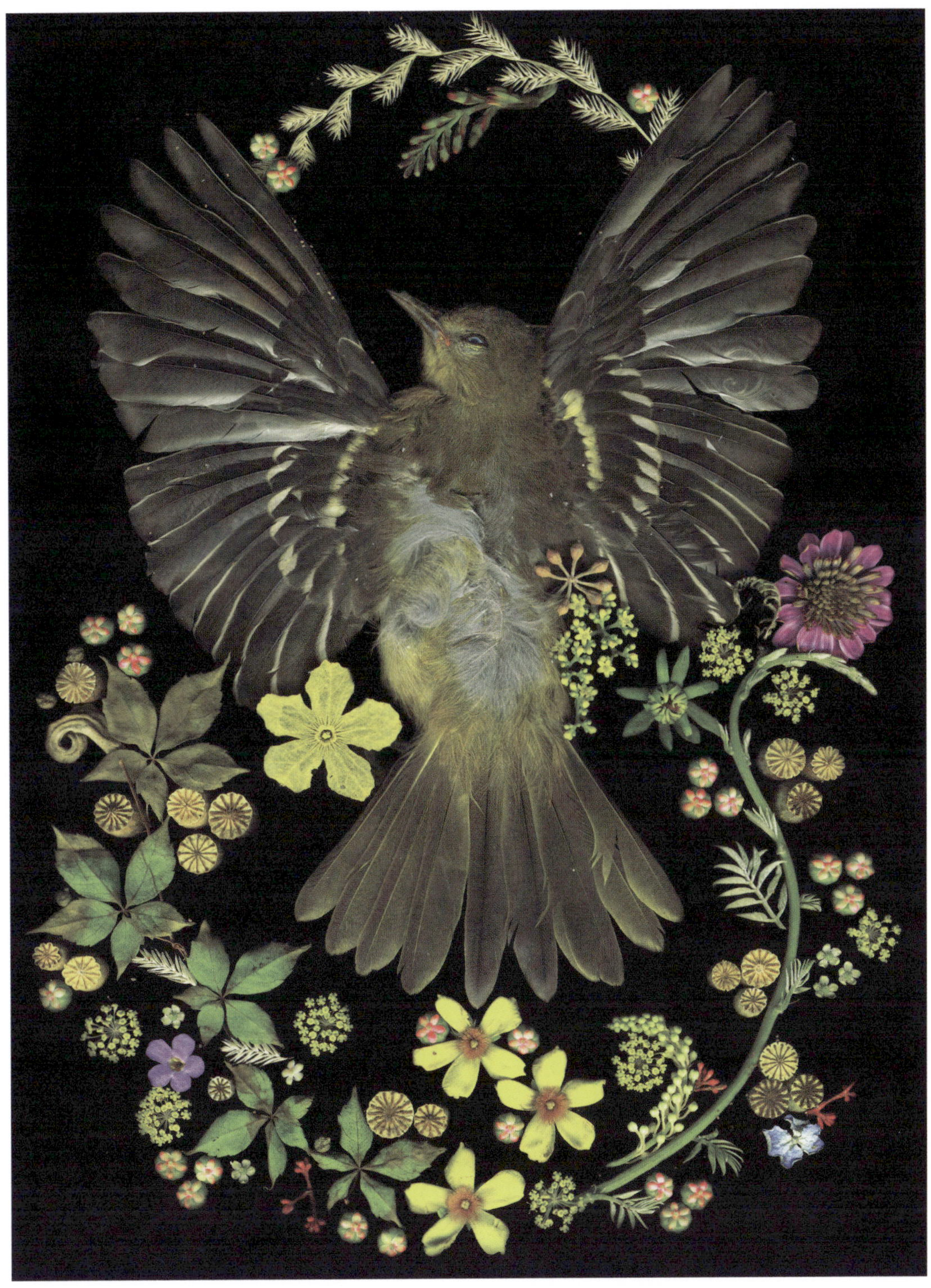

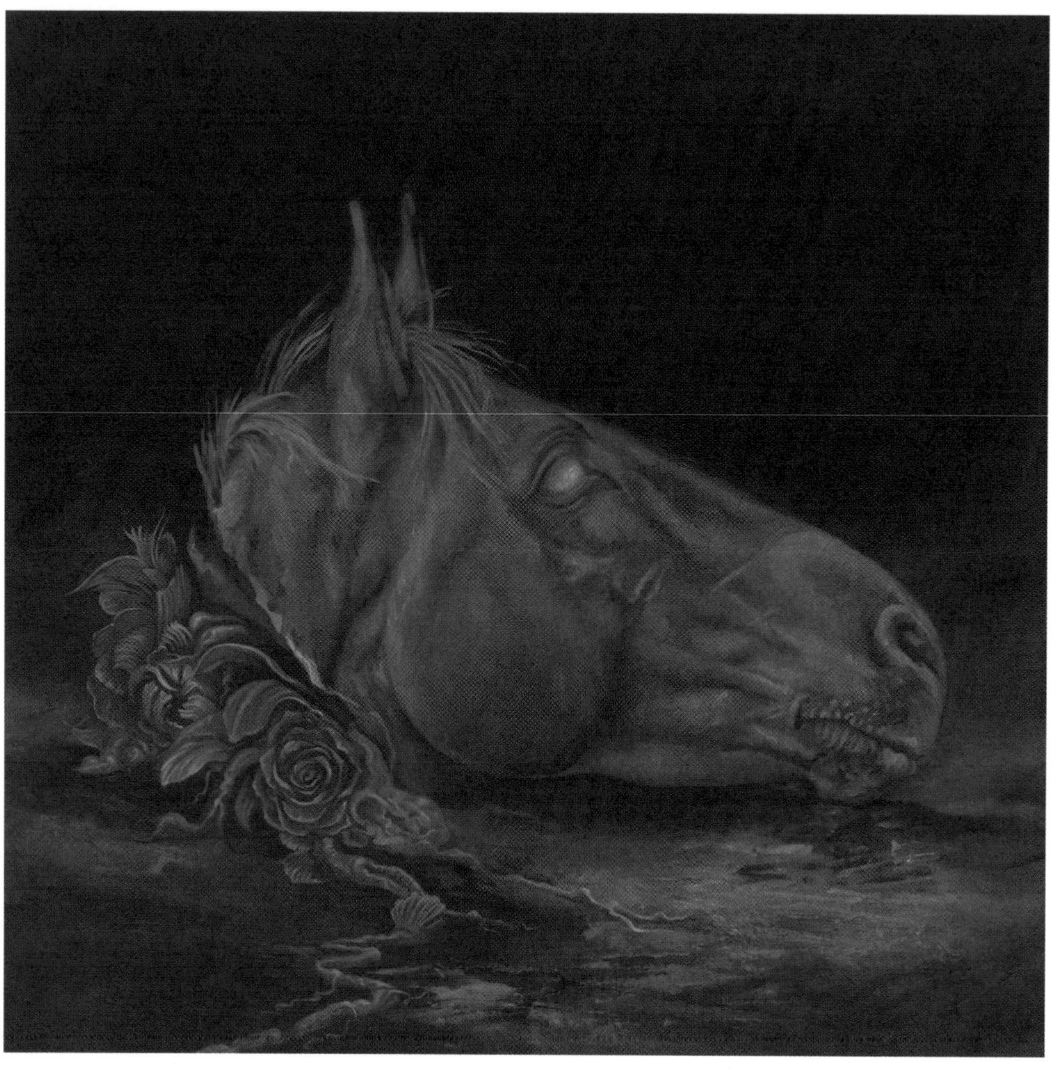

Above: Grey, Brittle, Paul Romano, 2013, oil on canvas.

American contemporary artist Paul Romano is interested in representationalism, not realism. In his works, imagination overrules reality, and accuracy is forsaken in favour of evocation. Thoughtful and enigmatic, travelling with ease between impossible dream worlds of shadow and half-light, Romano coaxes dark memories and strange sorrows into existence and immortalizes them as melancholic creatures and beings in abstract narratives that ask more questions than give answers. Filtered through allegory and archetype a disembodied horse head oozes flowers from its wounds, milky eyes gazing sightlessly into the dark and evoking a resigned sense of loss, and yet – there blossoms a strange, dusky gentle trust of hope as well.

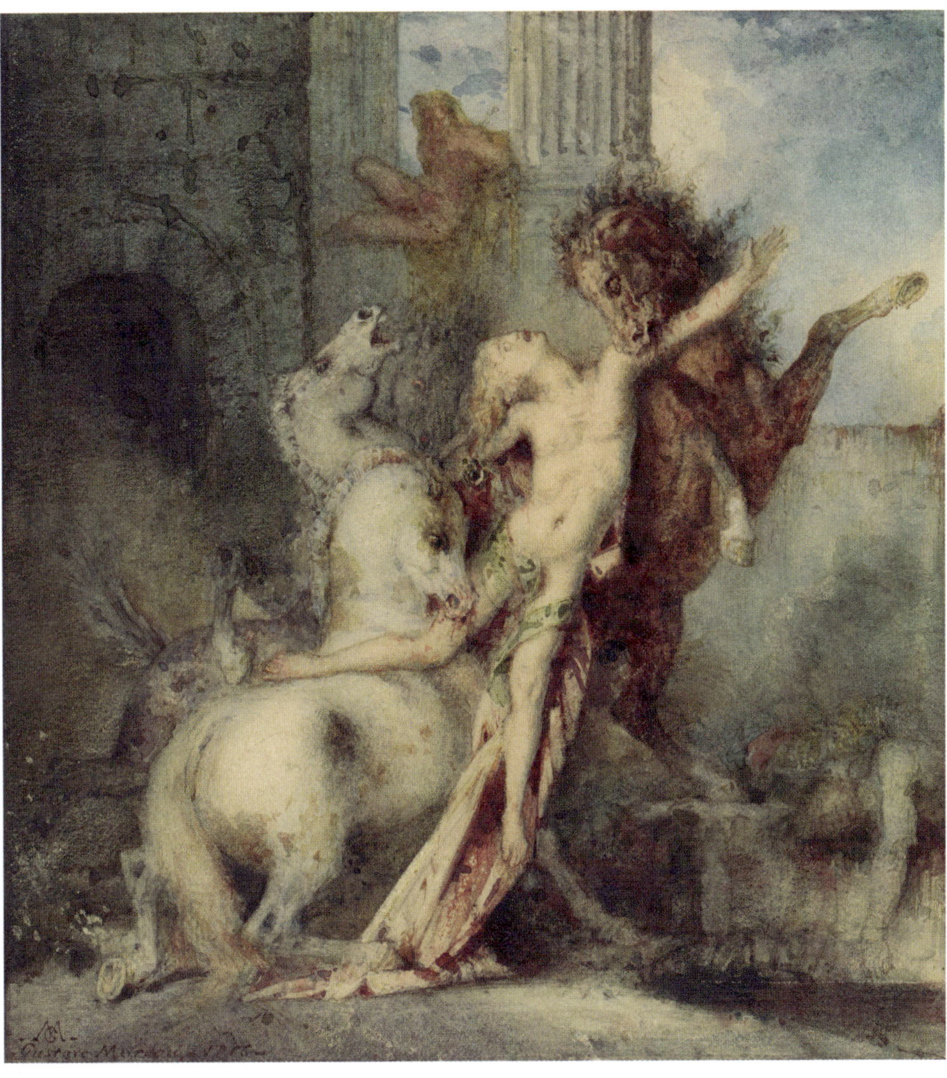

Above: Diomedes Devoured by his Horses, Gustave Moreau, 1866, watercolour.

The strange and poetic works of French Symbolist Gustave Moreau (1826–98) teem with the otherworldly and macabre and often depicted mythological themes and religious scenes, bringing new light and shadowy twists to popular and frequently illustrated iconography. Here he returns to the bloody saga of Hercules and his labours. As the shadowy figure of the demi-god lurks from between two columns in the background, four wild horses rip apart the slight body of King Diomedes in a scene which illustrates the dramatic climax from the eighth labour of Hercules, who was ordered to capture the four flesh-eating horses belonging to King Diomedes. Hercules killed the king in battle and fed his body to the horses, which tamed them. Gustave Moreau's fascination with violent, emotionally charged subjects portrayed in sensuous, jewel-like colours typifies mid-nineteenth-century French painting.

Right: A Good Catch
Kazuya Akimoto, 2007, acrylics.

The philosophy of contemporary Japanese Artist Kazuya Akimoto's art is: 'If it is not a masterpiece, then it is a waste of time, both for an artist who created it and those who are forced or happen to see it.' This enigmatic creator paints not to represent the outer world or the inner world, by giving free rein to feelings or by imitating the real world, but for his own sense of aesthetic languages and logics. This complicated statement is either illustrated in or even further obfuscated by such works as this monochromatic undersea cacophony, wherein shadowy fish and squid crowd around a fisherman's lure. Perhaps, then, it is both. Who are we to know an artist's mind?

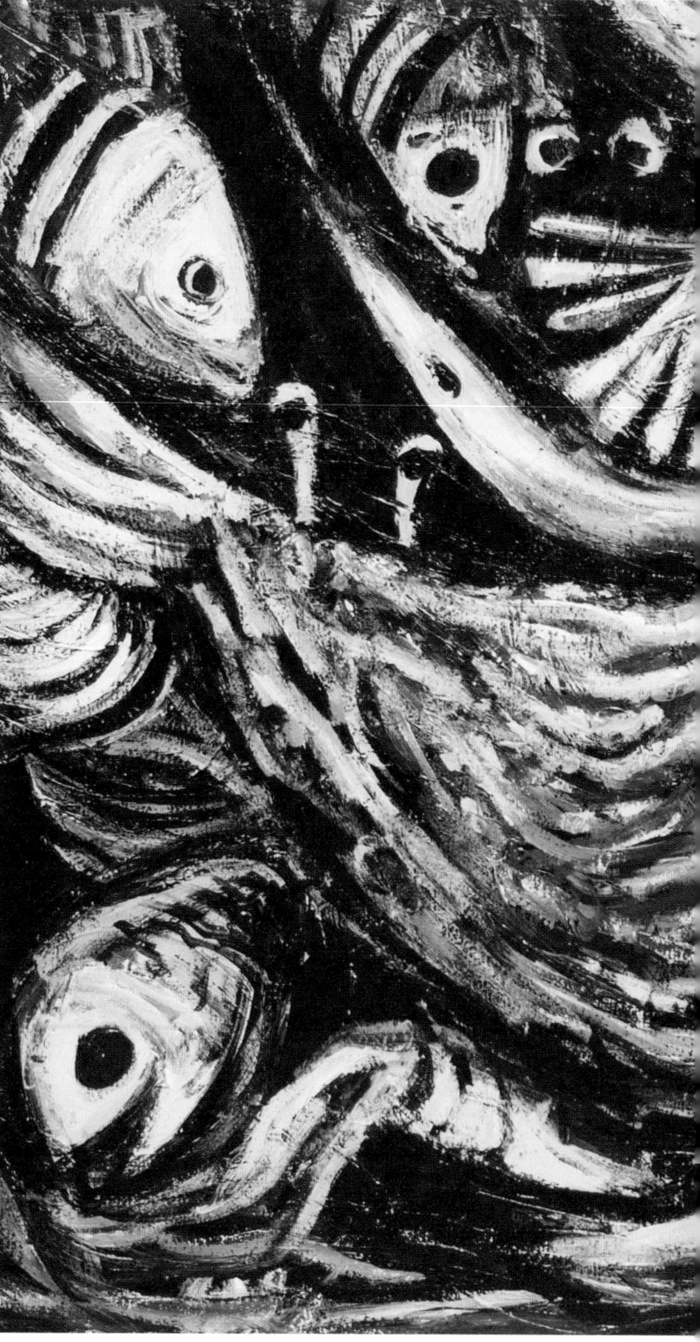

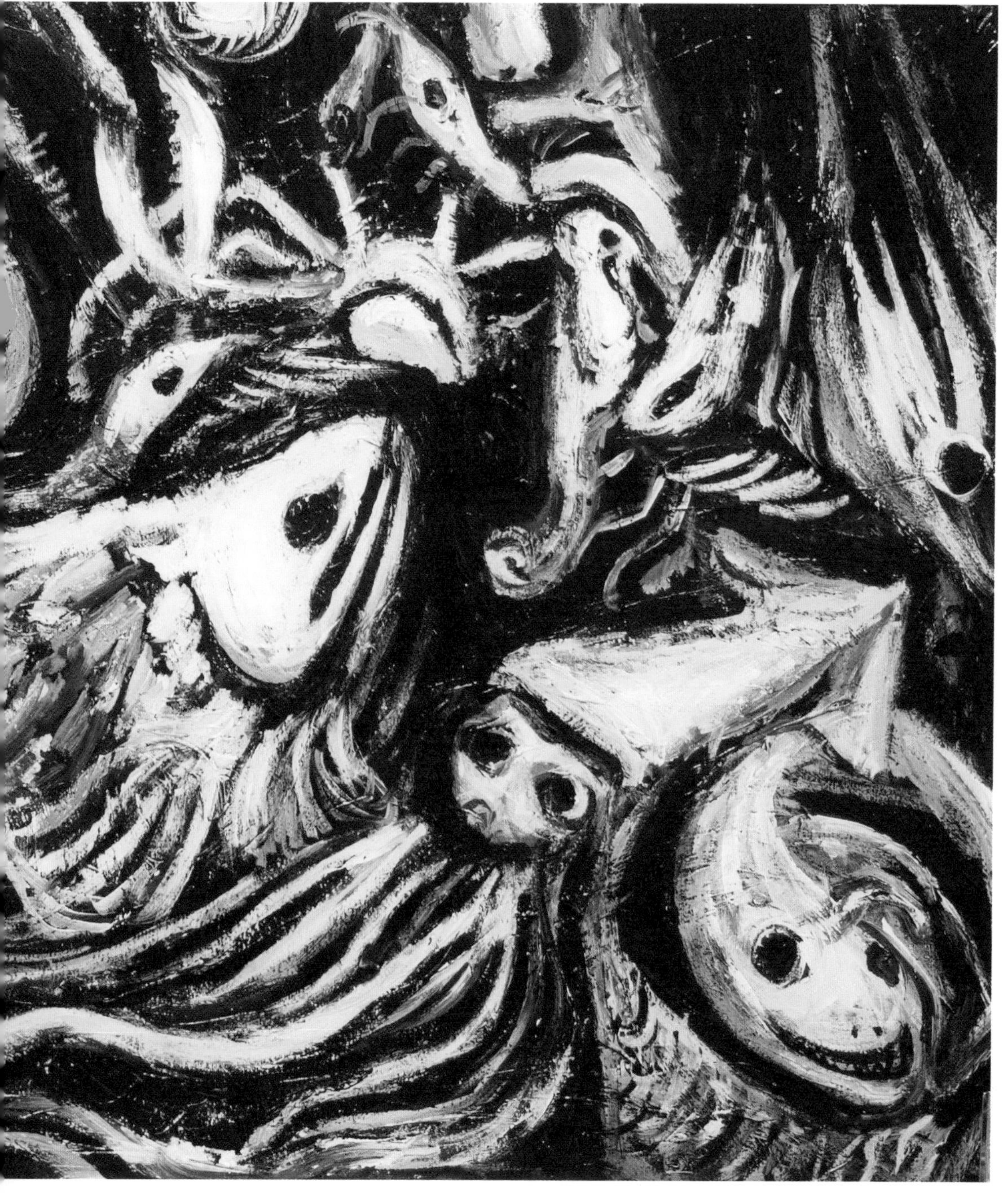

IX

Mysterious Landscapes, Ruins & Ravaged Places

'Midway in our life's journey, I went astray from the straight road and woke to find myself alone in a dark wood.'

– DANTE ALIGHIERI

Scenic vistas blazing with wild darkness and raw beauty, where a boundless sense of nature overwhelms, the atmosphere so intensely charged you can almost hear it crackle and hum. What lurks in the shadows of that thickly painted evergreen forest, or looms behind those crumbling columns choked with creeping vines? And why, even though these scenes feel fraught, fearsome, fatal – why do they still, despite everything, call to you? Why do we at times find ourselves desperate to crawl deep within these sombre scenes, to disappear forever?

These lonely landscapes and tenebrous topographies affect us and engage our senses through a variety of compelling features. Ancient lands inexplicable and mysterious, connecting us to the unknown distant past. Unquiet, natural forms used to unnerving effect, such as bleak expanses of heath and the borderlands where different worlds come together. Figures and objects or the lack thereof evoke the eerie and uncanny through secrets and suggestion. There is atmospheric effect: how weather, season, light and the time of day can impact a scene or space. As humans, we love a good mystery, and a combination of any of these visual cues and the visceral feelings they provoke is naturally compelling.

From the scratched markings into rocks appearing to be both art and cartography as early as 14,000 years ago, to the wall-painted landscapes and gardenscapes created by the Greeks and Romans, to the harmoniously contrived classical landscapes of the seventeenth century – humans are naturally drawn to vastness in scenery, and art and human geography have long been intertwined. The nineteenth century heralded many shifts in landscape art with the birth of landscape photography, which would considerably influence landscape painters' compositional choices. Despite a progression of technique and a reflection of changing values and sentiments in landscape art, the land itself remembers when things were not always so . . .

Do the places we inhabit have a memory of us after we disappear? Do they hold dreams of our past and a hint of our future? Does something of us remain caught in the branches, our phantom footprints in the grass, the ghosts of our breaths now haunting its walls? Scholars in a range of academic disciplines, including philosophy, geography and psychology, have long recognized the importance of 'place' in human experience – and there is a particularly haunting beauty in how we view and engage with places and spaces of architectural ruins.

Though the march of time lays waste to the triumphs of earlier civilizations, the moments seem to pause, shift and fold in these magnificent abandoned structures and this sense of disrupted time silently hints at a distant, glorious past. The depiction of ruins immortalized in art and semi-fictitious architectural paintings began during the Renaissance. The Corinthian pillars and colonnades of classical architecture attracted many artists; gothic construction also provided great inspiration for ruinscapes. Ruins serve as a portentous yet enthralling reminder of the Latin maxim, *sic transit gloria mundi* ('all glory is fleeting'), and we can find evidence of this sentiment in beautiful artworks depicting architectural decay in all its majesty.

Artists today engage with the twenty-first-century geography of our world by exploring themes of memory, belonging and human impact on nature. Sally Mann's photographs of the American South move from the landscape and its history to the people who inhabit it, to create a portrait of the emotionally charged and evocative geography that is Mann's home. Inspired by remote landscapes and environmentally sensitive locations, Zaria Forman's photorealist paintings with their grand proportions and glacial isolation, transport us to an area of the world where we are confronted with the effects of climate change and are reminded that these places are precious gifts that we can't afford to lose.

From the frozen landscapes of the Antarctic to the dilapidated haunted houses of childhood, the memory of places we experience is essential to a sense of self, and the art inspired by it is often a direct reflection of our dreams and memories and experiences. Sometimes the combinations of sensory information we view in these works may induce a sense of dread, an ambient murmur of light or shadow or seasonal shift that causes a frisson of fear, the hairs prickling at the back of one's neck. The next second we may glimpse a painted sunset on the horizon, incandescent, lurid with lilac and orange; unexpected, underserved and utterly sublime. The bleak, the beautiful, the peaceful and the exhilarating – one cannot gaze upon the awe-inspiring aspects of nature in a landscape or admire the timeless allure of ruins without the heady compulsion to step right through the frame and lose oneself completely.

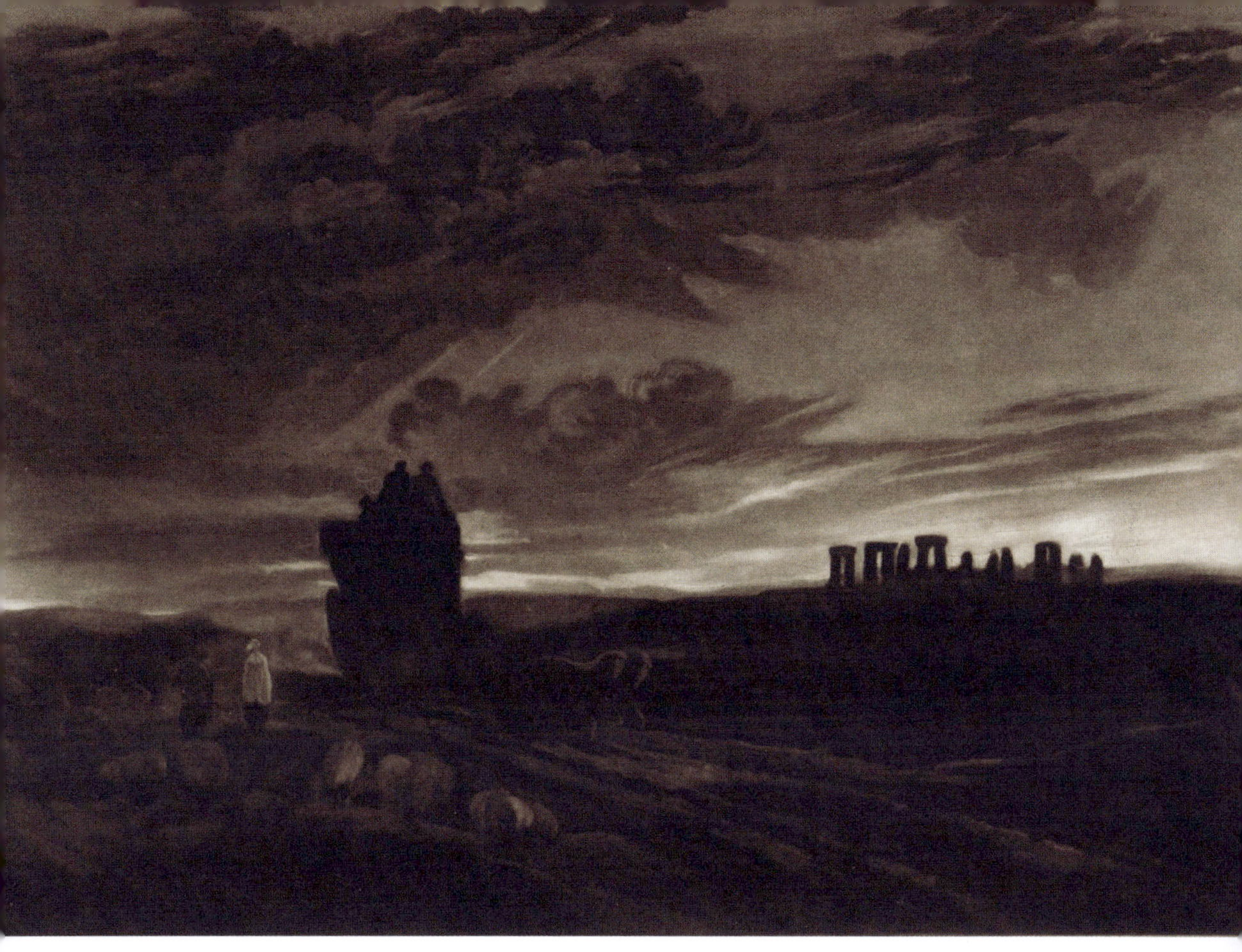

Above: Stonehenge, J.M.W. Turner, c. 1824, mezzotint.

Joseph Mallord William Turner (1775–1851) was an English Romantic painter and printmaker who made his reputation as a topographical watercolourist and who was denounced as much as he was lauded during his lifetime. He was determined to raise landscape painting closer in the hierarchy of genres to history painting, and his public status reflected both the criticism and admiration he received on these matters. In this image is a view of Stonehenge, looking to the east; towards the left, the silhouette of a stagecoach; in the foreground a woman, and sheep grazing. A great deal of mystery surrounds the remains of this famous landmark; however, given the circular pattern in which the stones are arranged, some theories suggest that the monument was once a burial ground.

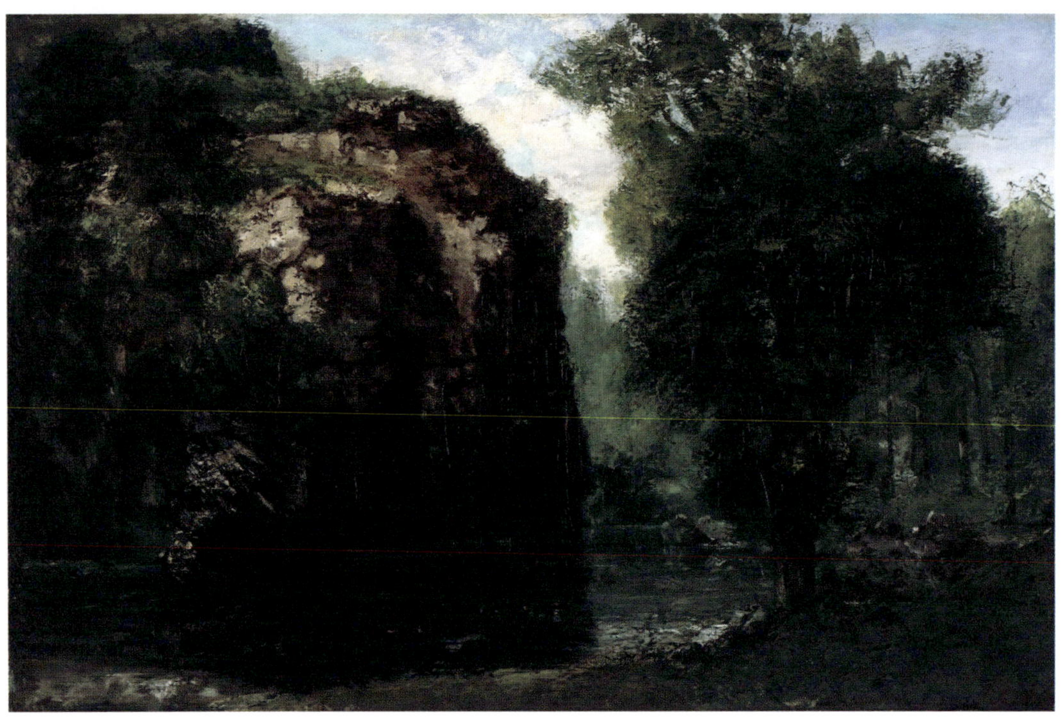

Above: The Silent River, Gustave Courbet, 1868, oil on canvas.

Gustave Courbet (1819–77) was a French painter who led the Realism movement in nineteenth-century French painting. Committed to painting only what he could see, he rejected academic convention and Romanticism. Landscape and the beloved terrain of his native France played a central role in Courbet's imagery. The distinctive limestone cliffs of the surrounding Jura Mountains provide the backdrop for one of his early self-portraits and he later developed a repertoire of landscape motifs rooted in his native Franche-Comté, including the Puits-Noir, or Black Well, which inspired a series of paintings that span more than a decade. In these canvases one can read nature's sombre poetry, smell the vegetal decay of wet autumnal leaves, feel the velvety texture of mossy rocks among the detritus of the forest floor.

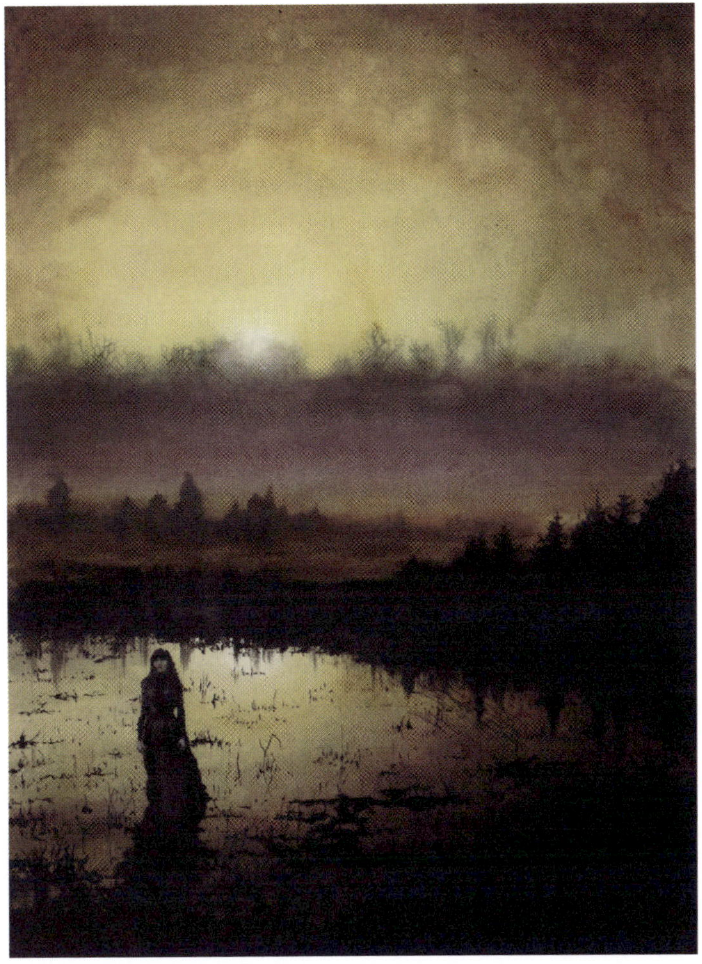

Above: Hagg Lake II, Adam Burke, 2019, acrylic on panel.

'Fantasy and dark subject matter,' remarks contemporary American artist Adam Burke, 'can access our deep needs and motivations, as well as present a sense of mystery or unknown in a world where the unknown seems to be ever shrinking.' This fascination with the myriad wonders of the natural world and the flora and fauna which inhabit it is expressed in the name of his website, nightjarillustration.com. According to Burke, nightjars are birds in the genus *Caprimulgus*. They are beautiful, but seldom seen, mostly nocturnal birds that have gorgeous markings and a distinct flight pattern. This fascination can also be glimpsed in his more personal works: dim-lit, moody landscapes of craggy cliffs and marshy bogs shrouded in mists, populated with woodland creatures and wanderers alike. All are seen through the vaporous veil suggestive of a haunting dream, perhaps an entirely different world. 'I think humankind's presence in this world is increasingly destructive and meaningless. I use art as a form of escape; to create a place or feeling that I wish existed or where I wish I was.'

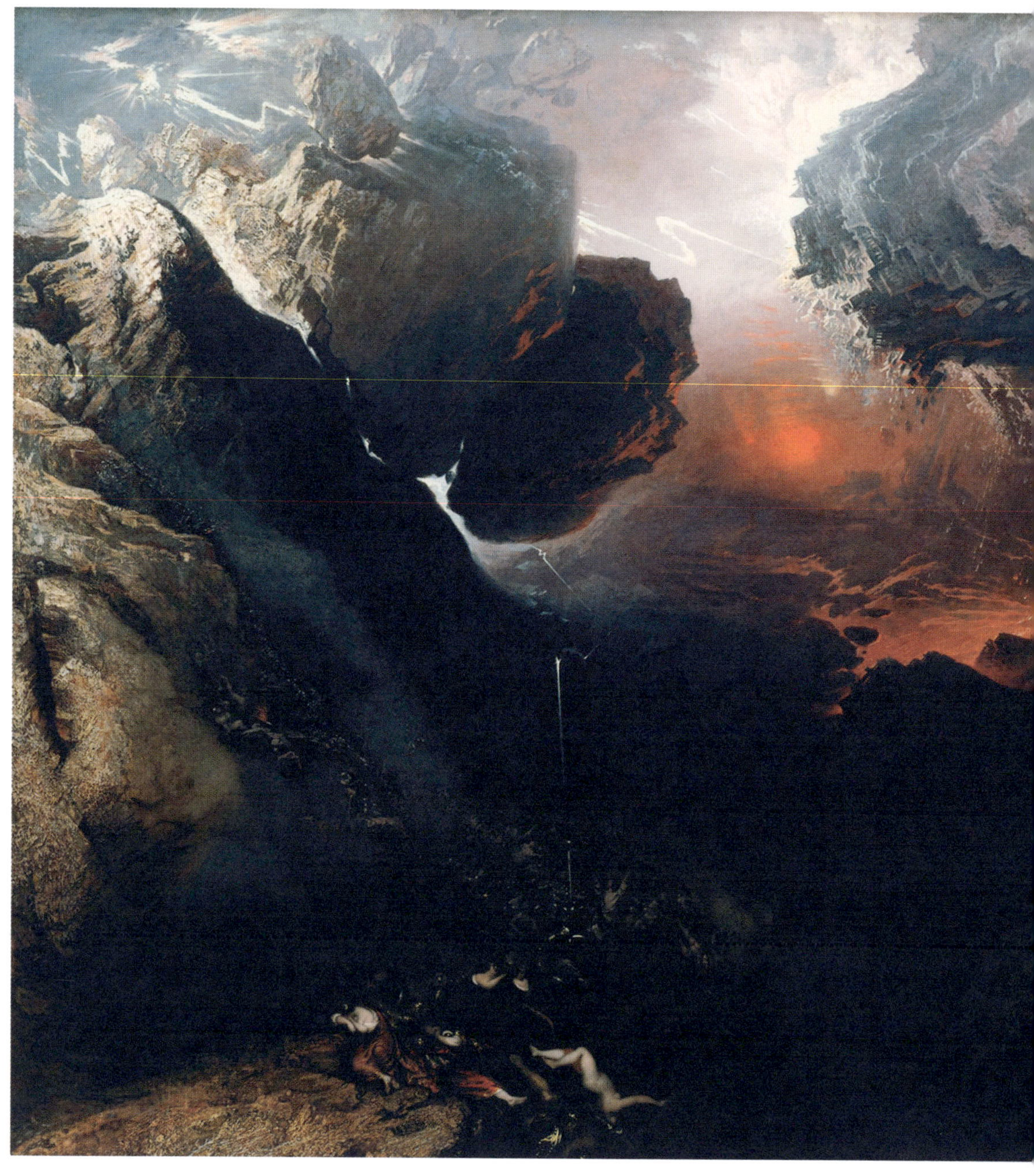

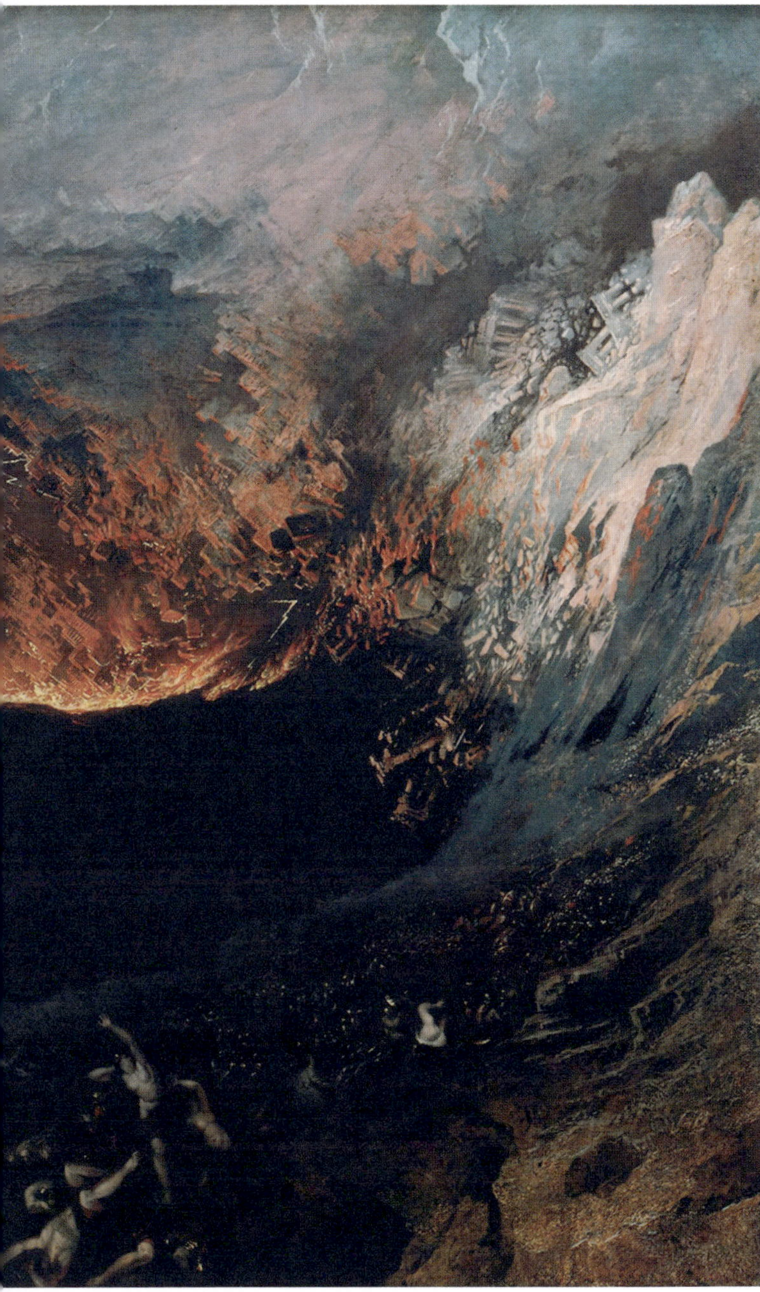

Left: The Great Day of His Wrath, John Martin, 1851–3, oil on canvas.

John Martin (1789-1854) was an English Romantic painter celebrated for his melodramatic paintings of religious subjects and fantastic compositions, imposing landscapes, exploding with pyrotechnic effects and supernatural intervention. This is the third picture in Martin's great triptych, known as the Judgement Series. Along with the other two vast panels, *The Last Judgement* and *The Plains of Heaven*, it was inspired by St John the Divine's fantastic account of the Last Judgement given in Revelation, the last book of the New Testament. Martin's aim in producing this series was highly Romantic: to express the sublime, apocalyptic force of nature and the helplessness of man to combat God's will. A blood-red glow casts an eerie light over the scene. The mountains are transformed into rolling waves of solid rock, crushing any buildings that lie in their wake. Lightning splits the giant boulders which crash towards the dark abyss, and groups of helpless figures tumble inexorably towards oblivion.

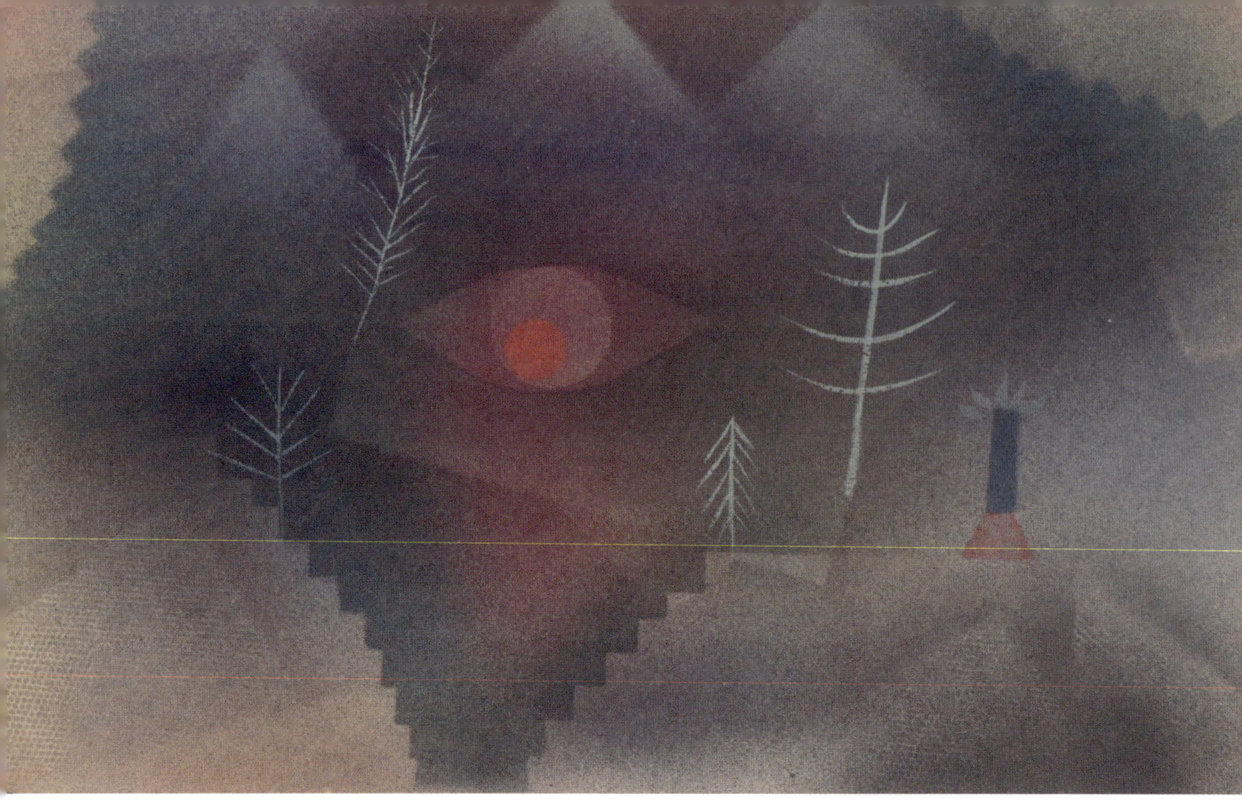

Above: Glance of a Landscape, Paul Klee, 1926, watercolour, sprayed through stencils and brushed, on paper, mounted on board.

Paul Klee (1879–1940) was born in Münchenbuchsee, Switzerland, and is considered both a German and a Swiss painter. His prolific body of work and singular style is associated with numerous groundbreaking twentieth-century movements, from German Expressionism to Dada – though it doesn't easily fit into any single category, with its movement, spontaneity and elements of magic. Are those trees or mystical hieroglyphs glimpsed through the haze of this foggy mountain landscape? And are we taking in the sights, or does that giant floating eye have us in its sights? These enigmas epitomize Klee's signature approach to artmaking.

Right: Winter Landscape, Sesshū Tōyō, c. 1470, ink on paper.

Generally regarded as Japan's most influential master of ink painting, Zen Buddhist monk Sesshū Tōyō (1420–1506) practised the art of sumi-e – literally, 'painting in Chinese ink' – a style that had a great influence on all later Japanese painting and remained in high demand for centuries after his death at the beginning of the sixteenth century. The ink, made by burning pine twigs, collecting the soot and mixing it with resin, is made into a flat stick, which is then rubbed in a small pool of water in an inkstone. By mixing in more or less water, the artist arrives at the desired value. This sparse technique seems entirely appropriate for rendering this icy mountain ridge amid a bleak, brittle winter landscape.

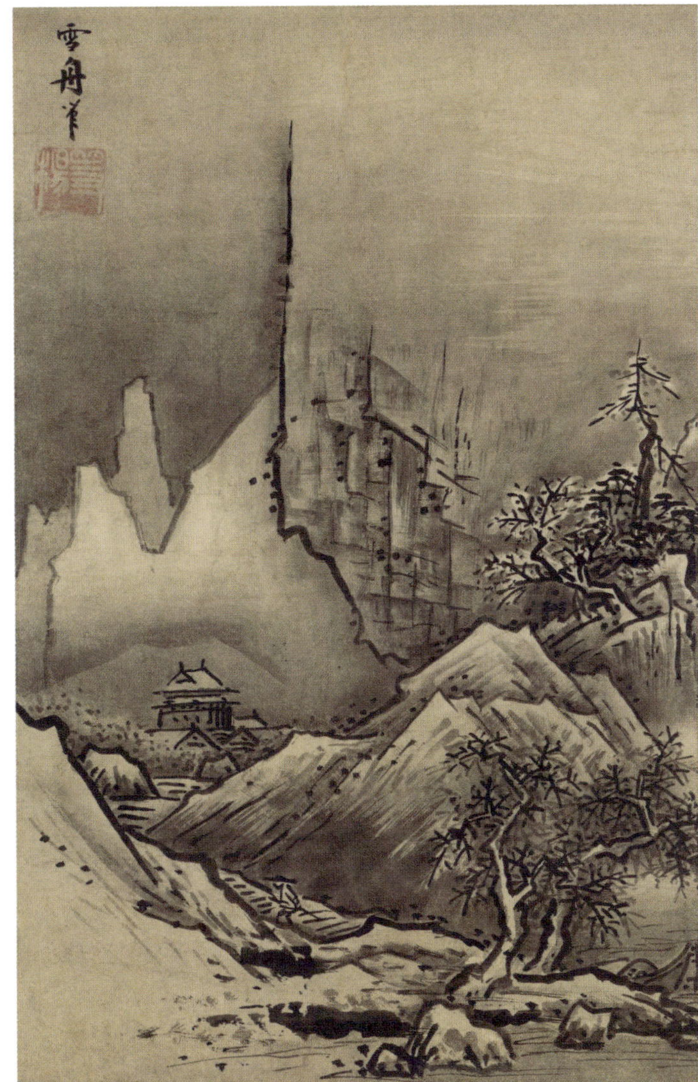

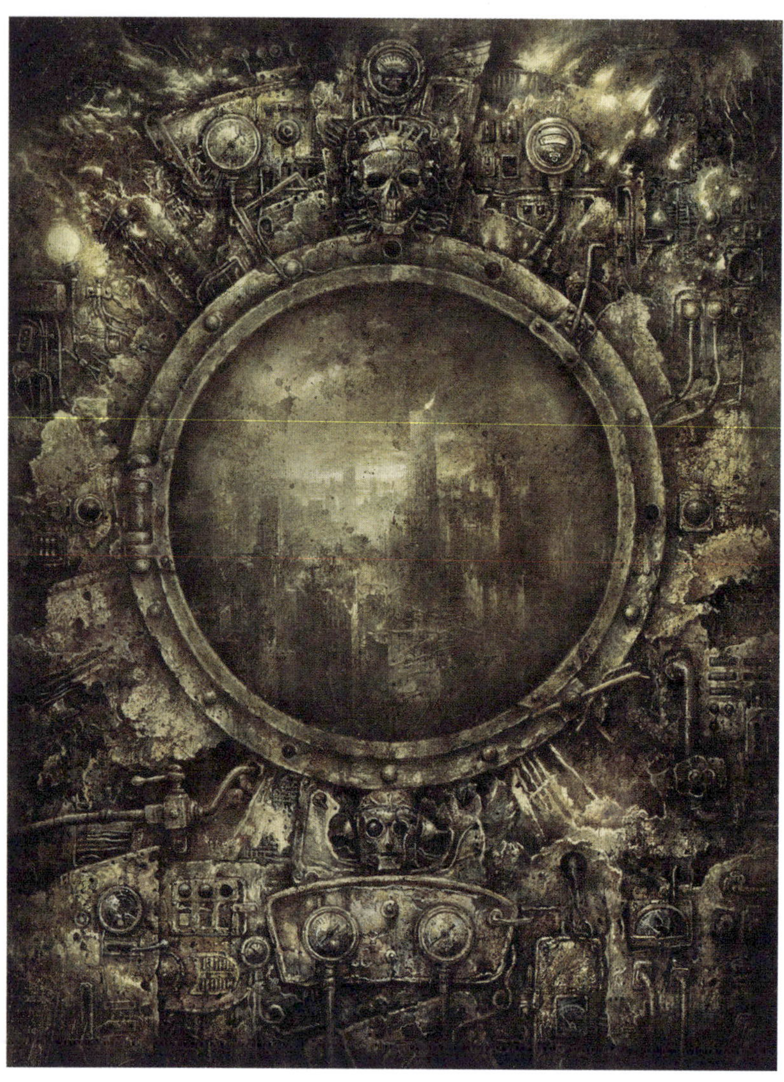

Above: Post Apocalypse Mirror, Yaroslav Gerzhedovich, 2017, acrylic on paper.

The paintings of Russian artist Yaroslav Gerzhedovich (b. 1970) are gloomy, often monochrome and surreal creations, featuring barren fields, ancient structures and fantastical compositions, and brimming with mystical intrigue. Inspired by the European masters from the fourteenth to the seventeenth centuries, Gerzhedovich's transfixing work reads like an escape from reality to a detailed and dark world of weird fiction, and is created on paper with acrylic, pencil, ink and occasional digital manipulation.

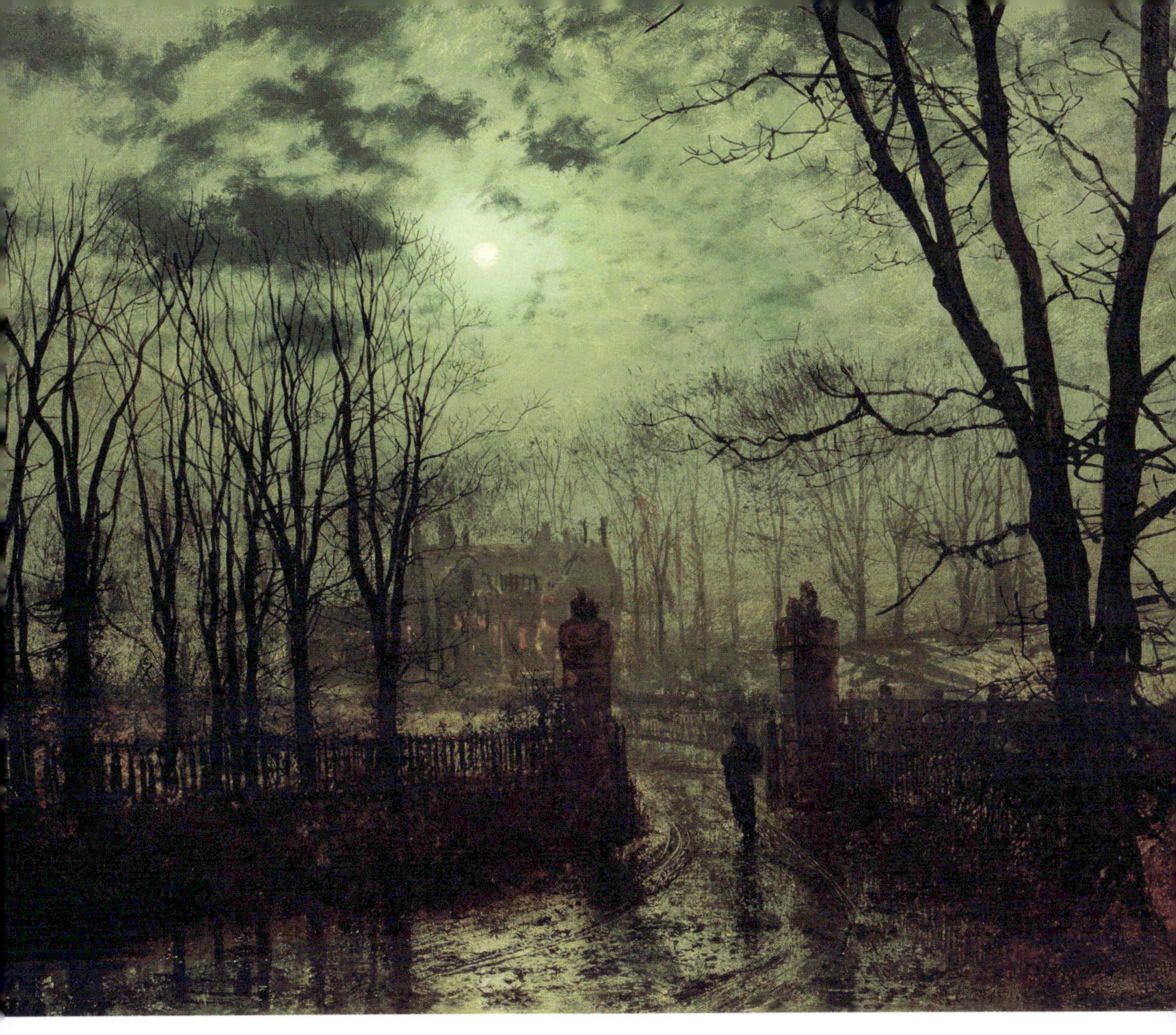

Above: At the Park Gate, John Atkinson Grimshaw, 1878, oil on canvas.

Best known for his introspective nocturnal scenes of misty, gaslit urban landscapes, John Atkinson Grimshaw (1836–93) is today thought of as one of the great English painters of the Victorian era, as well as one of the best and most accomplished nightscape and townscape artists of all time. Grimshaw's love of realism stemmed from a passion for photography – a novel medium at the time that struck people with excitement, disbelief or a mixture of both – and which would eventually lend itself to his creative process from the mid-1860s until the end of the decade when he decided to compose by imagination and observation alone. *At the Park Gate* is one of Grimshaw's many night-time scenes where he focuses on the light created by the moon.

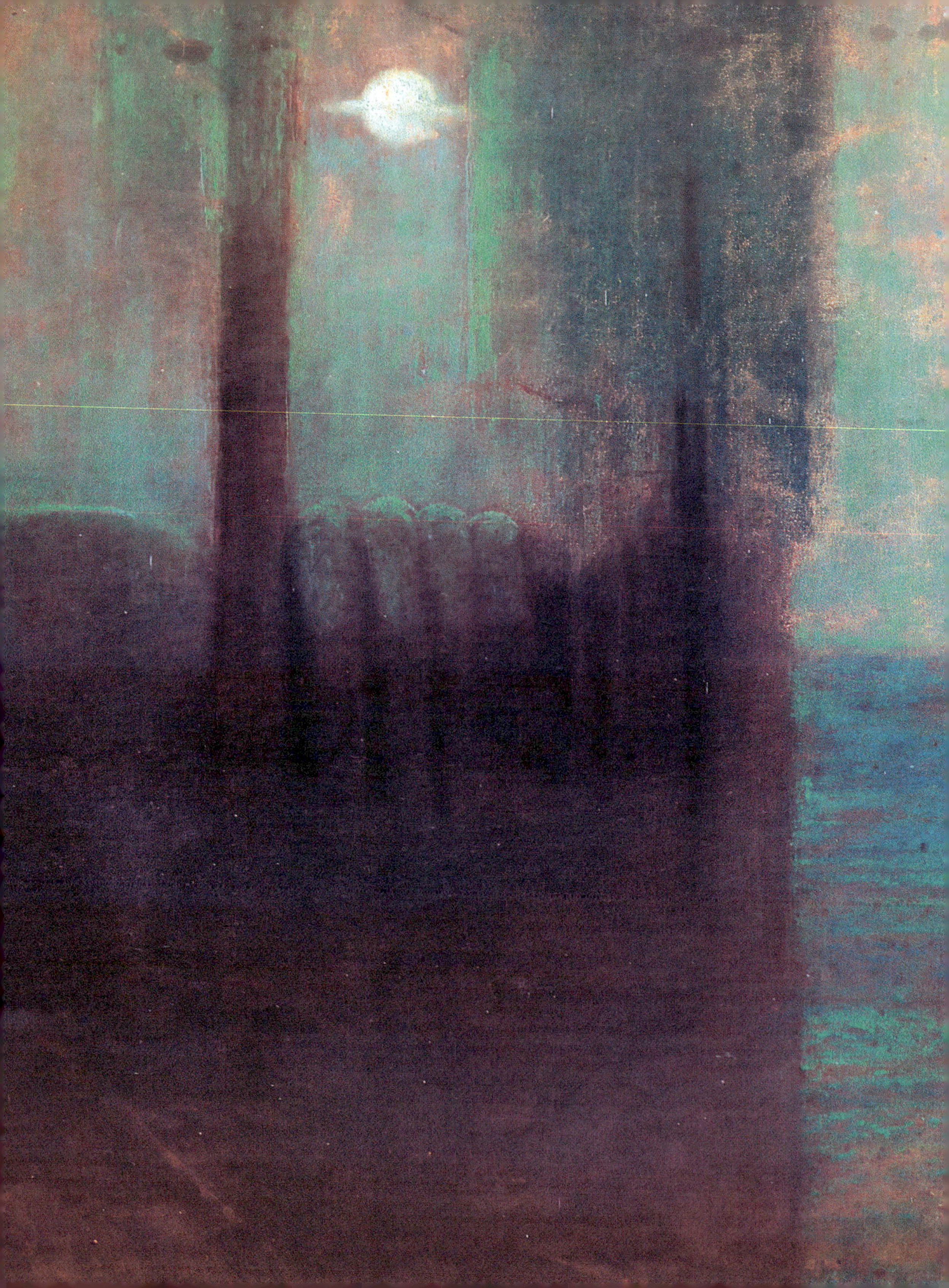

Right: Hades Grove, Natalia Smirnova, 2013, tempera on cardboard.

A qualified art-restorer, contemporary artist Natalia Smirnova brings that passion for antiquities and mysteries of the past to her esoteric art practice. Her ghostly enchantments and otherworldly visions glimmer from monochrome or sepia-toned shadows, conjuring a world of fairy tales and dreams and fabled tales in illuminated manuscripts, awash in the language of allegory and arcane symbolism.

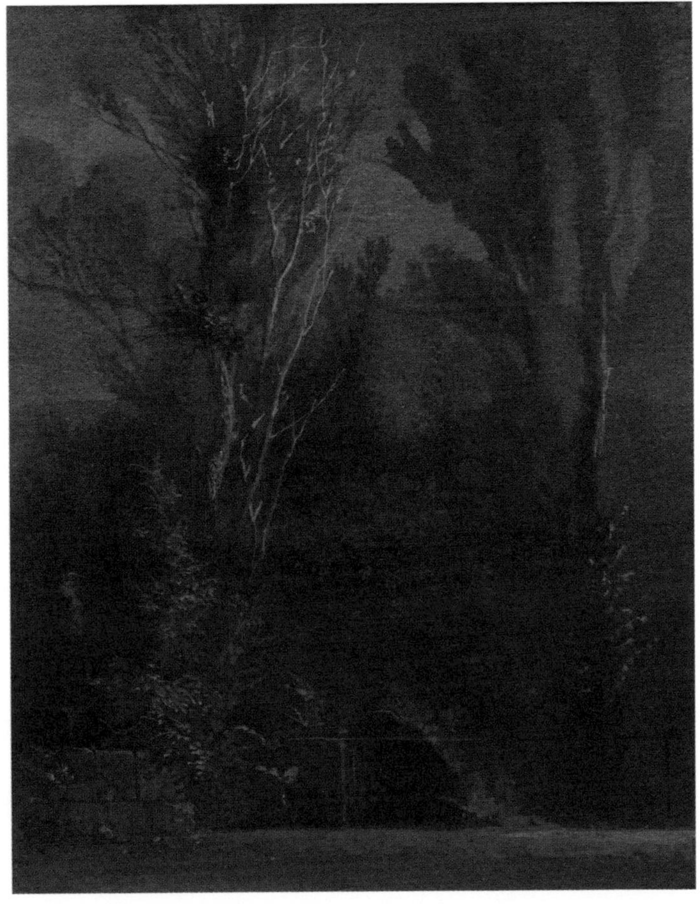

Opposite: Night, Mikalojus Konstantinas Čiurlionis, 1904, oil on canvas.

Lithuanian artist and composer Mikalojus Konstantinas Čiurlionis (1875–1911) was an intriguing figure in the history of European arts. Though he started as a musician finishing two musical conservatories (in Warsaw and Leipzig), he is better known for his otherworldly paintings - and one of the interesting aspects of these creations was that he incorporated musical theory into his artworks. The artist is noted as having said that he enjoyed painting with pastels as it reminds him of playing an instrument - how it becomes alive under the fingers. And he treated his paintings as such - as live beings that are awakened by his fingers. Almost like a still frame from a moving picture, how would *Night*, awash in a jewelled veil of nocturnal hues, sound? Low and sonorous, perhaps, with an almost imperceptible but deeply unsettling swoop of theremin sounds as the moon appears in the sky.

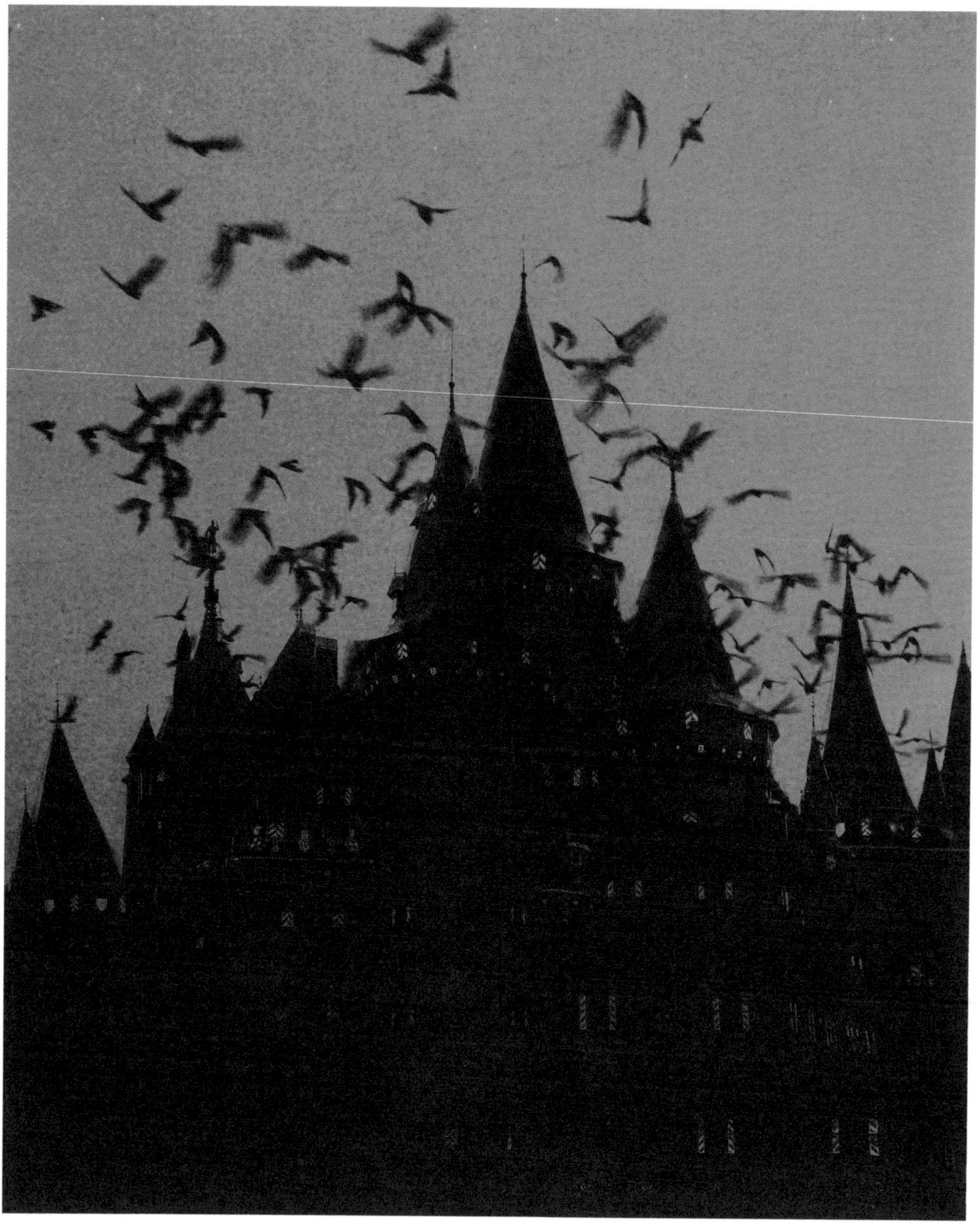

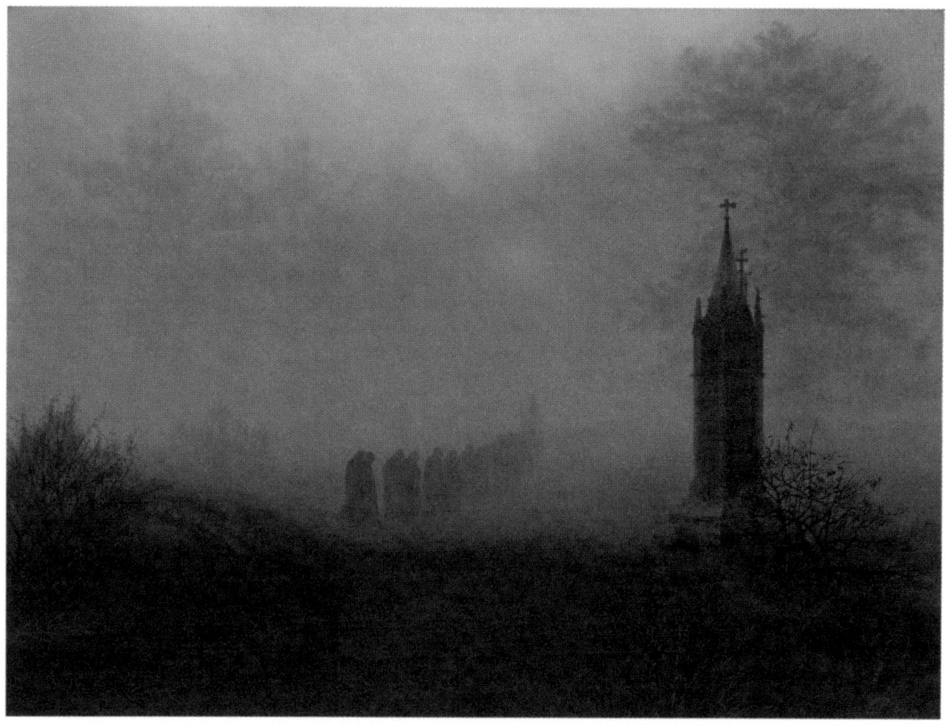

Opposite: When Night Comes, Nona Limmen, 2019, digital photography.

Nona Limmen is based in Amsterdam, but her photos grant us visions of a vast, mysterious dream world obscurely bordering our own. Wrought of shadows and secrets, this enigmatic kingdom with towering cliffs, dark caves, looming edifices and veiled inhabitants is revealed in snapshots of menace, mystery and magic. The analogue approach to photography adds another layer of mystique: the grain, multifaceted lenses and blurs gives you the sense that you're fortunate to receive glimpses of a place both magical and rare, somewhere no one has ever seen before.

Above: Procession im Nebel, Ernst Ferdinand Oehme, 1828, oil on panel.

Ernst Ferdinand Oehme (1797–1855) was a German Romantic painter trained at the Dresden Academy of Fine Arts who specialized in moody landscapes. Oehme studied with the highly regarded Danish painter Johan Christian Dahl, and through him met Caspar David Friedrich. The influence of both painters is evident in Oehme's sombre tones and 'gothic' settings; his most famous oil painting, the subtle yet darkly atmospheric *Procession im Nebel,* reveals a lonely, dreamlike reverie wherein shadowy cloaked figures disappear into fog-shrouded forest. Later in his career, Oehme shifted his focus from the symbolism and emotional content of his early landscapes to more naturalistic, unsentimental subjects.

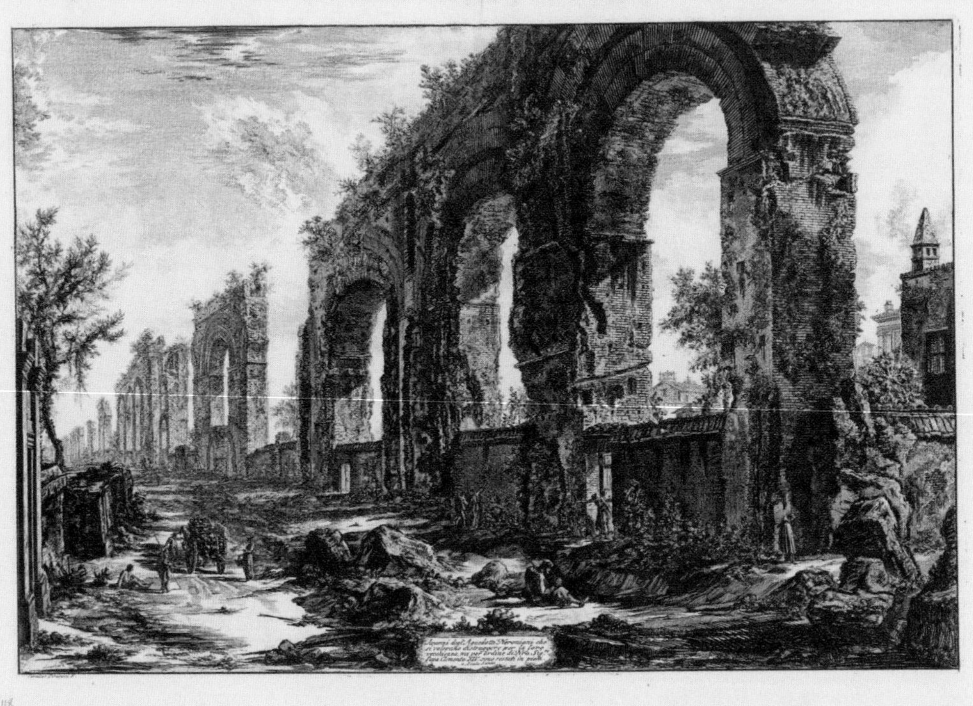

Above: Remains of the Aqueduct of Nero, Giovanni Battista Piranesi, c. 1760–78, etching.

Italian artist, designer, architect and theorist Giovanni Battista Piranesi (1720–78) was fascinated by the ancient architecture of Rome. Sometimes called 'Rembrandt of the ruins', Piranesi created etchings that employed dramatic angles, flights of spatial fancy and bold lighting effects to imbue crumbling structures with vitality and romance. 'I need to produce great ideas, and I believe that if I were commissioned to design a new universe, I would be mad enough to undertake it.' This statement, reported by one of his early biographers, in many ways sums up the man whose dreams of antiquity so often surpassed the reality of existing buildings; from his earliest etchings of architectural fantasies to the fanciful restorations of ancient remains that he produced at the end of his career.

Opposite: Gothic Church Ruins, Carl Blechen, 1826, oil on canvas.

German landscape painter Carl Blechen (1798–1840), without receiving any formal training, was appointed as a painting professor at Berlin's Academy of Arts – an unusual accomplishment for an academy outsider. As was distinctive of the Romantic movement, Blechen painted with an appreciation for the glories of nature, capturing its awe-inspiring beauty and divine essence, bringing both artist and viewer closer to God. Unfortunately, Blechen suffered from frequent bouts of depression and resulting stays in the hospital; he died aged forty-two.

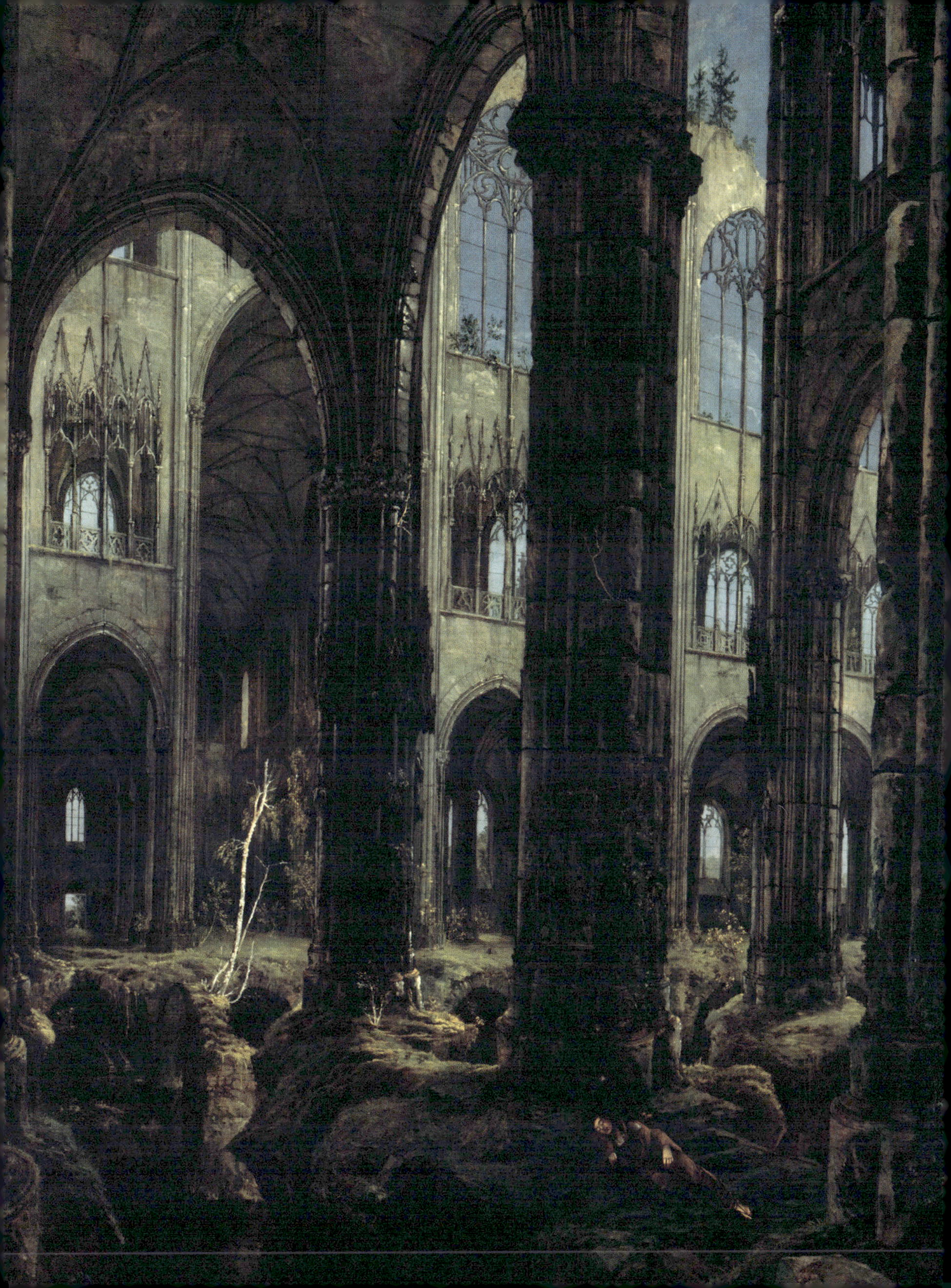

PART FOUR

—

Visions from Beyond

‘. . . there is something ghostly in all great art, whether of literature, music, sculpture, or architecture. It touches something within us that relates to infinity.’

– LAFCADIO HEARN

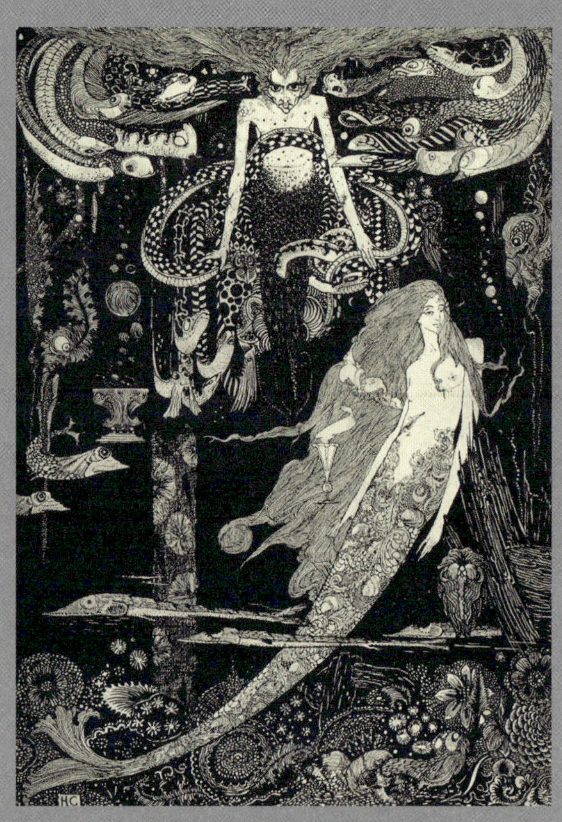

It seems as though there's always someone trying to convince us that we didn't see what we thought we saw, isn't there? That there is in fact some sort of 'rational explanation' for that otherworldly encounter, that antique cursed object or that elusive monster we glimpsed in the shadows.

In this age of science, the idea of the restless dead, the concept of magical happenstance or sometimes even just the thought of praying to whatever god we believe in . . . well, we've been led to believe it's the stuff of myth and story time. Fictional entertainment, for cheap thrills. But for many people the world over – and not even that long ago – these were real entities and experiences, that offered solace or inspiration, or of course elicited the expected and utterly genuine fright. In the following chapters, we will look beyond our own terrestrial reckonings into more nebulous worlds to discover how visual artists explore these realms of the unseen.

Folklore, mythology, mysticism and the occult, the paranormal and supernatural – while science and technology can certainly augment and improve our perception and understandings of how the world works, the bigger questions and perpetual wonderings whether we are alone in the universe, what is out there and what is our place in all of it, will always remain, no matter what new technologies are dreamed up or rigorous scientific studies are proving or disproving. It's all about what we believe – and there is a distinctly human desire to believe in something beyond ourselves, a timeless desire reflected in a myriad of works wrought by the hand of artists attempting to illuminate these beliefs across the centuries.

Depending on many of our religious beliefs – or lack thereof – we could claim a vast swathe of the art we are familiar with has been focused on supernatural concerns. Many of these works, after all, depict supposedly superpowered beings who likely may not even exist, performing acts that are rationally not possible. But for all the strangeness or sublimity of these canvases, many of these creators didn't consider these subjects paranormal – it was just the natural order of how the world worked. Or at least how these artists believed that it worked. So, we'll have to agree that 'supernatural' is a slippery and culturally specific term. For you, demons and witches, fantastical creatures and monstrous ghosts may constitute a horrific fear and certainly nothing you'd ever expect to encounter in waking life. But for someone

Opposite: 'I know what you want' said the sea witch, illustration for 'The Little Mermaid' from *Fairy Tales* by Hans Christian Andersen (1835), Harry Clarke, c. 1910, black and white photograph of engraving.

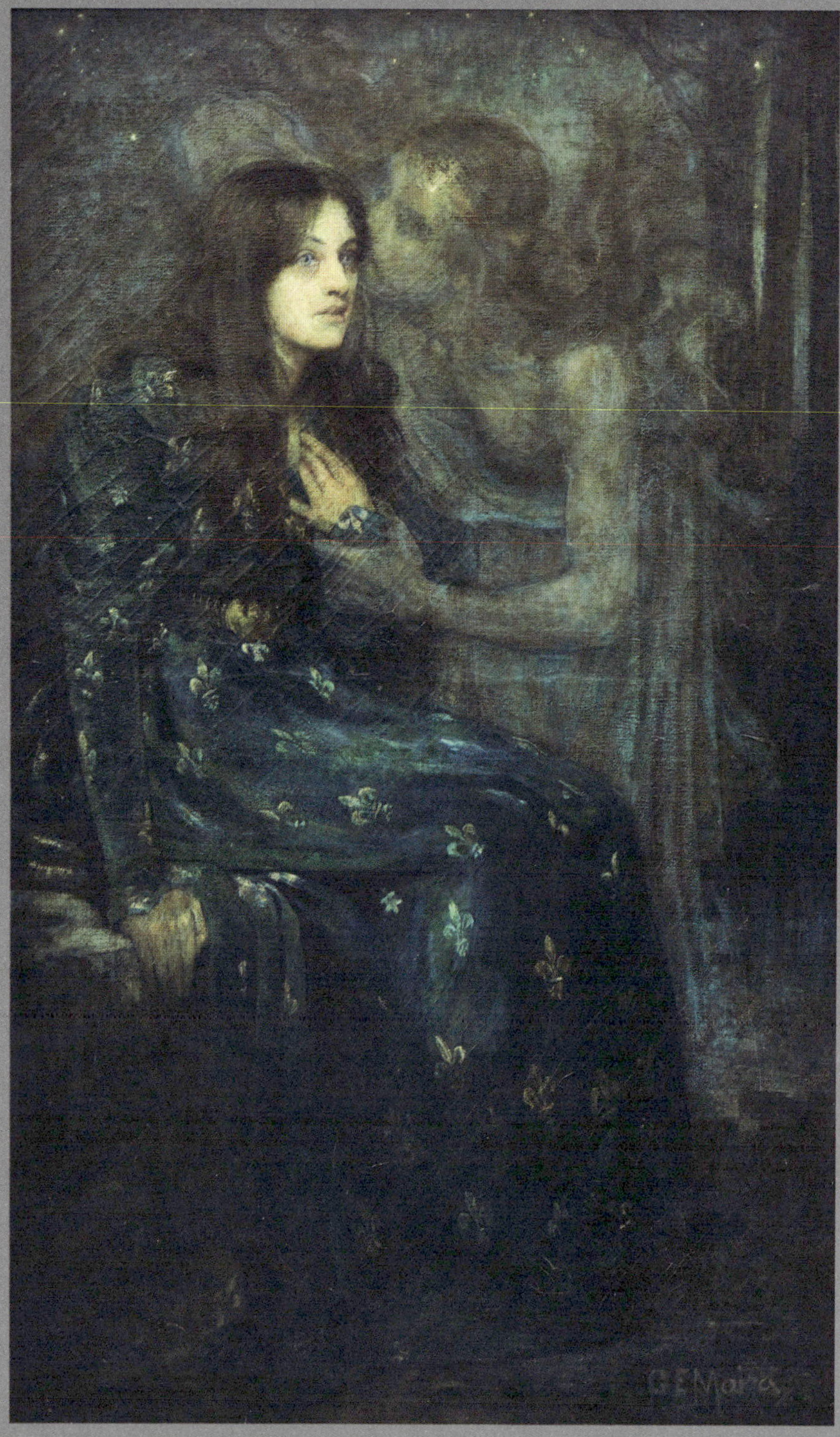
G E Maris

'It is an ill thing to meet a man you thought dead in the woodland at dusk.'

– ROBERT E. HOWARD

else, seeing a fairy or a goblin, or nocturnally wandering spirit, might be par for the course. Just another day that ends in Y. When we observe these apparitions and manifestations in art, it might be an interesting exercise to see if we can sense a spirit of pragmatism in the brushstroke, or did the artist infuse the work with a mood of horror and revulsion? Or . . . is that just what you see because that's what you believe?

Whether your faith lends to a sureness regarding the uncanny and unexplained; whether you see ghosts as messengers of guidance and comfort; or if you are merely intrigued with artwork that rings with all things weird and eerie, these artworks and visions from beyond remain vital and relevant reminders. They paradoxically teach us about the very real day-to-day world that we live in, both in terms of past and present; they reveal the darkness and wonder in their own, shadowy psyches; and they demonstrate the gaps in our understanding of just about everything, and encourage us to keep asking those big, deep questions.

Opposite: The Silent Voice, Gerald Moira, 1892, oil on canvas.

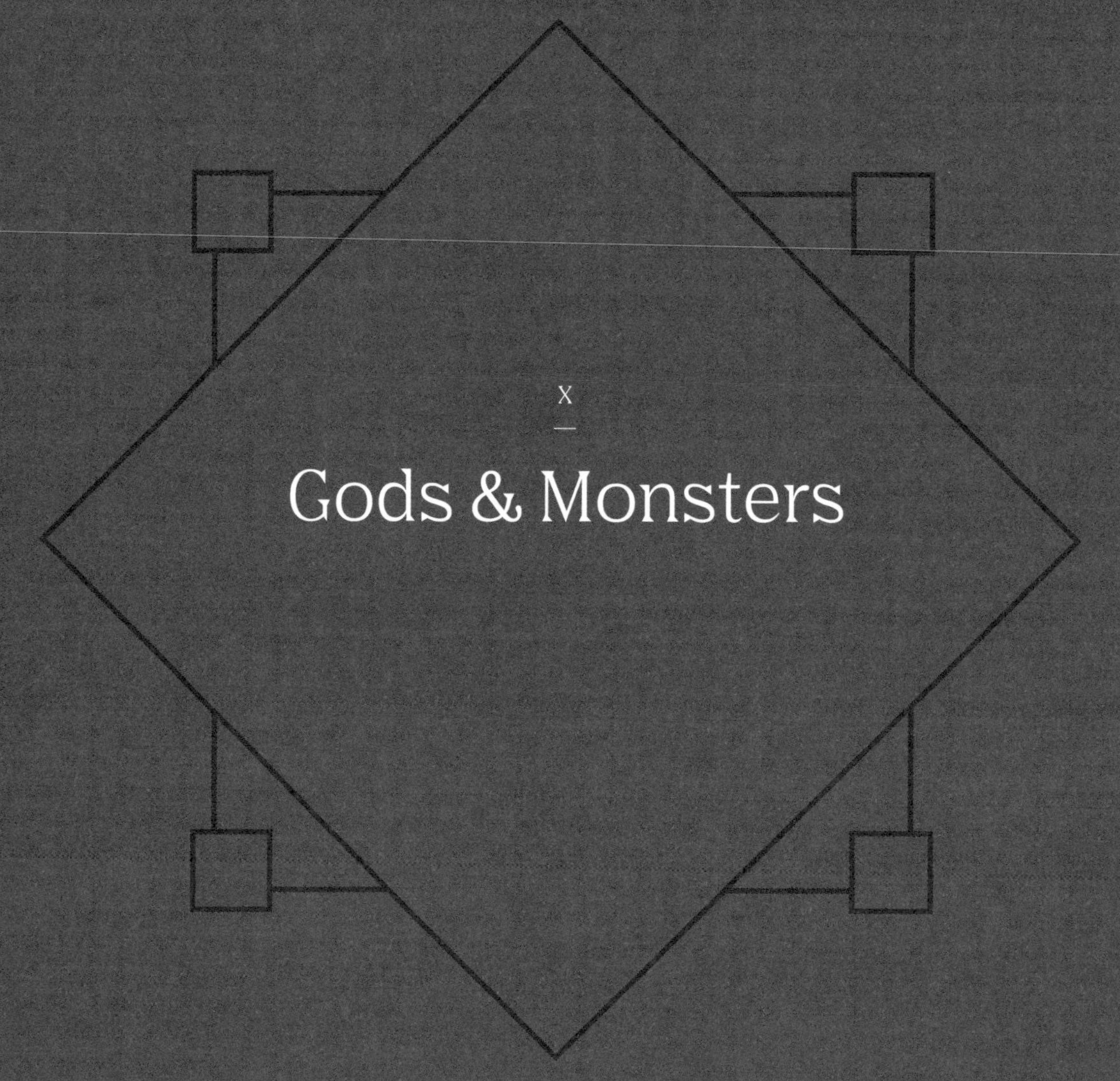

X

Gods & Monsters

'As flies to wanton boys are we to the gods.
They kill us for their sport.'

–GLOUCESTER, *KING LEAR*

If the gods, demi-gods and other members of divine hierarchies and religious mythologies were people like you and me, if they walked among us, do you think they'd really be doing anyone any favours? No, I think they're the sort to break their competitor's kneecaps; the avenging angel who exacts retribution on their sleeping spouse; or the trickster who attempts to enlist their old university pals on multilevel marketing pyramid schemes. As we hear so often on celebrity reality shows they are 'not here to make friends'. No, these divine beings act on mercurial personal whims, they don't care about morality and are no better than we are.

Of course, it's always the worst of these dastardly, despicable tales that leaves the most lasting impression on us. We, being the nosy humans we are, always insatiably sniff the darkness of these myths for dirt and drama, eternally hungry to gobble them up. And, unsurprisingly, the naughty stories of mythical and religious deities – sometimes sublime, sometimes shocking – have long inspired artists.

Artistic explorations of the gods' exploits, even in those mythic tales where atrocious, appalling things happen, can sometimes help us to think about justice, grief, love and the heroic. Gods, artists, the regular person on the street, nobody is just one thing – light or dark, good or evil – and once examined, such works can offer a window into creativity, imagination and beauty. Indeed, badly behaving gods and demi-gods are at times depicted as brave, intelligent and kindly disposed towards humanity. At other times they are shown to be spiteful, vengeful and utterly morally corrupt. This dichotomy has inspired artists and titillated viewers for centuries. From the petrifying gaze of the Gorgon and the bloodthirsty Minotaur to the carnal temptations of the Prince of Darkness – these sacred, sublime and wholly terrifying encounters with dazzling divinities have been compellingly retold in every type of visual art, from ancient painting and sculpture, to installation and video art today.

Peter Paul Rubens (1577–1640) found the pain and suffering in classical mythology a constant source of inspiration throughout his career. Pre-Raphaelite artists such as John William Waterhouse and Edward Burne-Jones mined classical mythology and religion for the theme and allegories which they portrayed through their nuanced lenses, brimming with luscious colours and meticulous details. Leading light of the Symbolist movement,

Gustave Moreau channelled mythological iconography as well as the Old Testament in works of exquisite, emotive drama. Contemporary artists continue to interpret the plethora of the problematic deities and their mythic misdeeds, sometimes allegorically, sometimes through the lens of psychology, and often re-envision them entirely, in settings that pay homage to the original stories while reflecting modern narratives.

What does any of this mean today, in an era where vast swathes of humanity revere the concrete evidence of science in place of the sacred and profane mysteries of the gods? In a world that feels like it is constantly, apocalyptically burning down around us, we are beset at every turn by crises of a political, social and environmental nature. Our emotional and spiritual wellbeing tested to its limits on a daily basis, we sometimes feel we are being ripped apart at the seams. So many of these issues are deeply systemic and it will take a massive amount of breaking down to affect any real change. Even with all our logic and reason we still think of such things as 'Sisyphean tasks', or something that will take a 'Herculean effort'.

Below: Satan, Sin and Death (A Scene from Milton's *Paradise Lost*), William Hogarth, c. 1735–40, oil on canvas.

Best known for his series paintings of 'modern moral subjects', of which he sold engravings on subscription, William Hogarth (1697-1764) was a painter, printmaker, pictorial satirist, social critic and editorial cartoonist. His engravings were so plagiarized that he lobbied for the Copyright Act of 1735 as protection for writers and artists. During the 1730s Hogarth also developed into an original painter of life-sized portraits and created the first of several history paintings in the grand manner. Hogarth's unfinished oil sketch is a dramatic illustration to John Milton's epic poem, *Paradise Lost*; Satan, on the left, confronts Death who bars his way from hell to earth. Between them is Sin, who apparently can't mind her own business.

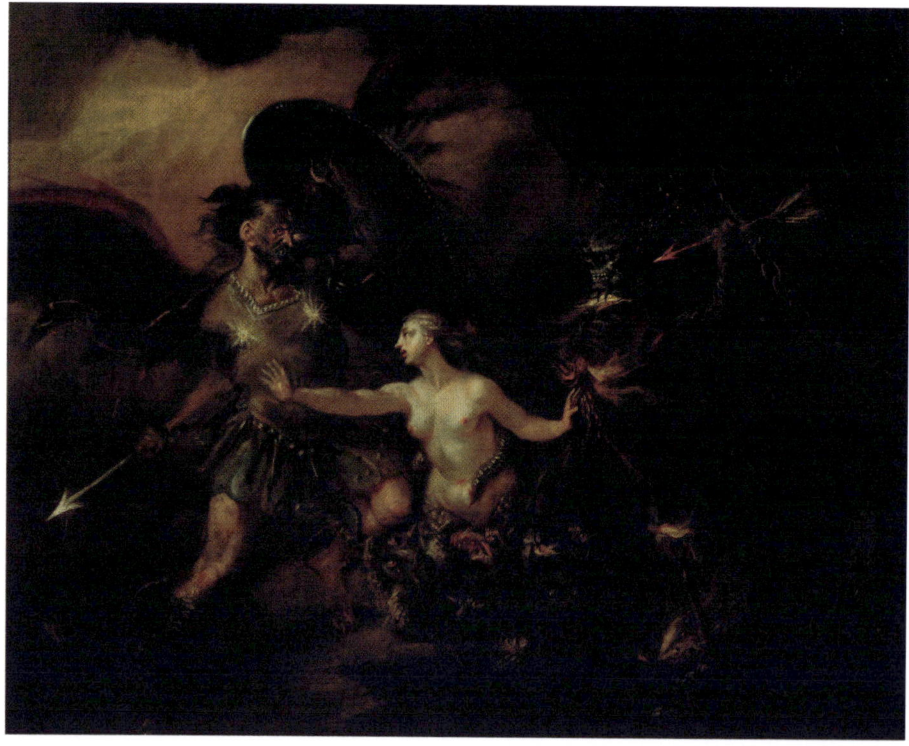

Right: Jupiter and Semele, Gustave Moreau, 1894–95, oil on canvas.

Renowned for the mystical and enigmatic quality of his paintings of biblical and mythological subjects and lensed through his own unusual interpretations, Gustave Moreau (1826-98) has created the massively stunning but thoroughly overwhelming *Jupiter and Semele* which will stop you in your tracks and hold you utterly transfixed. It portrays the classical myth of the mortal woman Semele, mother of the god Dionysus, and her lover Jupiter, the king of the gods. Semele, on some bad advice from the goddess Juno, Jupiter's wife, asked her lover to appear before her in all his divine splendour. Jupiter obliged but, in so doing, brought about her violent death by his divine thunder and lightning. It's easy to get lost in the exquisite beauty of the imagery, but it's wise to remember that there are some aspects of the world best left unrevealed.

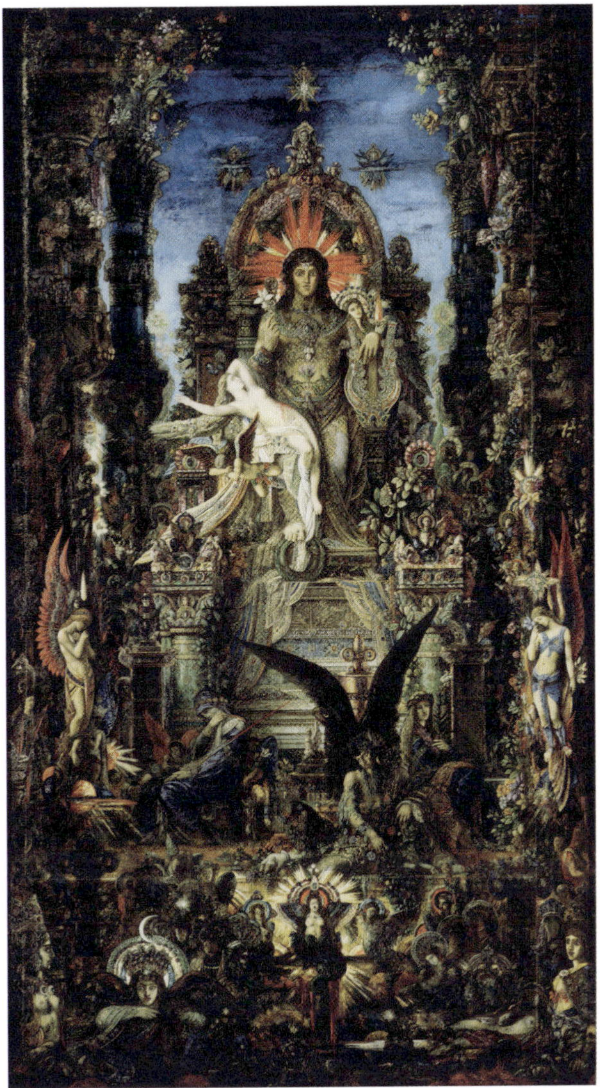

Is it possible that we need these gods and their narratives of disruption and havoc now more than ever? Do we rely on these agents of death and rebirth, destruction and creation, commotion and confusion, and total, glorious chaos? After all, are not all these challenging energies necessary for growth? When darkness consumes us, perhaps we must be prepared to face, embrace, and devour it – and I can't wait to see the art arising from *that* story.

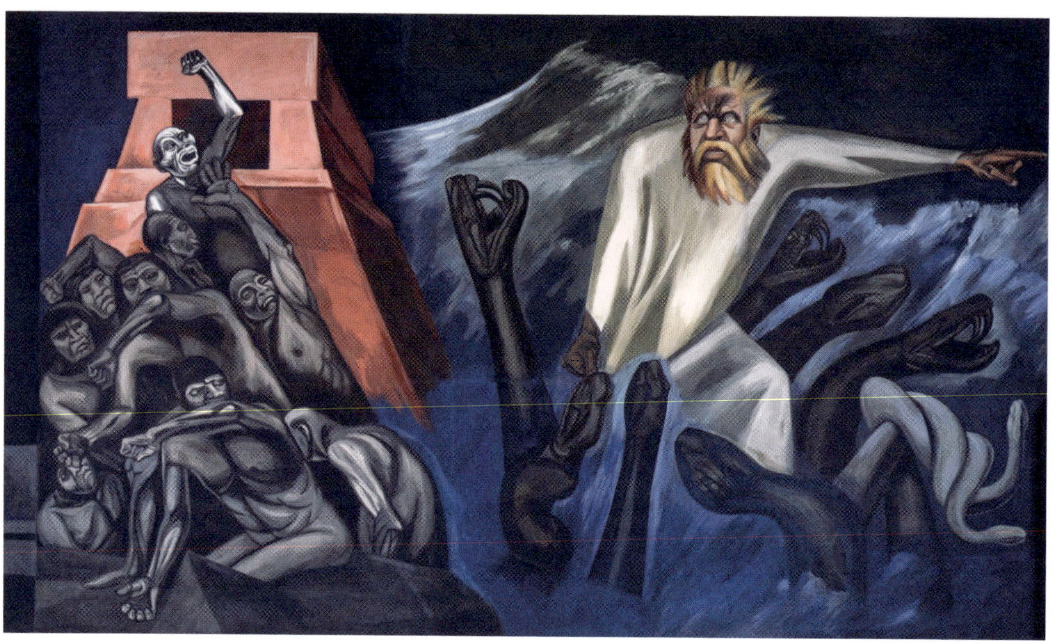

Above: 'Departure of Quetzalcoatl', from *The Epic of American Civilization*, José Clemente Orozco, 1932–34, mural.

José Clemente Orozco (1883–1949) was a painter who helped lead the revival of Mexican mural painting in the 1920s. Orozco's complex and often tragic works were powerful expressions of political revolt, often depicting subjects related to political and historical events and allegories of the ongoing human struggle for freedom and justice. In the autumn of 1949, Orozco completed his last fresco, and he died in his sleep of heart failure soon after. Throughout the 1960s and 70s, he was hailed as a master of the human condition. As Orozco himself insisted, 'Painting . . . it persuades the heart.'

Opposite: The Blind Queen, Chet Zar, 2013, oil on canvas.

Contemporary artist Chet Zar (b. 1967) has an interest in the darker side of art and all things macabre and strange, which began early in life. These fascinations fostered a deep connection to horror movies, where he could relate to the feelings of fear, anxiety and isolation being conveyed through the fearsome stories and gruesome medium. Challenging the assumption that darkness is a negative outlet, the artist does not shy away from these personal and societal fears, but rather explores the darker recesses of human consciousness, in his unsettling, yet empathetic oil paintings of monsters that one might think are an invitation to connect with their 'shadow sides'. While that is partially true, the artist has also noted that he just plain likes to paint monsters, that they are more fun and satisfying to create. 'I also like to play the game of creating something that is traditionally considered "ugly" or "dark" and making a beautiful painting out of it. I like the dichotomy.'

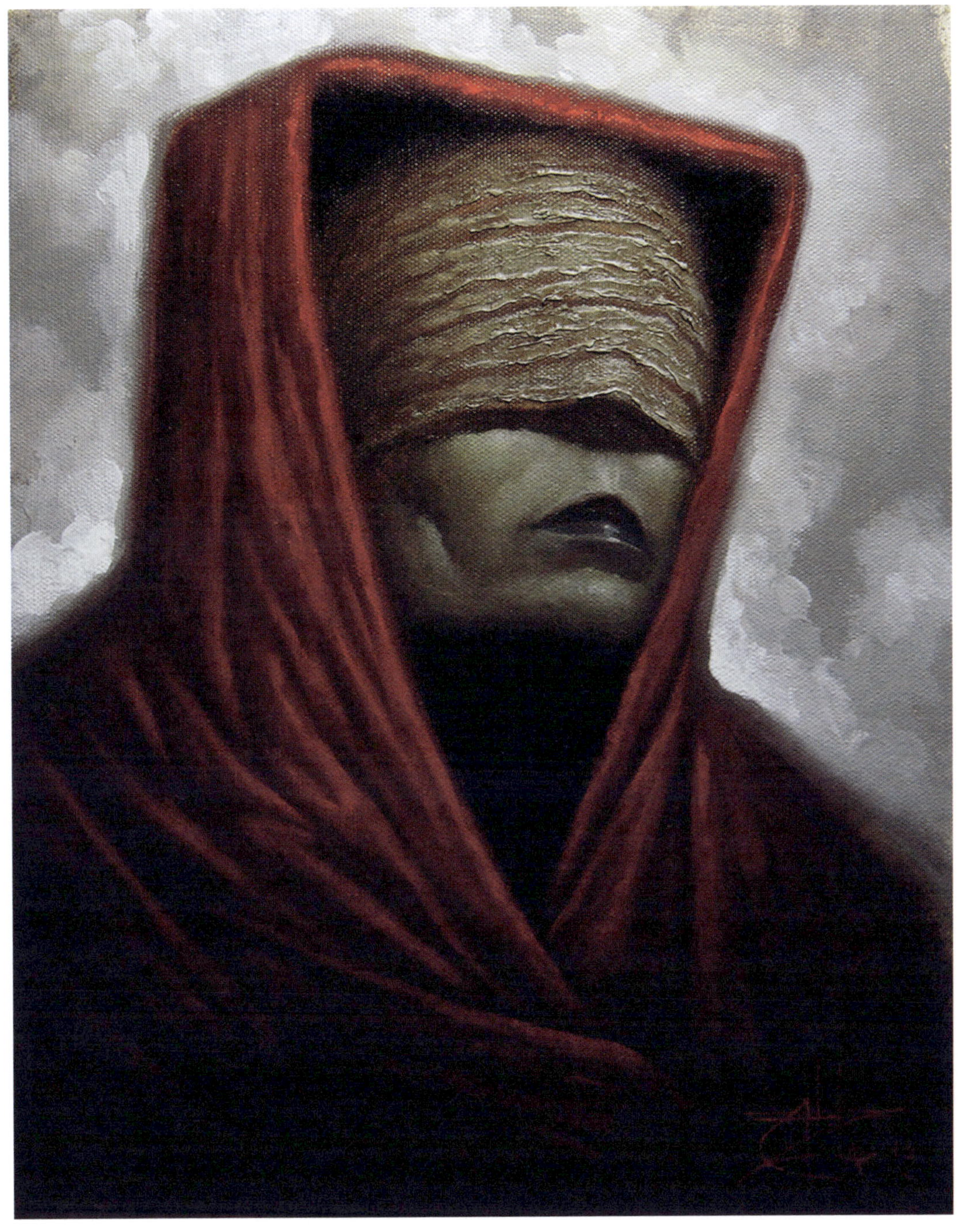

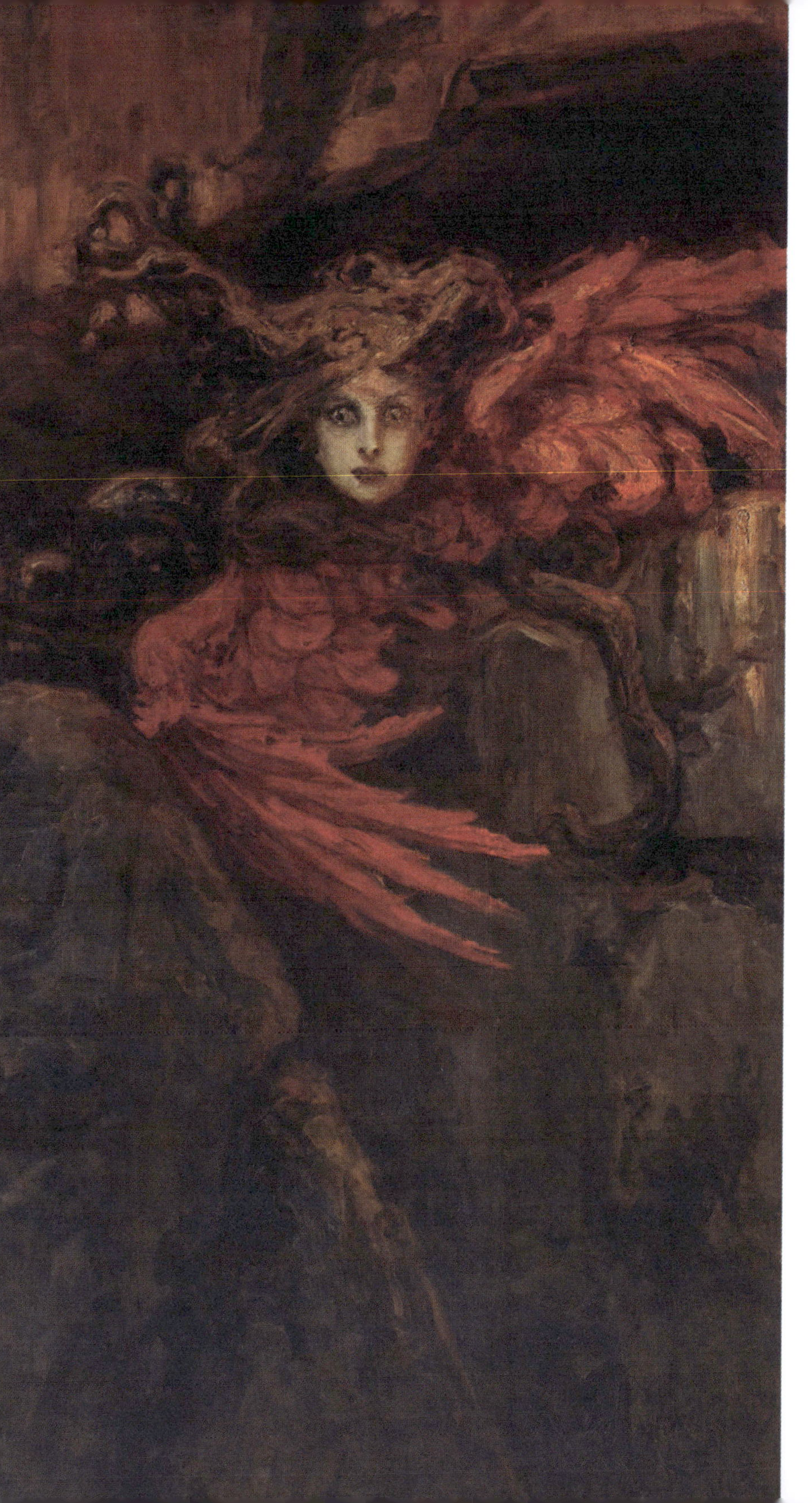

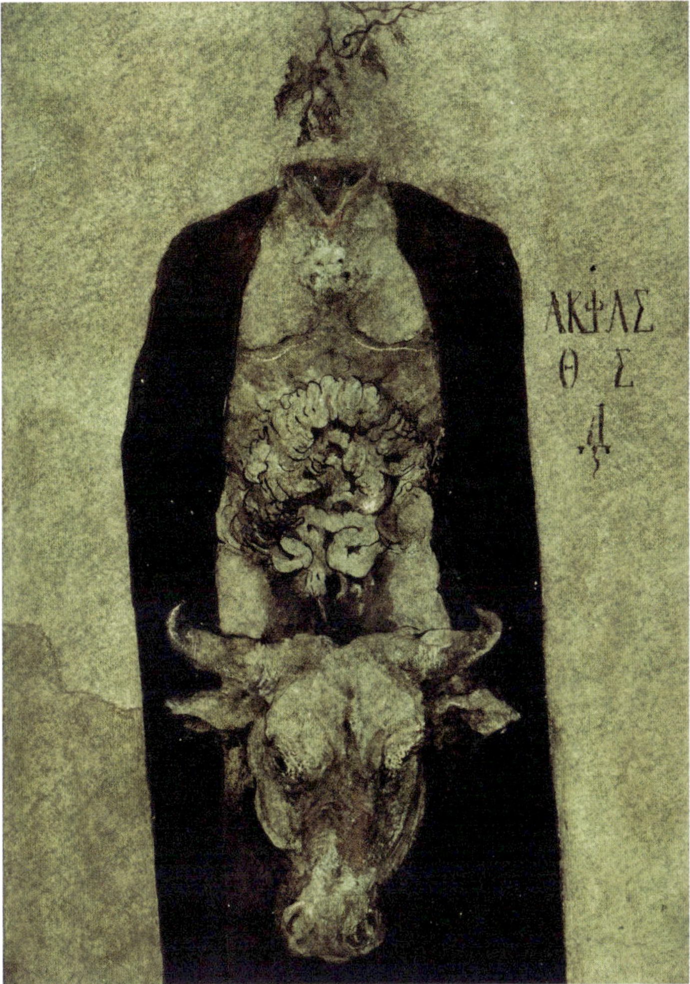

Left: Study for Entrance to the Labyrinth, Denis Forkas Kostromitin, 2014, ink on paper.

The cryptic paintings and drawings of Russian artist Denis Forkas Kostromitin (b. 1977) live in the liminal spaces, the shadowy pathways outside of time, the leap before the infernal plummet . . . or the flight to the stars. Drawing on mythology, poetry and philosophy, Forkas believes '. . . there's no beauty without mystery and there's no mystery without threat'. In the maze of the labyrinth, it is said that you do not lose yourself – you find yourself. From the glooms of the labyrinth emerges the minotaur, a strange hybrid creature, a twin form of bull and man; in Forkas's version we get the sense that we are observing this figure in the moments before divine revelation, a mystical threshold imbued with potent symbolism and sacred mystery.

Opposite: Medusa, Vasily (Wilhelm) Alexandrovich Kotarbinsky, 1903, oil on canvas.

Vasily Alexandrovich (Wilhelm) Kotarbiński (1849–1921), a Polish Symbolist painter of historical and fantastical subjects, was not the first artist to depict the fierce image of Medusa on the canvas, nor will he be the last. An avatar of feminist rage and empowerment, Medusa is a nuanced and complex character and an instantly recognizable figure from ancient Greek art. She represents a dangerous threat meant to deter other dangerous threats, an image of evil to repel evil. Her face, whether fierce and grotesque or feminine and composed, appears in virtually all media in varying contexts, and her gaze fills us with a heady mixture of fear, desire, fascination and horror, and is a timely motif that transcends era and genre.

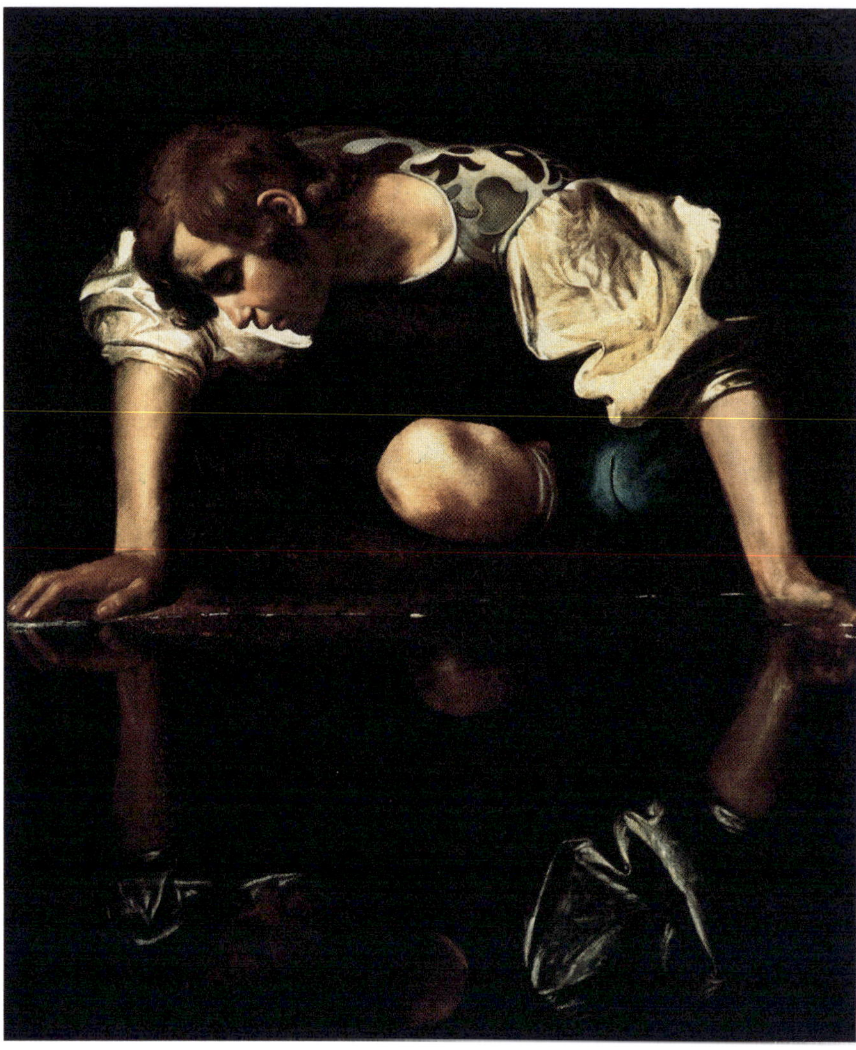

Above: Narcissus, Michelangelo Merisi da Caravaggio, 1600, oil on canvas.

Italian baroque master artist Michelangelo Merisi da Caravaggio (1571–1610) painted the classical Greco-Roman mythological story of a Narcissus, a handsome, vain young boy who falls irrevocably in love with his own reflection, then lost the will to live, no longer eating or drinking, and eventually died. Legend has it that a beautiful yellow narcissus flower then bloomed where he spent his last moments and was named in his honour. This tale is the origin of the word 'narcissism', where someone is fixated with themselves and their attributes. Here, Narcissus is depicted seated by a pool of water, leaning over and fascinated by his reflection, and in this painting there is nothing but Narcissus and his reflection, highlighting the obsessive focus of the youth and the dark infinity of such all-consuming self-love. Everything else has faded from his attention.

Right: Madame Satan, Georges Achille-Fould, 1904, oil on canvas.

In this charmingly lurid canvas by French painter Georges Achille-Fould (1868–1951), Madame Satan beckons to us with pink roses in full bloom in one hand, glittering jewels dangling in the other. Smiling invitingly, draped in a rich, luxurious gown, we almost miss the shadowy wings unfolding behind her back, the smoke billowing in the background as if to suggest that all the time the gates of hell were but a few steps away. Who could resist such treats? Who could blame us for pooh-poohing the eternal flames for a mere sniff of that perfect blossom? Some might even suggest in this risk/reward relationship that such pleasures are worth it.

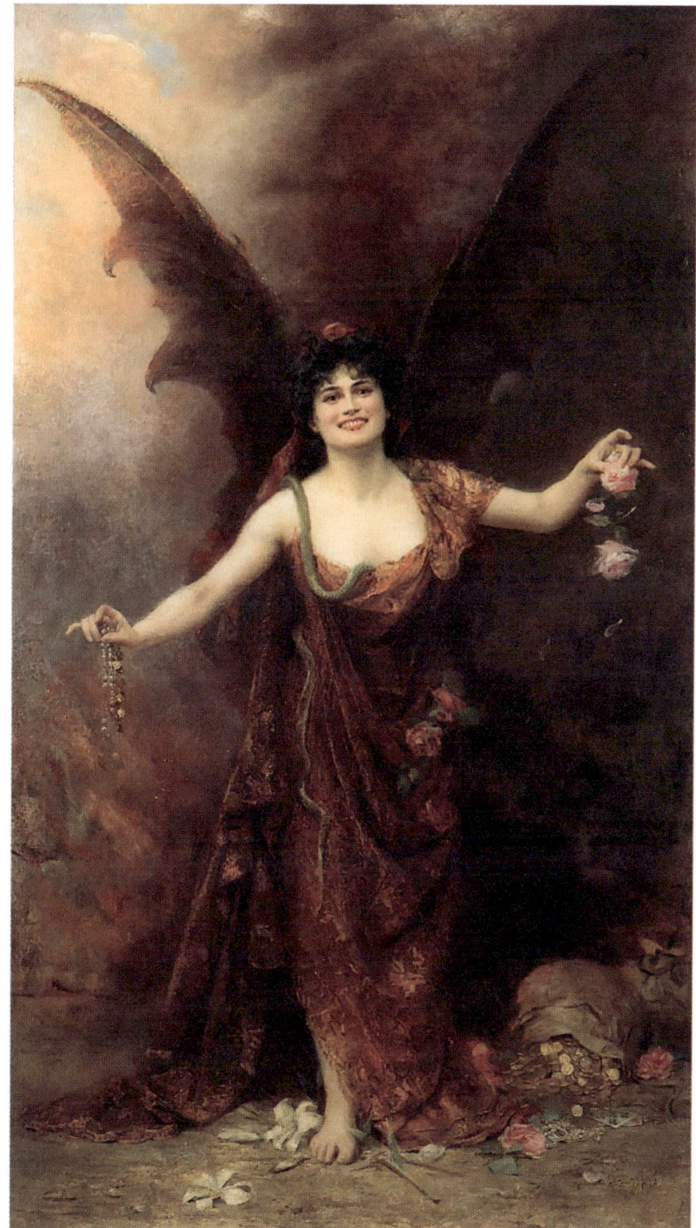

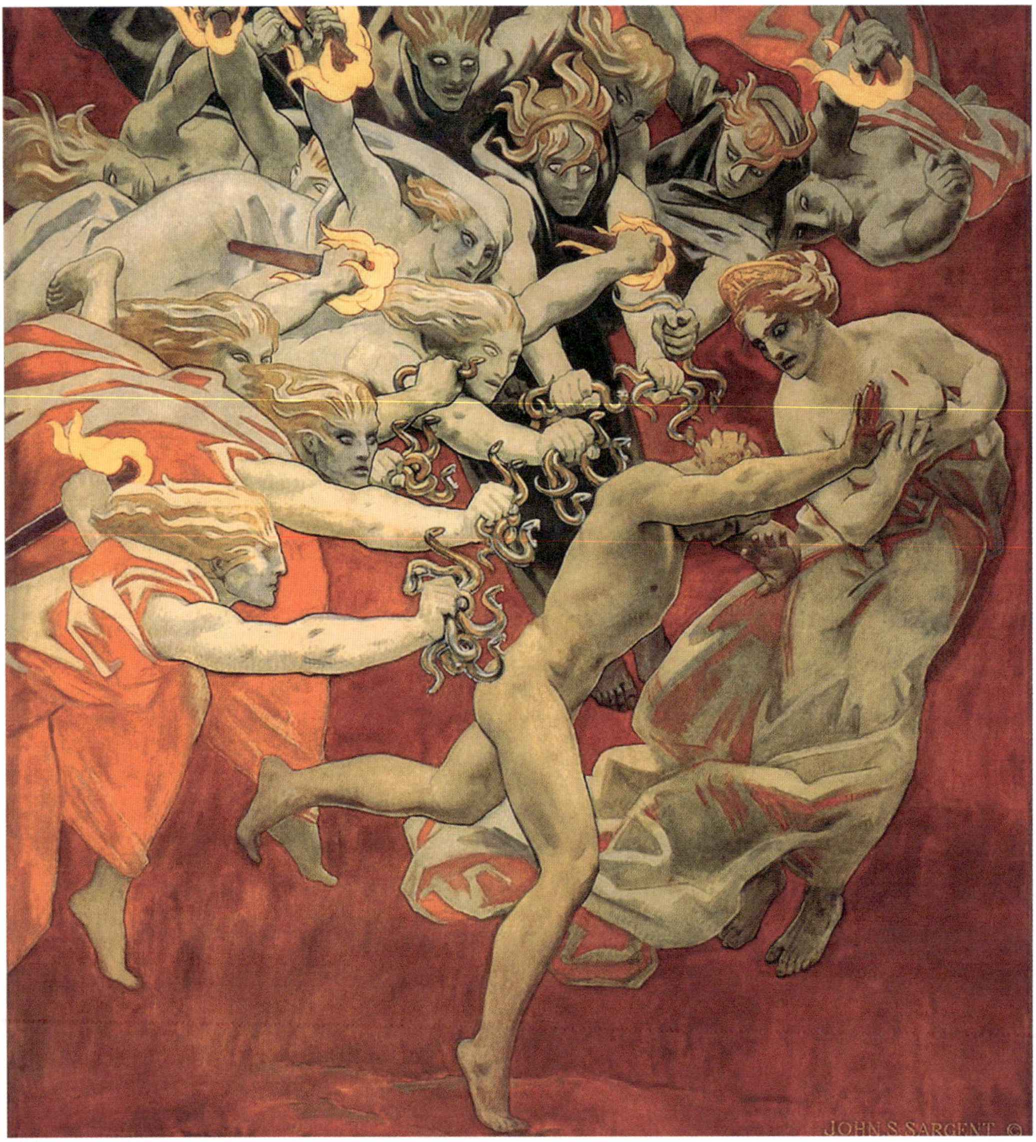

Above: Orestes Pursued by the Furies, John Singer Sargent, 1921, oil on canvas.

Noted by novelist Henry James as having an 'uncanny spectacle' of talent, English artist John Singer Sargent (1856–1925) was generally thought to be the most successful portrait painter of his era. In 1921, the Museum of Fine Arts in Boston commissioned Sargent to paint an installation on the ceiling of its Huntington Avenue stairway. This large masterpiece was one of the last paintings that he completed before he died in 1925. Aeschylus's *Oresteia* is a trilogy of plays following the spate of murders and tragedy in the lives of Agamemnon, the King of Argos and commander of the Greek forces that destroyed Troy, and his son, Orestes. The third play, *The Eumenides* (one of the euphemistic names for the Furies), opens with the Furies hunting Orestes down, haunting and tormenting him to drive him mad, because of these murders. Over its 100 square feet (more than nine square metres) of canvas, it shows a young Orestes cowering under the attacking swarm of the Furies, as he attempts to outrun their fearsome wrath.

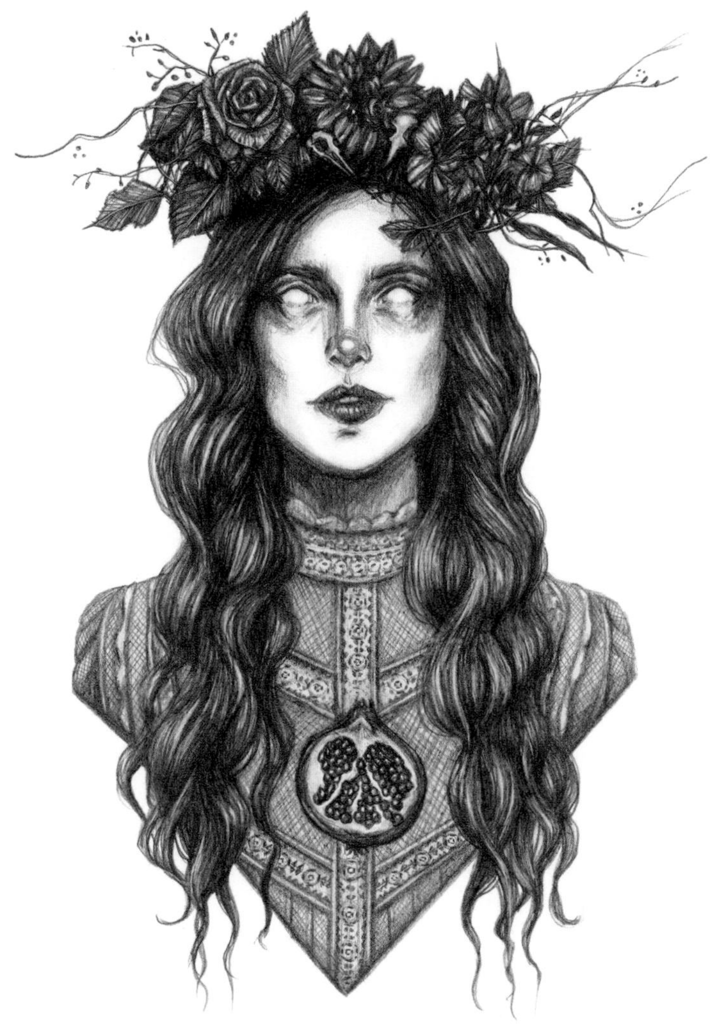

Above: Persephone, Caitlin McCarthy, 2020, pencil on paper.

Contemporary artist Caitlin McCarthy illustrates spectral beauties, sibyls and seers, witches and widows that gaze impassively at the viewer, their delicate and bloodless visages hinting at a bygone era of melancholy and loss and ringing with otherworldly resonance and mysteries glimpsed from beyond the veil. Modern art and poetry romanticize the heart-wrenching tale of the abduction and subsequent rape of Persephone, the innocent goddess of spring, at the hands of Hades, the grisly king of the Underworld. Persephone is then doomed to eternally shuttle between her abductor/husband in the Underworld and her mother on the fertile earth; there is no escape for her without disturbing the balance of the seasons. McCarthy's subtle rendering of the wraith-like goddess's sadness and resignation makes the heart clutch in grief and sympathy.

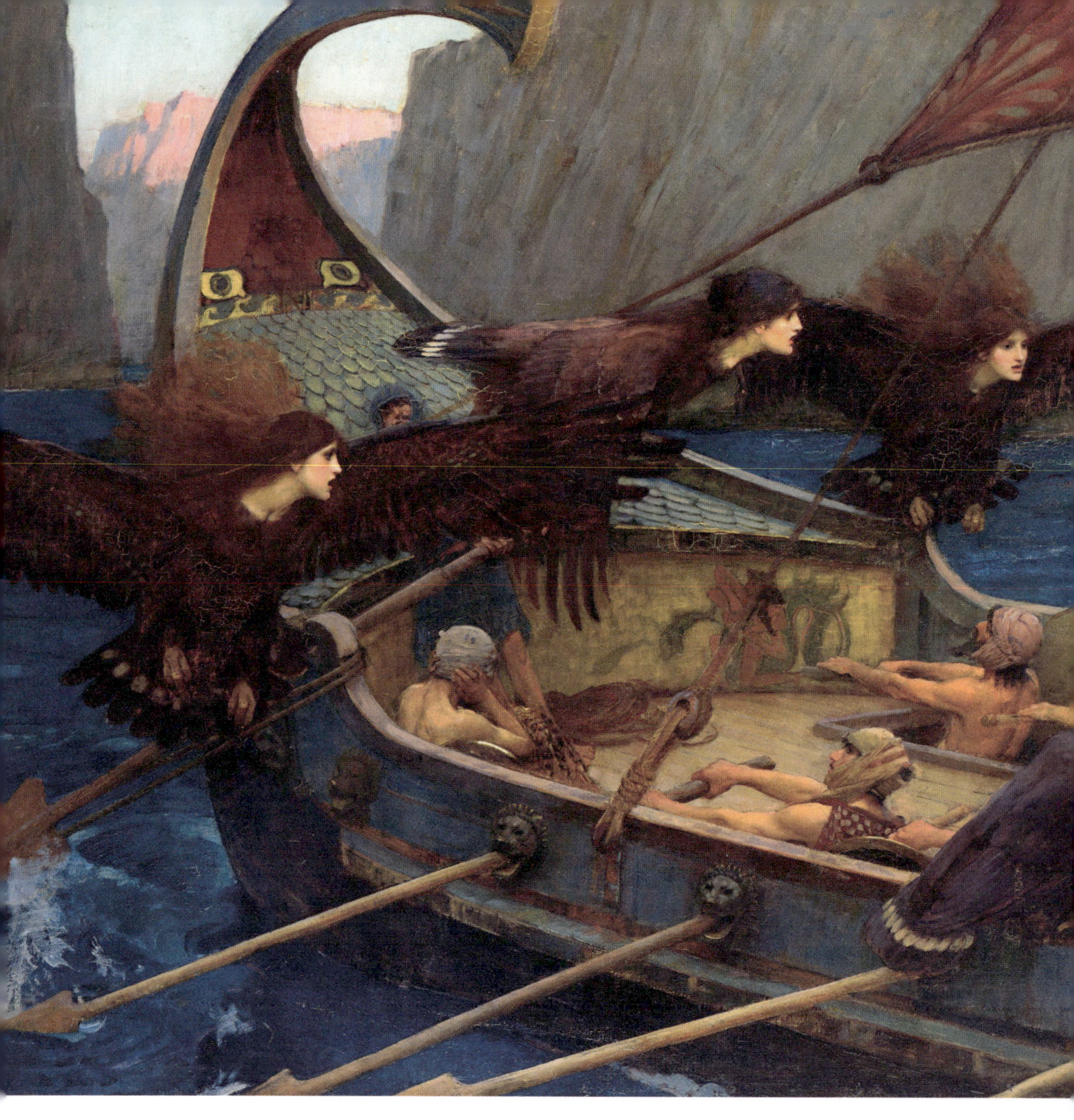

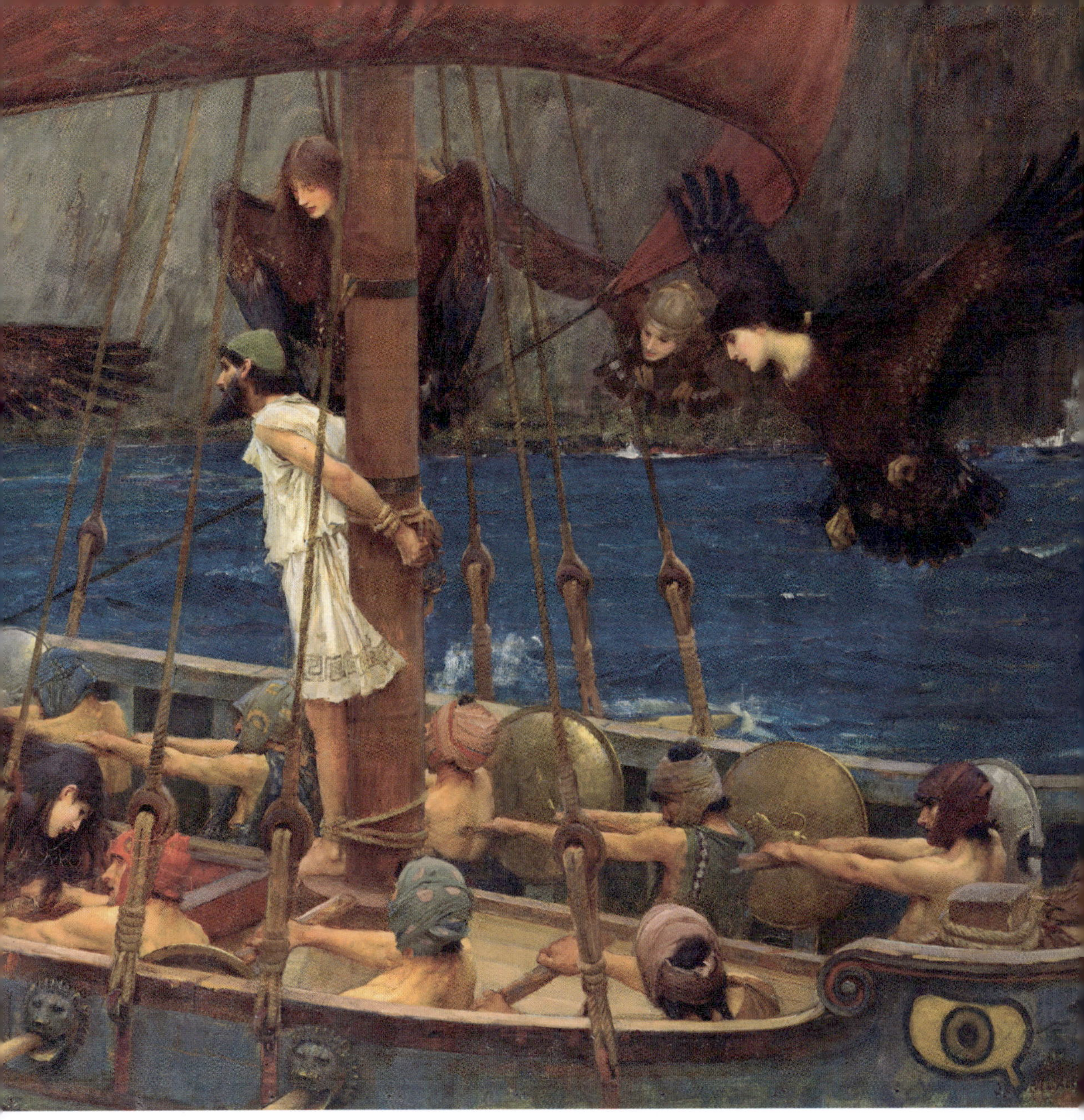

Above: Ulysses and the Sirens, John William Waterhouse, 1891, oil on canvas.

Ulysses and the Sirens by John William Waterhouse (1849–1917) dramatically illustrates a fraught scene from the Greek hero Odysseus's (Ulysses in Latin) journey home after the Trojan War in which he attempts to pass by the Sirens, infamous for luring unwary sailors towards perilous rocks and their doom by singing enchanting songs. Waterhouse uses this myth to create an inspirational and compelling composition. The Sirens, as birds, flock around the ship singing with their melodic voices, the men gazing at them with awe. Ulysses himself, arms and legs tense and tethered, faces towards the menacing, mythical creatures with longing. Waterhouse's sirens were surprising to Victorian audiences, who were more used to seeing these mythic creatures portrayed as mermaid-like nymphs.

XI

The Restless Dead & Other Eerie Entities

'I think ghosts want to be seen. They want to be reassured that they truly exist.'

–EMILY X.R. PAN, *THE ASTONISHING COLOR OF AFTER*

The trembling thrill and lonesome terror that tingles our spines when we've glimpsed shapes moving just outside our periphery of vision. Strange, creeping shadows on the walls of our bedrooms, late at night. The desolate flash of grief, guilt or memory that overtakes us when we believe we hear a loved one's voice calling mournfully, even though they've been gone for years. There's a space between breath and heartbeat in the nexus of these many realities where what's past is present, the dead speak, and disbelief and doubtlessness simultaneously exist.

If you have ever experienced the frozen moments of ghostly phenomena or supernatural encounters with mysterious beings, you certainly wouldn't wish it on anyone else. And yet, knowing that another someone has seen something they cannot explain can help one to feel less desperate and alone. After we've endured the shivery wonderments of the otherworldly and unexplained, it is in our very natures to seek out evidence that we are not alone in these frightening experiences tainted by sorrow, melancholy or loss. Even better if these occurrences have been interpreted through an artistic lens.

The 'supernatural' and 'paranormal' refer to experiences and phenomena beyond scientific explanation, suggesting the existence of entities beyond the observable universe. But even for the most level-headed among us, there's something irresistible about the eerie (im)possibility of haunted houses and forlorn spirits. 'I know that ghosts have wandered on earth', opines the tormented hero Heathcliff in *Wuthering Heights*, and he's not alone in that knowledge. Whether or not we live in a particularly haunted culture, as humans we are all haunted by something – a dream, a memory or even maybe a literal phantom or two – and artists have always sought answers for why ghosts return, spirits remain unsettled and apparitions arise to appeal to our emotions. Their enduring prevalence in art and literature bears witness to their persistent power to terrify and inspire. Our notions of ghosts – the fears that they provoke, the forms they take – vaporously embody our shared past, reminding us of our own histories, ancient stories and timeless terrors that refuse to die. You might be inclined to think that visual representations of ghosts and ghouls haven't changed much over time. But if we peek behind the veil of art history, we'll see that the dead, too, are capable of change. Medieval wall-paintings represent ghosts not as ethereal spirits, but as walking corpses that go about offering unsolicited but probably well-intended advice, such as 'As we are now, so soon you'll be – so straighten up or you'll be sorry!' In illustrations accompanying ballads of the seventeenth century, ghosts wore the shrouds they were buried in – it was much later that they began to wear the voluminous white sheets that we associate with our last-minute childhood Halloween costumes and ineffectual Scooby Doo villains. Contemporary artist Angela Deane even has a bit of fun with this idea, painting comical ghouls over eerie found photographs. For Pre-Raphaelites Dante Gabriel Rossetti and John Everett Millais, ghosts illustrated explorations of intense, psychologically charged situations, introducing a heightened dimension to the dark, human dramas of their drawings and paintings.

Japanese ukiyo-e woodblock art is crawling with the eerie drama of all kinds of supernatural beings that you wouldn't want to meet after dark, such as the ghostly *yurei* and the grotesque *yokai*. And since we're contemplating creatures of the night, we cannot forget the vampire's artistic legacy of bloodthirsty seduction and danger, their sense of elegance and mystery captivating the minds of artists such as masters Philip Burne-Jones, Edvard Munch and Leonor Fini. A more diminutive supernatural threat is posed by creatures that we don't always associate with malefic darkness, but let's not kid ourselves; whether you cross them, or whether it's just in their mercurial nature, fairies can be both fanciful and fearsome. Fairies of folklore were blamed for all manner of mischief and ills, ranging from petty vandalism and theft to outright murder. A fascination with fairies and the supernatural was a phenomenon of the Victorian age and resulted in a distinctive strand of art depicting fairy subjects drawn from myth and legend.

Ghosts mournfully seeking out our company; tiny, winged beings enticing us into the lost-time of the misty fairy lands; or bloodsucking fiends hanging around just outside our doors looking for an invitation to dinner – these are a needy bunch. The appearances of these spirits and apparitions in the art we create and consume can tell us a great deal about our cultures and about the self, invisibility and otherness. But mostly, I think, it reveals the unescapable truth that, even in death, there is no respite from loneliness.

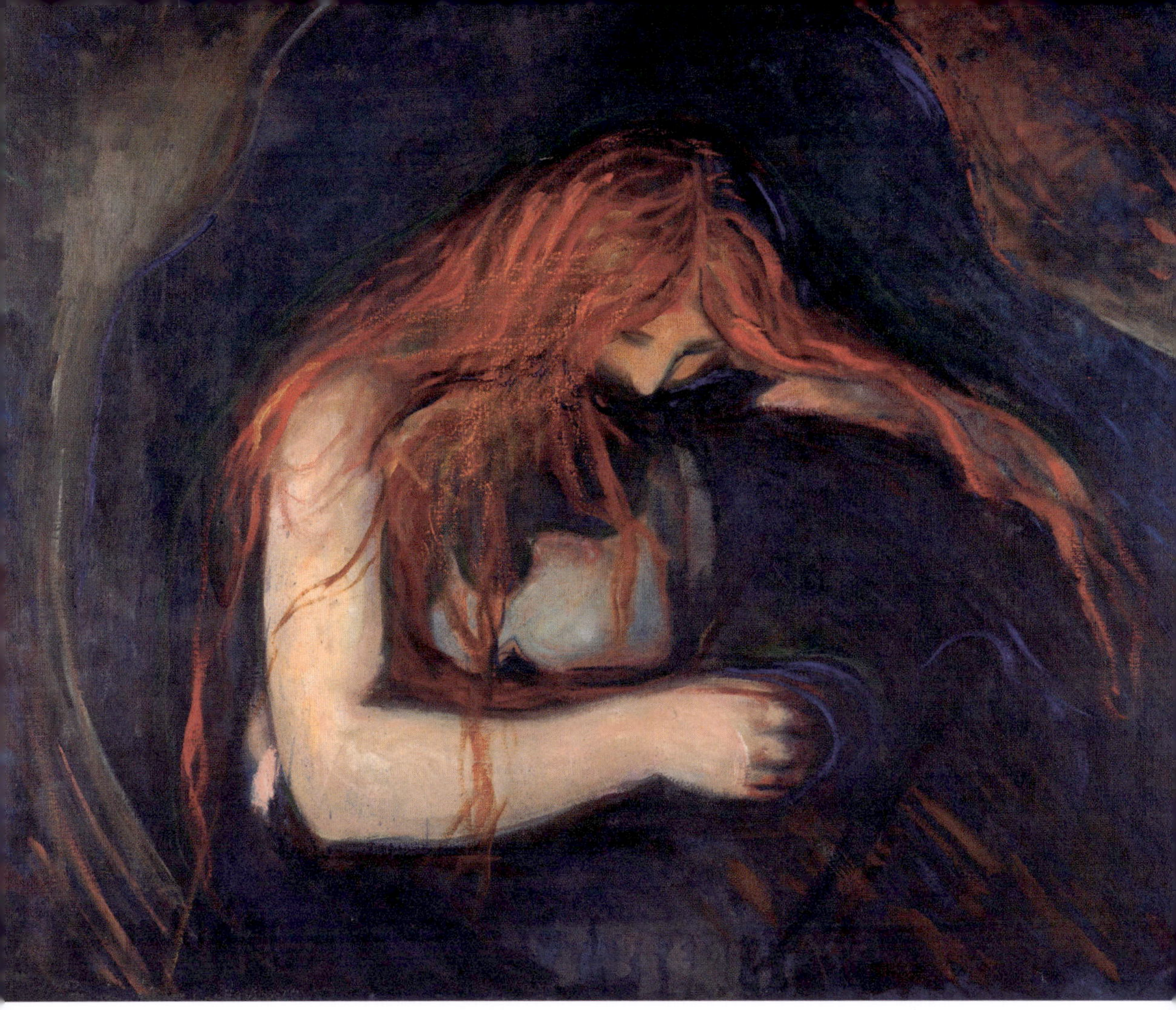

Above: The Vampire, Edvard Munch, 1895, oil on canvas.

As it happens, Edvard Munch (1863–1944) did not title this painting *The Vampire*. He originally called it 'Love and Pain' and it was only later that it picked up the name and interpretation of a man locked in a vampire's embrace. The painting depicts a black garbed man and a woman with flame red hair, her arms wrapped around him, as she bends towards his neck for a vampiric nibble. But perhaps she is tenderly laying her face on his shoulder to offer solace to his anguished form? Some thought it may have been about his visits to prostitutes, others saw in it a macabre fantasy about the death of his favourite sister. The Nazis declared it morally 'degenerate'. Munch himself remained ambiguous about the work's deeper meaning and maintained it was nothing more than a woman kissing a man on the neck. In typical Munch form, it incorporates melancholic themes of angst, love, sex and death, and the rest, one supposes, can be left to personal interpretation.

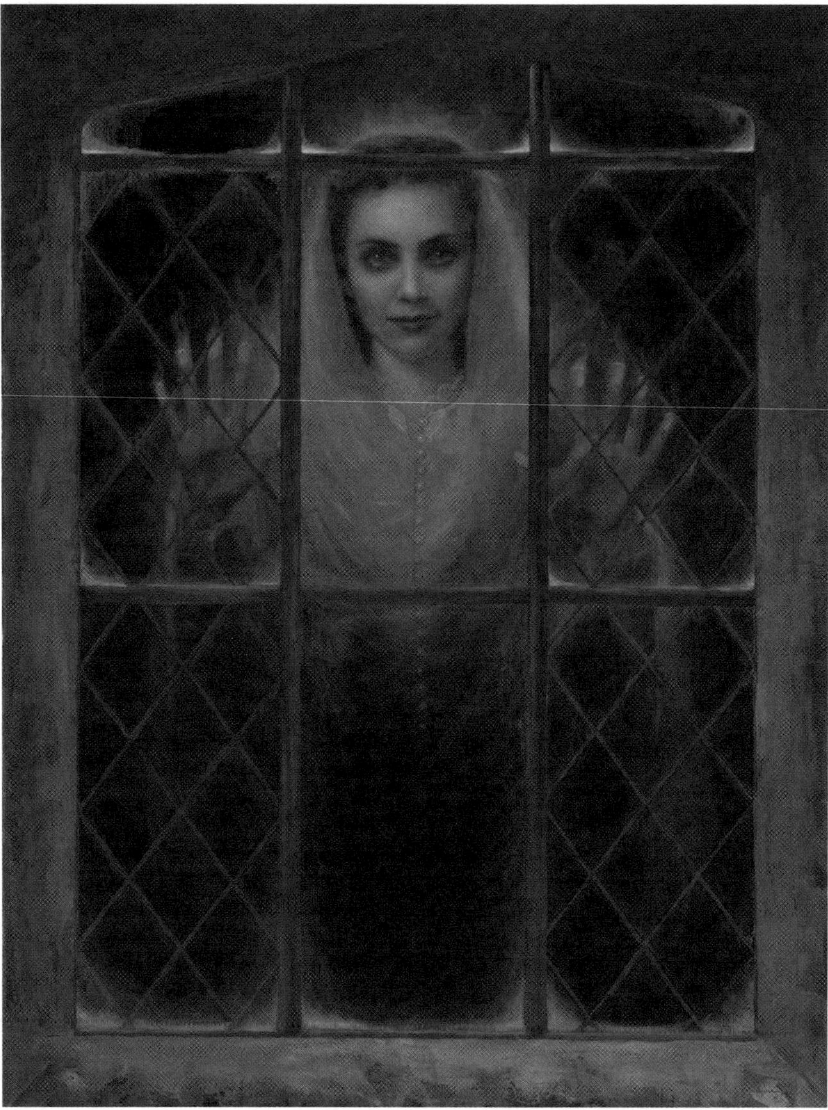

Above: Cathy's Ghost, Laurie Lee Brom, 2015, oil on canvas.

American Laurie Lee Brom (b?) is an artist who grew up in the historical town of Charleston, South Carolina, and her imagination has always been informed by the local ghost stories and folk tales of the swampy Low County. Her work today carries with it a similar spirit, with all manner of curious ghosts and odd characters in her mysterious portraits and paintings. The American Southeast is quite a way from the ghostly wanderings of menacing spirits that inhabit the windy moors of *Wuthering Heights* where the spirits of Cathy and Heathcliff and their wild, abandoned love lingers – but Brom's spectral canvas of luminous yearning can make us believers that ghosts of the unforgiven and the unforgettable do indeed wander the earth.

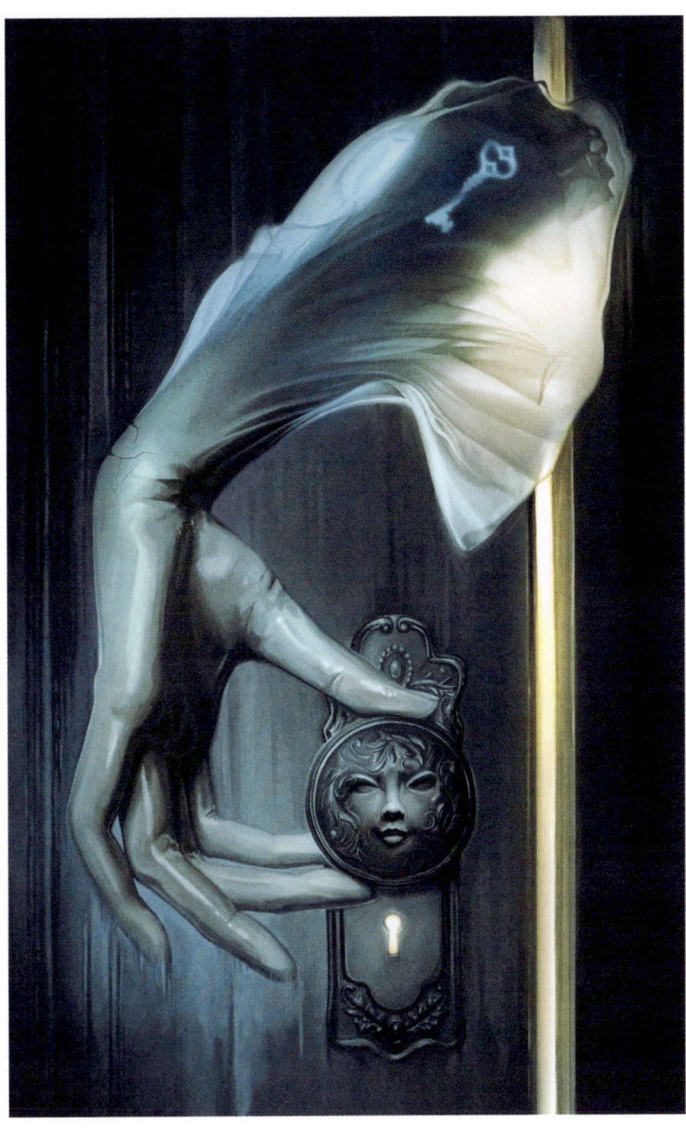

Above: The Uninvited, David Seidman, 2018, hand-embellished digital painting.

David Seidman conjures the unsettling stories hidden deep in the walls of the spaces we haunt. Rooted in a universe both dark and fantastic, his work examines the fragility of the human condition while offering glimpses of the beauty and terror that shift and shimmer within the darkness of the unknown. Seidman, though well studied in more traditional forms, uses digital painting techniques to create his dreamlike images of houses and bodies - and the bleak interiors of both - gloomily, silently, watching, awaiting the oblivion which sooner or later takes us all.

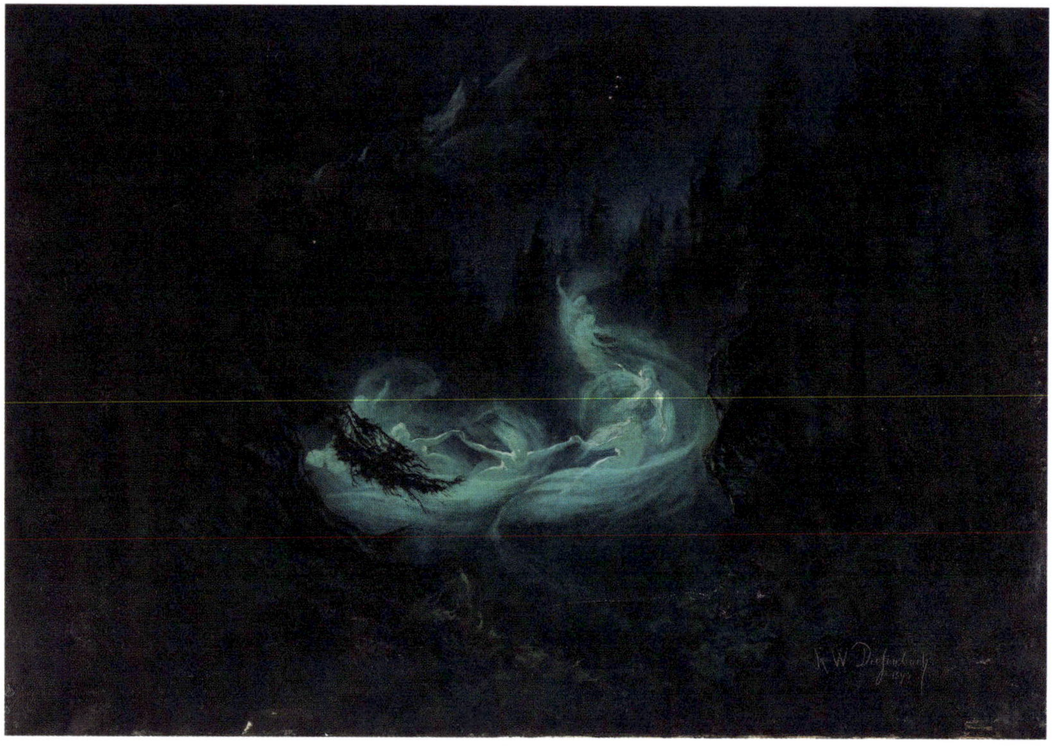

Above: The Fairy Dance, Karl Wilhelm Diefenbach, 1895, oil on canvas.

Opposite: Ballad of Lenore, Emile Jean-Horace Vernet, 1839, oil on canvas.

Do ghosts wear clothing? Do fairies? Did Karl Wilhelm Diefenbach (1851–1913)? This eccentric German Symbolist artist and social reformer, after a severe case of typhoid fever, converted to vegetarianism and gave up cigarettes and alcohol. Abandoning the Catholicism that he had been brought up in, he began to follow his own brand of bohemian spirituality, centred on free love, nudism and oneness with nature. In this swirling moonlit forest scene, we are treated to a vaporous frolic of fairies, a celestial celebration of the mystic strangeness of the nocturnal natural world.

Born into a family of artists, Emile Jean-Horace Vernet (1789–1863) was predestined for art by familial inheritance. A Romantic painter, Vernet was inspired by a ballad telling of a fantastical ride of two lovers between the worlds of the living and the dead written by German author Gottfried August Bürger around 1770. In the poem, it is 1763 and the end of the Seven Years' War, and Lenore is waiting for her fiancé. He appears in the night on a black horse, promising to marry her before dawn. But upon arriving at the cemetery, the horse rider is revealed to be a skeleton wearing armour. Surprise!

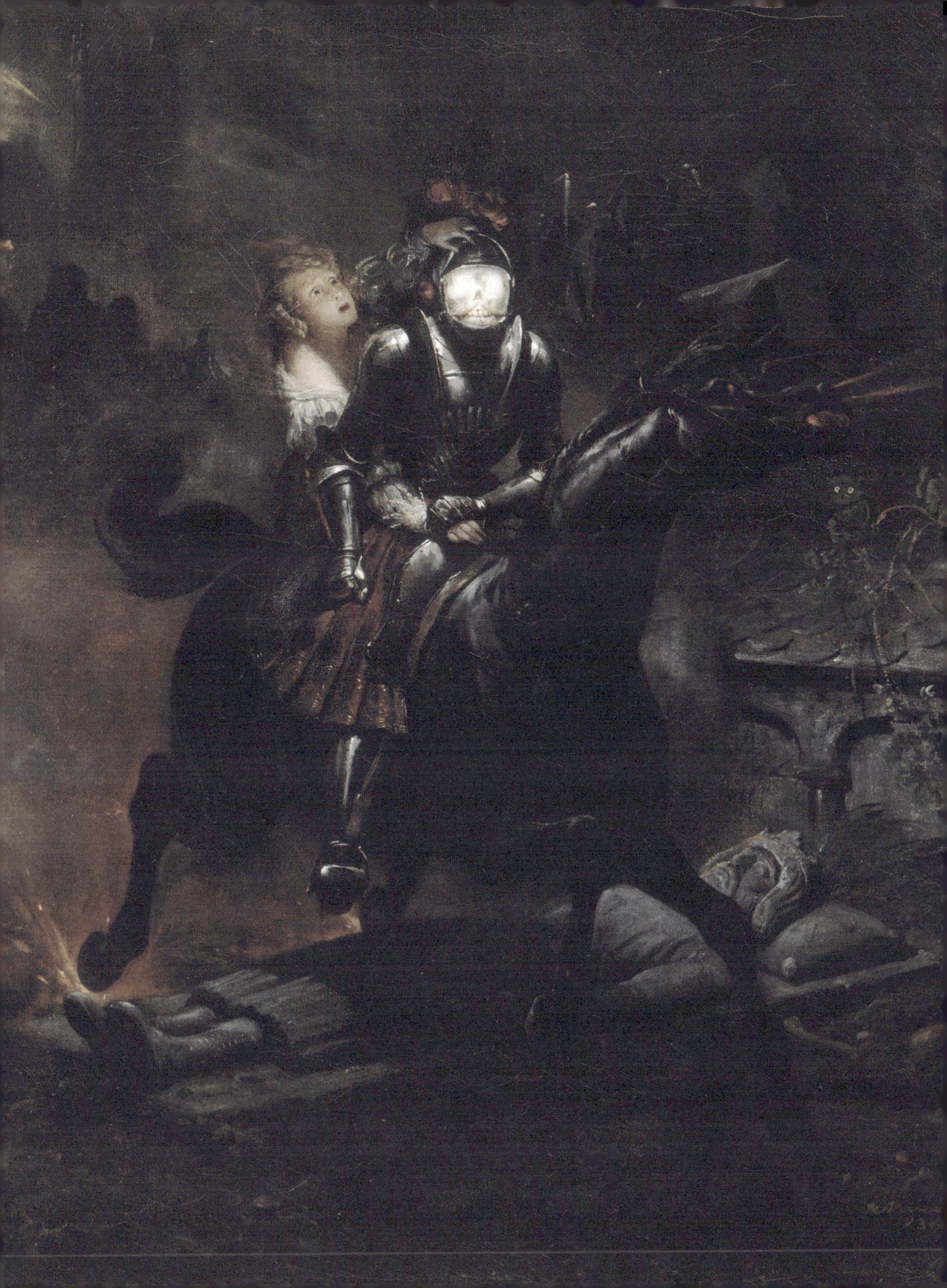

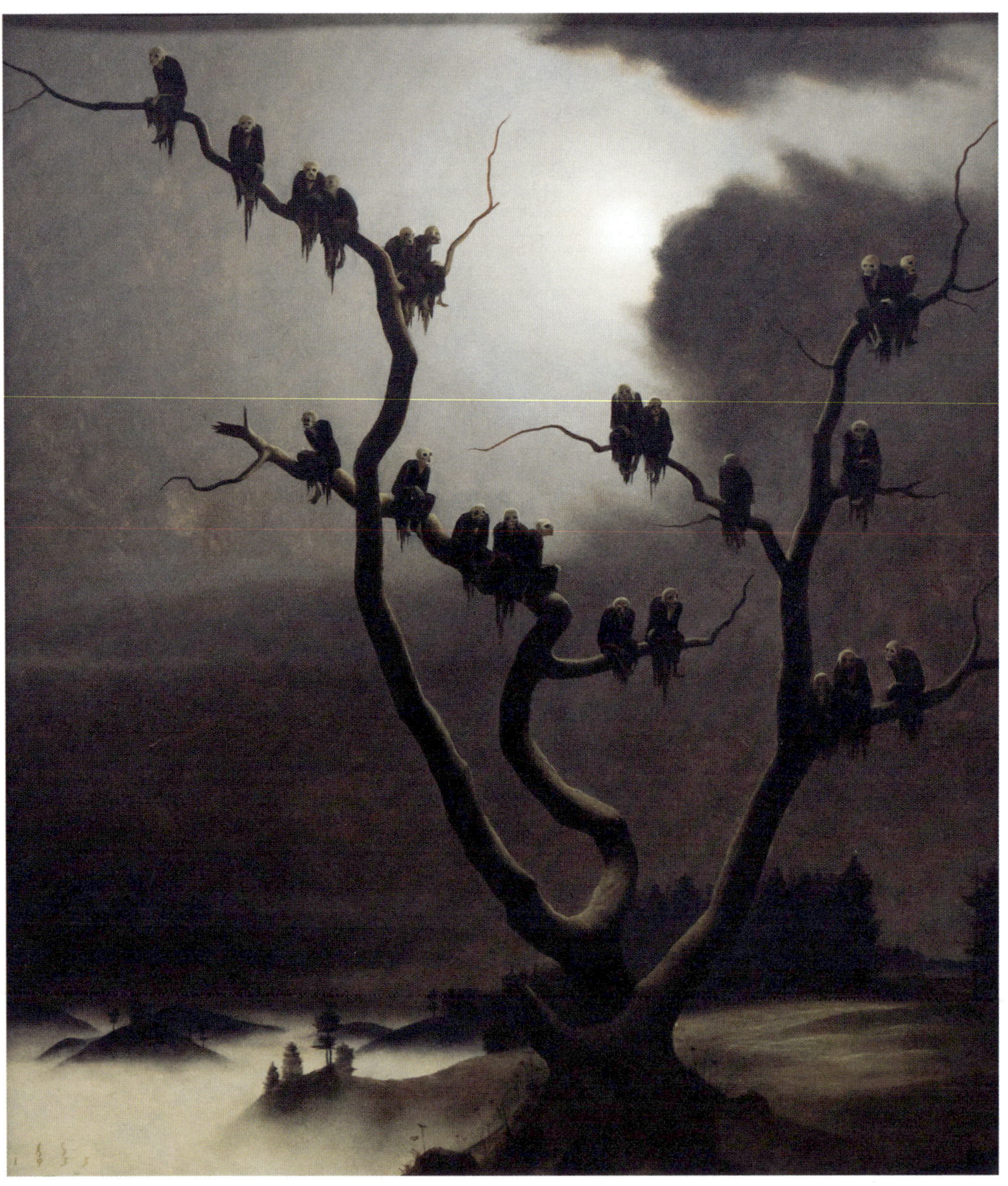

Right: Through the Thinnest of Veils, Marci Washington, 2009, watercolour and gouache on paper.

Contemporary artist Marci Washington describes her work as illustrations for a book that has never been written. Had it been, it would tell tales of terror following a cast of characters through a dark world of haunted manor ghosts, bloody handwritten letters, poisoned betrayals and all the dark spaces between. Interested in building a fictional narrative with connections to history as well as to the present, if this imaginary novel were to exist, it would probably be a lot like *Wuthering Heights*, *Jane Eyre* or *The Turn of the Screw* – novels that function as social commentary as well as haunting epics of supernatural romanticism.

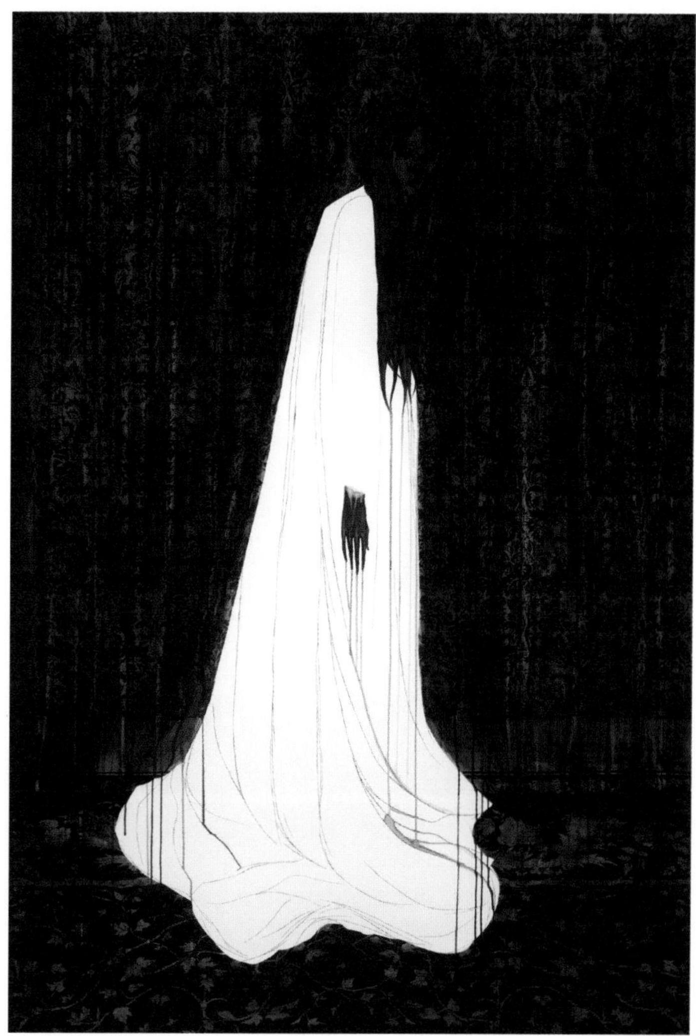

Opposite: Ghosts in the Tree, Franz Sedlacek, 1933, oil on canvas.

Franz Sedlacek (1891–1945) was an Austrian painter whose fantastically surreal works are considered to be in both the New Objectivity and Magical Realism styles. Thought of as one of the most outstanding Austrian artists of the inter-war period, his mysterious and still-fascinating work resists common classifications. 'Viennese Painter Revels in the Grotesque' was how *Life* magazine categorized his paintings in 1937, and it's hard to argue with that assessment, with the creepily bizarre hybrid creatures populating the strangely lit, lonely and utterly ominous landscapes and an overall mood both melancholic and threatening – no doubt exemplifying the widespread alienation and loneliness of the time.

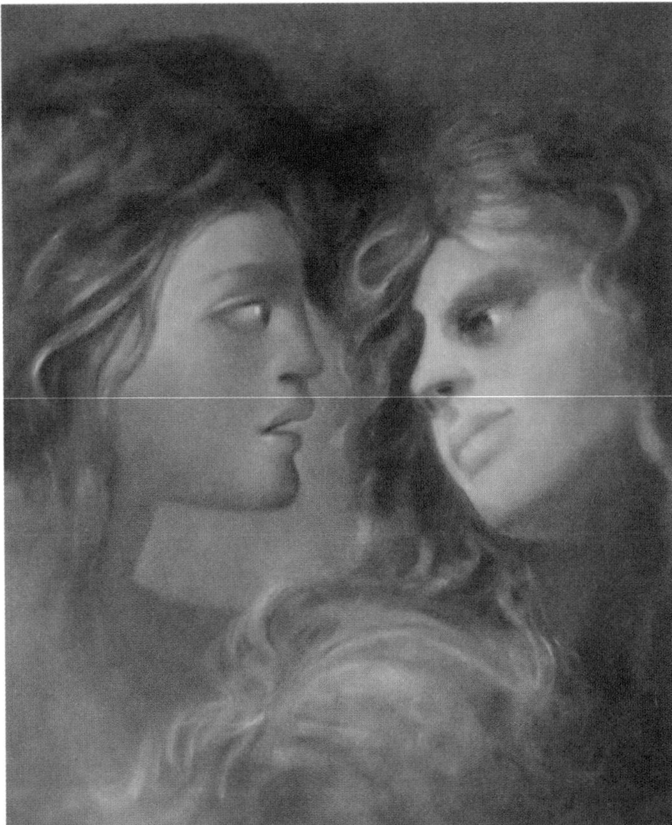

Left: Carmilla #1, Leonor Fini, 1983, colour lithograph.

Argentinian Leonor Fini (1907–96), painter of the surreal, illustrator of books, theatre designer and writers was driven by passion and a sense of liberty, and lived by unrestrained desires and staunch individuality. Merging various influences in her languid brush strokes and lavish palette along with her interests in psychoanalysis, philosophy, mythology and sorcery, Fini's centring of woman as a sexual creature – and often a cruel dominatrix or predator – led Surrealism in new directions. In 1983 Leonor Fini, in collaboration with her friend, the art publisher Arianne Lancel, created a series of eight paintings for *Carmilla*, Sheridan Le Fanu's 1872 gothic novel of vampirism and transgressive desire. Predating Bram Stoker's *Dracula* by 25 years, Carmilla is the first known vampire novel, and Fini's paintings were used as the basis for a new edition of the book's silk-screen illustrations.

Opposite: Vögguvísa, Becky Munich, 2015, colour pencil on paper.

It's the rare well-dressed, bloody-faced siren that causes one's jaw to drop to the floor and exclaim, breathlessly: 'I'll wear what that vengeful red-carpet ghost is wearing!' The gruesome muses, looming spectres and lurking shades of Becky Munich evoke that very reaction – and more. On the surface these sinister, ethereal wraiths and monstrous femme fatales simultaneously menace and beguile, but in a strange and playful twist, there's sly and creepy-clever mischief to be found in the details and its clear to see that this artist takes her spooky business quite seriously while winking at us playfully at the same time.

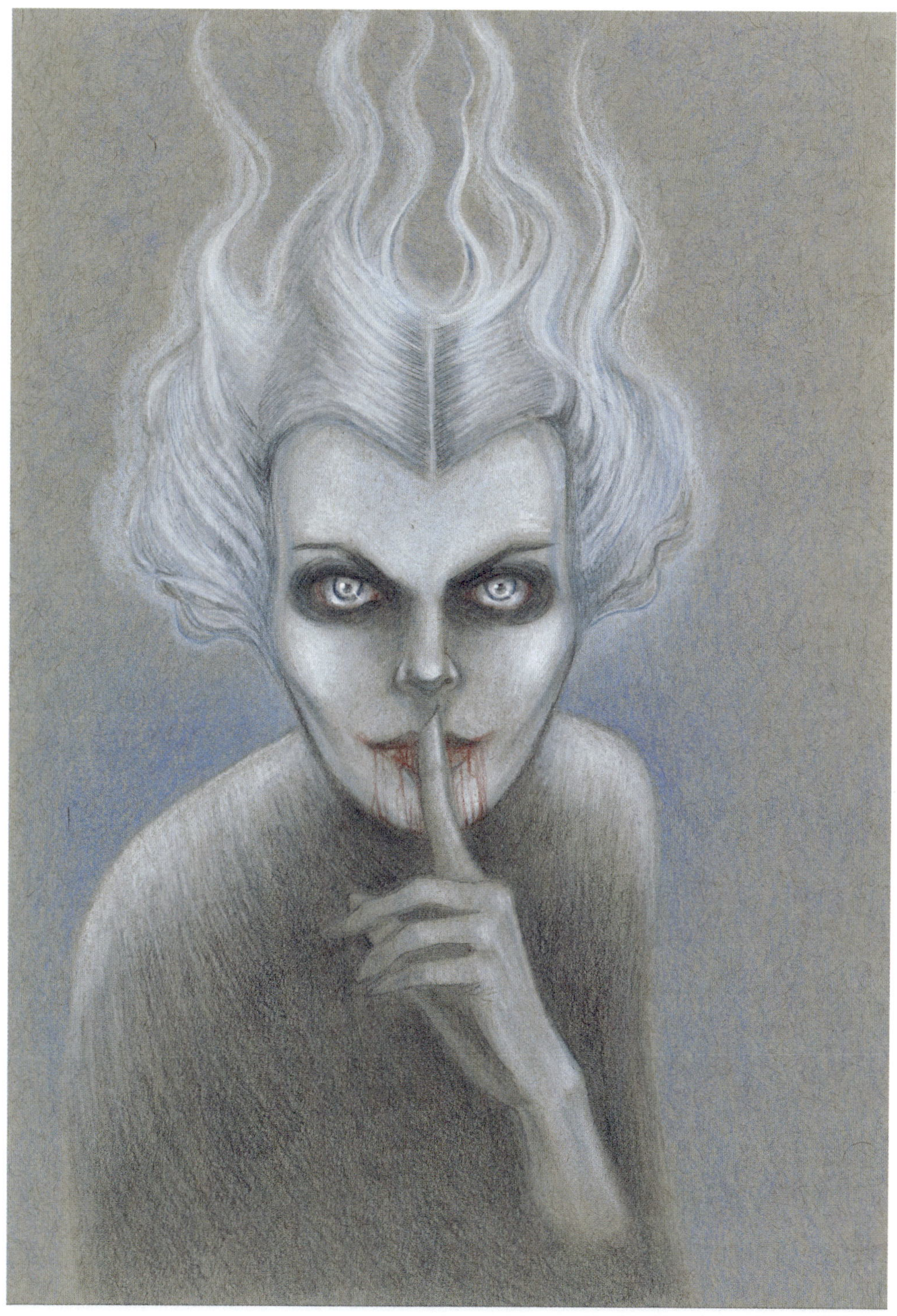

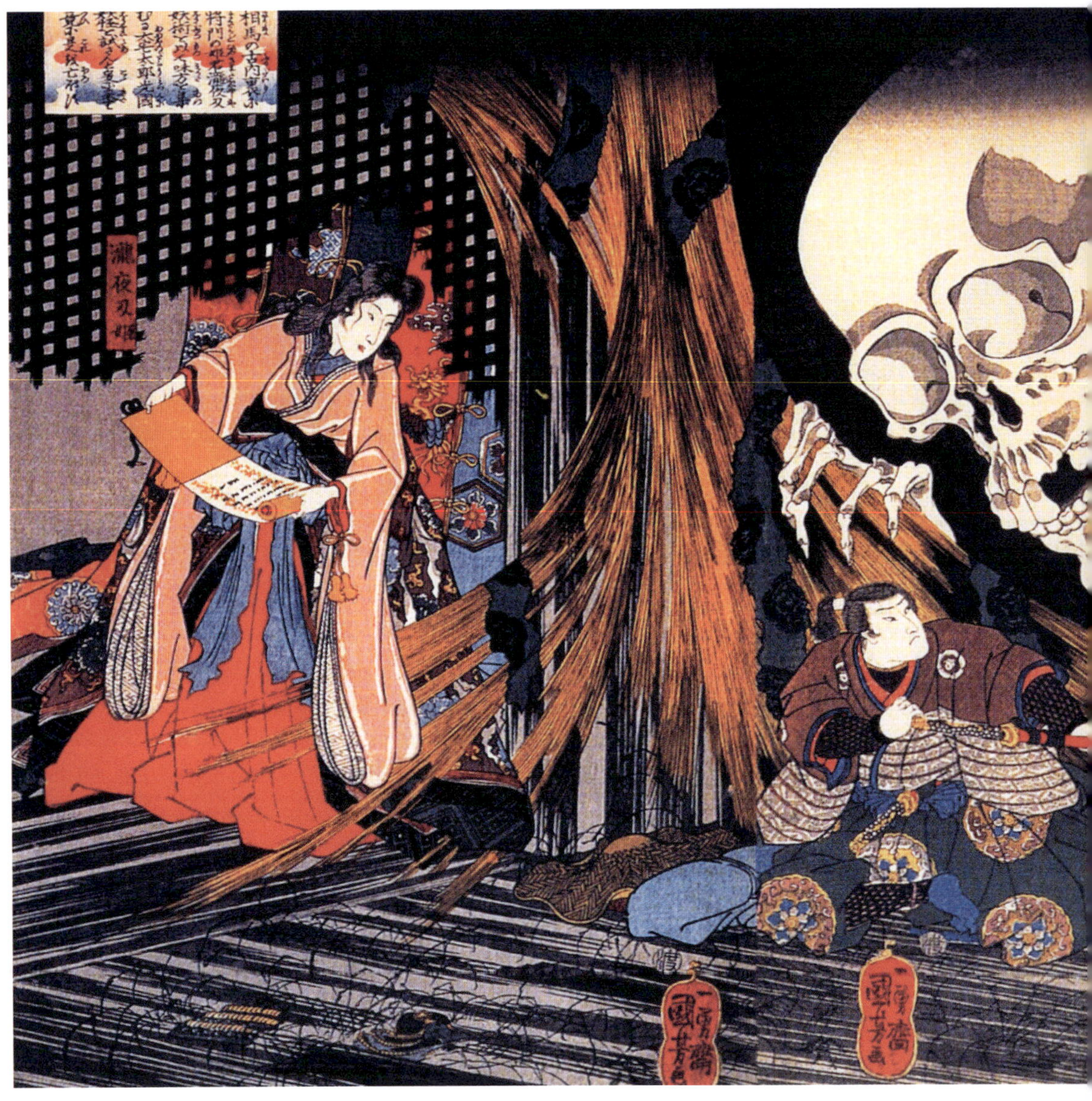
瀧夜叉姫

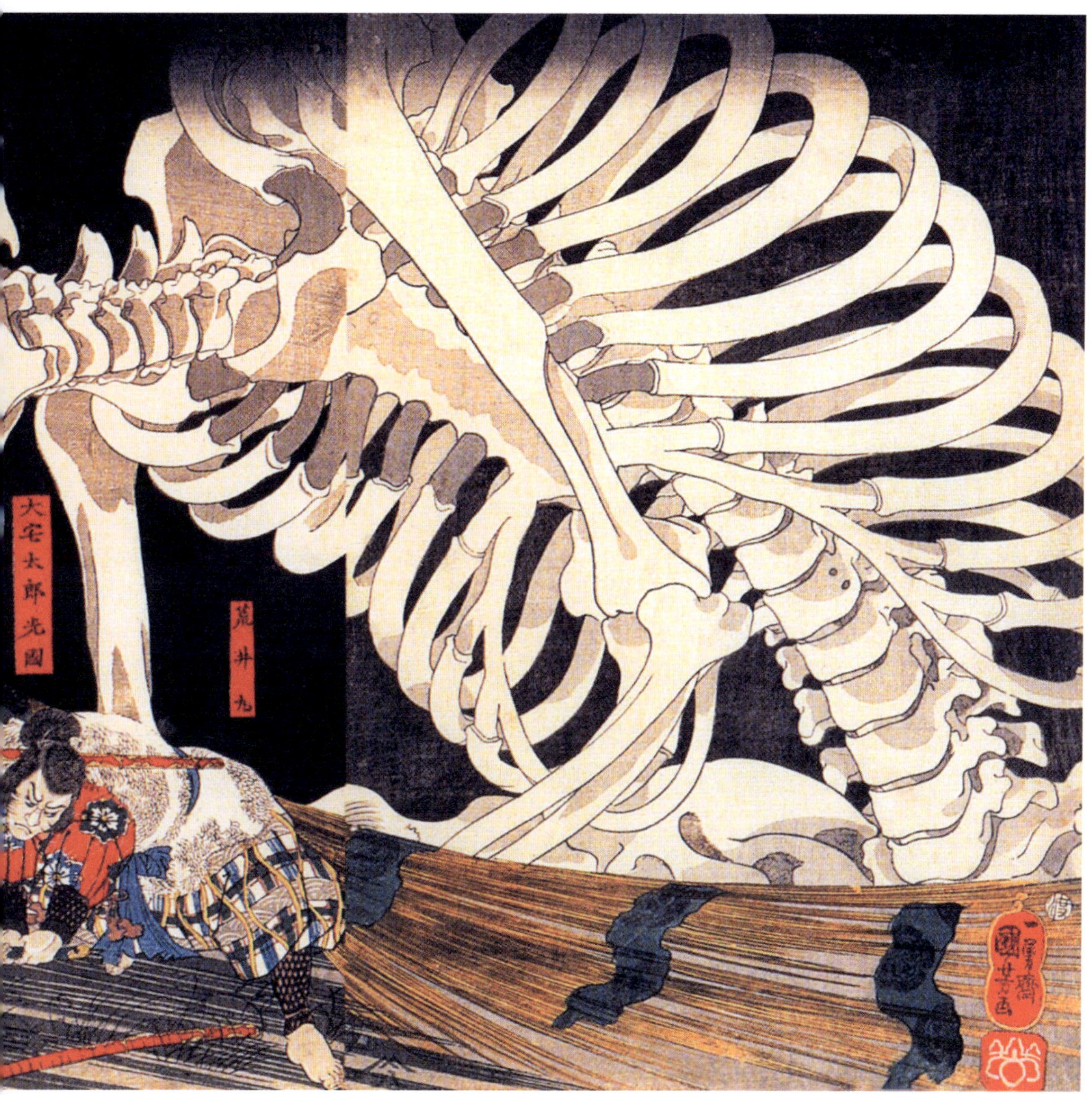

Above: Takiyasha the Witch and the Skeleton Spectre, Utagawa Kuniyoshi, c. 1844, woodblock print.

Takiyasha the Witch and the Skeleton Spectre is a woodblock print by the Japanese artist Utagawa Kuniyoshi (1798–1861), who was especially renowned for his depictions of historical and mythical scenes. This delightful horror story is from the *Story of Utō Yasutaka*, written in 1807 by the Edo poet Santō Kyōden. In this print we see the princess on the left, framed in the broken palace blinds. She grips a magic scroll, reading the spell to summon a Gashadokuro, monstrous yōkai of Japanese imagination appearing as gigantic skeletons, assembled from the combined bones of famine victims, or in this case, the bodies of the doomed soldiers that followed the samurai warlord Taira no Masakado to their deaths. These gargantuan spirits were believed to haunt lonely country roads, snapping up solitary travellers to bite off their heads and slurp their blood as it spouted.

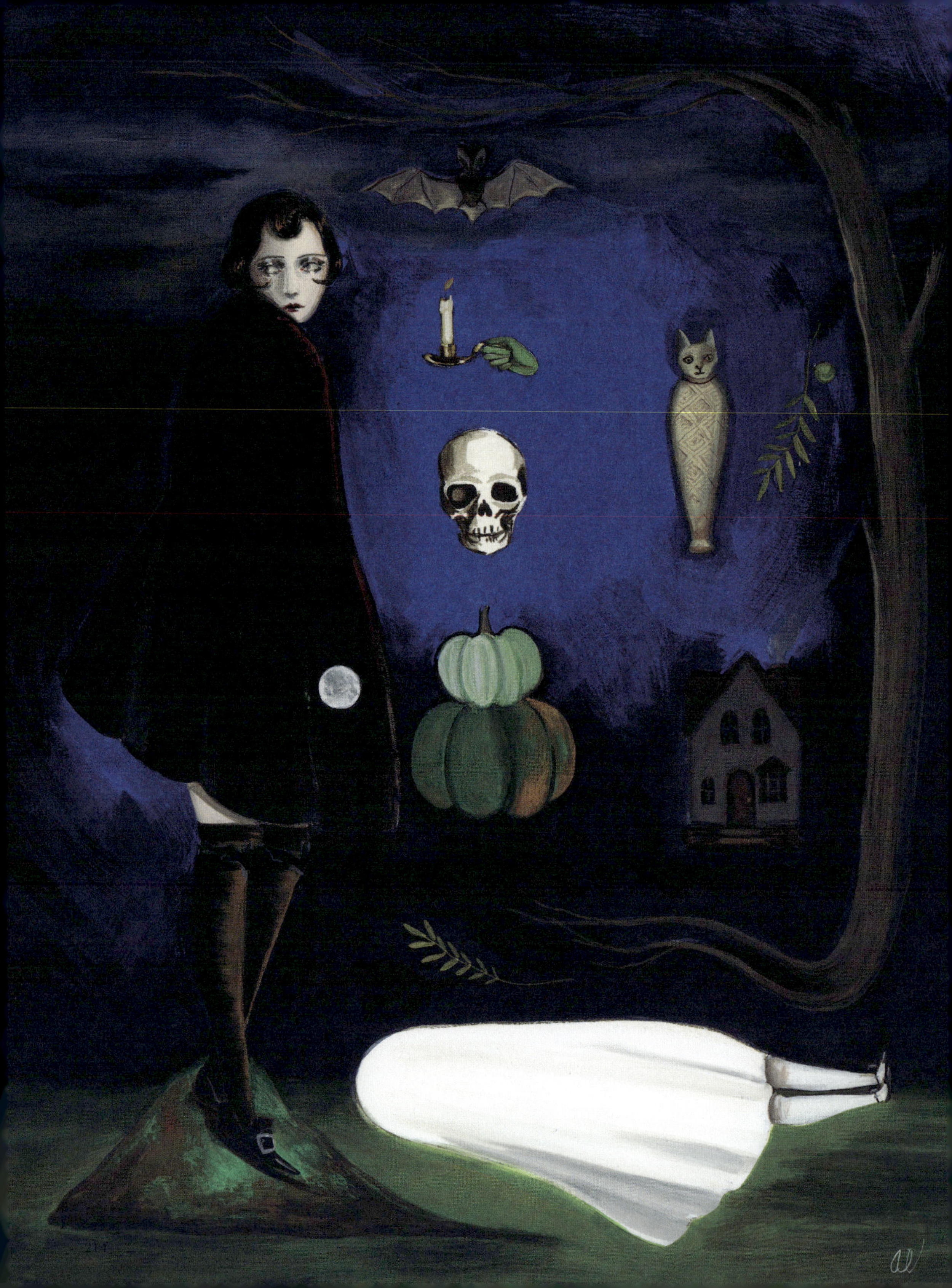

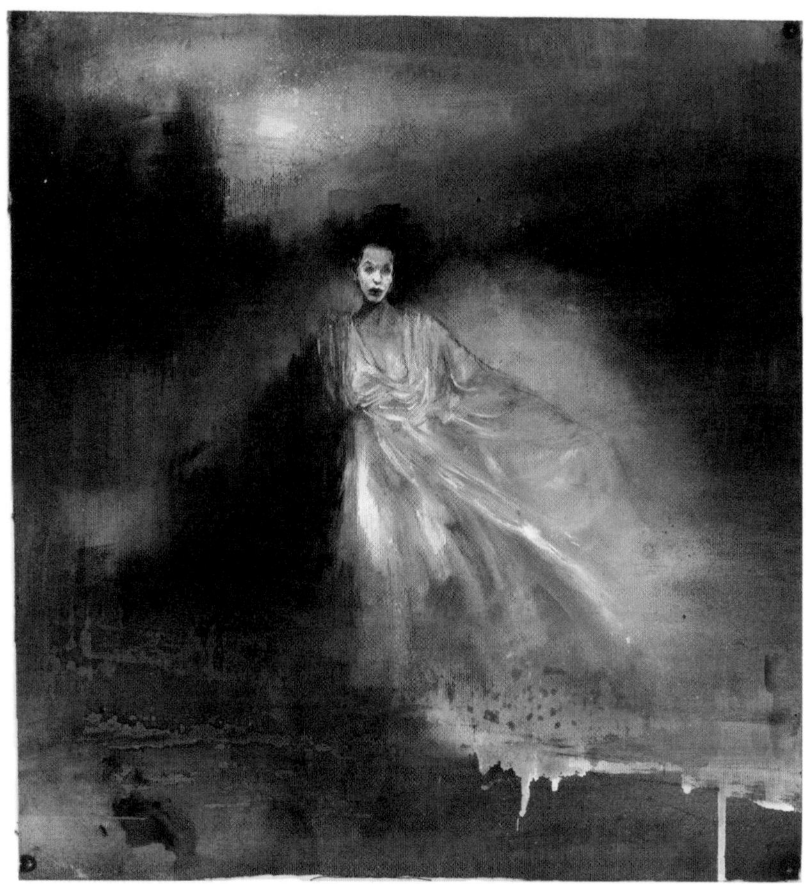

Opposite: Disbelief, Amy Earles, 2021, gouache.

US-based artist and expert daydreamer Amy Earles paints figures floating and flickering through the otherworlds of perpetual autumn daydream. These vignettes brim with foreboding fancies and gentle perturbations, delicate disturbances and vague unease that we can't quite identify or put a finger on. Earles notes that most of her inspirations and influences are connected to older things: antique objects and various histories, and reveals that she is always enamoured by language (archaic words in particular); certain words or phrases can inspire whole universes, and these fascinations inform every eerie, elegant brushstroke.

Right: Hel, La Rouille, 2017, oil and spray on canvas.

La Rouille (b. 1981), whose name artfully translates to 'rust', is a French street artist whose creations encompass the dissolving silhouettes inspired by forgotten and abandoned urban landscapes and buildings in decline. Working in dark contrasts and muted colours, and attracted to the moody atmospheres emerging from these spaces abandoned by man, this self-taught artist focuses on conveying feelings of melancholy, regret and nostalgia and connecting them through history and time with his own ghosts and those who haunt these various modern-day ruins.

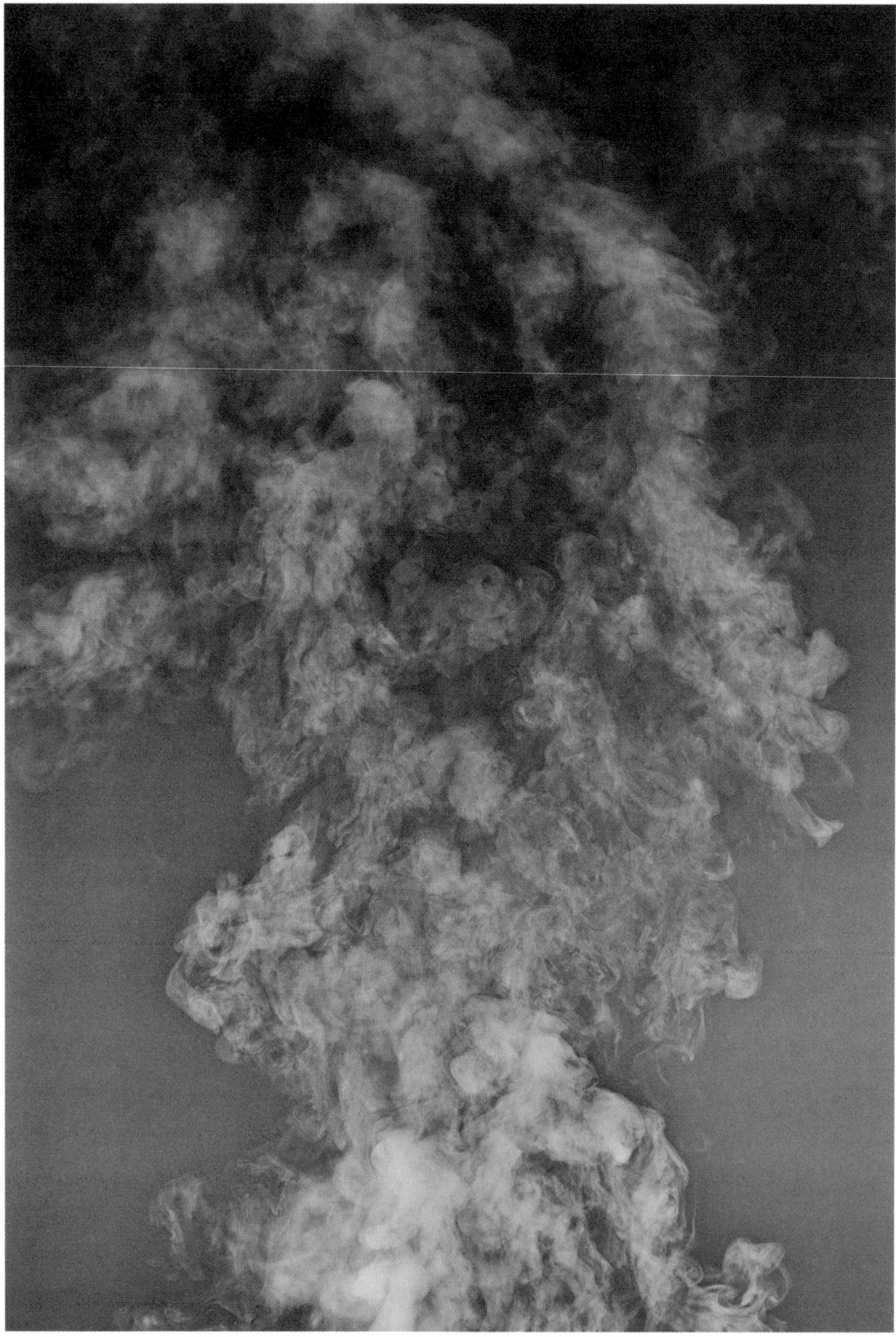

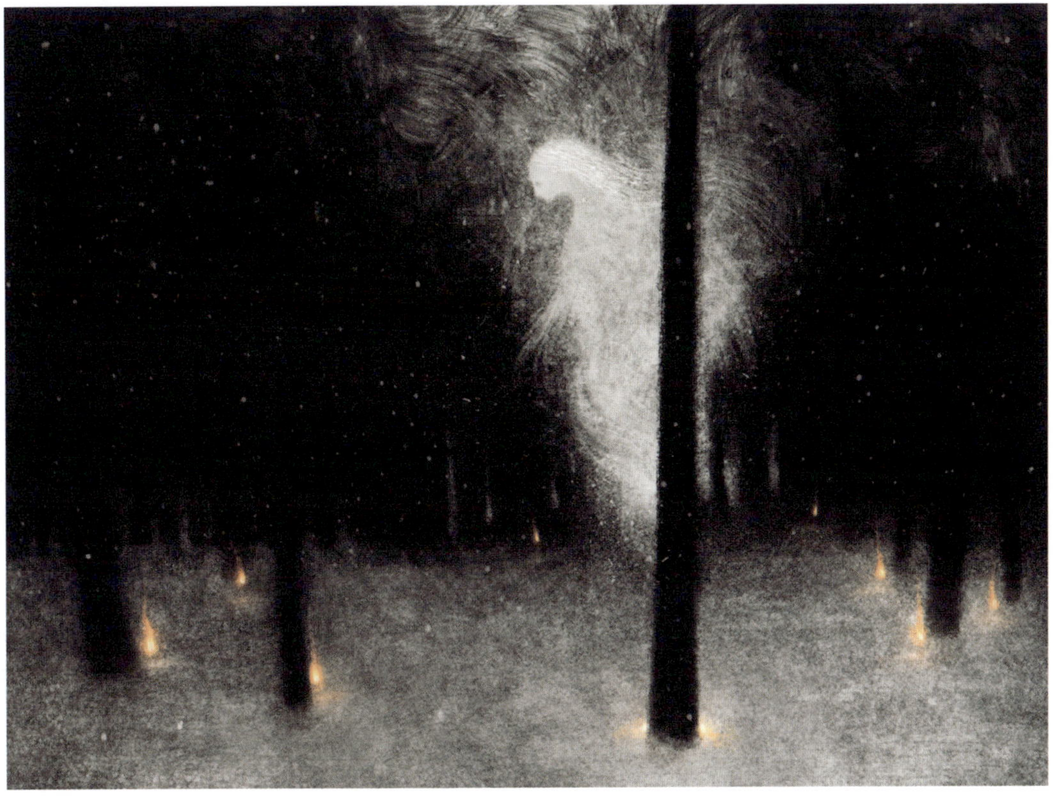

Opposite: From the series My Ghost, Adam Fuss, 2001, gelatine silver print photogram mounted on muslin.

British photographer Adam Fuss (b. 1961) grew up in rural England, where he first began to document the natural environment through photography. Experimentation with unconventional photographic processes led to his eventual abandonment of the camera altogether. Fuss has since become known for his ethereal images created using photogram techniques of light flashes on a sensitized surface, through which he achieves these ghostly manifestations of light and shadow and poetry.

Above: Kreis, Benjamin König, unknown date and medium.

Benjamin König (b. 1976) has been enamoured with drawing and painting since his earliest years, when countless beautifully and creepily illustrated children's books inspired his artistic passion. Currently a freelance illustrator in Upper Bavaria, Germany, König feels that this creative compulsion is his calling, citing a strong bond to the magic of fairy tales, (old) children's books, myths and almost everything that sparks a very deep and certain intuitiveness within one's heart.

XII

Dark Arts & Forbidden Mysteries

'All creative art is magic, is evocation of the unseen in forms persuasive, enlightening, familiar and surprising.'

–JOSEPH CONRAD

By candlelight a shadowy form brews elixirs of inexplicable hermetic significance and pages through a brittle, leather-bound tome. A solitary figure stares intently into a blackened mirror and through the murky glass a face not their own emerges from its depths. The shadowy covenants made at the midnight crossroads, the folk magic of crones cackling at their cauldrons, the enigmatic visions and proclamations of the soothsayers and fortune tellers. All this imagery is familiar throughout every culture and age, though the details may look different depending on our upbringing and our different geographies; everyone knows the trappings of magic and mystery when they see them. And all too frequently we find these magical beings fearful.

Circe, Morgan Le Fay, Cassandra. Witches and enchantresses, sorcerers and necromancers. From seers and prophets to evil fairy queens and the curses of wicked stepmothers, these icons and archetypes are framed as mystical, mysterious beings – and yes, their stories are often shrouded in darkness. But there may be another side of the story here, and if we shine a light on these narratives, what might we find there? Perhaps they've poisoned young maidens, they've swapped your child for a changeling, they've predicted the fall of your city and the death of your entire family. But were these individuals born bad to the bone or did a series of unfortunate circumstances and cycles of trauma shape their evolution? What did their journey look like? How did they get there? And if in the end they are simply irredeemable, their hearts corrupt through and through, what can we learn from them? How can we recognize, reconcile and reckon with this darkness within ourselves? Let's not kid ourselves that the villainous enchantments that we see reflected in works of art weren't found first in our real-world human behaviour and attitudes, reactions to our sometimes irrational fears and limiting beliefs. Were these stories rooted in people being afraid of women wielding a little power or even just exercising their basic rights as human beings? Gaze even for a slight moment at many of those canvases and that's exactly what you'll see: women being humans in a world that wants so much less for them.

Since the dawn of human creativity, magic and art have gone hand in hand. The practice of magic and the creation of art come from the same desire to better understand the world around us and our attempts to exercise control over important aspects of our existence and our environment. Myths developed as stories that attempted to explain natural events. Rituals, spells and alchemical experiments all grew as ways of trying to influence the course of nature by harnessing inner powers and supernatural forces. All these things point to our vast human capacity for imagination and our deep yearning for poetic beauty – an eternal sense of seeking and dreaming that continues to stir and inspire our minds. These are topics that often neither science nor philosophy can fully address.

Practitioners and wielders of these magical forces have long been artistically depicted in intensely, and sometimes disturbingly, vivid imagery. Whether the subject is a troubled king consulting a necromancer for guidance in a shadowy canvas by Salvator Rosa, or a menacing scene of mesmerism wrought by visionary artist Sascha Schneider, or that famous trio of Shakespearean witches that almost every artist has taken a crack at portraying – these worlds of forbidden knowledge, the occult and esoteric, have long fascinated us. In the imagined bodies and fantastic rituals that have haunted the margins of religion and spirituality for thousands of years, we find our hopes, desires and anxieties mirrored in the transgression and allure of these images.

Whether wronged since birth, violently shaped by fate or shunned for sharing the sorts of omens and predictions that powerful people definitely did not care to hear, whether persecuted for practising harmless healing or merely for being different – the stories of magical practitioners are threaded by themes of protest and expression that remain relevant today. In contemporary society, witches and witchly artists embrace and reimagine those stories, channelling their darkness into creations addressing the struggle for bodily autonomy, anti-capitalism and patriarchal resistance.

Art allows us to reflect on, and sometimes even heal through, subject matter that often neither science nor philosophy can fully manage or fix. It provides a portal through which to better understand the motivations and stories – fearsome, fierce or fanciful – of those dark archetypes, magic movers and shadow shakers. And in these reflections, we gain a better understanding, appreciation and acceptance of our own histories and experiences. This, too, is a kind of magic.

Opposite: La Magie Noire (Black Magic), René Magritte, 1934, oil on canvas.

René Magritte's (1898–1967) enigmatic, thought-provoking works helped define the imagery and philosophy of the Surrealist movement. In the captivating elegance of La Magie Noire, or Black Magic, a woman leans against a block of stone, in a dusky, unidentified landscape. No ordinary woman, though – this is Magritte's model, muse and wife, Georgette Berger. Georgette's upper body appears to be celestial and otherworldly, while her lower body remains earthly. One way we can interpret this split is that as humans we are often mentally lost elsewhere, our heads in the clouds, while our bodies remain firmly rooted in reality. What does it mean? What does Magritte say? Well, from the artist, himself: '. . . when one sees one of my pictures, one asks oneself this simple question "What does that mean?" It does not mean anything, because mystery means nothing either, it is unknowable.'

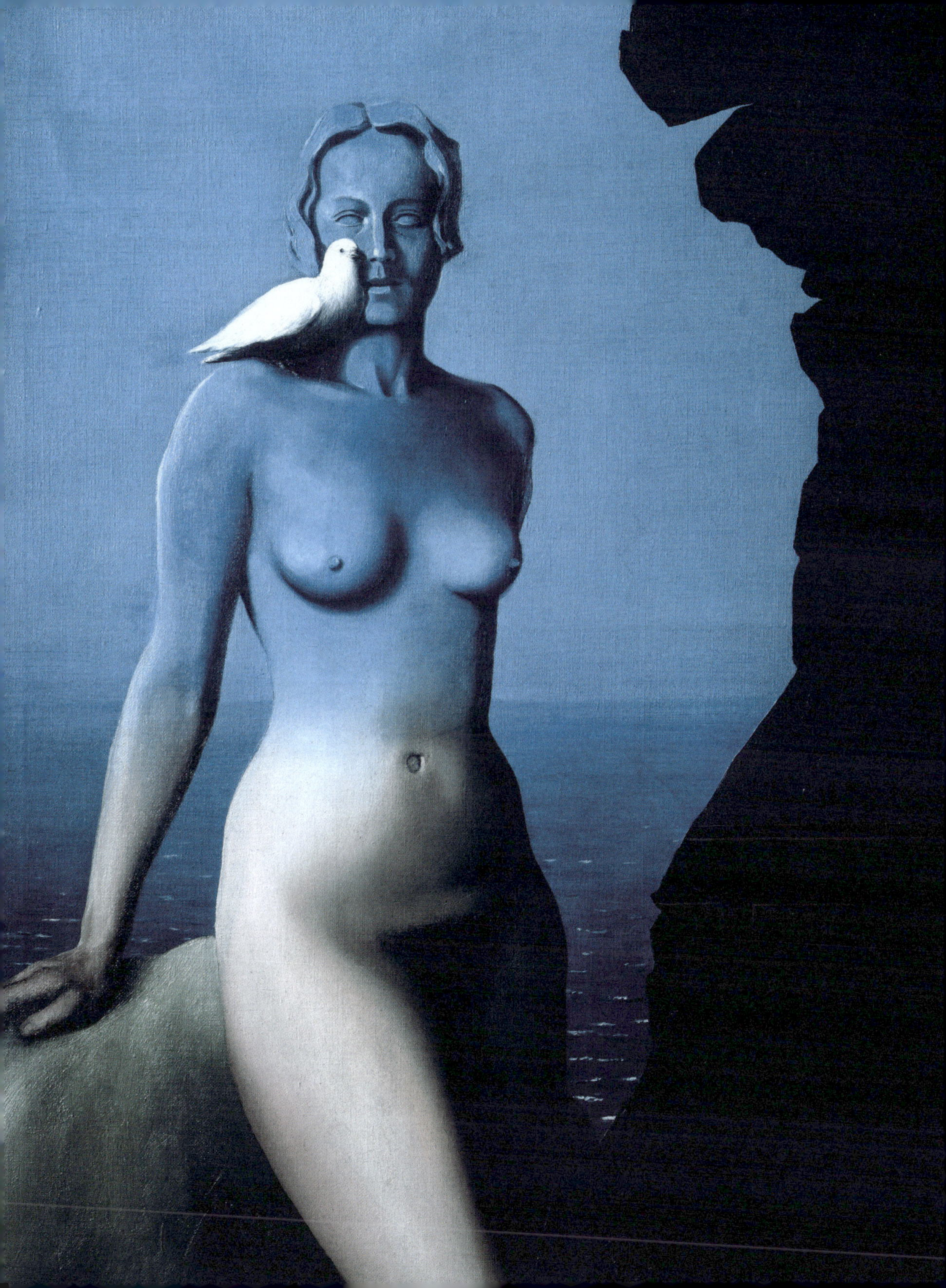

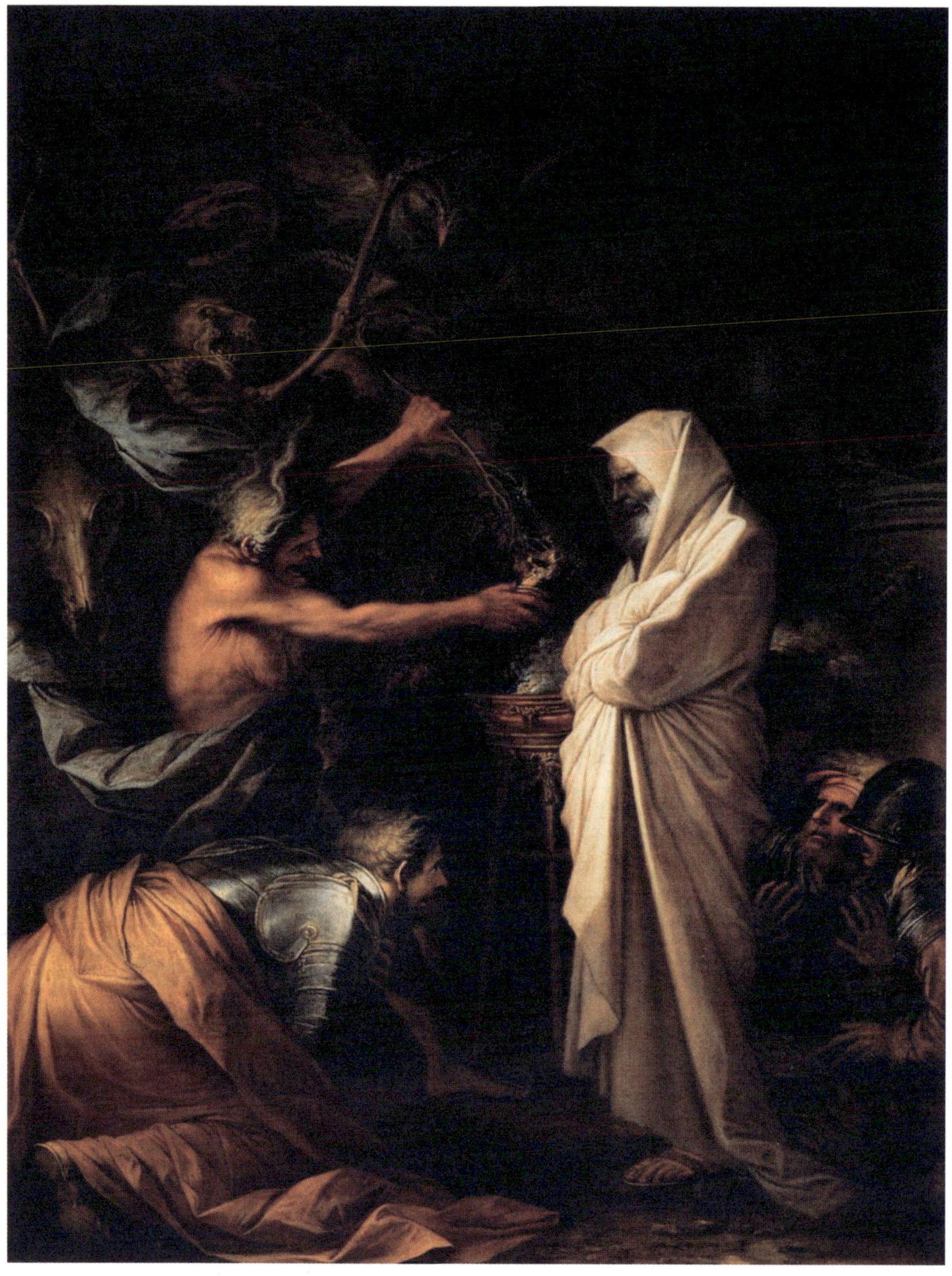

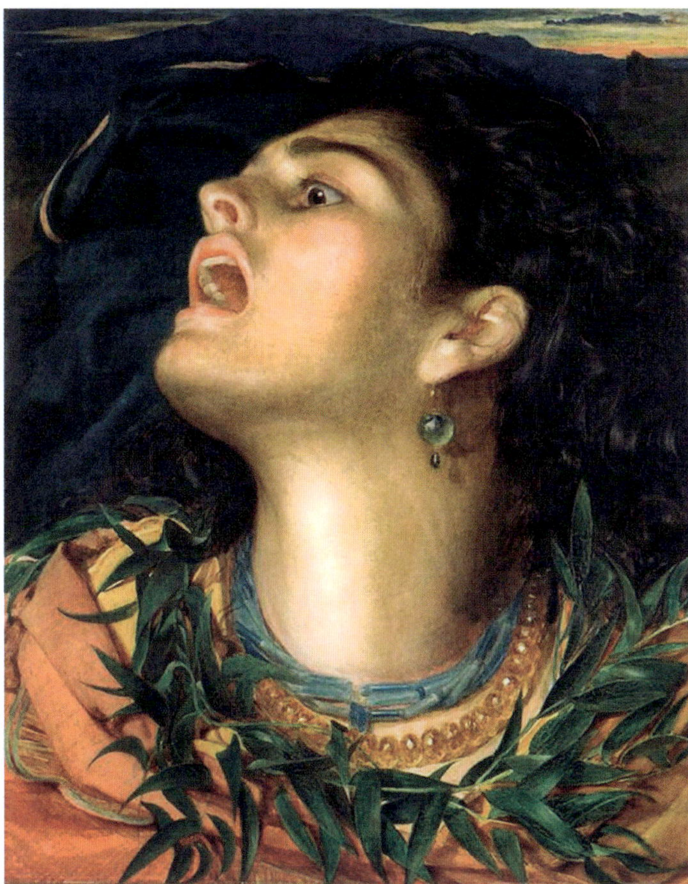

Left: Cassandra, Anthony Frederick Augustus Sandys, c. 1863–4, oil on board.

Anthony Frederick Augustus Sandys, usually known as Frederick Sandys (1829-1904) was a British painter, illustrator and draughtsman, associated with the Pre-Raphaelites, who focused mainly on mythological subjects and portraits. *Cassandra* is one of Sandys' portraits of legendary female figures. The daughter of King Priam of Troy, Cassandra caught the notice of Apollo, who bestowed upon her the gift of prophecy. Which was apparently one of those conditional, cursed sorts of gifts, for when she spurned his advances, Apollo avenged himself by ordaining that her prophecies should never be believed. The myth of Cassandra has been used by contemporary philosophers, psychologists and political scientists to explain the condition of valid truths being disregarded and disbelieved. In this fraught image, Cassandra, afflicted by visions of terrors and devastation to come, branded treasonous and mad, is depicted with her mouth in a painful, silent scream. You would scream too if you were harassed by a god and gas-lit by your own people.

Opposite: The Shade of Samuel Appears to Saul, Salvator Rosa, 1668, oil on canvas.

Salvator Rosa (1615-73) was an unconventional seventeenth-century Italian master whose work seethes with darkness, and though mainly a painter of landscapes (most of which were awfully dark and weird), he also depicted scenes of witchcraft, revealing his interest in the irrational and less-conventional intellectual preoccupations of his age. In this story from the Old Testament on the eve of a battle, Saul, the king of Israel feeling forsaken by God in a critical hour, visits a necromancer, the witch of Endor, to discover what the future holds. He directs her to call up the spirit of the prophet Samuel who, during his lifetime, had been Saul's mentor and had himself anointed Saul as their first king. Cranky at being recalled from the Shades, Samuel foretold the worst, that Saul would perish with his entire army in the coming battle. In Rosa's painting Saul is shown on his knees before a shrouded Samuel risen from the earth, while wraiths and monsters hover in the gloom.

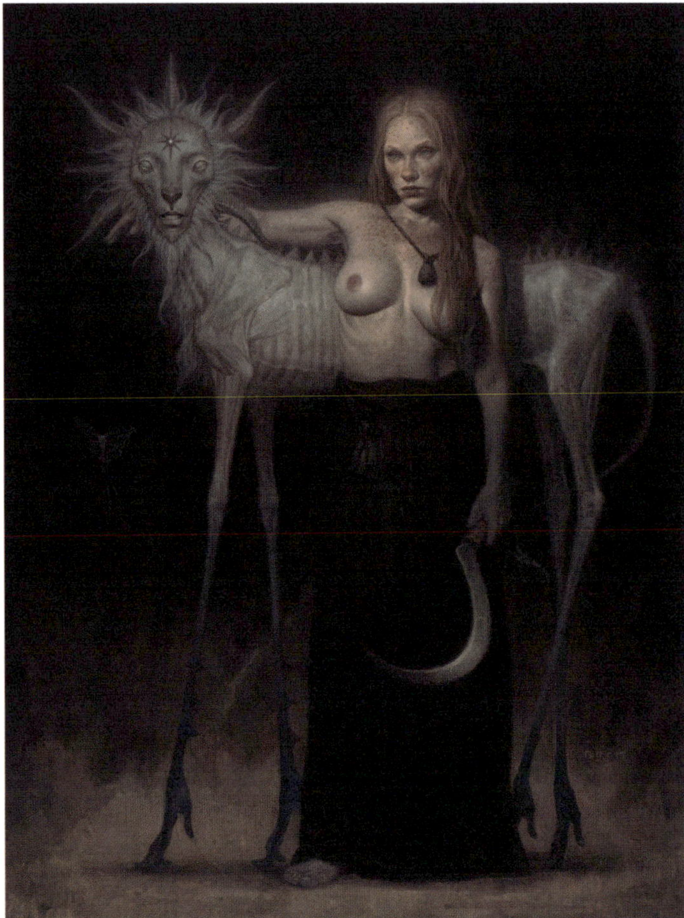

Left: Star Witch, Brom, 2019, oil on canvas.

From as far back as he can remember, artist Brom (b. 1965) has been obsessed with the creation of the weird, the monstrous and the beautiful. He has since gone on to lend his distinctive vision to all facets of the creative industries, from novels and games to comics and film. Fascinated by the hidden realms of spirits, the spectral evidence of ancient beings and their rites and deeds both wicked and noble, this artist has spent a career heeding the calls of these characters and giving the voice to both the monstrous and the beautiful through his distinctively haunting work.
In *Star Witch*, a sickle-wielding sorceress, her arm slung casually around a strange, shining creature, regards us languidly. One presumes from her impassive appearance, we're simply not worth the trouble to pursue.

Opposite: Les fleurs du mal (Death Flowers), Achille Calzi, 1913, oil pastels on paper.

There is little accessible information on Italian painter and ceramicist Achille Calzi (1873-1919) but we do know that, after attending technical and drawing school in Faenza, he moved to Florence to continue his studies at the Institute of Fine Arts. He became a drawing teacher at various art schools, and once back Faenza, he worked alongside the director of the art gallery Argnani and devoted himself to local art and culture through research and publications. A multifaceted and receptive personality, it has been noted that only his untimely death interrupted his tireless stylistic research. The illustration opposite, imbued with macabre and mysterious suggestion, and rendered in muted contrasts and sinister shimmers, is supposedly from Charles Baudelaire's scandalous and sensual *Les Fleurs du Mal*.

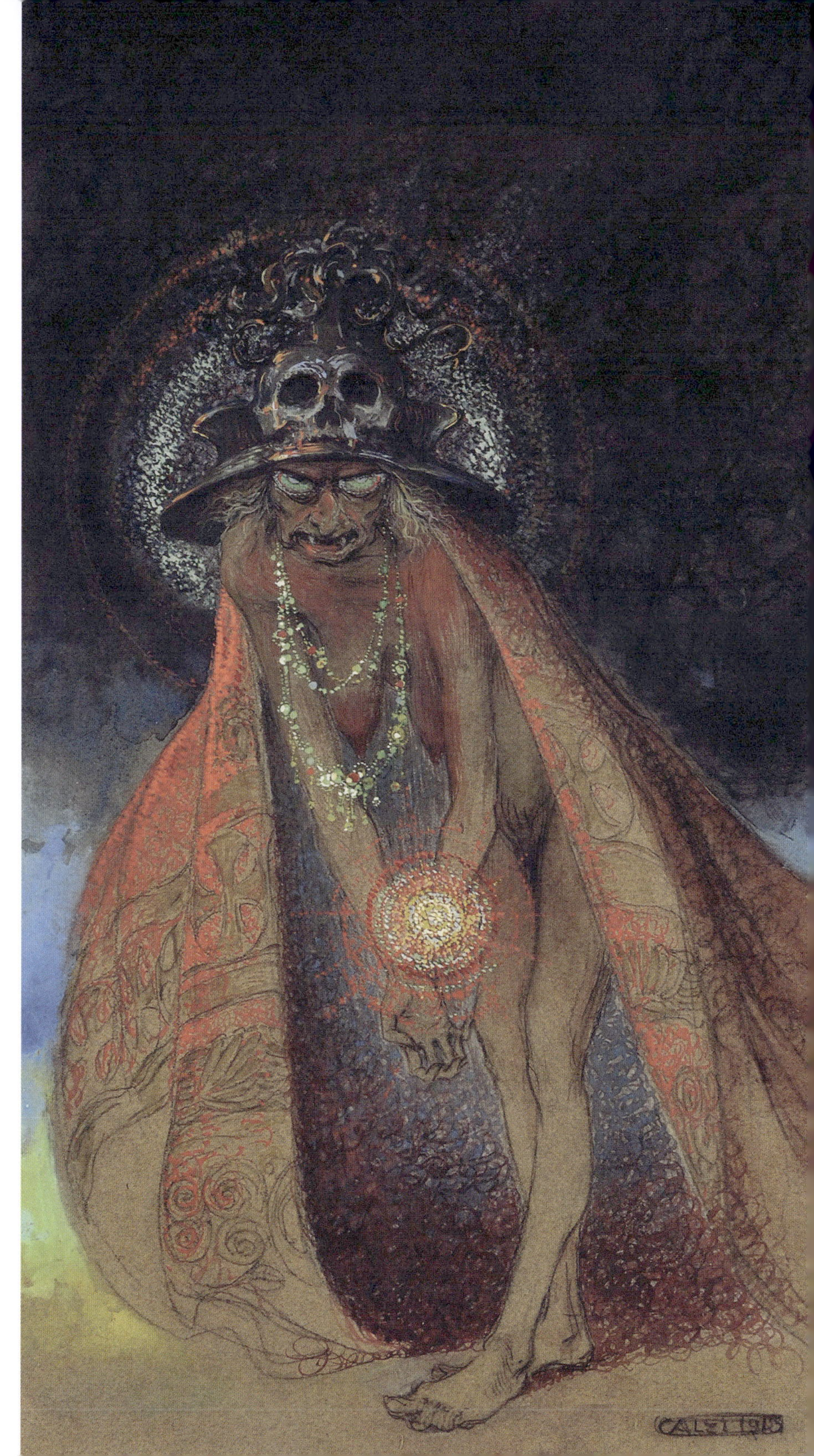

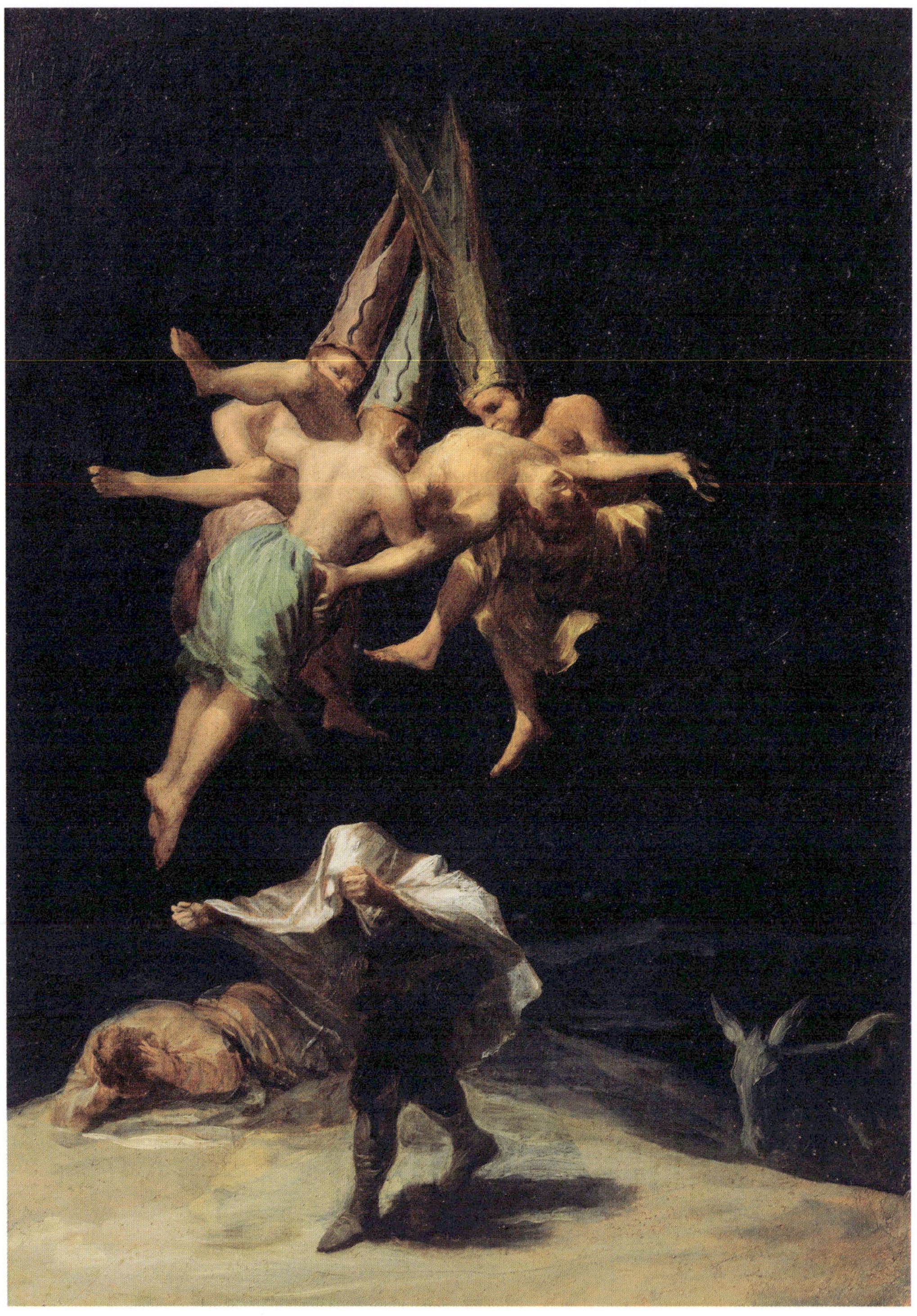

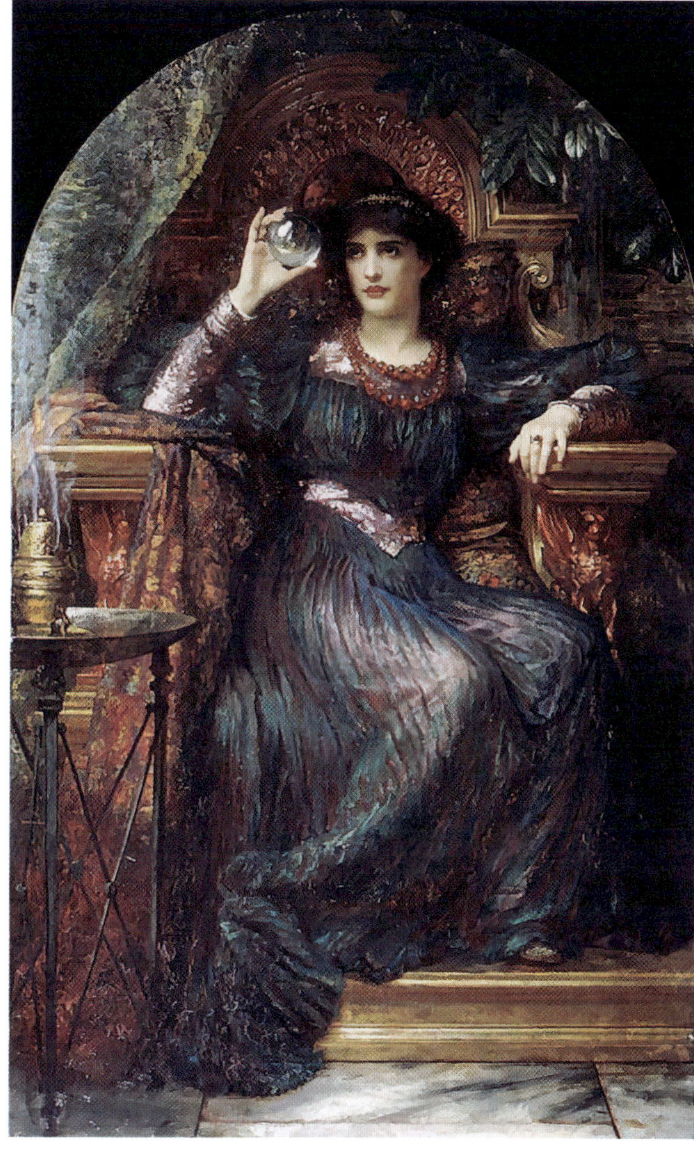

Left: *The Magic Crystal*, Francis Bernard Dicksee, 1894, oil on canvas.

The English Victorian Romantic painter, draftsman and illustrator Francis Bernard Dicksee (1853-1928) was best known for his Romantic historical scenes, often embellished by imagination rather than based on a particular event or literary source, and employing sumptuous technique and bold and unusual lighting effects. He was also a noted painter of portraits of fashionable women, which helped to bring him success in his own time, and a keen sensibility which is certainly seen to great effect in the detailed costumery of his mythic motifs. Mysticism is at the heart of Romanticism, and in this scene we observe a woman intently staring into a crystal orb which she is holding aloft in a sunbeam. Is the young woman a witch? A sorceress? Or is she merely meditating upon the play of light through the quartz and daydreaming, enrapt in reverie?

Opposite: *Vuelo de Brujas* (Witches in Flight), Francisco Goya, 1797–98, oil on canvas.

This powerful and disturbing painting by the Spaniard Francisco Goya (1746-1828) grants us a vision of three bare-chested witches struggling with a figure as they levitate in mid-air. Another character lies on the floor, covering his ears in terror, while a sixth figure flees, his head covered with a white cloth. With his hand, he makes the gesture intended to protect him from the evil eye. At the right of the scene a donkey, unfazed, stands out against a pitch back sky and completely bare ground. No stars, clouds, grass or trees are shown, and there is no horizon. *Witches in Flight* has been interpreted as an attack on the power of the church, organized religion and its 'holy men' rather than a criticism of witchcraft itself.

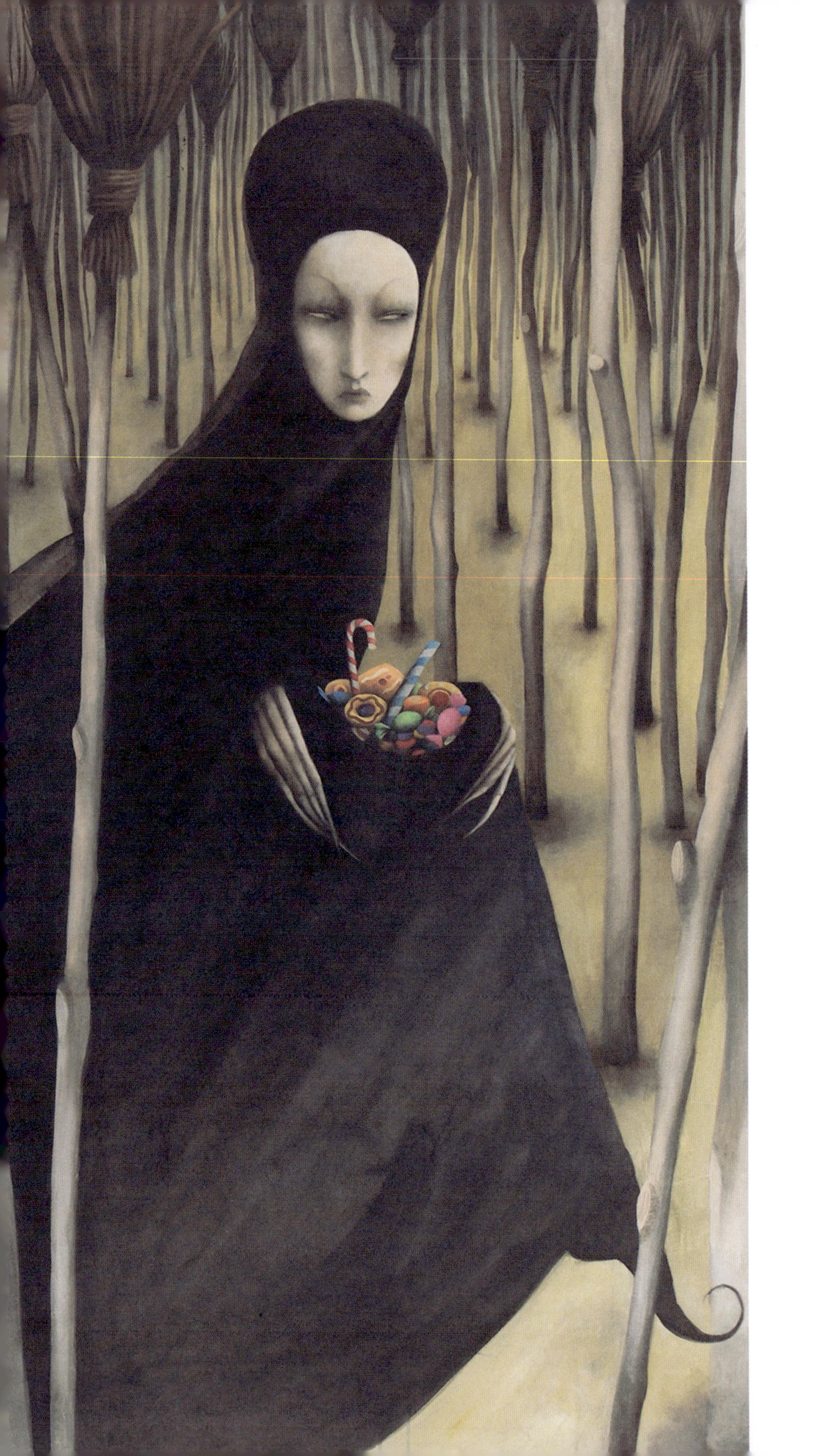

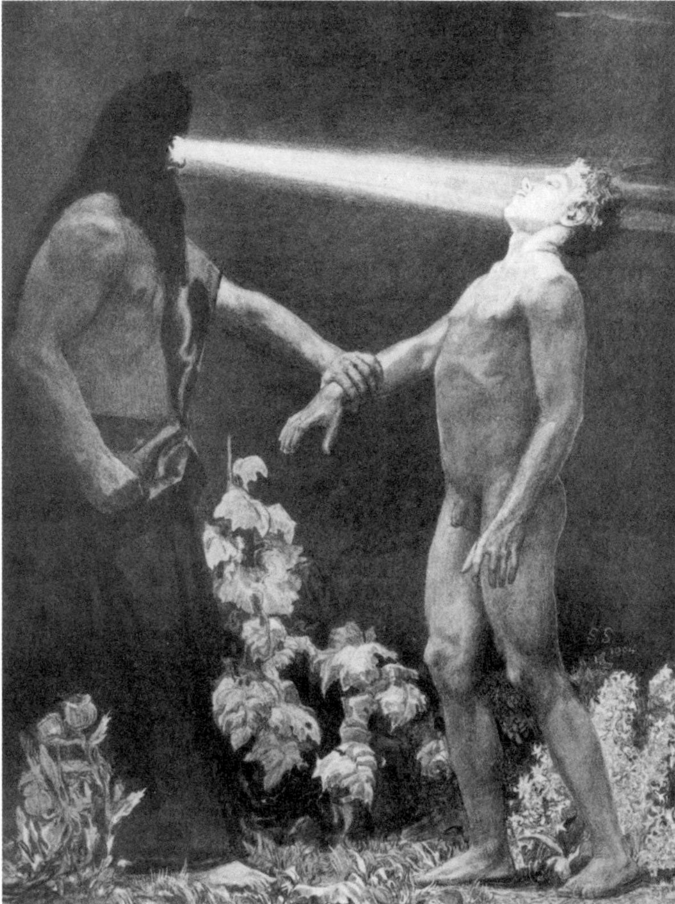

Right: Hypnose, Sascha Schneider, 1904, etching.

Sascha Schneider (1870–1927) was a visionary artist whose dreamlike works full of potent symbolism achieved success in turn-of-the-century Germany despite its striking homoeroticism. This period of German history saw the Health and Hygiene Movement, or Freikörperkultur, which advocated for a return to classical ideals, traditional exercise and healthy living pursuits, involving a plethora of natural efforts and, among other things, nudity. Schneider, who actually constructed a body-building studio in his atelier, was an adherent of this classical ideal. And since this attitude towards mental and physical development was by no means an exclusively homosexual one, it was Schneider's charcoal and oil creations of striking muscular bodies and his abashed depiction of male beauty that made his art, paradoxically, so mainstream. However, German society proved that, while it was willing to accept homoerotic imagery, it was not yet willing to confront and accept homosexuality. On account of his, he was forced to resign from his post at Weimar University and fled to Italy in the early 1900s.

Opposite: Roundabout the Witch, Ana Juan, 2007, acrylic on canvas.

Ana Juan (b. 1961) is a Spanish artist who lives and works in Madrid, where she illustrates, paints and tells stories through her drawings. In her poster art for the opera *Hansel and Gretel* at the Metropolitan Opera House in New York in 2007, Juan illustrates the predatory witch looking down at the children with patient hunger, entwining her clawed fingers with anticipatory glee as they strain towards her web of hanging treats.

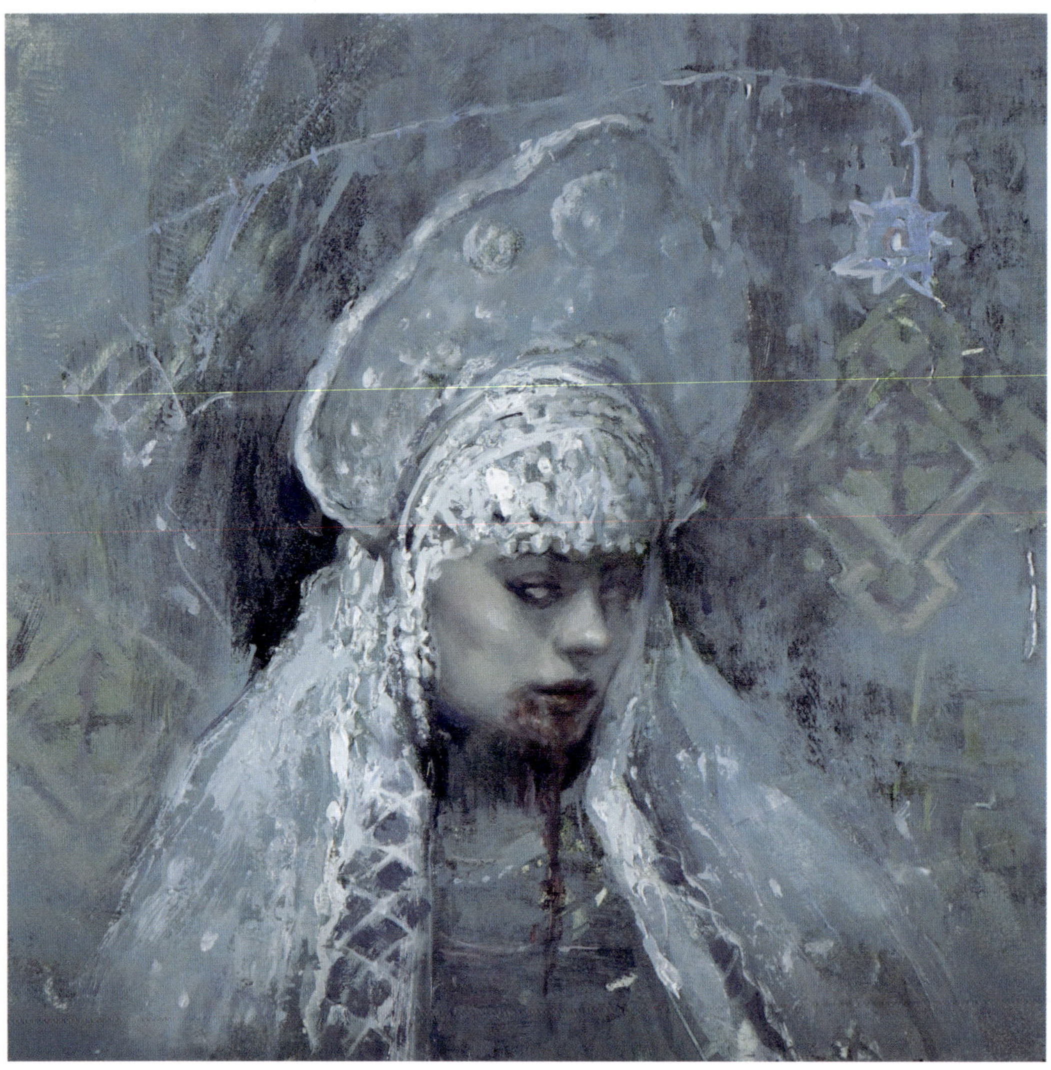

Above: Young Yaga, Nadezda, 2019, oil on panel.

Nadezda (b. 1985) is a Russian-born artist focusing on narratives carefully mined from the mysterious world of the imagination and transformed into dreamscapes. In turn, these multifaceted artworks are intimate windows into the inner world of the peculiar characters and creatures she creates. In this hazy portrait, we catch a glimpse of young Baba Yaga, Russia's most infamous witch, an intriguing folkloric entity who is both benevolent and dangerous, and ultimately more unpredictable than evil. Baba Yaga has her own motivations, which are beyond the understanding of us mortals.

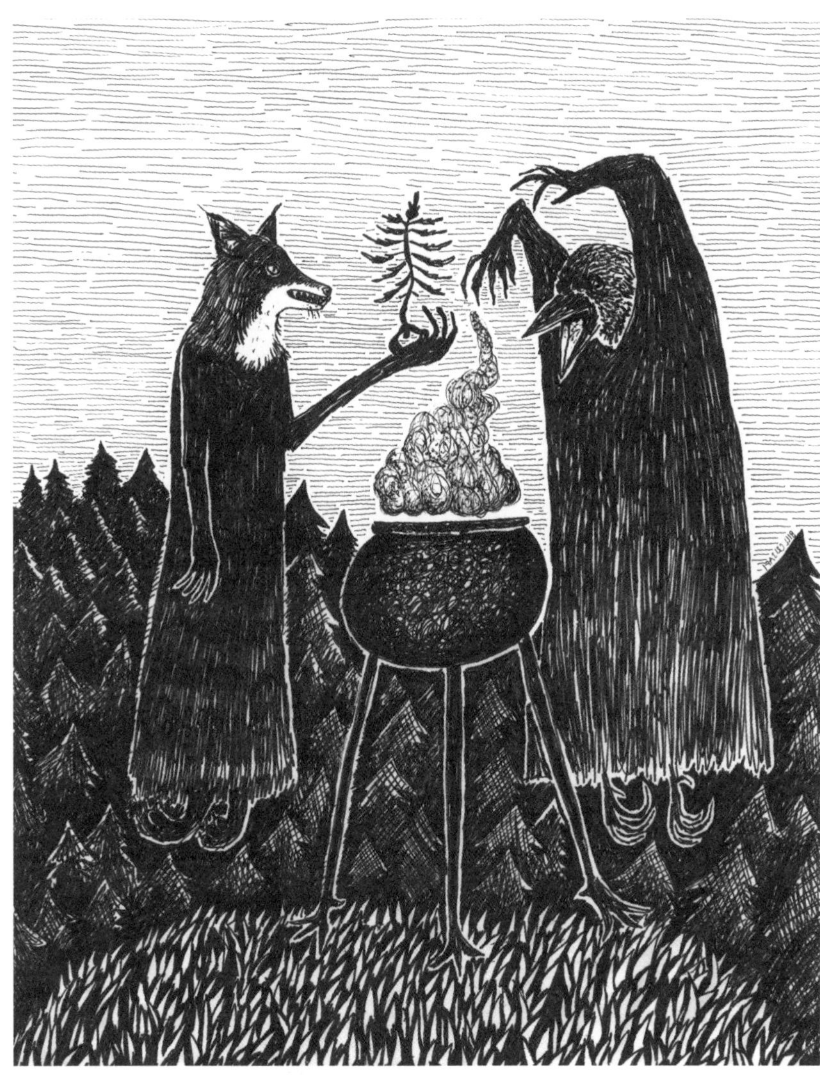

Above: Atop The Brocken, Bill Crisafi, unknown date, pen and ink.

Contemporary American illustrator, photographer and sculptor Bill Crisafi moves with ease between media, and in doing so summons his uncanny inner narrative into powerful visions made manifest. Crisafi draws inspiration from nature, feminine strength and energies, and the 'remaining echoes of the Victorian era that haunt the landscape' of his native New England. Crisafi shares this otherworldly imagery with the viewer through a variety of lenses, both literal and figurative. Feral witches and their familiars frolic, mystical woodland rituals are illumined, and the deeply dreaming, fog-shrouded forest holds sway over all in his starkly surreal, whimsical illustrations and eerie woodland photography.

Right: Lightning Struck a Flock of Witches, William Holbrook Beard, mid–late nineteenth century, oil on cardboard.

American artist William Holbrook Beard (1825–1900) is noted as having been one of the most talented painters in Buffalo during the pre-Civil War era. His older brother, James Henry Beard (1811–93), was also an artist and both worked as portrait painters. William earned a reputation for his animal paintings, and he often used satire to convey each creature's cultural meaning – a practice that dates to antiquity and was especially popular in nineteenth-century European and American art. This canvas, then, teeming with wizened witches, airborne, toppling and tumbling through the clouds, white-shocked hair streaming wildly in the frozen moment of the canvas, is a curious mystery given that there is nary an animal in sight, not even a witch's familiar.

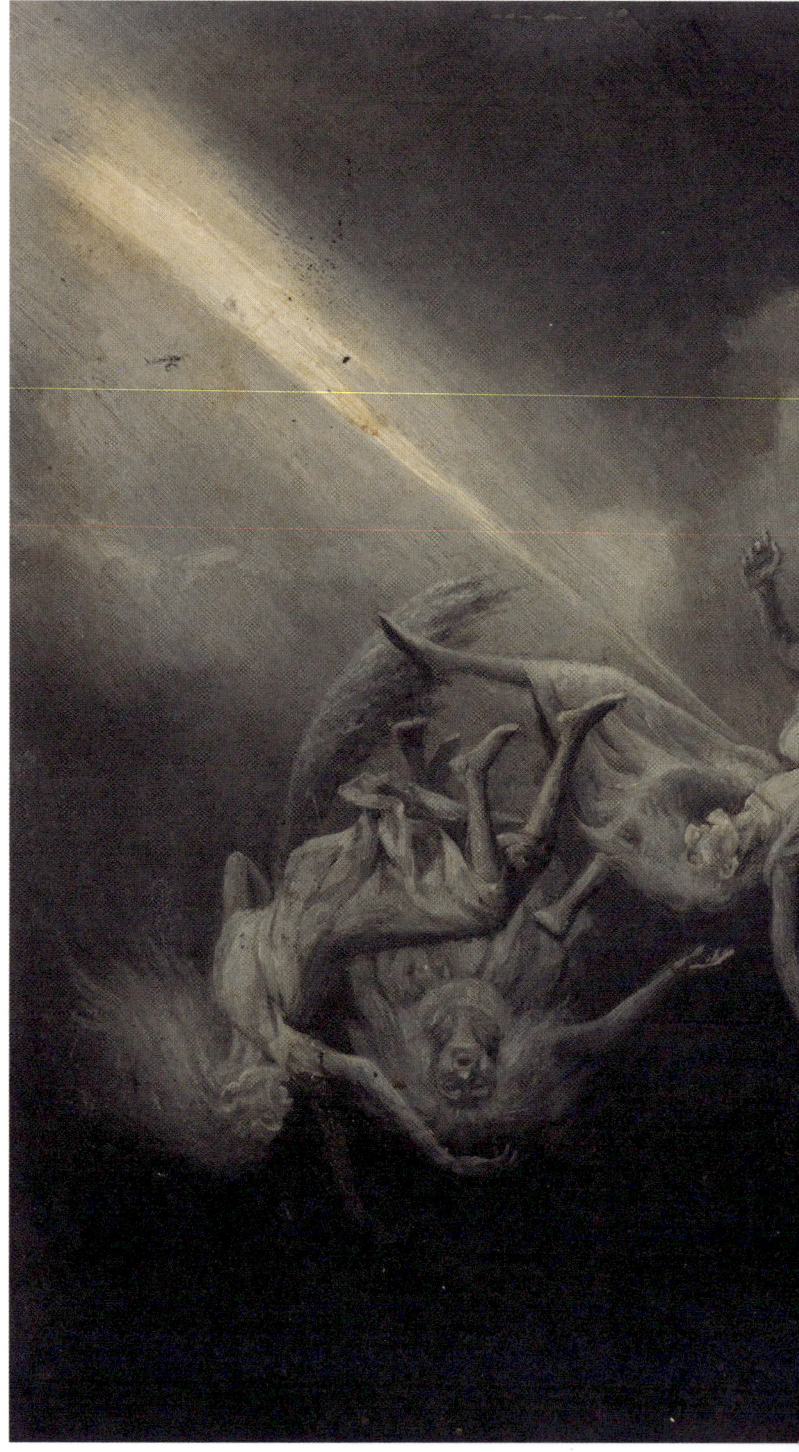

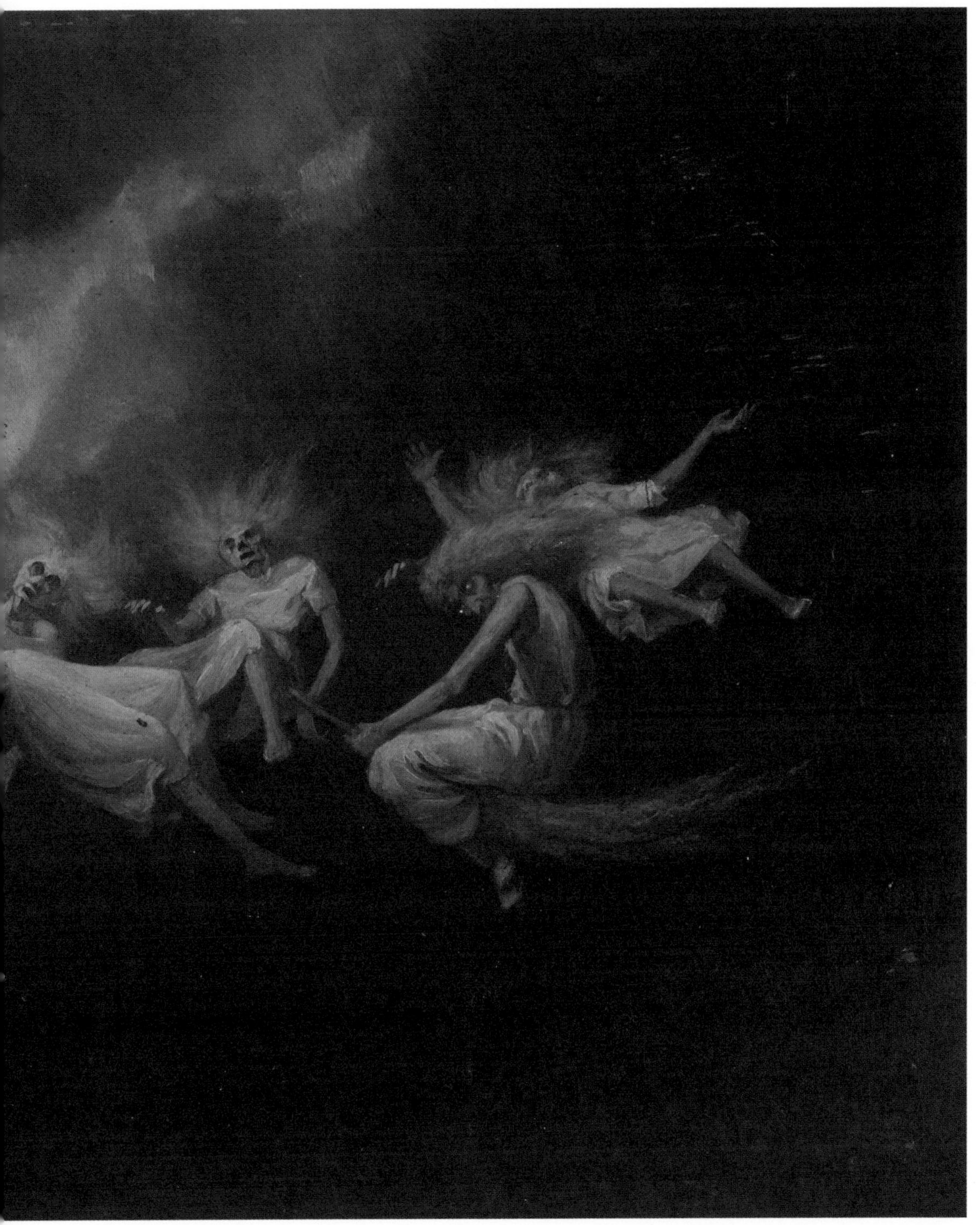

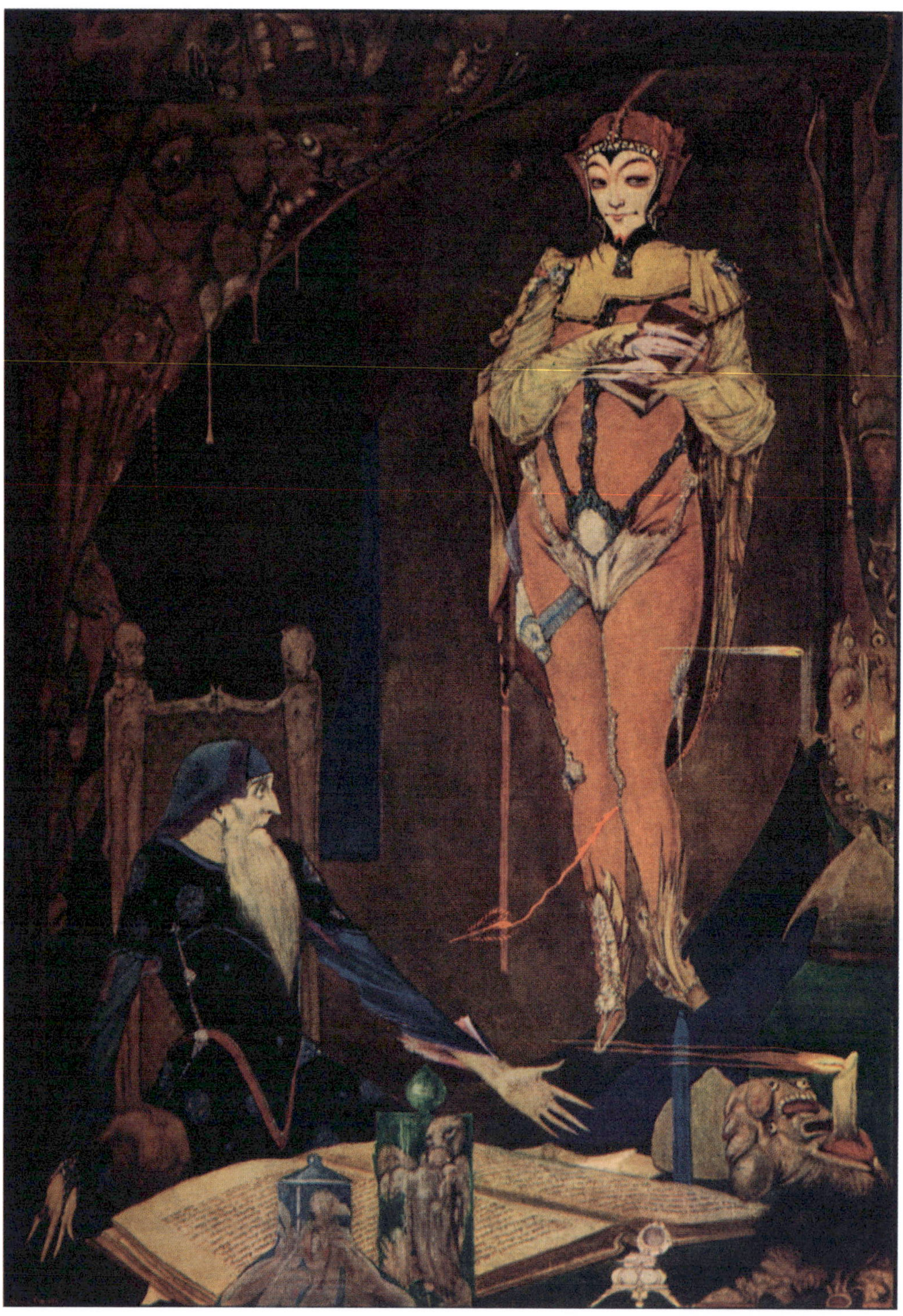

Right: Tears, Jana Heidersdorf, 2018, digital.

Jana Heidersdorf is a fantasy and horror illustrator located in Berlin, Germany, whose moody and surreal work is often inspired by the mystery and unpredictability of wild things and the natural world, as well as facets found in fairy tales and the fantastical. She notes an undeniable romantic side to her understanding and appreciation of flora and fauna that idealizes the rawness and chaos of nature, especially opposed to our need as humans to categorize and order everything. One gazes at the nocturnal being in this work and wonders if it's a timeless elemental spirit emotionlessly observing us or just a human being out past their bedtime; what covenants are they weaving their dreams into, what midnight magics are they communing with or conjuring forth?

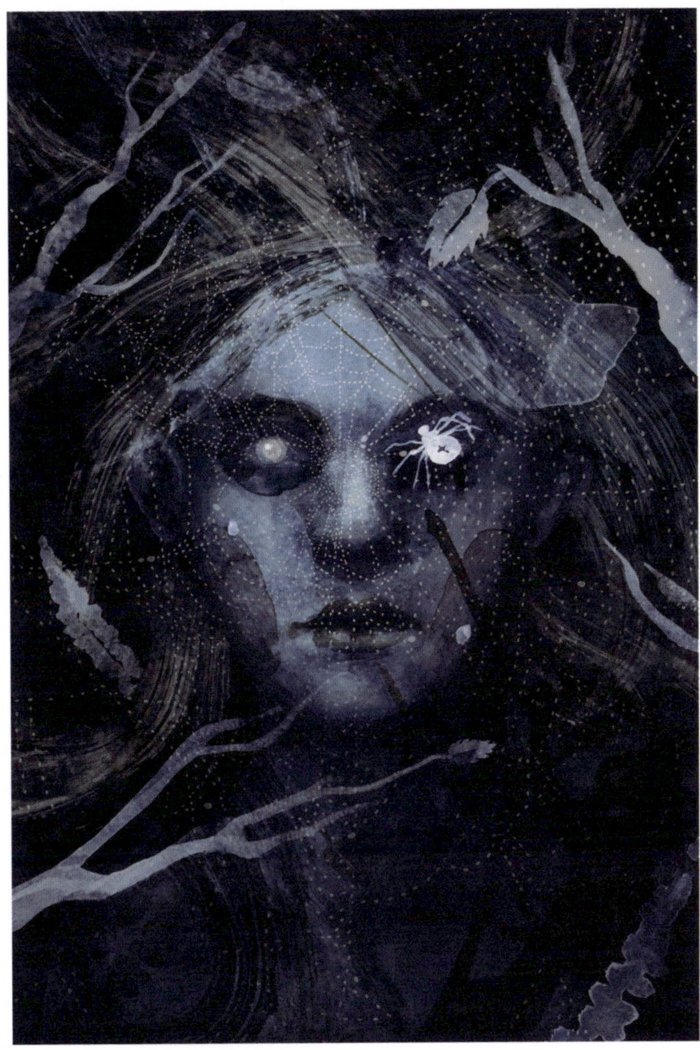

Opposite: Faust, Harry Clarke, 1925, colour book illustration.

In 1925, Irish-born stained-glass artist and book illustrator Harry Clarke (1889–1931) was commissioned to illustrate a special edition of Goethe's *Faust*. Clarke's unmistakable aesthetic, with its intricate line and often ghoulish tone, lends the Goethe masterpiece an additional dimension of haunting beauty. Clarke considered the edition his best work, but confessed in a letter to Thomas Bodkin that his publisher felt the illustrations were 'full of stench and steaming horrors'. Faust is the protagonist of a classic German legend, based on the historical Johann Georg Faust. Scholarly Faust is highly successful yet dissatisfied with his life, which leads him to make a pact with the Devil at a crossroads, exchanging his soul for unlimited knowledge and worldly pleasures.

Further reading

There are books in the following list that you may enjoy if you wish to read further about something mentioned or alluded to within *The Art of Darkness*. There are also books included in this list that I enjoyed while writing these pages.

Age of the Succubus by Nona Limmen, 2021

Altars by Nona Darla Teagarden, 2022

Be Scared of Everything: Horror Essays by Peter Counter, 2020

Body Horror: Capitalism, Fear, Misogyny, Jokes by Anne Elizabeth Moore, 2017

Dark Archives: A Librarian's Investigation Into the Science and History of Books Bound in Human Skin by Megan Rosenbloom, 2020

Darkly: Blackness and America's Gothic Soul by Leila Taylor, 2019

Dead Blondes and Bad Mothers: Monstrosity, Patriarchy, and the Fear of Female Power by Jude Ellison Sady Doyle, 2019

Disability and Art History by Ann Millett-Gallant (Editor), Elizabeth Howie (Editor), 2017

Down Below by Leonora Carrington, 1972

Dracula by Bram Stoker, 1897

Femme Fatale: Images of Evil and Fascinating Women by Patrick Bade, 1979

Field Guide to Getting Lost by Rebecca Solnit, 2005

Goldmining the Shadows by Pixie Lighthorse, 2018

House of Psychotic Women: An Autobiographical Topography of Female Neurosis in Horror and

Exploitation Films by Kier-la Janisse, 2012

In the Dream House: A Memoir by Carmen Maria Machado, 2019

It's OK That You're Not OK: Meeting Grief and Loss in a Culture That Doesn't Understand by Megan Devine, 2017

Kwaidan: Stories and Studies of Strange Things by Lafcadio Hearn, 1904

Leonora Carrington: Surrealism, Alchemy and Art by Susan Aberth, 2004

Odilon Redon: Prince of Dreams by Douglas W. Druick, 1994

Powers of Horror: An Essay on Abjection by Julia Kristeva, 1980

Rebecca by Daphne du Maurier, 1938

Remedios Varo: Letters, Dreams, and Other Writings by Margaret Carson, 2018

Salt Is For Curing by Sonya Vatomsky, 2015

Savage Appetites: Four True Stories of Women, Crime, and Obsession by Rachel Monroe, 2019

Scream: Chilling Adventures in the Science of Fear by Margee Kerr, 2015

The Astonishing Color of After by Emily X.R. Pan, 2018

The Book of Disquiet by Fernando Pessoa, 1982

The Devil: A Very Short Introduction by Darren Oldridge, 2012

The Man of Jasmine & Other Texts by Unica Zürn, 2020

The Memory of Place: A Phenomenology of the Uncanny by Dylan Trigg, 2012

The Picture of Dorian Gray by Oscar Wilde, 1890

The Witches Are Coming by Lindy West, 2019

Underland: A Deep Time Journey by Robert Macfarlane, 2019

Yurei: The Japanese Ghost by Zack Davisson, 2015

Index

Page numbers in italics indicate illustration captions.

Picture credits

The publishers would like to thank the institutions, picture libraries, artists, galleries and photographers for their kind permission to reproduce the works featured in this book. Every effort has been made to trace all copyright holders but if any have been inadvertently overlooked, the publishers would be pleased to make the necessary arrangements at the first opportunity.

4 Bridgeman Images; **7** agefotostock/Alamy; **8** Wikicommons; **11** Wikicommons/National Gallery of Norway; **13** Bridgeman Images; **18** IanDagnall Computing/Alamy; **19** © The Trustees of the British Museum; **20** Bibliothèque nationale de France; **21** The Metropolitan Museum of Art; **22** Christophel Fine Art/Getty Images; **23** Masterpics/Alamy; **24–5** Wikicommons/Robert O. Muller Collection; **26** Stephen Mackey; **27** David Whitlam; **28** Bridgeman Images; **29** Wikicommons; **33** The Metropolitan Museum of Art/Art Resource/Scala, Florence; **34** Wellcome Collection; **35** Art Collection 4/Alamy; **36** ©Tracey Emin RA; **37** Antiquarian Images/Alamy; **38-9** © Fine Art Images / Bridgeman Images; **40** Private collection, Paris; courtesy Andrew Edlin Gallery, New York & Ubu Gallery, New York; **41** © Musée cantonal des Beaux-Arts de Lausanne; **42-3** © the Estate of William Kurelek, courtesy of the Wynick/Tuck Gallery, Toronto; **45** Photo Schalkwijk/Art Resource/Scala, Florence; **48** © The Estate of Francis Bacon; **50** ZUMA Press, Inc./Alamy; **51** Aleksandra Waliszewska; **52-3** JJs/Alamy; **54** Darla Teagarden; **55** Wikicommons; **56-7** Courtesy of the artist and Eli Klein Gallery © Cui Xiuwen; **58** Karen Cronje; **59** Wikicommons; **60-1** Aron Wiesenfeld; **64** The Picture Art Collection/Alamy; **67** © Christie's Images/Bridgeman Images; **70** Wellcome Collection; **71** Ailsa Mellon Bruce Fund; **72** Wellcome Collection; **73** Barbara Hepworth © Bowness; **74** Atkinson Art Gallery Collection; **75** The Picture Art Collection/Alamy; **76** Courtesy of Chris Boïcos Fine Arts, Paris; **77** Wikicommons; **78** Wikicommons; **79** © Peter Willi/Bridgeman Images; **80** © Imperial War Museums/Bridgeman Images; **81** Courtesy of the Estate of David Wojnarowicz and P P O W, New York; **82** Realy Easy Star/Alamy; **83** Wangechi Mutu/Victoria Miro; **84** © Susan Gofstein; **85** Wikicommons; **89** Bridgeman Images; **90** National Trust Photographic Library/Bridgeman Images; **91** Wikicommons; **92-3** Paul Mellon Collection; **94** Joseba Eskubi, from the book INSOMNIA, published by Belleza Infinita; **95** The Picture Art Collection/Alamy; **96** © Paula Rego; **97** Darla Jackson; **98** incamerastock/Alamy; **99** Wikicommons; **100** © Gordon Roberton Photography Archive/Bridgeman Images; **101** Wikicommons; **102-3** Wikicommons; **106-7** The National Trust Photolibrary/Alamy; **108-110** The Picture Art Collection/Alamy; **111** Caitlin MacCormack; **112** © Damien Hirst and Science Ltd; **113** National Gallery of Art, Washington, DC; **114** Fine Arts Museums of San Francisco; **115** © Shirin Neshat. Courtesy Gladstone Gallery, New York and Brussels; **116** Artefact/Alamy; **117** Wikicommons; **118-9** akg-images/Cameraphoto; **120** Adagp Images, Paris/SCALA, Florence; **121** Susan Jamison; **122** Paul Koudounaris; **123** Rebecca Reeves; **126** The Metropolitan Museum of Art; **128-9** Leeds Museums and Galleries, UK/Bridgeman Images; **132-3** Wikicommons; **134** The Picture Art Collection/Alamy; **135** Santiago Caruso; **136-7** Tate Images; **138** © Chris Mrozik; **139** National Gallery of Art, Washington, DC; **140** Jaime Aelavanthara; **141** Marco Mazzoni; **142** Rachael Bridge; **143** Jana Brike; **144** © Gordon Roberton Photography Archive/Bridgeman Images; **145** Agostino Arrivabene; **148** Dipper Historic/Alamy; **149** The Uffizi Gallery; **150** Stefano Politi Markovina/Alamy; **151** Artefact/Alamy; **152** Wikicommons; **153** The British Museum; **154** Charley Harper; **155** Courtesy of the Van der Grinten Galerie, Cologne © Ruth Marten; **156** Dylan Garrett Smith; **157** Frances Pelzman; **158** Paul Romano; **159** The J. Paul Getty Museum; **160-1** Kazuya Akimoto; **165** Royal Academy of Arts, London; **166** classicpaintings/Alamy; **167** Adam Burke; **168-170** Wikicommons; **171** Tokyo National Museum, Japan; **172** Yaroslav Gerzhedovich; **173** Wikicommons; **174** Artefact/Alamy; **175** Natalia Smirnova; **176** Nona Limmen; **177** © Staatliche Kunstsammlungen Dresden/Bridgeman Images; **178** The Minnich Collection; **179** Wikicommons; **182** Lebrecht Authors/Bridgeman Images; **184-9** Wikicommons; **190** Hood Museum of Art, Dartmouth College; **191** Chet Zar; **192** Heritage Image Partnership Ltd/Alamy; **193** Denis Forkas ; **194** Wikicommons; **195** Artepics/Alamy; **196** Painters/Alamy; **197** Caitlin McCarthy; **198-9** Wikicommons; **203** Wikicommons; **204** Laurie Lee Brom; **205** David Seidman; **206-7** Wikicommons; **208** Azoor Photo/Alamy; **209** Marci Washington; **210** Leonor Fini; **211** Becky Munich; **212-3** Album/Alamy; **214** Amy Earles; **215** La Rouille; **216** The Metropolitan Museum of Art/Art Resource/Scala, Florence; **217** Benjamin König; **221** Bridgeman Images; **222** The Picture Art Collection/Alamy; **223** Painters/Alamy; **224** Brom; **225** MIC Faenza; **226** Heritage Images/Getty Images; **227** Artepics/Alamy; **228** Ana Juan; **229** Wikicommons; **230** Nadezda; **231** Bill Crisafi; **232-3** Heritage Images/Getty Images; **234** The Print Collector/Alamy; **235** Jana Heidersdorf

Acknowledgements

To my eternally patient Yvan; to my silly, supportive sisters (even though you are both so badly behaved in my dreams); to my BGF who will make me laugh and feel good about myself and gossip with me when I need snark and sarcasm most; to my thoughtful, sensitive Mikey, for your suggestions and recommendations and always making me kinder and more compassionate; to the fantastic creatives and friends who inspire me endlessly; to the infinitely insightful and incredibly encouraging editorial team at Quarto: thank you all for bearing with me. Again.